The Hendon Foot

A to Z

David Ballheimer

London League Publications Ltd

The Hendon Football Club A to Z

© David Ballheimer and other contributors: Colin Tate, Simon Lawrence and Peter Lush

The moral right of David Ballheimer, Colin Tate, Simon Lawrence and Peter Lush respectively to be identified as the authors of their contributions has been asserted.

Front & back cover design @ Stephen McCarthy.

All photographs are from private collections unless otherwise credited to the photographer or provider of the photo. No copyright has been intentionally breached; please contact London League Publications Ltd if you believe there has been a breach of copyright.

Front cover photo: The Hendon FC team that won the Middlesex Senior Cup in 2018 (Derek Beech Photography). Back photos: 1912–13 Hampstead Town team (courtesy Kim Parker) and Hendon supporters at Claremont Road (Peter Lush)

A CIP catalogue record for this book is available from the British Library.

Published in October 2019 by London League Publications Ltd, PO Box 65784, London NW2 9NS

ISBN: 978-1-909885-23-3

Cover design by Stephen McCarthy Graphic Design
46, Clarence Road, London N15 5BB

Editing and layout by Peter Lush

Printed and bound in Great Britain by Ashford Colour Press Ltd, Gosport, Hants PO13 0FW

Foreword

After flirting with professional football with Brentford FC and Queen's Park Rangers for five years, I then played non league football for 16 years, with a number of clubs. I signed for Hendon FC in 1985, not knowing much about the club, but the offer was good. We avoided relegation in my first season with an epic game at Slough Town to guarantee survival.

The next season, still under the legend that is Ted Hardy, who had joined the club during my first season, we reached the League Cup Final and the GMAC Final, which we lost to Kettering Town. The next season we won the Middlesex Charity Cup at Wembley Stadium...brilliant!

Little did I know that I was to spend six wonderful seasons at Hendon, with varying levels of success. A number of great players passed through and now, looking back at 59 years of age, I realise the club and my experiences there have helped to shape who I am today, for which I am grateful. Simon Lawrence, David Ballheimer and Steve Lytton amongst others, who now are the life blood of the club, would turn up supporting us in all weathers wherever we played midweek. That's commitment!

Hendon FC is not just a football club, it is a community hub, inclusive, and helping those less fortunate. In recent months my company has provided some sponsorship for the club, which is rewarding for me and which I regard as pay back for the positive impression Hendon FC has made on me and the enduring friendships it has provided me with. Hendon FC has a rich history and I'm proud to have been a small part of it.

Colin Tate

Colin Tate played for Hendon from 1985 to 1992. He made 284 appearances and scored 83 goals. He is the director of PP Wealth Limited, one of the cub's major sponsors.

Claremont Road to Townsend Lane

Claremont Road to Townsend Lane is a journey of less than four miles. On a good day, it takes less than 10 minutes to get there by car. When Hendon FC left Claremont Road in September 2008, we didn't expect it to take nearly 10 years to get there but it did.

The 2008–09 season saw the beginning of fans ownership of the club and the end for Claremont Road. One of my first and, thus far, saddest tasks as Chairman was to help manage our eviction from the ground that I had known and loved since I saw us beat St Albans 3-1 in August 1970.

That nomadic 2008–09 season saw us play matches at Wembley, Harrow Borough, Northwood and even Staines Town before we settled in to a formal groundshare arrangement with Wembley which lasted four seasons.

Personal highlights of that period would have to be our FA Cup runs – making the fourth qualifying round in each of those seasons and the first round proper twice with the absolute highlight being our stunning victory at home to Eastbourne Borough and "that" goal by Isiah Rankin.

Next stop was Earlsmead where we enjoyed a much more harmonious relationship with our friends at Harrow Borough over the following three seasons. This included the fabulous 2014–15 season where we won two cups but narrowly missed out on promotion, losing the play-off final after Aaron Morgan was, wrongly, sent off after just 18 minutes. On-field success, however, couldn't mask the fact that our finances and prospects for long-term sustainability were looking increasingly precarious.

Enter Rob Morris! I knew of, but had never met Rob and it became obvious at our first meeting in late 2013 that he was someone who could help transform the club's fortunes. Sure enough, over the next two and a half years, Rob – aided by Tom Stockman – worked tirelessly to rebuild a crumbling Silver Jubilee Park in order to meet the ground grading requirements. That moment at the end of season Awards Night in May 2016 when I announced that we would be playing at SJP for the 2016–17 season, is a moment I'll never forget.

The 2016–17 season will not live too long in the memory, but the final game certainly will. A heavy defeat in our first home League game at SJP sadly turned out to be a taste of things to come and eight months later we found ourselves having to gain a draw on the last day to ensure survival. What happened next was about as tense as it gets but, thanks to Casey Maclaren's 46th minute goal, we lived to fight another Step 3 day.

The last third of the 2016–17 season laid the foundations for an incredible 2017–18 season in which we went closer to promotion than ever before, losing on penalties in the play-off final. The highlight of that season for me was our 4–0 demolition of Folkestone Invicta in the play-off semi-final when all of the "fearsome foursome" got on the scoresheet and the game was over by half-time. That play-off final loss proved to be the catalyst for massive change – as Gary McCann moved onwards and upwards, taking with him Freddie Hyatt, Mark Findley and the rest of his coaching staff together with a number of players. Slowly but surely, the rest of the first team squad also headed off to pastures new. If that wasn't enough change, the FA moved us from the Isthmian League – in which we had competed since 1963 – to the Southern League.

I don't think that the scars of that close season will ever heal, but I will never forget the unstinting support provided throughout that summer from Daz Bloor who had joined the club as Secretary at the start of the 2017–18 season replacing club legend Graham Etchell who "moved upstairs".

2018–19 was another roller coaster of a season. A brand new side managed by Jimmy Gray leapt out of the blocks and into a play-off position. While Jimmy worked hard to steady and improve the squad, performances and results deteriorated and we once again found ourselves facing a relegation battle that was again only won on the final day of the season.

At the time of writing, it's too early to see how 2019–20 will turn out but, as I write, we've had a mixed bag of performances and results as well as some much-needed success in the FA Cup. Let's hope that come 25 April we're reflecting on an enjoyable and successful season and that we're looking forward to the future with confidence and enthusiasm.

Simon Lawrence

Simon has been a Hendon supporter for almost 50 years and is currently club chairman. He played a key role in setting up and developing the Supporters Trust which saw the club survive the change in ownership and departure from Claremont Road.

About the author: David Ballheimer

Disillusioned with professional football, David fell in love with Hendon FC in 1972. His first big Hendon match was the 1972 Amateur Cup final at Wembley and, three dozen years later, he has spent more time and certainly more money than a sane human being should on a pastime. David has come to the conclusion that being pessimistic is the best way for a football fan: when the worst happens it is nothing less than was expected; when there is glory it can be celebrated even more.

A book editor, journalist, Hendon FC press officer, occasional author and total sports junkie, especially football, cricket, rugby league, baseball and American football, David loves numbers and was quite pleased that he reached his personal half-century in the same year that his beloved Football Club reached 100. He thinks it is entirely appropriate that he has lived in only two areas in his life: Golders Green and Hendon. He co-wrote the Hendon Football Club History with Peter Lush. This book is largely based on articles he wrote for the Hendon Football Club match programme.

About this book

David Ballheimer and London League Publications Ltd would like to acknowledge the Hendon FC website, which has been an important source of statistical information. However, any errors are our responsibility.

We had limited access to photos for this book, and hope this does not spoil readers' enjoyment of it. Our thanks to people who did provide photos, in particular Derek Beech and Kim Parker.

We would like to thank Colin Tate and Simon Lawrence for their contributions.

Peter Lush wrote the following pieces: Bobby Cantwell, London's (other) professional clubs, Middlesex Wanderers and The Olympic Games.

The choice of players and matches to be featured in a book like this is always problematic. Our apologies if your particular favourites are not included, but it ended up being considerably longer than originally planned anyway.

David Ballheimer and Peter Lush

Contents

Part 1: The Hendon A to Z

Part 1: The Hendon A to Z

The FA Amateur Cup

Only two Peter Anderson (s)

Arsenal

The Athenian League

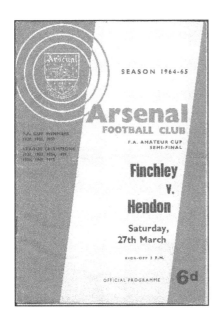

The programmes from two famous wins in the FA Amateur Cup – 4–1 against Finchley in the semi-final at Highbury in 1965 and 2–0 against Enfield in Hendon's last final appearance in 1972.

The FA Amateur Cup

The Amateur Cup was once the second biggest knock-out competition in English football. The Football Association Amateur Challenge Cup, to give the competition its full name, began 15 years before Hendon's first season in 1908. The first three winners covered the full gamut of football, an old boys team – Old Carthusians; a future Premier League club – Middlesbrough; and the most successful team in the competition's history – Bishop Auckland. It was set up because the FA Cup, once dominated by the amateur teams that made up the FA in its first 20 years of existence, was now won by the professional teams of the Football League and Southern League. This trophy was created to offer a national competition for the amateur teams.

Hendon won the trophy three times, as did Bromley, Leytonstone and Stockton – a record bettered only by Bishop Auckland with 10, Clapton and Crook Town with five each and Dulwich Hamlet with four. It took a long while for the club to make a serious impact on the Amateur Cup, which for Hampstead Town began on 5 October 1912, when they faced Luton Albion, a week after losing 2–1 at York Road, Maidenhead, in their FA Cup debut, but there was no success in this competition either as they were beaten 4–2. Twelve months later, there were victories over Wood Green Town, Luton Trinity and Luton Amateurs before Enfield ended Town's run, 4–1. Hampstead's debut in the Athenian League had already been curtailed by the outbreak of the First World War, but the Amateur Cup continued and Town were given byes until November. Sadly, it was one and done as Page Green Old Boys won 4–2.

Hampstead reached round two in 1921–22 before losing 5–0 to Cardiff Corinthians. Four years later, they went one better, going out 4–0 in the north-east to Ferryhill Athletic. After the name change to Golders Green in 1933, there were two more third round appearances, and exits, at the hands of ICI Alkali in 1935–36 and Sutton United, three years later, both by 4–2 scorelines. The club became Hendon in 1946 and, in the last 28 years of the Amateur Cup, few teams were as consistent. The Greens reached their first quarter-final in 1947–48, losing 4–1 to Leytonstone and they went one better three seasons later when a missed penalty against Pegasus in the semi-final at Highbury, meant a replay, which the Oxbridge club won 3–2.

The incremental improvement continued and this meant a first Amateur Cup final in 1954–55. Unfortunately, the opposition was Bishop Auckland and, in front of the last 100,000 crowd at Wembley for an Amateur Cup final, it ended 2–0 to the Bishops. Five years later, there was no mistake. Vauxhall Motors 3–0, Wimbledon 2–1 and Redhill were brushed aside in the first three rounds before the Greens beat

West Auckland Town in a quarter-final replay at Claremont Road. The semi-final was against Enfield and Brentford's Griffin Park was the venue. Laurie Topp and Brian Figg were the goalscoring heroes as Hendon booked their second Amateur Cup final appearance at Wembley. Kingstonian seemed to have their hands on the trophy when they led 1–0 with just a couple of minutes remaining, only for Terry Howard to equalise and Topp snatch the winner. Hendon were Amateur Cup winners for the first time.

Season 1964–65 was Hendon's finest ever, with the Isthmian League title and the Middlesex Senior Cup joining the Amateur Cup in the trophy cabinet. Exempt to the first round proper, Sutton United, Leytonstone and Carshalton Athletic were despatched before Hendon had to make the long trip to Whitley Bay, but there were no mistakes at Hillheads Park as the Greens came away 3–1 winners. The semi-final saw a second visit to Highbury in the season and the Greens scored four times to beat Finchley 4–1, thanks to a David Hyde double, a Dave Emson own goal and Peter Slade, before Jim Cooley grabbed a consolation for the Finches.

In the final against Whitby Town, Hyde again bagged a brace and Jimmy Quail got the other as Hendon became two-time Amateur Cup-winners. Twelve months later, Wealdstone beat Hendon 3–1 in the final. A year after that, there were three semi-final matches against Skelmersdale before the northerners prevailed.

There would be one more Amateur Cup trip to Wembley, in 1972, when Enfield were the opponents, this after Wycombe were memorably beaten 2–1 in the semi-final at Brentford. An own goal from Mick Smith, deflecting a John Baker shot, and Tony Bass, late on, gave Hendon a 2–0 victory over the Es. The final season of the Amateur Cup was in 1973–74 and Hendon played nine matches, but won only twice. They need four matches to beat Harwich & Parkestone, two to overcome Tilbury before Leatherhead won a third round second replay 1–0 at Wycombe's Loakes Park. It was a frustrating end to the club's often glorious history in this competition.

Only two Peter Anderson (s)

Hendon had two players, whose similarities ended with wearing the green shirt with distinction, dark hair (very different styles) and the same name.

Peter Anderson, the winger, was one of the last amateur players to leave Hendon for a career in the professional game – and he made a huge success of it, at Luton Town and Sheffield United, as well as spells in the USA and Belgium. He joined Hendon as a 19-year-old from Barnet, and made his debut on the opening day of the 1968–69 season.

He scored his first goal in the next game, a 1–0 win at Ilford. Tony Harding had left the club in the off-season after scoring 61 goals in 85 appearances, but Peter was not a straight replacement for him, being much more a creator of chances than an out-and-out finisher. Hendon had their worst finish –at that time – in the Isthmian League in 1968–69, sixth place, but Peter made only 28 League appearances. It was a different story in cup competitions, the highlight of which was the London Senior Cup final at his old hunting ground, Underhill, where Hendon beat Dagenham 1–0.

In 1969–70, Hendon came close to another Football League scalp with a 2–2 draw against Millwall in the London Challenge Cup. Peter didn't score against the Lions, but he had done when Barnet were beaten 2–0 in the previous round. Another disappointing League campaign was more than compensated by cup success as the Greens reached the second round proper of the FA Cup. Peter scored in all but two of Hendon's seven ties, including a hat-trick in the 7–2 second round qualifying replay demolition of Rainham Town at Claremont Road. In all, Peter missed just three of 58 matches and scored 24 times.

There was talk, even at the start of the 1970–71 season, of Football League clubs trying to sign Peter. He continued to contribute to the Greens' cause, scoring the first goal in a 2–1 victory at St Albans City which took Hendon into the FA Cup first round proper, where Aldershot won 2–0 at Claremont Road. He had scored a hat-trick in the League in a 6–0 win at Clapton in that September and signed off for Hendon with a double against Staines Town in the Middlesex Senior Cup on 6 February 1971. His Luton Town debut came just seven days later. Although not signed primarily as a striker, he scored 58 goals in 125 games, almost a goal every other game.

The second Peter Anderson joined Hendon from Ilford in July 1976. A tall, thin defender, Peter looked like a centre-half, but was equally accomplished at right-back, where he spent much of his Hendon career, Alan Campbell and Peter Deadman claiming priory in the middle of the back four. That Hendon defence, left-back Gary Hand was the other member, was one of the best in non-League football, and, maybe a fourth-place finish was disappointing, but Hendon have only once finished higher than that since 1974. Stopping goals is the prime concern for defenders, but Peter and Alan together scored 12 goals in Peter's first season at Claremont Road. They managed an astonishing 17 – neither was a penalty-taker – the following campaign.

Peter missed only four League games in 1976–77, one of which came after he helped the Greens to win the Middlesex Charity Cup. He suffered a cut to his head that bled so profusely that three separate attempts to staunch the flow of blood failed and when his white shirt became almost as red as the Uxbridge ones, the referee effectively ordered him off. It would be the first of two medals Peter won that season as he was part of the team which won the Isthmian League Cup with a 1–0 defeat of Barking at Earlsmead.

The following season was a disappointment as Hendon slipped to 13th in the Isthmian League but they did reach the first round proper of the FA Cup, losing 2–0 to Watford, and came up short in both the Middlesex Senior and Charity Cup finals. Peter won his second Middlesex Charity Cup winners medal the following season, as a substitute against Harrow Borough at Earlsmead, his last cup final for Hendon. In fact, cup and League success was pretty thin on the ground in the latter part of Peter's career, and his absence in the FA Cup first round proper replay defeat away to Wycombe Wanderers was key to the Chairboys' success. Peter did play in the Greens' first ever venture onto the Astroturf, the 5–1 defeat of Taunton Town at QPR's Loftus Road ground, and he scored the final goal, too. Sadly, Peter's Hendon days ended just a few weeks later when spending cuts resulted in senior players being released following the FA Trophy defeat at Witton Albion. Overall, he made 265 appearances and scored 31 goals.

Arsenal

Arsenal are one of the biggest clubs in England, against which Hendon played on several occasions.

One of the most famous nights in Hendon's proud history came in October 1964 when the Greens visited Highbury in the London Challenge Cup. The competition was open to all London's professional clubs, plus the last four in the previous season's London Senior Cup – the top London competition for amateur clubs. In most cases, the professional clubs put out a mixture of first-team squad players and youngsters.

Arsenal put out a very strong team, including new £62,500 signing Ian Ure, a full Scottish international who was now English football's costliest defender, and another full international in Northern Ireland's Eddie Magill. Also in the XI – there were no substitutes – were future internationals Bob Wilson, Peter Storey and John Radford, as well as Peter Simpson, David Court, Jon Sammels, Tommy Baldwin all of whom went on to have very long careers in England's top division. Simpson spent a short period at Hendon in the 1970s.

The Gunners made a flying start, in front of a 2,352 crowd, and Radford bagged a nine-minute hat-trick inside 18 minutes. Many teams would have capitulated, but not Hendon, who hit back with a stunning goal from Danny Lakey, who beat Wilson from a very acute angle, and a header from David Hyde, who outjumped Ure to net from Elved Price's cross. John Swannell had struggled with his footing on the lush Highbury turf, so he changed his studs at half-time and was at his best in the second half, making a number of excellent saves. Wilson was less successful, being beaten again in the 59th minute, when Hyde finished off a move involving Roy Sleap and Peter Slade. With 13 minutes to go, Hyde cut in from the left and drilled the ball past Wilson. His hat-trick had taken 34 minutes longer than Radford's, but fine Hendon defending ensured the Greens walked off victors 4–3. Six months later, Hendon returned to Highbury to comfortably beat Finchley 4–1 in the Amateur Cup semi-final.

It wasn't Hendon's first victory over Arsenal. That had come 13 years earlier, when the Greens became the first team ever to win a competitive floodlit match in England. Hendon played three matches at Highbury in 1951. The first visit was a hugely disappointing Amateur Cup semi-final draw with Pegasus – a combined Oxford and Cambridge University team. The pitch was very muddy, but Hendon coped well with the conditions and took the lead with a 70th-minute 25-yard drive from Roy Stroud. Pegasus equalised, but in the last couple of minutes, Bob Avis was tripped in the penalty area. Dexter Adams took the penalty, but Brown made a fine save. The replay, at Crystal Palace's Selhurst Park, was won 3–2 by Pegasus. Two months later, Hendon were back at Highbury and lost 4–3 after extra time to Bromley in the London Senior Cup Final.

The floodlit victory came in the 1951–52 season, in the London Challenge Cup. As they would in 1964, Arsenal put out a very strong side, with a number of first-team regulars in the Gunners' XI. There was a hint of good fortune about the 1–0 Hendon victory, because Arsenal finished with just nine men, Colin Grimshaw being concussed and Arthur Shaw suffering a leg injury. With two minutes to go, Stroud crossed and Arthur Phebey – a fine cricketer who spent many years as Kent CCC's opening batsman – scored past Wales international goalkeeper Jack Kelsey. Hendon went on to beat West Ham in the next round, before losing a semi-final replay against Charlton Athletic, when they were without players on amateur international duty.

Hendon made two more appearances at Highbury in the 1950s, losing the London Senior Cup Final in 1955 to Walthamstow Avenue and in 1959 to Tooting & Mitcham.

In 1999, there was a "what might have been" meeting in the FA Cup. Hendon lost 2–0 at Blackpool in the second round proper and, the following day, the Tangerines were rewarded with a trip to Highbury. One cannot understate how different Hendon's history would have been had they won at Bloomfield Road because the earnings from a full house at Highbury would have secured the future for years to come.

The links between the two clubs really developed after the Second

World War when Arsenal played London Midweek League matches at Claremont Road in the 1950s. From 1947 until the late 1950s, the Gunners were regular opponents for the Will Mather Cup and – to thank the Greens for their hospitality – they usually sent very strong teams for the match.

As well as these matches, there have a number of players who played for both teams. Probably the most famous were Hendon boys Denis and Leslie Compton – both top cricketers as well as international footballers. More recently, one of Hendon's best players of the 1970s and 1980s, the late Dermot Drummy, was an Arsenal product who went on to play almost 350 times for the Greens.

The Athenian League

This piece features the only other League Hendon FC played in until 2018 – and it was the only one in which the club played as Hendon, Golders Green, Hampstead and Hampstead Town – the Athenian League. Many of the titles of leagues for amateur clubs had classical references – Athenian being a citizen of Athens. Spartan, Isthmian, Delphian and Corinthian are other examples.

Hendon joined the Athenian League in time for the start of the 1914–15 season, the third in the competition's history, but played only two matches in their first five years of membership. This, of course, was due the outbreak of the First World War. The two matches were both away from home and both were drawn, 2–2 at Barnet & Alston, in which O. Warren and Arthur Humphreys scored, and Humphreys also got the goal in a 1–1 draw away to Summerstown.

If history had been only a little different, Hampstead Town might never have played in the Athenian League or their membership would have ended after those two matches because, in the spring of both 1913 and 1919, the club applied to join the Isthmian League, but were rejected on both occasions; Enfield suffered the same fate. The War ended in November 1918, and leagues reformed for a half-season, unofficial competition beginning in January 1919.

This meant that the club's first full season was 1919–20. Only once in the first six seasons were Hampstead Town outside the top five, but they never finished in the top two. As Hampstead, in 1926–27, the team finished one off the bottom, four points clear of West Norwood, but five behind Summerstown. There was slight improvement the following season, but in 1928–29, Hampstead finished runners-up, eight points behind Leyton – it was two points for a win throughout the club's days as Athenians.

The Athenian League was, probably, just about the second strongest competition in the south of England, for amateur clubs, with the

Isthmian a tiny bit ahead – the gap grew significantly after the Second World War. Hampstead and Golders Green made numerous applications to join the Isthmians, between the Wars, but were rebuffed in 1920, 1928, 1929, 1930, 1931 and 1933.

The last season as Hampstead was also the best, because Walthamstow Avenue took the title by two points from Hampstead, but had the team won their home match in March – it was 1–0 to the Avenue at Claremont Road – or the 2–2 draw at Green Pond Road in early May, the championship might have come to Claremont Road.

Golders Green, in the years before the Second World War, finished between third and 10th in the 14-team competition. The 1939–40 season ended after two matches, the Green having beaten Barnet 6–4 at Claremont Road and played a goalless stalemate with Southall at Western Road. The last season as Golders Green, 1945–46, was the club's worst, finishing 12th out of 14 teams. The club became Hendon in the summer of 1946, and the change of name led to a change of fortune, with the club not finishing lower than eighth, with three runners-up spots, until the title was won for the first time in 1953. The Greens lost only twice in 26 matches and finished five points clear of the chasing pack, led by Wealdstone.

This was Hendon's golden era – it lasted around a quarter-century, 1949 to 1974 – and Hendon were clearly one of the country's leading amateur sides. The Greens' first three cup final appearances at Wembley Stadium were as members of the Athenian League, in the 1945 Middlesex Red Cross Cup (now Middlesex Charity Cup), the 1955 and 1960 FA Amateur Cups. Tufnell Park were beaten in 1945, and Kingstonian were downed in 1960, but Bishop Auckland won in 1955.

Hendon's continued to be a powerful force in the Athenian League, too. After winning the 1953 title, the Greens were champions again in 1955–56, and were never out of the top five until a disappointing eighth place finish in 1959–60, a season in which they won as many games as they lost – nine – but drew 12 times. The rebound was emphatic as Hendon topped the table in May 1961, finishing a point clear of Wealdstone. David Bell's goal at Claremont Road on April Fools Day 1961, proved the key as it gave the Greens a 1–0 win over the Stones.

The Greens' 49-year membership of the Athenian League (37 seasons of play) ended at the conclusion of one of the most frustrating seasons, 1962–63, in League history as the big freeze decimated the campaign and left teams without fixtures from before Christmas to mid-March. Hendon, by this stage had announced their intention to stand for election to the expanding Isthmian League, and this time – along with Sutton United, Hitchin Town and Enfield – were given the green light. It meant the final two seasons' eighth place finishes were quickly distant memories.

The Athenian League became even more clearly the second amateur league in the south, even though it expanded to three divisions. One notable achievement by the Athenian League was to become the first league competition to receive sponsorship: Kingsmead Hotels were the company to back the League. Sadly, the Athenian League became weaker and weaker and its final season was in 1983–84.

The programme from Barnet versus Hendon in April 1963
– the last Athenian League match between the clubs.

B

John Baker

The Barassi Cup

Barnet FC

Dale Binns

Borrowed Grounds for FA ties

**Brothers, fathers and sons
(and uncle and nephew)**

James Burgess

Jamie Busby

Roy Butler

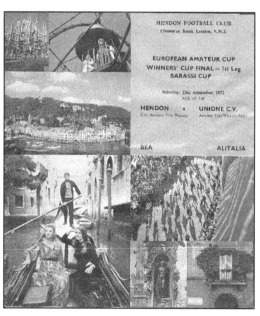

Right: The programme
from the home match in
the 1972 Barassi Cup,
which looked like a travel
brochure.

10

John Baker

Among Hendon's top scorers since the club joined the Isthmian League in 1963, John Baker reached double figures in goals in all seven of his seasons at Claremont Road and scored more than 20 in five campaigns.

His Hendon career stands up against all of the greats to wear the green and white. In seven seasons, he won the Isthmian League title, as well as gaining winners' medals from the FA Amateur Cup, Barassi Cup, Middlesex Senior Cup and Middlesex Charity Cup. And, at the end of the 1973–74 season, during which the Greens played Newcastle United in the FA Cup third round, John won the Supporters Association Player of the Year award. John joined Hendon as a 19-year-old in summer 1969, signing from Isthmian League rivals Kingstonian, this after being released by Brentford a little earlier.

He started his Hendon career with a bang, scoring in all of first three games of the season and two in the fifth match. The goals continued to flow in the FA Cup, where John's goal against Cambridge City booked Hendon's place in the first round proper. He scored twice as Carshalton Athletic were beaten 5–3 at Claremont Road, but the FA Cup run ended against Brentwood Town at the next stage. John finished his first season with Hendon as 26-goal top-scorer, a return that proved to be his best at Claremont Road, though he was top-scorer in 1970–71 with 21 goals.

Between August 1971 and May 1974, John played 164 times and scored 56 goals, a return of better than one goal every three games, but not as prolific as his almost one in two return from his first couple of campaigns. The difference was that he was not centre of attention for defenders in quite the same way, especially in 1971–72 and 1972–73, when the leading scorer was an old-fashioned target man centre-forward, Tony Bass. John and Tony, assisted by John Connell in the first of those seasons, made for a fearsome attacking line-up and amassing 70 goals between them (and this doesn't include the 23 from midfield provided by Rod Haider). Bass's quality in the air – at 6ft 3in he towered above most defenders – suited John's game perfectly because he could run onto to knock-downs or sniff out chances on the rebound. John's style was built on incredible bravery, speed and strength, which made him a handful for any defender. Fans of that age remember John chasing a lost cause at Granleigh Road, Leytonstone, where he was knocked off balance and careered head-first into the concrete wall surrounding the pitch. He was desperate to continue, but wiser heads – no pun intended – prevailed.

In the 1971–72 FA Amateur Cup run, John scored in only the quarter- and semi-finals. Wembley authorities at the time, gave John the credit for the Greens' opening goal in the 2–0 Final defeat of Enfield, but it is more generally recognised as an own goal by the man trying vainly to stop him, Mick Smith. John's shot caromed off Smith's leg and looped over Andy Williams' head into the net. The following season was fantastic for championship-winning Hendon, but not quite so good for John, who missed almost a quarter of the campaign and ended with only 11 goals from 46 appearances. But he was back towards his very best in 1973–74, the season Hendon reached the third round of the FA Cup proper. John scored in the 3–0 defeats of Leytonstone and Merthyr Tydfil in the first and second round proper. He didn't score against Newcastle, but it was his flick-on of Tony Jennings' free-kick that set up Haider for the equaliser. The run ended at Watford's Vicarage Road in the replay. John played in 64 of Hendon's 67 games, as the Greens missed out on a second consecutive Isthmian League championship by only two points – a title that would have been Hendon's based on goal average and two points for a win. In each of the last three seasons, John added Middlesex Senior Cup glory to the other successes.

Baker – along with John Swannell – went to Leatherhead for the following season, where he enjoyed a run to the fourth round of the FA Cup. He was back at Claremont Road for the following season, and collected his only Middlesex Charity Cup-winner's medal. He hadn't lost his taste for goals, grabbing 23 in 55 appearances. John then spent more than three seasons away, but returned for a last hurrah in October 1980. Now in his 30s, and suffering for his craft – he had a chronic hip problem – he made only 21 appearances in six-plus months, but still managed a dozen goals.

The Barassi Cup

On 15 October 1972, Hendon became European champions – or so the club was dubbed by the British media. This is the story of the Greens' only official competitive match outside Great Britain.

Ottorino Barassi was one of European football's most influential officials, being a member of the FIFA Executive Committee for almost 20 years and one of the founders of UEFA in 1953. More famously, he held the Jules Rimet Trophy – the first FIFA World Cup – for longer than most countries. As head of the Italian Football Federation, in 1939, he was charged with the safe keeping of the trophy, won by Italy in 1938, during the Second World War. He decided that he did not trust its safety in a bank, which might have been raided by the Nazis, so the trophy was stored in a shoebox under his bed during the conflict. When the War was over and the World Cup resumed in 1950, he handed the trophy back to FIFA.

He was the guiding light behind the Barassi Cup, which began in 1968. It was a special challenge match between the winners of the

Amateur Cup and the Italian equivalent. Leytonstone were the first winners, and no English team had been beaten, North Shields sharing the trophy in 1969. Sadly, Sr Barassi died in November 1971, but the organisation of the competition continued under the leadership of Gigi Peronace, a well-known football agent, who had negotiated major Anglo-Italian transfers of prominent British players such as Jimmy Greaves and Denis Law.

Hendon, thus had a great deal of British honour to defend as the 1972 Amateur Cup winners. Their opponents, early the following season, were Unione Calcistioa Valdinievole from the town of Monsummano Terme, between Pisa to the south-west and Florence to the south-east, about 20 miles inland from the Mediterranean coast. Unione were like many clubs, *nouveau riche* thanks a new backer and they had done the double of promotion and the Italian Amateur Cup, and their squad contained not only a couple of Italian Amateur internationals, but also 39-year-old goalkeeper Giuliano Sarti, who, in a storied professional career had won eight Italian caps, the Serie A title with both Fiorentina and Inter Milan, the European Cup (twice), European Cup-winners Cup and the Coppa Italia.

Calling the Barassi Cup the European Amateur Championship was actually a bit of a stretch; more accurately it was the Anglo-Italian Amateur Cup-winners Cup, but it was nonetheless very prestigious. Hendon had enjoyed playing Italian opposition a year earlier, when they met Torino at Claremont Road. The Italians had been preparing to face Tottenham Hotspur in a European tie and used the game against Hendon as a warm-up. The Greens led 1–0 at half-time, but Torino put out a much stronger team after the break and ran out 3–1 winners. Manager John Evans thus had an inkling of what to expect from Unione and, as always, he had the Greens perfectly prepared.

It certainly wasn't beautiful football on 23 September 1972. Unione were adept at the darker arts of defensive Italian football of the era, but Hendon made them pay for their indiscipline. After 10 minutes, Bobby Childs curled in a free kick and Rod Haider headed the ball past Sarti, who injured himself trying to make the save and went off – he spent the rest of the match signing autographs. Hendon continued to set the pace and they got a second goal soon after half-time, a 35-yard special from Childs. The match finished 2–0.

Hendon Supporters Association ran a coach to Italy for the return – it left slightly earlier, by two days, than the one to Dulwich Hamlet a fortnight before – and there were 34 fans on board. Hendon's players were already in their hotel in Pisa when they were astonished to learn that the Hendon supporters' coach had turned up and they greeted the fans warmly.

It was a gloriously sunny October Sunday in Italy – and the atmosphere in the ground was hot and tense, too – when Hendon completed the job. I was 14 and could not travel to Italy – the match programme is one of the rarest of all issues for Hendon games. It wasn't easy, especially after John Baker retaliated to a Unione foul and, along with Mazzacane, was sent off. The Italians grew more and more frustrated as Hendon kept them at arm's length. Then, three minutes from time, Gary Hand raided down the left wing, delivered a perfectly-weighted cross and Tony Bass applied the coup de grâce. A minute later substitute Rossi equalised – much to the Greens' frustration – but they could not get another goal and Hendon were European champions.

The Barassi Cup continued for two seasons after the end of Amateur era with Isthmian League second-tier champions Staines Town and Tilbury representing England, before the semi-professional Anglo-Italian Cup effectively succeeded it.

The Hendon teams in the Barassi Cup were:

Home: John Swannell, Tony Jennings, Gary Hand, Peter Deadman, Phil Fry, Rod Haider, Bobby Childs, John Connell, John Baker, Jimmy Wilsonham, Walter Koller. Unused subs: Arthur Paisley (gk), Graham Thomson, David Poole.

Away: Swannell, Jennings, Hand, Deadman, Alan Phillips, Haider, Fred Pudney, Wilsonham (Childs), Tony Bass, Baker, Fry. Unused subs: Paisley, Koller.

Barnet FC

One of Hendon's longest-lasting rivalries is with Barnet FC. Hendon were based in what is now the London Borough of Barnet for most of the club's first 100 years. Hendon Borough Council had become part of Barnet in the 1965 London local government reorganisation. Our rivalry with Barnet FC – in both clubs' different guises – has lasted longer than a century. The first meeting was at Hampstead Town's still new Avenue Ground – they had moved in to their home for 14 years at the start of the season – on Saturday 30 November 1912, in the Middlesex League. Arthur Humphreys made his debut against Barnet & Alston and celebrated with a goal in a 5–1 win; the others coming from Ollie Sumner with two, Henry Pennifer and Billy Denham. Town went on to win the title that season.

Two seasons later, on 12 September 1914, we made our debut in the Athenian League with a match away at Barnet & Alston. Warren and Humphreys were the Town goalscorers in a match which counted for nothing because, a few days later, the competition was suspended as a result of the outbreak of the First World War.

After the Athenian League resumed in September 1919, the two teams – Barnet having dropped the Alston – were regular opponents. The teams met every season between the wars, with the Bees having the better of things in the 1920s and Hampstead/Golders Green on top in the 1930s. In 1927–28, two matches were abandoned, a league game at Underhill – Town trailed 1–0 – and a Middlesex Charity Cup tie at Claremont Road. The latter game was rather controversial because Barnet led 6–1 with 10 minutes left – Hampstead lost 8–2 against Leyton a week later. The match was not replayed for four months and then Hampstead won 4–1.

The biggest winning margin in the inter-war years was Golders Green's 7–0 victory in 1935–36, Dave Walker, three, Tommy Evans, two, Cyril Drinkwater and Billy Breagan scored. The teams were paired together in the Middlesex Senior Cup eight times in 11 seasons, with Barnet winning six of them, but in the 1931 semi-final, an aggregate crowd of 7,000 watched Hampstead draw 2–2 and win the replay 6–1 with two from Freddie Evans and one apiece from Harry Walsh, Bill Morton, Potter and Frank Dean. Just as in 1914, the 1939–40 season was abandoned after two matches, the first of which saw Barnet providing the opposition. The Green won 6–4, Jock Ellison and George Bucci scored twice each and Arthur Wright and Roy Evans once.

After the Second World War, there were regular Athenian League meetings until 1962–63, an era which Hendon dominated – despite a 5–4 defeat in the last qualifying round of the 1948–49 FA Cup. The Greens came close to not losing to the Bees in the 1950s – finally going down in April 1958 – including an 8–2 victory in September 1956, when Miles Spector scored a hat-trick. The rivalry pretty much came to an end when Hendon joined the Isthmian League in 1963. Barnet joined the semi-pro Southern League in 1965.

The clubs did not meet competitively until 1969, when Bobby Wilson and Peter Anderson scored in a 2–0 London Challenge Cup victory at Underhill. Two years later, the Bees knocked out the Greens in the FA Cup, and both these results were reversed over the next two seasons. Barnet were the only non-League team to beat Hendon in the first half of the 1972–73 season and, 12 months later, a Roger Connell hat-trick gave the Greens a first round proper place in the FA Cup. That run ended against Newcastle United.

There have been just two FA Trophy meetings, Barnet won in a replay in 1980–81, and Hendon gained revenge 2–1 on a snow- and frost-bound Claremont Road in December 1981. In the Middlesex Senior Cup, Hendon beat Barnet, now based at The Hive in Queensbury, 2–0 in the semi-final in February 2018. Hendon went on to win the Cup.

There have been only four friendlies since December 1981. In November 1991, Barry Fry sent a team to Claremont Road for a fund-raising friendly after the ground had been closed a few weeks earlier; the Bees returned to Claremont Road for an August 1997 pre-season friendly; they played again in 2011 – Dave Diedhiou scored in a 1–1 draw – and Hendon was the second club to play Barnet at The Hive in 2013, when Anthony Thomas scored in a 4–1 defeat.

Between 1974 and 1996 there was very little player movement directly between the clubs, with probably the most notable being Phil Gridelet, who left the Greens for Underhill in 1990. Former Bees favourite Frank Murphy became Hendon manager in 1997, but he had left Barnet for Dulwich Hamlet before coming to Claremont Road and he signed a number of former Barnet players, including Richard Nugent and Tony Lynch. More recently, former player and present Bees boss Darren Currie starred for Hendon, while working for Dagenham & Redbridge. Maltese international Luke Gambin, England non-league player Wes Fonguck, Mauro Vilhete and Ryan Gondoh all have had brief loan spells with Hendon in the past decade. Going in the other direction, on a permanent deal in summer 2018, striker Josh Walker stepped up two levels after a superb eight months at Silver Jubilee Park.

Dale Binns

Dale Binns began his career as a teenager at Hendon and who has since gone on to become a most respected player and a fan favourite where ever he has been.

He made his debut more than three months before his 18th birthday, a second half substitute replacing Steve Bateman, who had won an Isthmian League winner's medal before Dale's third birthday. There was not much to the teenager, quiet to the point on introverted off the pitch, but a livewire on it. A flying winger, he terrified defences with his extreme pace, but he had to wait a number of years before he nailed down a first-team place.

His first manager, Frank Murphy, who had played in Dale's debut, was infatuated with his game-changing speed and it meant that 43 of the 83 appearances he made in the 1999–2000 and 2000–01 seasons were as a substitute, taking advantage of tiring defenders. Dale's first start was overshadowed by Bontcho Guentchev, also in his first start for the Greens and the spectacular overhead scissors kick in the 3–2 defeat of Canvey Island. It is hard to imagine two more different football characters than Dale and Bontcho, but the former learned a huge amount from the latter. The 1999–2000 season saw Hendon reach the second round of the FA Cup and Dale started in three of the first four matches, coming off the bench in the defeat of Margate. In the first round victory at Bath City, he was Hendon's brightest attacking force for much of the game before late goals from Dominic Gentle and Guentchev won the tie. It was something of a surprise Dale was omitted for the game at Blackpool, won 2–0 by the Tangerines. Three weeks later, Dale scored his first Hendon goal, the fourth in a 4–3 win at home to Basingstoke, and he was on the scoresheet again a week later at Aylesbury.

Murphy's last season at Claremont Road was Dale's most productive and he netted 18 goals in 50 appearances, 22 of which were as substitute and he scored the last goal of the weather-accursed curtailed campaign. It should also be noted, Dale – who won the Supporters Association Player of the Year Award – played in all 19 of the League matches between 3 March and 5 May. Under Dave Anderson, Hendon's football was less expansive, but Dale was a key component, starting 43 matches and only David Hook and Simon Clarke (40 apiece) appeared in more than his 39 League games. His nine goals were also second at the club and included two, off the bench, when the Greens came from 4–3 down to beat Billericay 6–4 at New Lodge. At the end of the season, Dale won his first medal with Hendon, in the Middlesex Senior Cup, and he netted the last goal as the Greens beat Northwood 4–2 after extra time at Hayes.

Dale's style of play left him susceptible to injuries and in 2002–03 he suffered a groin injury in the 4–4 draw at Canvey Island and missed three months. In terms of League position, this was Hendon's best season since 1973–74, with the Greens finishing third. And there was more silverware too, the Middlesex Senior Cup being retained with a 2–0 defeat of Enfield Town at Northwood. More than half of Dale's 35 appearances (20) in 2003–04 were as a replacement, but this was because his fitness was monitored much more closely and risks simply weren't taken when he wasn't 100 percent. The Greens finished closer the League champions than they had 12 months earlier but finished one place lower. If Hendon won the last game, at Kettering, they would have been runners-up, and if Dale hadn't been suspended, it might have been different. These are ifs and buts, and, sadly, it was buts that were Dale's downfall because, in the Middlesex Senior Cup final victory over Uxbridge at Yeading, he had lowered his head towards John Swift and been sent off.

Before the start of the following season, most of the Hendon playing and management staff decamped to AFC Wimbledon, but Dale didn't. However, the fact that Hendon had decided against taking their place in the new Conference South, and the way that new manager Tony Choules wanted him to play, meant that after 45 minutes of a friendly at Berkhamsted – he wore the number 3 shirt – Dale elected to move on. Since then, Dale has played at the highest level of non-league football for a number of clubs, and made a brief return to Hendon in the 2016–17 season, playing five games. In 2019, he won the FA Vase with a Chertsey Town side managed by former Hendon boss Dave Anderson, and including several players very familiar to Hendon supporters.

For Hendon, Dale played in 217 matches, scoring 41 goals.

Borrowed Grounds for FA ties

Hendon have long been pro-active in getting matches played, especially in FA competitions, so there have been a number of grounds staging ties when the club's home venue was unavailable.

This is not a new phenomenon, nor a real surprise given the regularly bog-like state of the pitch at Claremont Road from the 1950s.

In every decade from the 1960s, there have been Hendon home matches which have been played at either neutral venues or at the opponents' ground. On 4 February 1961, a week after overcoming Carshalton Athletic in a replay, Hendon, the defending cup-winners, faced Walthamstow Avenue at Claremont Road. However, the pitch was so bad that the game was abandoned. With bad weather continuing, it was decided to move the match to a former Olympic Games and future World Cup venue, the White City. Hendon's grip on the trophy was wrested away by the Avenue, 2–0, and they went on to succeed the Greens at Wembley in the spring. Consolation for Hendon was that they won the Athenian League title at the end of the season.

The next time Hendon moved an FA competition fixture, it was – mainly – by choice. The winter of 1973–74 was memorable for power cuts caused by striking mine-workers leaving power stations without coal to operate. Hendon enjoyed their best ever season in the FA Cup, beating Barnet in a fourth qualifying round replay, then Leytonstone at home in the first round proper and Merthyr Tydfil at Penydaren Park in the second round, all three victories by 3–0. The third round saw Hendon travel to First Division Newcastle United, where Rod Haider's goal secured a 1–1 draw. With thousands of fans interested in attending the replay, the Greens sensibly decided to move the tie to Watford, where more than 18,000 fans filled Vicarage Road on a Wednesday afternoon. There was no fairy-tale as Hendon became the last amateur club to play in the FA Cup – irrespective of paying wages from 1974 on, all clubs were considered to be semi-professional – losing 4–0 to the eventual runners-up.

Fast forward to another bad winter, that of 1981–82. A cold snap meant that Hendon played only once in December before, on 22 December, local referee Alf Buksh ruled that the snow-covered, icy pitch was playable – in the modern era of health and safety, the frozen terraces would have ensured the game was off, irrespective of the pitch's state – so we went ahead with our game against Barnet in the first round. A late Martin Sperrin goal, fumbled over the line by Gary Phillips, who slipped as he tried to catch the ball, gave Hendon a 2–1 win and a tie against Taunton Town. Claremont Road was unusable on 9 January 1982, the match was postponed and there was no chance of the game going ahead in midweek. To assist Taunton and prevent them making a vain trip on 16 January, pulling strings, the Greens were able to hire the Omniturfed Loftus Road ground of QPR. Rangers were canny about using their weather surface and, on the morning of Sunday 17 January, Barnet and AP Leamington played out a truly dire goalless draw in the Alliance Premier League (now the National League Premier Division).

The afternoon saw Hendon play the men from Somerset. Assisted by Tony Currie's loan of the kit-room key to his brother Paul, it allowed the Greens to wear the boots designed for use on the all-weather surface. On paper, Hendon should have won comfortably; on Omniturf they did, 5–1. The Greens' goals came from Bobby Gough, Sperrin, Dermot Drummy, Pat Morrissey and Peter Anderson. The next round took Hendon north to Northwich, where Witton Albion won a contentious tie 1–0.

All our FA ties in the 1990s due to be at Claremont Road were played there (sometimes in desperately poor conditions), even if ties in other competitions were moved, but Hendon were forced to move matches in both 2000 and 2002 – the former due in no small part to the November 2000 FA Cup tie against Dagenham & Redbridge going ahead. Worcester City were Hendon's opponents and the pitch was never going to recover for this game, so it was moved to the Clarence Park home of St Albans City.

Here a Dale Binns goal forced a replay, which Hendon won 3–2, but then went out in the following round, bogged down by Tiverton Town, whose route one tactics succeeded. The following season, after Hendon had forced a 1–1 draw with Cambridge City, the replay was postponed when the pitch was found to be covered in glass, the result – probably – of a broken beer glass being dropped into a pile of sand waiting to spread on the pitch.

With Claremont Road out of commission for a couple of weeks as the glass was painstakingly cleared, on the day of the next round Hendon were grateful to St Albans City for hosting the replay and, courtesy of a Martin Randall double, Hendon advanced to travel to face Gravesend & Northfleet, who beat the Greens 2–1.

Brothers, fathers and sons
(and uncle and nephew)

This piece could fit into a section in the Dream teams category, because, in the past 20 years alone, Hendon could put out two teams made up of brothers.

A few years ago, there was a story in the papers about a brother who was dismissed for a foul on his sibling. As Hendon has a strong reputation as a family club, I was confident that I could name a team made up entirely of brothers? In fact, with a little cheating, I found enough for a second team, too, and all played for the Greens in this century. Then I thought about fathers and sons. For time-scale reasons, however, this two-generation team goes back a little further, but still in Isthmian League days.

These are the two teams of brothers. The first is limited either to pairs of brothers who were selected by Gary McCann in the same team or the brother who made more appearances than his sibling. For the second team, Goalkeeper Ben Goode and midfielder Daniel Brathwaite were both registered to play for Hendon, but did not make any competitive appearances. In the 2014–15 season, in London Senior Cup semi-final against Harrow Borough Charlie Goode was on the bench for Hendon (unused) and Ben was in goal for Borough; neither brother could recall ever having appeared on opposite teams before.

Team 1: James Reading, James Burgess, George McCluskey, Charlie Goode, Elliott Brathwaite, Casey Maclaren, Lubomir Guentchev, Davis Haule, Brian Haule, Carl McCluskey, Byron Bubb.
Team 2: Ben Goode, Dave Reading, Mark Burgess, Sam Page, Daniel Brathwaite, Kevin Maclaren, Iavor Guentchev, Bradley Bubb, Jack Page, Charlie Mapes, George Mapes.

There were a number of occasions when Hendon named three pairs of brothers in the same 16, but there does not seem to be any occasion when all six were on the pitch at the same time. The three pairs of brothers did not include either of the Maclarens (whose third brother Conor played in a pre-season friendly) or the Burgesses who, between them, made 993 appearances.

In 2007–08, as Hendon battled for the play-offs, missing out with a final-day defeat against Wealdstone at Claremont Road, they could not have come closer. The starting line-up contained Sam and Jack Page, Lubomir Guentchev and Davis Haule. On the bench were Iavor Guentchev, who replaced Jamie Busby and Brian Haule, who replaced … Davis Haule after 36 minutes. By the way, James Burgess wore the number 2 shirt and Casey Maclaren number 12, but was not used. Ben Hudell came on for James.

Four of these 22 players are identical twins: the Burgesses and the Readings. James and Mark Burgess made a number of appearances together, but Dave and James Reading played in just two games, and the only time they both started, on Saturday 16 April 2011, the Greens lost 3–0 at home to Horsham.

On Saturday 21 March 2015, in the Evo-Stik Southern League Midland Division match between Aylesbury FC and Bedworth United, Aylesbury had four former Hendon players in the starting line-up and another in the dugout as manager: Danny Murphy and Bradley Wadkins, plus Davis and Brian Haule, all playing for Steve Bateman, whose two sons have both played for him. Midway through the second half, Brian and Davis jumped for the ball and it was not clear if Brian was shown a second yellow for an elbow on Davis or the Bedworth player who was also involved. The *Non League Paper* report at the time, said Brian had elbowed his brother, though it was Bedworth who were awarded the free-kick.

Below is the father and son/uncles and nephews team, together with a few substitutes. I could almost have added Scott Cousins senior and junior, but Scott senior played only in the reserves. I have cheated with the last of the substitutes: Tony Currie, brother of Paul and uncle of Darren, made a handful of appearances for the Greens in the 1985–86 season, playing alongside the brother of another pretty good player, Steve Wilkins, brother of Ray – a third brother Graham, another former Chelsea regular, also made nine appearances for the Greens 1983–84.

In the 2018–19 season, no less than three sons of former players appeared for the Greens. Admittedly Matty Harriott's father Les appeared only in pre-season games, but Dereck Brown had two spells with Hendon, and Bayley joined midway through the campaign. As youth team secretary in the very early 1990s, I signed Scott McGleish (as well as Darren Currie and Tobi Morrissey, son of Pat), but he left for Edgware Town in the autumn. The son of 1970 and 1980s striker Jock McGleish, Scott had a hugely successful career in the Football League, and joined the club just before Christmas. At the age of 44, he finally made his first-team debut. And, in the 1936 Olympic Games, Bernard Joy, who played a couple of times for Hendon, appeared in the same team as Jackie Gardiner of Queens Park; his grandson Jacob Gardiner-Smith joined the club in January 2019.

Father and sons team: Gary McCann, John Deadman, Paul Currie, Peter Deadman, Steve Butler, Dereck Brown, Lubomir Guentchev, Roy Drake, Roy Butler, Bontcho Guentchev, Darren Currie. Subs: Julian Drake, Max McCann, Bayley Brown, Iavor Guentchev, Tony Currie, Jock McGleish, Scott McGleish.

James Burgess

In modern football, loyalty is almost a dirty word. Breaking the mould were the Burgess twins, Mark and James. On 2 February 2002, James came off the bench to replace Eugene Ofori in the dying moments of a 2–0 FA Trophy replay victory against Cambridge City at Clarence Park, St Albans. At right-back that afternoon was identical twin Mark and all three of James's appearances in that campaign came with Mark also in the team. One had to feel sorry for a rather bemused assistant referee at Hayes when the twins came off the substitutes' bench a minute apart at the end of a 5–1 Hendon victory in the Middlesex Senior Cup. And both played the full 90 minutes when Hendon's interest in the League Cup ended away to Aldershot Town. It turned out to be James's last appearance of the season.

The following season, James became a regular in Dave Anderson's team, amassing a total of 40 appearances – including the Middlesex Senior Cup final when he collected a winner's medal – but in 2003–04 it was Mark who played regularly while James played sporadically.

As well as being identical – more than one supporter has seen one of the twins come out of the dressing room a few seconds after the final whistle and wondered how they could have got changed so quickly. James confided in me that there was an easy way to tell them apart, provided you knew where to look – and the difference was easy to spot even if they were walking down the street together!

It is said that identical twins think alike and act alike – and the Burgess boys proved that argument in their style of play. Both were defenders or midfielders, tough tackling, no nonsense and ready, willing and able to help out team-mates in distress. This, unsurprisingly, got them into trouble with referees and they set an unwanted record when both saw red cards in a 2004–05 FA Cup tie at Stevenage, though one of the red cards was rescinded on appeal. Their combative nature made it difficult for the Hendon management team to have both players on the pitch at the same time, so Mark left during the 2005–06 season.

The twins' similarity went further than playing style, because the way they took penalties was also identical: a 40-yard sprint to the ball and a shot at full power. Feltham's goalkeeper in a 2003 penalty shoot-out screamed at the referee that James was taking two in a row, but the referee shouted "This one is 3, the last one was 2." Mark put his attempt in exactly the same spot, with the bamboozled goalkeeper paralysed with indecision and fear, given the speed of the ball.

Despite their ability from the penalty spot, neither twin was noted for their goalscoring prowess. Mark scored only once, in September 2005, but James had to wait even longer, until he was well past his 30th birthday. Although he wound up with a Hendon career total of three goals – aggregate yardage for the trio being approximately six – the first came in his 231st first-team outing, on 15 October 2008 against Harrow Borough at Northwood. For almost every fan there it was the most memorable of the match. James also scored Hendon's last goal of the League season, a stoppage time consolation at home to Carshalton Athletic. James's third and final goal came in the dying moments of another victory, 3–0 at home to Maidstone United, only this goal was not celebrated by every player – Craig Vargas was left as the only regular outfield player not to score, and Burgess had applied the coup de gras to his goal-bound effort.

James proved to be a valuable servant to manager Gary McCann, playing in a variety of positions in all of his first six seasons. He made at least 22 appearances in every campaign from 2004–05 to 2010–11. In 2011–12, James was a peripheral figure and made only two appearances, both memorable. He was a substitute in the FA Cup fourth round qualifying at Luton Town and his final appearance in a green shirt – so far – was at AFC Wimbledon in the memorable 2–1 London Senior Cup semi-final victory over the Football League newcomers. He left Hendon to join Harrow Borough, and then in 2013–14, James joined Northwood, where Mark is manager. After four seasons at Northwood, he subsequently joined Uxbridge.

Jamie Busby

Jamie Busby made his debut in Gary McCann's first full season in charge and played for more than six seasons. He gave Hendon great service, but had no winners' medals to show for it. The Greens won two London Senior Cups, but he missed the 2009 success because he was on holiday – the final being delayed until after the League season – and was injured in 2012.

Always a midfielder, Jamie had an exceptional scoring record, averaging better than one goal every five games 58 in 258 matches. Rail-thin, Jamie was very strong and quick, a good clean tackler and an above-average passer – a pre-requisite for a Gary McCann midfielder. He was also a superb striker of the ball, either at a set-piece or in open play. His goal in the 1–0 victory at Bury Town, in the second game of the 2011–12 season, stands out: a low tracer shell that Marcus Garnham wasn't close to saving as it arrowed inches inside the post.

Jamie's Hendon debut came during the relegation battle of 2005–06, when the Greens only avoided the drop because of another club's financial woes. He joined from Hillingdon Borough just before the 31 March signing deadline and made his debut at Maldon Town on 1 April. His first three appearances were all as a substitute – replacing Lee O'Leary in the 2–2 draw at Park Drive. His first start also resulted in

Hendon's first win in 12 League outings – a 4–0 crushing of Leyton at Claremont Road. Jamie also started the last three games of the season, including the 3–2 London Senior Cup final loss against Fisher Athletic at Tooting.

Buzza's first Hendon goal was the last one in a 4–0 FA Cup victory over Arlesey Town in mid-September 2005. His next one – three months later – was more important, the winner against Worthing at Claremont Road. Hendon started the following season in spectacular form, scoring goals for fun. With Brian Haule, Belal Aite-Ouakrim and Wayne O'Sullivan sharing 58 goals between them, there weren't many opportunities for others to register and Jamie had his lowest return in a full season, just four goals in 48 appearances, and half of those were in the 11–1 victory at Leyton. Hendon reached two cup finals in spring 2008, losing to 3–0 Hampton & Richmond Borough in the Middlesex Senior and 3–2 to Tooting & Mitcham United in the London Senior and Jamie picked up a second runners-up medal in the former, missing the London final with an injury.

The 2008–09 season served as Jamie's coming out party as a goal scorer. He netted 15 in 44 games, to finish the campaign as leading scorer and winner of the Supporters Association Player of the Year Award, the first of two he would receive. It was a difficult season for Hendon, the club's 101st and the one when the Greens lost their Claremont Road home. A 16th-place finish showed how tough things had been, but the 69 goals scored were fifth-best in the Division. There was another runners-up medal at the end of the season, the 2–0 loss to AFC Hayes in the Middlesex Senior Cup, but he was away for the London Senior success.

Jamie missed almost one-third of the 2009–10 season, but still managed to score eight goals – all in the Ryman League. The following season was probably Jamie's best for Hendon, as he won his second Supporters Association Player of the Year Award. He netted 18 times in 53 outings, including two in the FA Cup first round proper, when the Greens lost narrowly 3–2 to Chelmsford City.

Sadly, Buzza's Hendon career ended the following season, one which saw him suffer a number of injuries, easily the worst of which was the broken cheekbone during the FA Cup fourth qualifying round at Luton. He played in only 27 matches, though he did score seven goals, the last of which was a penalty-spot equaliser against Carshalton at Vale Farm in late March An ankle injury soon after half-time proved to be his last action of the season – and to date his Hendon career, though he is still only 28 years old. In the summer of 2012, Jamie announced – that with a young family and work commitments taking up more and more of his time – he was taking a break from football.

Roy Butler

Roy Butler was a Hendon player who epitomised 100 per cent effort. Nothing says more about Roy Butler's contribution to the Hendon cause than the fact that he was named as Supporters' Association Player of the Year in 1978–79, a season during which he went through more than Greenwich Mean Time (in his case five days short of six months) without scoring a single goal. For those who don't know his name or much about him, Roy was a big, bustling striker, an old-fashioned No. 9. Another big plus against his name is his personality and the fact that when he found out that fans – myself included – could not get to Hayes for a Boxing Day game (public transport, i.e. bus and underground connections, were almost non-existent in some parts of London in those days), volunteered to go out of his way to pick them up and took them to Church Road.

What Roy was very good at, however, was soaking up pressure, making a complete nuisance of himself with opposing centre-halves and normally took the main defender out of the equation to deal with him. In 1978–79, this mean that Mick Garrini, a signing from Tring, and a very close friend of Roy's was given the time and space to bang in 19 goals. Despite Roy's goal drought that winter, from 21 October 1978 to 16 April 1979, he did manage to score a total of 10 goals during the season.

Roy's career at Hendon was in two parts, a brief spell as a young man in the great 1971–72 team, and then as a battle-hardened forward in the late 1970s. A signing from Ruislip Manor, where he had represented the Athenians in an inter-league fixture, his debut came in the cauldron of a local derby against Enfield, just after Christmas 1971 – and there were well over 1,000 fans in attendance – a match Hendon won 1–0 thanks to a goal from Roy. He got a run of consecutive games and scored in four of his first five matches for the first team. He ended the season with five goals from 12 appearances, 11 of which were starts – there was only one substitute available in those days. Although Hendon reached three finals that season, he was an unused substitute only in the London Senior Cup defeat against Enfield and thus missed out on winners' medals in the Amateur Cup and Middlesex Senior Cup.

In the summer of 1972, Roy moved on to St Albans City, before moving on to Hayes, where their fans, like those of Hendon, loved his never-say-die attitude and made him their player-of-the-year. In October 1976, Hendon paid Hayes then the princely sum of £1,000 to secure his services and his second debut came in a 1–1 draw, coincidentally against Enfield, a match which ended in a 1–1, defender Peter Anderson scoring. Roy scored only five goals in 34 appearances, but picked up Isthmian League Cup and Middlesex Charity Cup winners' medals. The following season, Roy missed a quarter of the season, appearing in only 32 Isthmian League fixtures, but 17 out of 20 cup-ties. He won a runners-up medal as Hendon lost to (the old) Hillingdon Borough in the Middlesex Charity Cup Final in May 1978.

In 1978–79, Roy scored in Hendon's first and last fixtures, both in the Middlesex Charity Cup. The opener was on 5 August, in a 3–1 defeat of Finchley in a group match, the last one was on 14 May, the final goal of the season, the third in another 3–1 victory this time over Harrow Borough in the final, here at Earlsmead.

In his final Hendon campaign, 1979–80, Roy couldn't add to his medal count and again missed a quarter of the league season, appearing only 31 times. He scored nine goals from 46 appearances, but Hendon's league form had been mediocre during the last three seasons, with 13th, ninth and 13th place finishes – never really in relegation danger, but never in the hunt for the title.

After leaving Hendon, Roy went to Boreham Wood, then Slough Town. He moved into management and had some success at Berkhamsted Town. Playing for Hendon is, for some players, a multi-generational thing, and Roy's son, Steve, followed in the footsteps of many others – Darren Currie, John Deadman and Roy Drake, to name but three – by wearing the same colours as his father.

C

Alan Campbell

Bobby Cantwell

Careers – Shortest

Bobby Childs

Christmas

Claremont Road

Simon Clarke

Mickey Cooper

Scott Cousins

Alan Campbell

Alan Campbell is a particular hero of our club chairman, but well justifies his place in this book anyway. He was a typical 1970s centre-half, and a very good one. Signed from Finchley in the summer of 1976, it would be fair to say that he had a lot to learn about defending in the Isthmian League top division. He was blessed with an outstanding central defensive partner in Peter Deadman – more a sweeper than a stopper-centre-half – but one of the best central defenders of his era, having been a good enough footballer to be an international midfielder earlier in his career.

His debut came in a Middlesex Charity Cup tie in August 1976, a 1–1 draw with Wembley, and his league bow followed two weeks later, a 2–0 defeat away to Kingstonian. There was no questioning the 22-year-old's desire, commitment or potential, but he was still very rough around the edges. In November that season, he slid in to score after 50-odd seconds of an FA Cup tie at Waterlooville, a great goal, but tactically, should a centre-half be in that position to score from open play? Sadly, the Greens lost 4–1, though they gained revenge in the FA Trophy three months later. The season ended with two pieces of silverware, the Middlesex Charity Cup – in which Alan scored the opening goal of a 2–0 defeat of Uxbridge – and the Isthmian League Cup, where he netted in the last 16 game and semi-final. In that season, Alan scored his best Hendon goal, a magnificent overhead scissors kick away to Slough Town.

More than half of Alan's 31 Hendon goals came in his first two seasons at Claremont Road. He followed his seven – in 54 appearances – in 1976–77 with an astonishing 10 in 59 games the following campaign. In 39 cup ties those two seasons, he scored more than a goal every four matches. Alan's whole-hearted commitment meant he was never an ever-present, indeed only once, in 1977–78, did he play in more than 35 League games. However, amazingly, he was never used as a substitute in his nine seasons with the club.

Financial issues meant that when Dagenham came calling for his services, Hendon couldn't say 'no', so in January 1981, Alan moved to Victoria Road. This was followed by a spell at Barnet, before Ted Hardy and Alan's best friend in football Roger Wade – who will be featured later in this series – persuaded him to return to Hendon in 1986. That 1986–87 season saw Hendon play 75 matches – Alan played in 60 – but there was no silverware at the end of it, just a pair of cup final defeats in the Hitachi (League) and GMAC (Premier Inter-League) competitions.

After scoring 28 goals in his first spell of five seasons, the older and wiser Alan Campbell – he was 32 when he rejoined the Greens – concentrated more on defence and managed only two goals in 127 appearances in his three years back with Hendon. The highlight of this second spell with the Greens came on 2 June 1988, when he was in the team which beat Wembley 2–0 in the Russell Grant Middlesex Charity Cup final, watched by more than 3,000 fans at Wembley Stadium. After a fantastic start to the 1988–89 season, fuelled by the prolific Iain Dowie, things disintegrated following his departure and Alan followed him out of Claremont Road in March 1989.

However, it was not quite the end, as manager Gwyn Walters brought Alan back in November 1991. Hendon's financial woes came to a head, resolved by the takeover by Victor Green a few weeks later and it was Mr Green who dismissed Walters and appointed Barrie Williams manager, with Alan as his assistant. That was cue for Alan to hang up his boots – he was 38 – but this spell ended in January when he asked to leave – although Mr Green announced he was leaving because of his impending wedding. It was an unfortunate end to a career that was certainly among the very best at Hendon in the past 35 years.

Bobby Cantwell

Bobby Cantwell was the Hendon captain in in two Amateur Cup finals – the 1965 win against Whitby Town and the 1966 defeat against Wealdstone. He made his Hendon debut in August 1964, having joined the club from Enfield.

His football career started with Barnet as a 17-year-old. He played in an Amateur Cup semi-final defeat to Woking in 1958, and then was in the Barnet side which lost at Wembley the following season. His team mates included Roy Sleap, Tony Harding and Roy Drake, who all went on to play for Hendon. In 1961, following two years in the Army doing national service and having lost his place at Barnet due to an injury, he moved to Enfield, at the same time that several Hendon players also made the trip round the North Circular to Southbury Road. He was part of the Enfield team that won the Athenian League in 1962 and 1963. He then played in the 1964 Amateur Cup Final for Enfield, a 2–1 defeat to Crook Town.

That summer he joined Hendon. He was a defensive wing-half, and became captain of the marvellous 1964–65 Hendon side midway through the season. He was a first team regular in the 1965–66 and

1966–67 seasons. After playing only 28 games for Hendon in 1967–68, he moved to Dagenham. He made a brief return to Claremont Road for the 1969–70 season, but left to return to Enfield. Overall, he made 170 appearances for the club in one of its most successful spells, scoring 13 goals.

He came close to winning an England amateur cap, and played in a trial match against Wycombe in 1965, but there was a lot of competition for places in the defensive half-back role, not least from former or current team mates Alf D'Arcy and Roy Sleap. However, he did play regularly for Middlesex Wanderers., making his debut in June 1959 on a tour of Uganda, Kenya, Tanganyika and Zanzibar. Interviewed by *EnfieldFootballTales* in 2014, he said that he enjoyed the tours with Middlesex Wanderers, playing in the Caribbean, the Far East, Iceland and twice in Africa.

Bobby Cantwell played for three of the best teams in north London amateur football – the Barnet team of the late 1950s, the Enfield team of 1961 to 1964, and the Hendon team of 1964 to 1967. He grew up in Islington, but then moved to Enfield. He became a Spurs supporter, and said in the interview that he admired Dave Mackay, particularly because he played in a similar position. Later he became friendly with Mackay, and was a Spurs season ticket holder after retiring as a player.

Understandably, the Hendon teams he played for are remembered by supporters for their attacking football. But without consistent defensive players like Bobby Cantwell, Hendon would not have been as successful.

Careers – Shortest

In October 2015, after Aryan Tajbakhsh was released following two appearances, lasting seven and 51 minutes. The question was: "Did Aryan have the shortest ever Hendon career?" The answer was an unequivocal "No," though his red card, seven minutes into his debut, was an unwanted quickest in that category. He has since played in the Football League for Crawley Town and caused a major fracas in a 2018 CONIFA World Football Cup match – getting himself sent off after the final whistle. (Do I bear a grudge? In his case yes.)

Going back to the season 2000–01, the following is the list of 29 players whose Hendon career was a single match, and that as a substitute (as always, with these statistical records, we are indebted to Chris, Steve and Phil Rogers, whose diligence in producing and storing the information on www.hendonfc.net is a priceless help). It is worth noting that all of these players made their sole Hendon appearance in a competitive match.

Junior Adeoye (2007–08, FA Cup, 90th minute)
Ricky Pattenden (2006–07, FA Cup, 89th minute)
Josh Hunte (2006–07, League[†], 89th minute)
Gianni Marotta (2009–10, League, 88th minute)
Paul Dunne (2000–01, Full Members Cup, 88th minute)
Greg Joseph (2003–04, League, 87th minute)
Jon Turner (2001–02, Middlesex Senior Cup, 87th minute)
Adam El-Haddad (2005–06, FA Cup, 86th minute)
James Morrison (2004–05, League, 86th minute)
Sofiane Mehdi (2005–06, League, 83rd minute)
Chike Nnatuanya (2005–06, League Cup, 81st minute)
Anderson Pinto Nogueiro (2017–18, London Senior Cup, 81st minute)
Elias Moses (2013–14, League, 78th minute)
Joshua Adusei (2012–13, London Senior Cup, 76th minute)
Andrew Francos (2000–01, Full Members Cup, 106th minute – game went to extra time)
Pitshou Ngopwani (2001–01, League, 75th minute)
Hassan Al Murtada (2017–18, League, 74th minute)
Daryl Atkins (2011–12, League, 73rd minute)
Lee Scott (2010–11, League, 64th minute)
Cheyce Grant (2018–19, Middlesex Senior Cup[††], 63rd minute)
Jamal Stewart (2013–14, Middlesex Senior Cup, 62nd minute)
Husein Kharas (2006–07, League[†], 61st minute)
Craige Tomkins (2012–13, League, 60th minute)
Mehmet Unal (2003–04, London Senior Cup, 60th minute)
Boris Bogdanov (2006–07, Middlesex Senior Cup, 46th minute)
Michael Kalu (2013–14, League, 46th minute)
James Rogers Oben (2016–17, League, 46th minute)
Jordan Payne (2018–19, Middlesex Senior Cup[††], 46th minute)
Jon-Jo Bates (2010–11, Middlesex Senior Cup, 78th minute – game went to extra time)

[†] = same match, Away versus Horsham, lost 4–1
[††] = same match, Away versus Harrow Borough, lost 3–2

Five players on the list, however, don't really belong because of the circumstances surrounding their games. Firstly, Paul Dunne played in a Full Members Cup tie 20 win at Harlow in October 2000, when the club named no starters for an FA Cup fourth round qualifying tie Hendon were due to play against Dagenham & Redbridge three days later, though at least Bontcho Guentchev and Marvyn Watson would have been in contention. Secondly, Jon Turner was Dave Anderson's assistant manager and Dave put out an experimental team in a 6–0 rout of Kingsbury at Silver Jubilee Park. Finally, all three of Anderson

Pinto Nogueiro, in 2017–18 (at home to Balham, lost 2–1) and both Cheyce Grant and Jordan Payne, in 2018–19 (away to Harrow Borough, lost 3–2), were in experimental teams in London Senior Cup ties.

However, here are three players who deserve special mention on the demerit side:

David Speedie, a former Scottish full international, in 1996–97, made five appearances for Hendon and received five yellow cards. He made his debut on the opening day of the season, a defeat against Sutton United, and finished the match in goal after Scott Ashcroft suffered a career-ending injury. There was one match in which he did not see yellow, but his final appearance saw two of them and his reaction the dismissal resulted in his immediate subsequent departure.

Simon Quail, another veteran player, albeit on the non-League scene, made two substitute appearances in 1995–96. He came off the bench on 16 and 19 December 1995, home defeats against Kingstonian, 3–0, and Hitchin, 2–1, and could not have looked less interested.

Rhys Paul made his only Hendon appearance on 14 October 2013, against Dulwich Hamlet in the London Senior Cup, a match the Greens lost 3–1. Paul, who had conceded the penalty which gave Hendon an equaliser in the FA Cup tie against Eastbourne Borough a year earlier, was substituted after 64 minutes, giving him a Hendon career six minutes longer than that of Tajbakhsh.

From the above, it is clear that there is one player who has the shortest Hendon career in recorded history, coming on in the 90th minute or in additional time. The reason recorded history is so relatively recent is that, prior to 2000, the times of substitutions regularly were omitted from statistics.

Junior Adeoye was the last of the Hendon substitutes in the 3–2 FA Cup first round qualifying replay victory over Aveley at Millfield on Wednesday 19 September. He came on for Ben Hudell, but did not earn a mention in the match report.

Bobby Childs

Bobby Childs was one of my all-time favourite Hendon players, who died tragically young. His statistics don't tell the true story of his contributions to Hendon. The only competition he didn't win in six seasons at Claremont Road was the London Senior Cup, but he did get a runners-up medal in 1972. Bobby had left Hendon much earlier in the season the Greens won the League Cup, the first season they entered the competition. He also played in the Hendon teams that drew at Newcastle United in 1974 and beat Reading in 1975. Bobby never led the club in appearances or goals but was second-top goal scorer in

1975–76. Before he joined Hendon, Bobby won an FA Amateur Cup-winners' medal in 1966, scoring twice for Wealdstone in the final against Hendon at Wembley.

A case could be made that Bobby was the final piece in the jigsaw as John Evans moulded one of the most dominant teams of the time. In modern terms, Bobby would be considered a winger or wide midfielder, having previously been more of an old-fashioned inside forward in the 1960s. Slope-shouldered, short and stocky, Bobby wasn't a will-of-the-wisp winger, but he combined great ball-control and strength with the ability to beat a defender inside or out and then deliver a dangerous cross. He was also a set-piece expert, either from the corner quadrant, from free-kicks or the penalty spot. From 12 yards, Bobby combined both power and placement; the one time it didn't work was an FA Trophy tie against Kettering Town in 1976, but the referee ordered the kick to be retaken and Bobby made no mistake second time around for the game's only goal.

Bobby's debut came against Hitchin Town in October 1971, a 2–0 victory, by which time Hendon had completed a large chunk of their League fixtures. He finished the season with 40 appearances, 19 of which came in cup-ties, including the finals of the FA Amateur Cup, London Senior Cup and Middlesex Senior Cup. He contributed five goals, three in knock-out matches, including the opener in the Amateur Cup semi-final against Wycombe Wanderers at Brentford and in the Middlesex Senior Cup final against Enfield. Bobby also scored in the Barassi Cup first leg against UC Valdinievole in autumn 1972. The 1972–73 season was the second most prolific of Bobby's Hendon career as he netted 12 goals in 51 appearances and claimed Isthmian League and Middlesex Senior Cup winners' medals.

Hendon couldn't repeat their League glory in 1973–74, but they more than made up for it in the FA Cup where victories over Barnet, Leytonstone and Merthyr Tydfil set up a third-round tie against Newcastle United. More than 30,000 watched the game at St James's Park, where Alan Kennedy had a torrid afternoon trying to keep Bobby quiet. A 1–1 draw led to a replay at Vicarage Road, Watford, and Newcastle made no mistake second time around, winning 4–0. A combination of long cup runs and power supply problems meant that midweek games were largely impossible during the winter months, which led to fixture congestion, and Hendon – worse affected than most – finished two points behind champions Wycombe. The only consolation was a third straight victory in the Middlesex Senior Cup Final, this time against Edgware Town.

The offseason saw almost all of the great team move on to pastures new and Bobby was one of those to go, returning to St Albans from where he had joined Hendon three years earlier. However, he returned to Claremont Road in February 1975, where finished the campaign with six goals in 14 appearances. Bobby might have made the difference in the Middlesex Senior Cup, where Hendon reached a fourth consecutive final, but the arcane qualification criteria of the time meant he was ineligible and the Greens lost in a replay to Staines Town.

Saturday 22 November 1975 is etched in Hendon history as the day the Greens first beat a Football League club in the FA Cup. Bobby was fouled on the halfway line at Claremont Road, Dave Metchick took the free-kick, John Baker flicked it on and Alan Phillips scored what proved to be the only goal against Reading. The following spring, Bobby won a Middlesex Charity Cup winners medal as Wembley were beaten 1–0 at Claremont Road. From a personal performance point of view this was possibly his best season, as 17 goals from 54 appearances and the Supporters Association Player of the Year award attest. It was also Bobby's last full season at Hendon as he left the club after making just 10 appearances in autumn 1976. Tragically, Bobby developed leukaemia, which claimed his life in his early 40s, a few years later.

Christmas

Christmas fixtures used to be a staple of football, specifically the matches played back-to-back on Christmas Day and Boxing Day. Football League matches on Christmas Day were played until 1957, but the Scottish League had matches for another 19 seasons. Some of the strangest scores in League history came on these back-to-back fixtures, most notably in 1935. Oldham Athletic beat Tranmere Rovers 4–1 on Christmas Day, but at Prenton Park a day later, the Latics scored four again, however, their defence was rather ripped apart as Rovers responded with 13 goals.

From what I can discover Hendon has the honour of having played in the last competitive Christmas Day fixture in England. It was in 1970, and Hendon's hosts were the same ones the club had played on most Christmas Days since 1928, Wealdstone. Games were not always played on Christmas Day or back-to-back on Boxing Day, mainly because there were a number of years when 25 or 26 December fell on a Sunday and Sunday football was not even considered. Bad weather, of course, was another issue and I remember hearing stories from Hendon fans who trudged through snow and ice, only to find the match at Claremont Road or Lower Mead was off.

Things would be very different today, especially as there is practically no public transport on Christmas Day and a limited one on Boxing Day. And, of course, for most of the years the Christmas and Boxing Day games were played, matches would have kicked-off no later than 2.15pm because floodlights were not installed.

The club's history with Christmas Day football dates back to 1912, when Hampstead Town played in the Middlesex League. Our opponents were Wood Green Town, not the club which has morphed into the present day Haringey Borough. It was the third meeting between the clubs in 1912, Town having won a Middlesex Senior Cup tie 4–3 in November and a London League fixture 2–0 in mid-December. Hampstead had to travel to Wood Green first, where Henry Pennifer, who had scored in both previous matches, netted twice on Christmas Day, with Arthur Humphreys and Herbert Pike getting the others in a 4–1 victory. The Boxing Day game, sadly, was abandoned with the game still goalless, but when it was finally played, almost three months later, Hampstead won 2–1 and went on to complete a double of London League and Middlesex League titles. They won all five meetings with Wood Green Town, Pennifer scoring in four of the games, netting seven in total.

Hampstead's first Athenian League season, 1914–15, was called off after three matches because of the outbreak of World War 1, so their first Christmas fixtures were not until in 1919, when George Blackburn scored the only goal in a 1–0 victory over Southall at Western Road. The following day, Town entertained Southall and won 2–1, with goals from F Burrage and J Croal. Christmas Day fell on a Sunday in 1921 as Hampstead enjoyed home games on both Christmas Eve and Boxing Day, winning 3–1 against Barnet and 2–0 against Luton Clarence. Records are incomplete for 1923, and there is no date given for the away game against Luton Clarence – a 3–1 Hampstead loss. On Boxing Day, Town crushed Clarence 9–0 at the Avenue Ground.

After playing Sutton United home and away in 1924 – quite a trek for Christmas in those days – and Barnet in 1926, the rivalry with Wealdstone started in 1928, the Stones' first season in the Athenian League. Hampstead won both matches in 1928, but the club does not have a record of the goal scorers in either the 3–1 win at Lower Mead or the 3–2 triumph at Claremont Road. The teams had Christmas meetings every year before the Second World War, with the exception of 1938, but Golders Green did not play between 17 and 31 December.

A strange feature of Hampstead, Golders Green and Hendon's Athenian League contests against Wealdstone was that all 23 Christmas

Day games were at Lower Mead and every one of the 25 games on 26 December were at Claremont Road – in 1949 and 1955 Christmas Day was a Sunday. The club's record against Wealdstone in these Athenian League contests, was pretty good, with 22 wins and 12 draws in 49 encounters.

Hendon joined the Isthmian League in 1963, a year before Wealdstone, and the Christmas rivalry continued annually from 1964 until the Stones joined the Southern League in 1971. The Isthmian League rivalry was completely dominated by the Greens who did not lose any of the 10 Christmas encounters – the other four games were postponed. Home advantage, however, did rotate from year to year.

On 25 December 1970, Hendon travelled to Lower Mead and returned with a point, John Wilson scoring for the Greens and Hugh Pentecost for the Stones in front of 975 spectators, the last Christmas Day fixture the Greens ever played. The Boxing Day return at Claremont Road was postponed. For the record, Hendon's overall record on 25 December – including Hampstead Town, Hampstead and Golders Green – is as follows: Played 32, Won 13, Drew 9, Lost 10, Goals for 66, Goals against 58, Points 35.

(The programme is the 1958 Christmas Day match at Wealdstone)

Claremont Road

Hendon's stadium for 82 years – Claremont Road – no longer exists as a football ground. The site is now a housing estate comprising Swannell Way and Haider Close (named after two of Hendon's 1960s and 70s legends (goalkeeper John Swannell and midfielder Rod Haider).

A new home stadium had to be found for Hampstead Town after the lease at the Avenue Ground expired in 1926 and Clitterhouse Farm on Claremont Road became available. The farm had recently closed and, in late 1925, Hendon Urban District Council had taken over the land, which they intended to use for playing fields. They agreed to provide a new home for the club. The fitting cost £1,500. Donations helped to reach this target, with a £100 donation from Lord Glendyne and support from the Mayor of Hampstead and Hampstead MP George Balfour. He was an MP and co-founder of the Balfour Beatty building company. The original rent was £225 a year.

On Saturday 18 September 1926, Lieutenant-Colonel C.D. Crisp, OBE JP – a future chairman of Chelsea FC – declared the stadium open. The first match was an FA Cup tie against Berkhamsted Town. Hampstead won 4–3, in front of a 3,500 crowd, with the honour of scoring the club's first goal at Claremont Road went to RT Sear. Another first season highlight was a 10–0 rout of West Norwood. Harry Shearcroft scored four and E Appleby got a hat-trick.

In 1935, a year after the formation of the Golders Green FC Supporters Association, the fans helped to erect terraces at Claremont Road. In 1938, Golders Green became landlords, welcoming Tufnell Park, whose ground had been commandeered by the Army for the laying of Air Raid Precaution Trenches. Another new feature of the ground was a loudspeaker system, a very useful addition, given that crowds topped the 2,000 mark for bigger matches. A year later, plans were unveiled for the building of a covered terrace opposite the main stand – but the outbreak of war ensured this did not happen until 1946 – the club had also unsuccessfully lobbied London Transport for the provision of a bus to go past the ground. This did not happen until the 1990s, when routes were changed to serve Brent Cross Shopping Centre which had opened in 1976.

After the end of the Second World War, the club changed its name again, to Hendon. The arrangement with Tufnell Park lasted only a couple seasons after the war, but there was a new club sharing the ground – albeit for their London Midweek League matches – Arsenal FC. This arrangement proved lucrative for the Greens as the Gunners sent strong teams to contest the Will Mather Cup at Claremont Road, in front of very large crowds. On 12 January 1952, Claremont Road's attendance record was broken for a 1–1 FA Amateur Cup tie against Bishop Auckland – the north-easterners got a 1–1 draw and won the replay 5–1. Ten months later, the record fell again, this time for the visit of Northampton Town. Quite how 9,000 fans squeezed into the ground is beyond me, but they witnessed a goalless draw and the Cobblers won the replay 2–0, in front of "only" 6,120.

The addition of seating in the main stand, the building of a new clubhouse and the erection of floodlighting apart – the ground changed little in character over the next 50 years. Numerous plans came and went for significant improvements to Claremont Road and – it must be said – that by the time the end of the millennium came around, this was no longer a top ground. I still loved it, but was deluding myself when thinking it was a great place for football.

By the time Claremont Road closed its doors for the final time, the cost of refurbishment was in the high six figures. Mother nature did her bit, such as the Claremont Road terracing (it had been between the grandstand and the Brent Cross end) overgrowing and becoming an almost unusable grass bank, apart from being home to a multitude of foxes. The terraces were starting to crumble, and the walls behind the goal – especially at the Brent Cross end – were not really safe. If, when the club had been prosperous in the 1950s, 60s and early 70s, the necessary improvements had been made, the club's history would probably have been very different.

One of the biggest problems was the pitch itself. The clay surface and poor drainage meant that rainwater would lie on the surface which meant that games regularly would be postponed. In wetter winters, it became a muddy bog, a surface that good footballers hated to play on. Even modern groundwork failed to remedy the situation and, at the end of one season, a visiting manager tried to get a match called off by burying a football in a large hole just outside the car park penalty area. The ball was removed, sand filled the void and the game was played.

But, in the 1950s and 1960s, the Football Association thought enough of Claremont Road to play two Amateur internationals at the ground, and there was an Olympic Games qualifier too. Also, in 1961, the Athenian League played out a 4–4 draw against an Iceland XI. The Olympics match was a qualifier for the 1968 Games against West Germany. Great Britain had won the first leg 2–0 so the 1–0 defeat was enough for Britain to advance to the next round. The last major representative fixture at Claremont Road was an Isthmian League XI playing the Combined Services in the mid-1990s, but the ground also staged cup finals for the League, Middlesex and London Football Associations.

Victor Green became club chairman in 1991–92. He planned to dramatically upgrade the stadium, which involved the purchase of some redundant playing field land, and building a new grandstand, with changing rooms, corporate hospitality and a bar. He obtained planning permission, but his involvement in the club lasted barely two years. His successor, Ivor Arbiter did start the renovation process, the building of a new clubhouse and banqueting centre in the mid-1990s. The banqueting suite helped to keep the club going for a few years.

There were also plans to move the pitch 10–15 metres away from Claremont Road, but the financing could not be achieved – had the Greens beaten Blackpool in the 1999 FA Cup second round, the third round tie would have paid for it – instead it was the seasiders who played Arsenal at Highbury. Ivor's health deteriorated and he died in the summer of 2005.

The ownership of the club passed to his son-in-law, and the writing was on the wall for Claremont Road. Hendon FC Supporters Trust took over the ownership of the club in the mid-2000s, but in the summer of 2008, they were notified that their eviction was imminent.

Memories of Claremont Road (photos: Peter Lush)

The main stand at Claremont Road (photo: Peter Lush)

On Saturday 20 September 2008, 82 years and two days after the first match at Claremont Road, Hendon lost 4–1 to Wealdstone, in front of 280 fans. Dave Diedhiou had the honour of scoring Hendon's last ever goal at Claremont Road and Stephen Hughes netted the final ever goal. Within weeks, squatters had moved in and eventually the final vestiges of our long-time home finally disappeared.

What is my favourite memory of Claremont Road? Oh boy … my goal for the Supporters Association against the club in 1982 – I can see still see the goalkeeper's arching back and dive getting nowhere near my dipping 25-yard volley (or was it from the Brent Cross car park?). For Hendon, beating Reading in 1975–76 FA Cup first round was very special, as was the defeat of Burton Albion in the GMAC Cup semi-final replay in 1987, but – in truth – there are too many to say.

Simon Clarke

Few players with 350 appearances have come as close as Simon Clarke did to be out of Hendon before his tally had reached 30. Simon joined the Greens after leaving Kettering Town, then a Conference club, having played three times for West Ham United in the old Second Division – now the Championship. Manager Mick Browne played him in midfield, sometimes on the left, sometimes in the middle, but he was a square peg in a round hole and his intricate control came to nought with his team-mates unable to support him. Throughout 1995–96, Simon was forced into unfamiliar midfield roles and was transfer listed by Mick Browne, then Neil Price, with no takers. Nonetheless, he appeared in all but four matches.

40

Simon scored 16 goals in his Hendon career, the most important of which came on 15 April 1997 when the Greens were in a desperate battle against relegation. Trailing 1–0 against Aylesbury at Buckingham Road, and lucky still to be in the game, Hendon fought back to equalise, then, in the dying minutes, Simon drilled a shot into the net to give the Greens three vital points. His consistency in a struggling team earned Simon the first of his two Supporters' Association Player-of-the-Year awards, not bad for a player who had been available for transfer early in the season.

Actually, subsequent managers Frank Murphy and Dave Anderson later made him available, so Simon had the unusual experience of being transfer-listed by four different managers at the same club. When Steve Smart was injured in the 1997–98 FA Cup first qualifying round match against Fisher Athletic at Claremont Road, Simon came off the bench and played at left-back. For most of his remaining time at Hendon, the number three shirt was his. He was the only Hendon player to appear in all eight FA Cup competition proper ties in the 1990s, and played his part in the glorious night at Brisbane Road on 25 November 1997 when Gary, Freddie and Junior combined to knock-out Leyton Orient.

Having played in more advanced roles, Simon thrived in Frank Murphy's attacking style and without neglecting his basic defensive duties; he was a dangerous player down the left hand side – often with Junior just in front of him. Another string to Simon's bow was his talent as an emergency goalkeeper; on a number of occasions he had to step into the breach. Football was in his blood and a cousin, Mel Capleton, played in the Football League for a number of years. The pair played against each other for the first time in a Full Members Cup tie at Park Lane, Canvey Island. On a rare foray forward, Simon accidentally kicked Capelton, who responded with, "Do you always kick your cousin." Simon looked around, somewhat shocked, as he hadn't noticed he was playing against a family member.

At the end of the season, Hendon won the Full Members Cup with a superb second half show against Basingstoke at Chesham's ground. Twelve months later, after an arduous campaign, the Greens retained the trophy, albeit in more functional style against Worthing at Gander Green Lane, Sutton. There was also Middlesex Senior Cup success.

The 2000–01 season was thoroughly unsatisfactory, mainly due to the bad weather and damage to the Claremont Road pitch. The Greens failed to complete their Ryman League schedule. Simon was the only player to start at least 30 League and 10 cup games, ending on 44 appearances, and he started six of the seven matches played in the final 12 days.

Things were somewhat different under Dave Anderson, but one that didn't change was Simon's level of performance. He collected his second supporters' Player-of-the-Year award, this despite the pressure of long commutes from his Essex base and also took home a Middlesex Senior Cup winners' medal, though only as an unused substitute. He also found himself wearing a number of different shirts, all too often those in the teens, but he saw time at right-back and in the middle of defence.

At the end of the season, the travel became too much for Simon and he left the Club. His love of the club was clear as when Hendon played at Bishops Stortford the following season, he drove to the game, just so he could catch-up with supporters, officials and former team-mates and to return the Supporters Association trophy. Simon came back to Hendon in October 2005, playing for Maldon Town, but he had left the Jam-Makers by the time of the return fixture in April – though the other Simon Clark did play for them at Park Avenue.

Mickey Cooper

Mickey Cooper was one of those players every successful club needs; a quiet, unflashy, reliable footballer who does the job well, in whatever position he is asked to play.

His Hendon career stretched from the mid-1960s to the end of the following decade, though he was considered a first-choice player for no more than three of his 15 seasons with the Greens, during which time he made 146 of his 416 appearances, and scored four of his six goals. In fact, although Mickey's Hendon career spanned 16 seasons, he made only one appearance in the Isthmian League championship campaign of 1972–73 and none in 1977–78. Indeed, he left the club on a number of occasions, normally returning a few months later.

Mickey was a full-back, and a very good one, winning three England Amateur international caps in 1972 on a tour to Scandinavia. He joined Hendon in the summer of 1964, an unheralded arrival, and spent the first half of the 1964–65 season in the reserves. On 30 January 1965, Mickey made his first-team debut, a 4–2 home victory against Tooting & Mitcham United. The debut would almost certainly have come earlier in the season, had substitutes been permitted, but that was still 18 months away. Mickey played twice more in the League during the rest of the campaign. The 1964–65 season was Hendon's finest with both the Isthmian League and FA Amateur Cup won, but Mickey's role was peripheral. His only cup tie was the quarter-final of the Middlesex Senior Cup, when he came in for regular left-back Roy Sleap in a 2–1 victory at Enfield – the Greens later claimed that piece of silverware too.

In the following season Mickey got the chance to shine at left-back and didn't let anyone down, making 27 League appearances and 11 more in Cup competitions, including at Wembley in the Amateur Cup

Final, where Wealdstone prevailed 3–1. In 1966–67, Mickey became the regular full-back. He also scored his first goal for the club and it could hardly have been more spectacular or important. The Greens were trailing 2–1 in the last minute of extra-time in their FA Amateur Cup semi-final replay against Skelmersdale United, at Birmingham City's St Andrews. Hendon forced a corner, which was half-cleared to Cooper who returned the ball, with interest, and it flew into the net. Mickey's reaction was, "the ball could have gone anywhere and my shots usually end up in the stand." Skem won the second replay 3–1, but the season ended with a Middlesex Senior Cup final victory over Enfield, 3–2 on aggregate. Mickey played in both legs to collect a winner's medal.

Not seeing much first-team action, Mickey briefly left, joining Slough Town in March 1968. However, when Ron Patterson replacing Bill Fisher as manager that summer, Mickey returned and, playing in midfield, he would be a near ever-present throughout the season, missing just one League game and a couple of cup ties. The season ended with another winners' medal, this one the London Senior Cup, as the Greens beat Dagenham 1-0 at Underhill.

John Evans' return to Hendon in 1970 saw Mickey revert to full-back, and there was improvement on the pitch, one of the highlights of which was an FA Cup run which saw Hendon entertain Aldershot in the first round proper, but there was no joy as the Shots won 2–0. It was the same score – to the opposition, too – in both legs of the Middlesex Senior Cup final as Enfield took home the trophy. Mickey made almost 50 appearances and seemed set for a long run in the first-team. However, a combination of knee injuries and new full-backs, Tony Jennings and Gary Hand meant Mickey found himself on the outside.

Indeed, it would not be until the 1973–74 season when Mickey played a notable part in the Hendon fortunes. He was the unused substitute in the 1–1 draw at Newcastle, and took over as the regular right-back when Jennings defected to Enfield in March. Many fans believe Hendon would have won the league that season had Mickey not broken a collar bone against Woking with four games left in the season. Two draws in the next two games proved the difference between champions and runners-up.

Another Middlesex Senior Cup winners medal was scant consolation. Apart from one season until 1979–80, Mickey remained a valuable squad member, rather than a regular starter. After just five appearances in autumn 1979, Mickey left the club. His brother Robbie had been at the club with him, but never made a first team appearance. Robbie actually watches Hendon occasionally, especially when the Greens are at Staines – his house backs onto their stadium.

Scott Cousins

Scott Cousins contributed much to Hendon, mainly as a player, but also as a coach. Scott joined Hendon from Chelsea in the summer of 2003, having found his path to the first team blocked by a multitude of internationals. He did have Hendon links as his father, also Scott, had made a handful of appearances for the reserves. His first manager at Claremont Road was Dave Anderson, who was aware of Scott's fiery reputation and I remember Dave telling me of a conversation he had with Scott when he had been with the club a few weeks – Scott missed the season-opener serving a suspension from the previous campaign. "Who is the better player, you or me?" Dave asked. "Me," replied Scott. Dave then asked, "If you are suspended and sitting in the stands, who is the better player?" The message got through, loud and clear.

In his first season at Hendon, Scott was an attacking left-sided player, who could beat a player on the inside and outside, then deliver a telling cross. He was also a superb striker of the ball, either in live play or from a set-piece. He scored and created numerous goals as the Greens finished fourth in the Ryman League Premier Division, only missing out on second place in the final week of the season. Scott scored eight goals, including a few penalties, in 51 appearances that season, both third-best at the club. One goal which stood out was at Northwood when, kicking up the hill towards the cemetery, he struck a 25-yard drive and buried it in the top corner of the goal. He then added a second half penalty in a 2–0 win. Hendon finished the season as Middlesex Senior Cup winners. At the end of the season, Dave's team moved *en masse* – 13 players and staff in total – to AFC Wimbledon, but not Scott. He played in the first preseason friendly, before signing for St Albans City, who he helped rise to the Conference National.

Sadly, Scott's career was derailed by a badly broken leg which he suffered playing for St Albans and he missed significant time. He left the Saints and signed for Carshalton Athletic in the summer of 2009, but returned to Hendon, now at Vale Farm, in October that year, making his second debut against Lowestoft in the FA Trophy, a 2–0 Greens victory. Scott was a different player now, certainly less combative, but smarter and still able to find teammates with passes few others would have even seen, let alone attempted. He was also regularly on the scoresheet, with five goals in 35 appearances. The 2009–10 season was an unusually barren one for Hendon whose interest in all cup competitions ended in the quarter-final of the London Senior Cup, but a comfortable mid-table finish of 10th was satisfactory after a disappointing first three months.

In 2010–11, Scott played a big part in Hendon's run to the FA Cup first round – the Greens went down 3–2 away to Chelmsford City – but he did pick up a runners-up medal in the London Senior Cup. The season started very promisingly and the play-offs seemed a possibility, but injuries meant the Greens coasted through the second half and finished in lower mid-table. Scott was appointed captain for the 2011–12 season and his leadership certainly helped the team. The arrival of Darren Currie gave the Greens a magnificent left-wing combination and it was little surprise that Hendon enjoyed a much better season, missing out on the play-offs by just three points, despite amassing a tremendous 72. Scott also had the honour of lifting the London Senior Cup after a comfortable 2–0 victory over Kingstonian at Imber Court. Scott also scored to date his last Hendon goal, at Lewes.

A rare moment of madness denied Scott the chance of leading out Hendon in the first round of the FA Cup at League Two Aldershot Town. He was sent off in the third qualifying round replay against Eastbourne Borough and was suspended for the tie at the Recreation Ground. Scott made 36 appearances in the League that season, but struggled with a groin problem that he could not shake off. This injury did not heal during the summer and Scott was limited to just five appearances in 2013–14, though his mentoring of Jack Bennett certainly made a difference to his career. When Junior Lewis left the Hendon coaching staff, Gary McCann had no hesitation in promoting Scott, a few weeks short of his 31st birthday, to the role of coach. He remained at the club in a coaching role until 2016.

D

Dagenham & Redbridge

Jon Daly

Peter Deadman

Defunct clubs

Dave Diedhiou

Disappeared grounds

Iain Dowie

Dermot Drummy

Dagenham Versus Hendon programme from 1955.

Dagenham & Redbridge

This piece is not just about Dagenham & Redbridge, a club Hendon have played only a few times. Instead, it is about the multitude of clubs which were sacrificed to create D&RFC. The full list is: Dagenham, Ilford, Leytonstone, Leytonstone–Ilford, Redbridge Forest and Walthamstow Avenue.

First matches:
Ilford: Hampstead Town met Ilford in the London League on 2 December 1911. Town won 1–0 with a J Davidson goal. The return result and date are not known.
The first League meetings with the other clubs were:
Walthamstow Avenue: In the Athenian League in 1929–30, Hampstead Town won at Claremont Road in March 1930, courtesy of an own goal, but the match at Green Pond Road ended 6–1 to the Avenue.
Leytonstone: In the Isthmian League in 1963–64, Hendon won 4–1 at Granleigh Road in November and 5–1 in the March return at Claremont Road.
Dagenham: Inaugural winners of the Isthmian League Second Division, we played the Daggers in 1974–75, losing 4–1 at Victoria Road in February and 2–1 at Claremont Road four weeks later.
Leytonstone–Ilford: Our Christmas and New Year opponents in 1980–81, we won 3–2 on Boxing Day at Claremont Road, but lost 2–0 at Granleigh Road on New Year's Day.
Redbridge Forest: This is slightly more complicated, because Leytonstone–Ilford remained the club's name even after the incorporation of Walthamstow Avenue. We played a pre-season friendly against LIFC with a programme cover which announced "inaugural season", and pictured their smiling captain with the League trophy they had won the previous season. Redbridge Forest played only two seasons of games against Hendon, the first of which was Hendon's first home game of the 1989–90 season, a 2–2 draw.
Dagenham & Redbridge: The first meeting was a Full Members Cup tie at Claremont Road, which Hendon lost on penalties in January 1997. A month later, we earned a 1–1 draw at Victoria Road, but won the return Isthmian League game 2–1 in late April.

The disappeared clubs' grounds could hardly have been more different:
Dagenham: Still being used by Dagenham & Redbridge, but pretty much unrecognisable from their days in the Isthmian League. I remember early matches at Dagenham having the crowd swollen in the

final few minutes when the adjoining factory hooter signalled the end of the shift.

Ilford: Lynn Road had a dilapidated pair of stands with good terracing either end, especially the far one. Peter Anderson – the centre-half, who left Ilford to join Hendon – recalled in the final season at Lynn Road being offered a very low price for a flat in the soon-to-be-built block coming to the site. He declined, as he put it, "I felt a bit like a cannibal."

Leytonstone: A three-sided stadium, Granleigh Road was shoehorned into a tiny space off Leytonstone High Road. Passengers standing on the platform at Leytonstone High Road station – Gospel Oak to Barking service – were almost directly over the corner flag. That side, however, mushroomed out to include a small stand and the clubhouse. The opposite wing backed directly onto gardens and had no spectator accommodation. Another strange feature was that the ground was on a slope, but the pitch was level, so fans stood above the pitch at the Station end and below it behind the High Road goal.

Walthamstow: This was a magnificent, large stadium – along with the old Champion Hill and Claremont Road, my three favourite ever in non-League football – with a very big stand, a long and deep covered side, cover behind the dressing room end goal and a massive open end. Every time I walked into the stadium, I felt I could hear the ghosts of the great players and matches at the ground. Irrespective of the crowd number, there was just an amazing aura about the place.

Hendon's last match records against the clubs are as follows:

Ilford: Isthmian League Cup, 6 November 1978 at Granleigh Road, lost 2–1. A huge shock result, but Hendon's players went straight to the game from assistant manager Bill Fisher's funeral.

Leytonstone: Isthmian League, 20 February 1979, at Granleigh Road, won 1–0, scorer Mick Garrini.

Walthamstow Avenue: Isthmian League, 16 March 1987, at Green Pond Road, won 1–0, scorer Neil Wolstenholme against his old club.

Leytonstone–Ilford/Redbridge Forest: Isthmian League, 5 January 1991, at Green Pond Road, won 2–0, goals from Mark Xavier and Gerry Solomon.

Dagenham: Isthmian League, 29 February 1992 at Victoria Road, won 1–0, scorer Mark Xavier.

Dagenham & Redbridge: London Senior Cup, 7 December 2005, at Claremont Road, won 2–1, scorers Jeff Campbell and Jimmy Froud.

(Programme is Walthamstow Avenue versus Hendon in 1951)

Jon Daly

Jon Daly is one of the many players who had more than one spell at Hendon. The signature of Jon Daly, in autumn 1992, wasn't down only to one of his closest friends in football, Barry Blackman – who had been with the Greens since the start of the season. Club manager Barrie Williams was far too astute to sign someone on the say-so of a player – but he did have a staunch ally. Daly and Blackman had been teammates at Croydon when that club had the best youth policy in south London non-League football. Jon first joined Hendon from Dulwich Hamlet, having previously played for Croydon, Tooting & Mitcham United and Whyteleafe. In May 1991, he was in the Sutton United team which played Wealdstone in the final senior match at Lower Mead; a decade later he was in the Hendon team when they played the final senior match at Enfield's Southbury Road ground – a unique if ghoulish double.

Jon was a powerful attacking midfielder with a good eye for goal, as a strike rate of a goal every 7.8 matches proves. His strength and fitness were excellent attributes, especially at Claremont Road around the turn of the century, when the pitch was in an awful state. Although not the fastest player around, he had the happy knack of appearing in the right place at the right time; his positional sense was also displayed on the odd occasion when he played in the middle of the back four. Jon's debut, against Basingstoke at Claremont Road, ended in a goalless stalemate, and his first goal came in a 2–2 draw at Wokingham in his fourth match for the Greens.

Hendon rather went off the rails in the second half of the season; Williams departed in the spring of 1993 and Bobby Makin took over for the rest of the campaign. Jon netted all of Hendon's last three goals, but none were in a winning cause and only one earned as much as a point. Peter Taylor took over in May 1993. It might have been a new dawn at Claremont Road – except Taylor left at the beginning of December and at the end of the month, chairman Victor Green pulled out too. He installed his wife Elaine as his replacement, with a massively reduced budget. Almost immediately, the team broke up and Jon moved on. He played for Kingstonian and St Albans before, in the summer of 1998, Hendon manager Frank Murphy, re-signed Jon for a four-figure transfer fee.

He joined a team which had been installed as pre-season favourites for the title, based on a great finish to the previous campaign. Those notions were disabused on the opening day when newly-promoted Hampton won 3–1 at The Beveree, but Hendon were a potent force with Paul Whitmarsh and Junior Lewis amassing 70 goals between them. Jon had one of his quieter seasons in terms of goals with only five in 58 appearances, but he did win both Middlesex Senior and Full Members Cup winners medals, after defeats of Wembley at Enfield and Worthing at Sutton. He also appeared in the FA Cup run to the first round proper, where Notts County won in a replay at Meadow Lane after a goalless draw at boggy Claremont Road. But Hendon under-performed in the Ryman League, and managed only a disappointing 13th place, 20 points away from both second top and second bottom.

In 1999–2000 Jon's performances earned him the Supporters Association Player-of-the-Year award – an honour he achieved at his last three clubs. He missed only one league match and finished with 55 appearances, including in the 2–0 defeat in the FA Cup second round at Blackpool. This was Jon's last full season as a Hendon player although he did play in the first and last games of the 2000–01 season. He had joined the Metropolitan Police – the third serving officer at Hendon, alongside on-loan keeper Richard Wilmot and defender Paul Towler. Jon's 36 appearances were his fewest in any of his last 12 senior seasons, during which time he played 617 times. Jon's final appearance at Claremont Road came four days after his 38th birthday, 24 September 2005, with his final club, Metropolitan Police FC, in an FA Cup tie the Blues won after a replay. He did not retire until April 2008, having – almost certainly – appeared in more than 1,000 senior matches. Oh yes, in December 2013, Jon played and scored for Met Police Veterans team.

Peter Deadman

Peter Deadman, to many experts, was the finest defender ever to play for Hendon. His record suggests that he had few peers amongst his contemporaries which 45 England amateur international caps shows. He was a fantastic reader of the game, predominantly left-footed, but a great tackler and very good passer.

His dedication to Hendon can best be shown by an event in April 1974. Peter received a call-up to play for the England Non-League team for a tournament at the start of May, but turned them down because the Greens were still in the running for the league championship. He would also have been the only player to be simultaneously an international at both non-league and amateur levels.

50

Peter joined West Ham United as a schoolboy, but his education took priority. He went to Loughborough University, where his football team-mates included John Evans and Dario Gradi. He played for West Ham United during a work placement year, for the 'A' team, alongside, amongst others, Frank Lampard Sr and Harry Redknapp. In his final year at Loughborough, Peter captained British Universities then, having completed his chemistry degree, returned to London and signed for Barking, whose player-coach was John Evans.

When Evans moved to Hendon in 1970, Peter followed him and made his debut in a shock 3–2 opening day home defeat to Woking. Peter scored his first Hendon goal in October, in a 4–1 League win at Hitchin Town, and scored twice in cup-ties, as Hendon finished runners-up in the Middlesex Senior Cup and sixth in the League.

Evans strengthened the Hendon team significantly for the 1971–72 season and it paid off handsomely as Hendon spent the next three seasons as arguably the strongest team in amateur football. Peter was a key player in some outstanding achievements. In the Amateur Cup semi-final, against Wycombe Wanderers at Brentford's Griffin Park, Peter scored the winning goal in a 2–1 victory that silenced the huge travelling support from Buckinghamshire. It was a magnificent long-range strike, which as Peter said came because, 'We were so angry at having conceded an equaliser.' In the 1972 Final against Enfield at Wembley, Peter was superb as Hendon were forced to defend for much of the game, but still won 2–0.

In the following season, Hendon won the Barassi Cup. But it was in the Isthmian League that the Greens rewrote the record books, going 38 games without defeat and storming to the title by a massive 18 points. The 1973–74 season was famous for that FA Cup run, which saw Hendon were drawn against Newcastle United. The Greens forced a 1–1 draw at St James' Park before succumbing 4–0 in the replay. There was no last-season Amateur Cup glory as Leatherhead won a third-round tie. More damagingly, however, the Greens needed nine matches to complete those three rounds and ended up with massive fixture congestion. This ultimately cost Hendon the title, losing by two points to Wycombe. Peter, however, was an ever-present in the League and finished the season with 67 appearances.

There was an exodus from Claremont Road in the summer of 1974 and Peter joined Ilford, managed by John Evans. He spent two seasons at Lynn Road before returning to Hendon, but the team was nothing like the powerhouse it had been half a decade earlier. He pick up a League Cup winners' medal and a number of Middlesex cup ones, but there were no titles and only occasional FA Cup competition proper appearances. On 18 March 1978, Peter made his only substitute appearance for Hendon, to go with 551 starts.

It all ended very suddenly for Peter at Hendon. The exit from the 1981–82 FA Trophy saw an immediate cut in the playing budget. First to go were senior non-contract players, Deadman, Peter Anderson and Paul and the high-priced Trevor Dark, Bobby Gough and Martin Sperrin. Peter went to play at Dagenham for Ted Hardy, but found the Conference – then called the Alliance Premier League – travelling too much, then Grays Athletic, before retiring aged 42. In 1995–96, when his son John played for half a season at Claremont Road, Peter came to watch a few times, but had no other involvement in football. His main sporting activity is now cross-country running, but he did attend the launch of the Hendon FC club history book in November 2008.

Defunct clubs

Writing this book, I have come to realise there are so many opponents that have ceased to exist.

One of Hendon's opponents in a cup match was a phoenix club – a team the club played more than 20 years earlier. Rushden & Diamonds were, when Hendon met them in the FA Trophy in September 1994, a team tipped for greatness. They had just risen to the Southern League Premier Division and were bankrolled by millionaire Max Griggs. He owned Rushden-based footwear company Dr Martens and later sponsored that League and was West Ham United's shirt sponsor. When the Greens travelled to Nene Park – and got a fantastic 0–0 draw, only to lose the replay 4–1 – it was only partially redeveloped from the homely base of Irthlingborough Diamonds. Only two side were all-seater, but by the time they had risen to the Football League, it was seating on all sides. Sadly, Mr Griggs's company hit the financial buffers and the lack of funding saw Rushden & Diamonds drop out of the Football League, then go bust, being replaced by the new AFC Rushden & Diamonds, whom Hendon defeated 1–0 in the first qualifying round of the FA Cup in 2014 and 3–0 two rounds and two years later.

Hayes & Yeading United are the result of a merger in May 2007 between two clubs with whom Hendon had a healthy rivalry over the years. Hayes, the Missioners, had been founded in 1909 as Botwell Mission (they changed to Hayes in 1929), and played for almost a century. Yeading, the Ding, were relative newcomers to senior football. Probably the club's most infamous match against Hayes was the 1988 FA Trophy tie at Claremont Road. It ended in a 3–3 draw – the Greens won the replay 2–0 – but it was notorious for a 20-man brawl which resulted in Hendon finishing with eight players and Hayes nine. Yeading only reached the Isthmian League Premier Division in 1992–93 and their first Saturday home game was against the Greens, who turned up – all players in suits – on a coach 90 minutes before kick-off. Overawed by Hendon's professionalism – Barrie Williams was the manager – the Greens strolled to a 3–1 victory.

A number of other Middlesex clubs have disappeared. These include Finchley – now part of Wingate & Finchley – their present home, Maurice Rebak Stadium, was called Summers Lane when Finchley played there – and Wingate, the team we beat 13–1 in 1958 for the club's record victory.

Two other of Hendon's most local opponents have also disappeared. Kingsbury Town moved out of Silver Jubilee Park and joined London Tigers at what was Viking Sports' ground in Greenford – the entrance in on the westbound carriageway of the A40. The superbly upgraded SJP is now Hendon's – and Edgware Town's – home. Willesden were based in the old sports stadium on Donnington Road – less than half a mile from Christ Church Hampstead's first ground. Hendon played Willesden in the Sports Centre, which was also the home of the Hockey World Cup in 1986. The club's last match against Willesden was actually in the park outside the ground, a Middlesex Charity Cup group match in 1977, Hendon won 2–1.

Both Hillingdon Borough – formerly Yiewsley – and Ruislip Manor have disappeared, the former now playing under that name was successor to Ruislip FC and play at the old Ruislip FC ground on Brakespeare Road North. Manor's ground is now the home of Wealdstone. In the east of the county, Brimsdown Rovers briefly disappeared – not long after they defeated Hendon in the London Senior Cup in 2009–10. Enfield FC is covered separately in this book.

Another league opponent has been Maldon & Tiptree, who were formed out of the merger of Maldon Town and Tiptree United. The Jammakers lost their ground in Tiptree and moved in with Maldon Town, with whom we played two Ryman League draws in 2005–06. Notable in this fixture was Maldon's teams containing former Hendon players Simon Clarke in one game and Simon Clark in the other.

Clubs which have been rebranded in relatively recent times include: Wimbledon, who became the MK Dons when they moved into the south Midlands; Hampton & Richmond Borough, who added the last three words to increase borough-awareness; AFC Hayes, who did likewise because Brook House was not well-known; Redbridge, who lost all backing from Ford Sports and were playing at Barkingside FC; and Walthamstow FC, formerly Leyton, Leyton-Wingate, Leyton-Pennant then Waltham Forest, who, after losing their Hare & Hounds ground to a new Leyton – themselves no longer in existence – moved into Wadham Lodge where they merged with Walthamstow Pennant. After a period away from Wadham Lodge, they are now back there, albeit playing in the Essex Senior League.

53

In addition to Leyton, two other clubs Hendon played in Gary McCann's management era – 2005 to 2018 – are Croydon Athletic, whose issues were the subject of unpalatable news stories, and Fisher Athletic. Both quickly reformed as phoenix clubs. And, finally, two more clubs who disappeared and became phoenix clubs: Aldershot, who folded in the early 1990s and returned as Aldershot Town; and Farnborough Town, both of whom Hendon have played in league matches, as well as a memorable first round FA Cup match at Aldershot.

Lastly, and very sadly, Hendon played their last match against Thurrock in spring 2018. The club built from nothing by Tommy South, pulled out of senior football as Tommy concentrated on his health following a very serious illness. Hendon's record at the never quiet Ship Lane, the stadium sat almost underneath the M25, after a first-season 3–3 draw and a 3–2 success six months later, was dire – one goal, two points – both goalless draws – and too many depressing defeats.

Dave Diedhiou

Dave Diedhiou was the last Hendon player ever to score at Claremont Road. Dave was 19 years old, and a recent migrant from Senegal in West Africa, when he joined Hendon in the summer of 2008, having previously played for Middlesex County League Willesden Constantine. Dave made his debut, coming on as an 86th-minute substitute against Sutton United at Gander Green Lane. A month later, on 20 September 2008, Dave wrote himself into the Hendon record books, though in a very sad way. His first goal for the Greens, midway through the second half of a 4–1 loss to Wealdstone, would be the last one scored by a Hendon player at Claremont Road. He also netted the last disallowed goal at Claremont Road – had it stood the score would have been 3–2.

Dave spent most of that first season on a dual registration arrangement with Wembley, so – although playing in the first match of the London Senior Cup run that season (a penalty-shoot-out victory over Bromley at Hayes Lane) – he was not involved in the Final victory against Croydon Athletic. A strong, physical presence, Dave has suffered for being so good in many different positions, in both defence and midfield, and this has probably hurt his career because he has never played more than 47 matches in a season and in seven campaigns – including the current one – almost a quarter of his appearances have been as a substitute, but for a defender/midfielder his strike rate is very good, a rate of a goal every 8.5 games.

In 2009–10, Dave was regular member of the squad and made 45 appearances, but it was a season of struggle for the Greens, with no cup success either. The following year was a different story; there was a trip to the FA Cup first round and a run to the London Senior Cup final. Dave missed half of the season, but was back for the London semi-final, when he scored the winning goal against AFC Wimbledon (who were battling for a Conference Premier playoff berth) at Kingsmeadow. Sadly the final turned out to be disappointing – a 3–1 loss to Wingate & Finchley. But, in just 28 appearances, Dave scored five times, his second best return for the Greens.

Hendon enjoyed their best season for many years in 2011–12. Aided by veterans, such as Darren Currie, Isaiah Rankin and, briefly, Frank Sinclair, together with new coach Junior Lewis, the Greens played some fantastic football and went all the way to win the London Senior Cup, giving Dave his first winners medal. The team performance in crushing Kingstonian 2–0 at Imber Court, Metropolitan Police was outstanding, as had been the semi-final victory over AFC Wimbledon, who were now a Football League club. As proof of his versatility, Dave was at right-back in the semi-final and in the centre of midfield in the final. Despite a flying finish to the campaign, Hendon missed out on the playoffs by three points and two places.

Dave missed much of the first of the 2012–13 season, and played little part in the run to the FA Cup first round, though he was an unused substitute in the narrow and heart-breaking defeat at League Two Aldershot Town. In the Ryman League, however, with Dave absent, Hendon struggled hugely and they would have gone bottom had they not beaten Thurrock in mid-December. In the second half of the season – during which time Hendon played two-thirds of their Ryman League fixtures, Dave was back and went on to play in 33 matches, though his goal return was down to just two goals.

The 2014–15 campaign was one of Dave's best for Hendon, both in terms of appearances and goals. He appeared in 47 matches and contributed nine goals, including the last one of the season against Margate. But if he had he been able to convert one more chance in that game, he would have been the fourth Greens player to reach double figures, along with Jefferson Louis, Leon Smith and Anthony Thomas.

Dave's continued importance to the team might have been best illustrated by the defeat at Dorchester Town in this season's FA Cup – Dave was sick and the Greens performance was lack-lustre in the 1–0 defeat. He has scored only four goals this season, but the one he scored against Leiston was the perfect example of all Dave best attributes: surprising speed, great strength, excellent anticipation and a magnificent technique.

Dave continued to be a powerful player in the Hendon midfield until the end of the 2017–18 season. As with virtually all his team-mates, he left the club, but headed north to Conference South side St Albans City, rather than south to Hampton & Richmond. But during his time with Hendon, when Dave Diedhiou was fit and playing well, Hendon were much harder to beat. In his 10 seasons with the club, he made a magnificent 380 appearances, scoring 43 goals.

Disappeared grounds

All the stadiums below, at some time, hosted senior football, and clubs competed in at least one of the FA Cup, Amateur Cup, FA Trophy or FA Vase. Not all of the grounds, thankfully, have disappeared permanently – Silver Jubilee Park, Middlesex Stadium (Breakspear Road North) Grosvenor Vale, Avenue Park, Maurice Rebak Stadium (Abrahams Stadium Summers Lane) and SkyEx Community Stadium (the former Yeading's The Warren) – have new regular users.

As well as far too many clubs disappearing, even more stadiums are now fallow, or have become housing estates or shopping centres. London, naturally, has seen the football landscape change dramatically with the desire for land for building. Middlesex, it appears, has suffered more than most. Ashford Town (Middlesex), Hampton (& Richmond Borough), Hanwell Town, Harefield United, Harrow Borough and Wembley are pretty much the only senior clubs (senior at some time between 1970 and 2015) not to have moved, even for one season. In fact, there are 21 Middlesex grounds listed below, but only 39 teams in the Premier League and Football League out of the current 92 have only had one home since 1970 – not all the clubs existed in that year.

These are the 21 Middlesex grounds: Wealdstone lost **Lower Mead** to Tesco; Enfield's **Southbury Road** is now a shopping centre; **Falling Lane** was the old Hillingdon Borough stadium; **Denbigh Road** was Hounslow's (another defunct club) ground until the adjacent school took it over; **Feltham Arena** is no longer used by Feltham; **Hall Lane** was Wingate's home before it was swallowed up by the M1 extension and they moved to Arkley in Hertfordshire, while Finchley played at **Summers Lane**, which was redeveloped; **Grosvenor Vale**, formerly the home of Ruislip Manor has also been significantly upgraded for their new hosts Wealdstone; Kentish Town briefly played at **Barnet-Copthall Stadium**, which was redeveloped as Allianz Park, the home of Saracens RUFC; Willesden FC, as mentioned in the defunct clubs piece, played at **Willesden Sports Stadium**, which briefly became the National Hockey Centre; **Breakspear Road North**, once Ruislip (Town) FC's was empty for a couple of years before new tenants, the new Hillingdon Borough moved in; the old **Honeycroft** disappeared, but Uxbridge now play at a new Honeycroft; Hayes no longer exist, nor does their **Church Road** stadium – it's a housing estate; Yeading, with whom Hayes merged in 2007; moved out of **The Warren** in that year, since when it went through a painfully long development before finally opening again for football a couple of years ago; in the same area,

Western Road, Southall, is another ground to have vanished; **Avenue Park** was Viking Sports' home, but after being vacant for a couple of years, is now used by London Tigers; the **Goldsdown Ground** was home to Brimsdown Rovers, Enfield Town and Enfield 1893, but was closed by Enfield Council on safety grounds; and adjoining it was the **Downs Ground**, J&M Sports ground, which the reformed Brimsdown are using in the Spartan South Midlands League Division One.

Last of all, **Claremont Road**, the club's home for 82 years and seven days, the **White Lion Ground** – Edgware Town's previous base – and **Silver Jubilee Park,** formerly Kingsbury Town's ground and Edgware's current and Hendon's current home.

Excluding the demolition of the grounds of clubs forming Dagenham & Redbridge – Lynn Road (Ilford), Granleigh Road (Leytonstone) and Green Pond Road (Walthamstow Avenue) – north-east London and Essex have also lost the Hare & Hounds (Leyton); Vicarage Fields (Barking's old home); Snakes Lane (Woodford Town), Sungate (Collier Row and Romford), Romford Greyhound Stadium (also Romford) and, completing a hat-trick for Romford (as well as Briggs Sports/Ford Sports/Ford United) Rush Green Road. Add to the list Catons Lane, formerly the defunct Epping FC's ground, the old Harwich & Parkestone ground, the Royal Oak, and Deri Park, home of long-gone Rainham.

Other Isthmian League grounds to have disappeared include Richmond Road, Kingstonian's old home – and they have also lost the use of Kingsmeadow; Sandy Lane, once Tooting & Mitcham United's fortress; the old Champion Hill, in Dulwich; both the Dolphin and Wexham Park homes of Slough Town. Aylesbury United have also lost two homes, Turnfurlong Lane and Buckingham Road. Oxford City no longer play at the White Horse Ground. Bedford Town – then Southern League – left the old Eyrie. Arlesey Town are another club with two former homes, but Hendon played only at the second one.

Looking upwards, at current Football and Premier League club grounds at which Hendon have played but no longer exist, there are: Highbury (Arsenal), Eton Park (Burton Albion), Ninian Park (Cardiff City), Layer Road (Colchester United), Baseball Ground (Derby County), The Lawn (Forest Green Rovers), The Den (Millwall), County Ground (Northampton Town), Manor Ground (Oxford United), Elm Park (Reading), Roker Park (Sunderland), Upton Park (West Ham United) Plough Lane (Wimbledon) and Loakes Park (Wycombe Wanderers). It is worth considering that not one Football League club changed grounds in the quarter century between 1955, when Roots Hall, Southend opened, and 1980 – the debut of Walsall's Bescot Stadium. In the 40 subsequent years, 53 have done so and Brentford are in their final season at Griffin Park, as possibly are AFC Wimbledon at Kingsmeadow, and their return to Plough Lane will be to the redeveloped greyhound stadium not the adjacent football ground.

Iain Dowie

Iain Dowie's place in Hendon folklore is assured, especially in the way he ended his career at Claremont Road. In November 1988, Luton Town paid Hendon a club record fee for the striker, who had already netted 27 goals in just 30 appearances.

When Iain joined the Club from St Albans City – he had also played for his hometown Hatfield Town and Cheshunt – at the beginning of November 1986, he was still a student, doing an engineering degree, with a focus on rocket technology. (which, of course, proves that football and rocket science go hand in hand). His place on the course was sponsored of BAE Systems in Hatfield, for whom he worked.

His Hendon debut came on a Tuesday night, close to his Hertfordshire home, at Top Field, Hitchin. It was more than successful as he scored twice in a 4–1 and one of the goals singled him out as a special talent. Attacking in the inside-right channel, he ran onto a through ball from Dermot Drummy, burst past a defender, who barely moved, and fired a rifle shot across the goalkeeper just inside the far post.

Ineligible to play in the League Cup – Saints had picked him earlier in the competition despite requests not to – he was able to take his place in the Hendon team for the run in the GMAC Cup, also known as the Premier Inter-League Cup. The Greens enjoyed a fantastic run in the competition's inaugural season, reaching the final where Kettering Town – then one of the strongest sides in the Conference – won 3–1 at Rockingham Road.

Iain had to miss the semi-final because the match was played on a Sunday and he had a finals exam that day. The club even looked at flying him up to the North Midlands, but he didn't make the 13 who drew 1–1 in a match that was not for the faint-hearted. He played his part in the replay and although he didn't score, the Greens won 3–1. Despite not playing for the first 10 weeks of the season, Iain completed his first Hendon campaign with 23 goals from 46 appearances.

The following season, Hendon made their final appearance at the old Wembley stadium in the Russell Grant Middlesex Charity Cup final, a 2–0 defeat of Wembley. The match on 2 June 1988 was his 56th match of the season, and he scored his 28th goal. But Iain wasn't satisfied with a strike rate of a goal every other game and he worked diligently throughout the off-season with coach Ronnie Duke, a hard taskmaster, but who had an outstanding technical and tactical mind.

All the hard work paid off handsomely as he banged in goals at a rate of almost one per match. The Greens made a great start to the Isthmian League campaign, but they were magnificent in the FA Cup, led by Dowie. He grabbed two hat-tricks, against Harwich & Parkeston and Bishop's Stortford, two in the defeat of Braintree Town and one against VS Rugby in a fourth qualifying round replay, which booked Hendon's trip to Reading.

By now a number of Football League clubs were showing great interest in the striker and it was clear that Iain's time at Hendon was coming to an end, though he agreed not to leave the club until the FA Cup run was over. Iain scored Hendon's first goal at Elm Park, but the Greens were beaten 4–2 by the Biscuitmen. Iain's final appearances came in the FA Trophy, an infamous tie against Hayes, in which five players were sent off at Claremont Road. Dowie scored twice in a 3–3 draw, but didn't find the net in the replay, which Hendon won 2–0.

As a professional, one of the few modern players not to use an agent, Iain appeared in more than 400 first-team matches, including 59 for Northern Ireland. Although born in Hatfield, Iain's parents were from Northern Ireland and they watched him play almost every week. His clubs included Luton, QPR, West Ham United, Crystal Palace and Southampton and he went on to manage QPR, Crystal Palace, Charlton, Oldham and Coventry, often with his brother Bob – who will appear later in this book – as scout or director of football. Iain is now a football pundit, seen regularly on Sky Sports.

Dermot Drummy

One of the pleasures of being a fan of a club such as Hendon is that when an exceptional player arrives, has success and moves on to pastures new, is that we can follow his subsequent career and think, maybe my club played a part in this success.

Dermot Drummy arrived at Hendon after being released by Arsenal without playing in the Football League for the Gunners. He had gone on loan to Blackpool, where he played a handful of matches.

Few players in my more than 40 years watching the Greens have had the level of skill and confidence that Dermot possessed. A genuinely outstanding winger, his party trick was a dummy when he dropped his hands either side of the ball and shaped to pick it up. Defenders, almost without exception, stopped – at which point Dermot would knock the ball past him, run on and cause chaos in the opposing penalty area.

He left Hendon to sign for Enfield, then in the Conference, and spent just under three seasons with the Es, winning the title in 1985–86. Malcolm Graves, the phantom bugler, was on the Hendon FC Committee in 1986, when Ted Hardy was manager, and he persuaded his fellow members to stump up the money to bring Dermot back to the club in autumn 1986.

His second League debut came in the same match that Iain Dowie made his Hendon debut, and they scored three of the four goals in a trouncing of Hitchin. On 2 June 1988, Drummy and Dowie were the scorers as Hendon beat Wembley 2–0 in the Russell Grant Middlesex Charity Cup final at Wembley Stadium, our last visit to the Twin Towers.

It was full circle for Dermot, who had made his Hendon debut in the same competition in a 5–0 demolition of Southall at Western Road in August 1980. The fathers of three future Hendon players were in that line-up: Peter Deadman, Paul Currie and Jock McGleish – Scott played in our youth team with Darren Currie in 1991–92. Other notable players in Hendon's eleven that night were John Swannell, Gary Hand, former Arsenal team-mate and Double-winner Peter Simpson and Alan Campbell. Three years later, Dermot scored for Hendon in the Will Mather Cup at Whitley Bay.

I have four vivid memories of that day at Hillheads Park. First was Dermot having a goal disallowed for calling for the ball in a London accent. The referee penalised him for calling out without giving a name and when he said to the referee, "I called my name" (he did – I was standing behind the goal and clearly heard "Dermot's"), the referee's responded with something along the lines that he hadn't understood.

That evening, the squad went back to their hotel on the Whitley Bay seafront – my stories about the Chinese takeaway and Royal Hotel are not for repeating here – but by the time another supporter and I had played a game of 10-pin bowling in the centre adjacent to the ground, we went back into the clubhouse to find the trophy sitting there. After looking around the clubhouse it was clear no Hendon people remained.

I spoke to the bar manager and told him of our predicament and asked if it was OK if we took it back to the hotel with us. He said it was OK, so the two of us walked the mile or so through Whitley Bay town centre, past the funfair and along the front and into the hotel proudly carrying the Will Mather Cup. Once we got into the hotel, the trophy was given to Hendon's manager Roy Ruffell.

But, back to Dermot. After brief spells player-managing Finchley and Ware – he shared the role with another former Hendon player Alan Roughan, he hung up his boots in 1996 and returned to work at Arsenal. He gave up driving his taxi and enjoyed much success with the Arsenal youngsters. Dermot joined Chelsea in 2009 and was in charge of their FA Youth Cup winning team in 2010. He subsequently managed Crawley Town. Dermot brought Hendon fans great enjoyment in his playing career and they were all proud of the success he had as a manager and coach. It was a sad day for the club and our supporters when we heard of his death in November 2017.

E

Uche Egbe

Enfield FC

England

Extra time

European Nations Cup for Amateurs

ENGLAND v. **AUSTRIA**

Wednesday, 26th October, 1966
Hendon F.C. Claremont Road,
London, N.W.2

1/-

OFFICIAL PROGRAMME

Uche Egbe

In his debut season Uche Egbe appeared for the Under-18s, reserves and first team. His first appearance for the first-team came in a mid-season friendly early in 1989. He had just turned 18, and had earned his call-up by scoring a hatful of goals for Hendon's Under-18s and reserve teams – and even more for his Sunday team, Barnet Youth, coached by the Greens' midweek youth team boss Jack Fisk. I remember nothing about the match, but I do remember watching Uche come into the bar after the match, because he was wearing a silver track-suit and was listening to music on a pair of silver headphones, out of which earpiece stood a tall aerial stick. The image was extra-terrestrial, his reputation other-worldly.

His official debut came in early March 1989, as a substitute for Neil Henry in a 2–0 loss away to Bognor Regis Town. It was easy to see why Uche would score 90-odd goals in the season for his four teams; at Under-18 level, he was a man in a boys' team but didn't really stand out in his half-dozen Isthmian League appearances. He was a shade over six feet tall and powerfully built, possessed two good feet, great balance and searing pace, especially over short distances. Uche had a striker's natural instinct and he marked his first start in the Isthmian League with his first goal, the Greens' second in a 2–2 draw against Dagenham.

The following pre-season saw Uche assert himself as a first-team regular and, on 19 August 1989, he helped Hendon make a winning start to the new League campaign for the first time in exactly 22 years. The Greens won 4–1 at Bromley and, for a few months at least, Hendon were among the League's pace-setters, though things went downhill after strike-partner Sean Baker suffered a season-ending injury just before Christmas. Hendon certainly weren't lacking in fire-power, and Uche was top scorer with 17 goals, though Baker's 14 goals proved irreplaceable, despite the best efforts of veteran Colin Tate, who managed 13. Hendon ended the season in a somewhat disappointing 12th place, this after picking up only 11 points in the last 13 matches.

In 1990–91, it was more of the 'what might have been' as Hendon again failed to pick up silverware. They did come close in the Premier Inter-League Cup, where they fell in semi-final against Aylesbury, losing 4–1, though Uche had given Hendon hope with an equaliser. It was a strange campaign for Uche, who finished two behind Tate in the goal scorers' chart with 12 in 52 appearances, but Uche had come off the subs' bench 18 times. However, his prowess had not gone unnoticed, and he was invited to pre-season training with Leyton Orient.

The Os decided not to sign him and it knocked his confidence back. Uche also suffered from an injury-hit 1991–92 season and finished with only five goals from 35 appearances. All in all, it was a season of struggle for the Greens, who finished only 10 points above the relegation zone in 17th place, to say nothing of the off-field turmoil which included the ground being closed by the local council and the club being taken over by Victor Green. Uche was not with the club in 1992–93, and returned late in the following season, making five appearances and scoring one goal. He also appeared in a Full-Members Cup last-16 tie, but not in the Final, won by the Greens 10 weeks later.

When Uche arrived for pre-season training in summer 1994, there was a strong possibility that Hendon might not actually start the season. Ivor Arbiter's take-over was completed the day before season opener – a famous 2–2 draw away to eventual runners-up Slough Town and Uche scored the first goal. The team was filled with players who had spent most of their recent careers a couple of divisions below the Isthmian League Premier Division so, at this level at least, Uche was one of the squad's most experienced members. The season of the kick-in was Hendon's salvation as manager Mick Browne's hard work in training on set-pieces paid dividends and the Greens spent only one week in the relegation zone, though their safety was only confirmed on the penultimate Saturday of the season. Sadly, four days before this, Uche had been sacked by the Chairman, effectively for caring too much. He considered Uche's furious reaction to being substituted – with the Greens trailing 2–1 at home to Harrow Borough – disrespectful. His goals, however, had been invaluable and Uche finished as joint-top scorer with 10 goals, despite appearing in only just over half the League games.

Uche still keeps in touch with the club – through social media – and will be remembered fondly by many fans for his loyalty to the cause in difficult times. Overall, he scored 46 goals in 186 first team appearances.

Enfield FC

When I started watching Hendon regularly, in the early 1970s, Hendon's biggest rivals were Enfield. County rivals, the teams met every season – excluding the Second World War seasons – for 60 seasons from 1921–22 until Enfield stepped up to play in top division of non-league football.

The first meeting between Hampstead Town and Enfield had come almost a decade before the Athenian League battles commenced, on Saturday 22 November 1913, when Enfield won 4–1 in the FA Amateur Cup, a match the *Hendon Times and Guardian* felt the Es deserved to win, but probably by only a single goal. There was very little to choose between the two clubs in the almost 40 years the clubs competed, but we did have slightly the better record with more runners-up finishes (five to one) and titles (three to two). Hendon also reached, and won the Amateur Cup final before Enfield, the Greens' first final coming in 1955, while the Es reached their first final four years after Hendon's first victory and a year before their second.

Without question, the two biggest meetings between the teams came in 1965 and 1972. Enfield and Hendon were elected to the Isthmian League in 1963 and while Hendon were runners-up in 1964, the Es were fifth. The following season, however, there was far less to separate them. Hendon held sway in knock-out matches, beating Enfield in both the London Challenge Cup in September and Middlesex Senior Cup in February, and, biggest of all, they won the Amateur Cup, beating Enfield's semi-final conquerors Whitby Town at Wembley. The Es, however, had reached the FA Cup second round, while Hendon went out – to Port Vale – a round earlier. In the Isthmian League, both teams finished on 63 points, Enfield winning 29 games to Hendon's 28, but when it came to goals, Hendon were 123–49, Enfield were 98–35. The Isthmian League rules at the time allowed for a play-off to decide the championship, so a 39th match was added to their schedules, on Friday 30 April – the day before Liverpool and Leeds met in the FA Cup final – at Dulwich Hamlet's Champion Hill ground.

The advantage was with Enfield because their goal average (2.8) was better than Hendon's (2.5), so if the match finished all-square, the title was theirs. However, this was the Greens' night. In front of a crowd of 4,900, David Hyde opened the scoring after 20 minutes, Peter Slade added a second after 57 minutes and Roy Drake made it 3–0 before Derek McDonnell pulled a goal back. Any Hendon nerves were stilled when Danny Lakey made it 4–1 near the end to give the Greens their first Isthmian League title.

Seven years later, the teams met at Wembley in the Amateur Cup final. Both teams were going for their third trophy. Enfield's first, mirroring 1965, had come at the expense of Hendon's semi-final conquerors Skelmersdale United in 1967. I remember watching John Baker run towards goal and shooting past Ian Wolstenholme, courtesy of Mick Smith's deflection. The scoreboard said it was Baker's goal and that was – and remains – good enough for me. The Es laid siege on the Hendon goal after that and the second half seemed to drag on for ever. However, with a couple of minutes to go, Hendon broke away, forced a corner from which Tony Bass headed home the second goal to give the Greens a 2–0 victory.

The advent of the "open game" era (clubs were no longer either professional or amateur) and, for both clubs, semi-professionalism in 1974 had a profound effect on the rivalry. Enfield had already signed Tony Jennings, Phil Fry and Derek Baker during the 1973–74 run-in.

Those defections probably cost Hendon a second straight Isthmian League title.

From 1974 to 1982, until Enfield joined the Alliance Premier League – subsequently the Conference, now the National League, they were the strongest and most consistent club in the Isthmian League – champions four times and runners-up twice in seven seasons. Victories against Enfield were always celebrated – and there was a memorable one in their final season in the Isthmian League, 3–0 at Southbury Road, with a double from Kevin Folan and one from John Baker. In the Conference, Enfield remained dominant, winning the title and the FA Trophy twice.

Enfield returned to the Isthmian League in 1990, but things deteriorated for them later in the decade, especially after their stadium was damaged by the use made of it by the Saracens Rugby Union team when they shared Southbury Road for a season. Boardroom and supporter friction led to the formation of Enfield Town, who worked their way up the pyramid to the Isthmian League Premier Division. Enfield, with only a handful of fans, moved out of Southbury Road in 1999 – Hendon were their penultimate opponents – and were relegated in 2003. Another relegation followed, then the club went bust. A new club, Enfield 1893, succeeded them, playing successively at Ware, Brimsdown, Harlow, Brimsdown and now back at Harlow, as Enfield FC, in the Essex Senior League. Hopes of a return to glory and a renewal of the rivalry with this version of Enfield FC seem sadly distant.

(Programme: The last match between Enfield and Hendon at Southbury Road)

England

There have been a number of men who earned England international honours as Hendon players, or before or after they were with the Greens. With one notable exception, these are all players who represented England in full internationals as an amateur, semi-professional or full-time professional. The "amateur" era ended in England in the spring of 1974, after which all players could legitimately earn wages as a player. Prior to then, amateurs were permitted only to claim only reasonable travel expenses, either to matches or training.

The first player mentioned is someone who will go down in the history books as, officially, the first black player ever to represent England (a strong case, however, could be made for Leeds United full-back Paul Reaney, who made his England debut in 1968, but he was what is now acknowledged as mixed race – his father was from Nigeria). His name was Ben Odeje, who represented England Schoolboys in 1971. His Hendon career was brief, he appeared in just three matches, starting with a 4–1 Rothman's Isthmian League defeat against Sutton United at Gander Green Lane on 4 January 1975. Nine days later, Ben's only cup appearance came in a 3–1 FA Trophy defeat – our first ever loss in that competition, at Falling Lane, the home of Hillingdon Borough. Ben's last appearance was also his only start in a 2–0 league victory, this time at Hayes Lane, Bromley.

In June 2015, Charlie Goode became only the second registered Hendon player to represent England at Non-League (England 'C') level, though he should have been the third. The Non-League team, until the rebranding, started playing matches just before the end of the amateur era, and Peter Deadman was selected for the team in spring 1974. With Hendon involved in a heated battle for the Isthmian League title, Peter declined the invitation. The player who did earn his colours was Phil Gridelet, selected by a former England Amateur and Non-League international (the former as a Hendon player), the late Tony Jennings. While he was with Hendon, Phil played twice, first in Italy, then against Wales at Kidderminster Harriers FC. It should be pointed out that there have been many other players who appeared for the Greens before or after winning England Non League caps.

In the past 30 seasons, I can recall only two former full England internationals who went on to play for Hendon. The first of these was Tony Currie, who made five largely unsuccessful appearances for the Greens in the 1985–86 season. Then 35 years old, Paul's brother – and Darren's uncle – made his debut in a 2–2 home draw with Worthing on 21 September 1985. He played in only four more league matches, all defeats – against Harrow Borough, Barking, Dulwich Hamlet and Windsor & Eton – during which time Hendon scored just twice and conceded 12 times.

The other player was Peter Taylor, player-manager of Hendon for the first four months of the 1993–94 season. Peter was already 40 years old, and joined Hendon from Watford, where he had been assistant manager. Soon after signing his contract, Glenn Hoddle approached him to become his Number 2 at Chelsea, but Peter said, "No." He went on to play 22 times in the league and cup, scoring seven goals. The team played some fantastic football and may well have been in the running for league honours had he not been lured by his home town club Southend United. Of course, since leaving Hendon, Peter has gone on to manage at the very highest level – one full international for England, many matches for the Under-21s and at all the top five levels of English club football, winning a number of promotions, more often

66

than not assisted by former Hendon star Junior Lewis – either as a player or coach. Junior also wore the England shirt while at Hendon, but this was for an FA XI in a match against British Universities at Soham Town Rangers' Julius Martin Way ground.

The list of England amateur internationals contains 17 names, including four of the most capped in history. The most-capped single-club international and the most overall are both Hendon men: John Swannell won all of his 61 England amateur international caps while at Claremont Road and the most-capped ever, Rod Haider won 55 of his 65 with the Greens (the first 10 coming at Kingstonian). Mike Pinner played nine matches for England while he was with Hendon, and played 50 times in all; he also played for Manchester United in what was then the Football League First Division and various other Football League teams. The fourth member of England's elite is Deadman, who won 25 of his 45 England amateur caps as a Hendon player. Other Hendon players to win England Amateur international caps are: Dexter Adams (18), Tony Bass (4), Eric Beardsley (3), Mickey Cooper (3), Freddie Evans (1), Jeff Harris (4), David Hogwood (7), Terry Howard (5), David Hyde (6), Roy Sleap (10), Roy Stroud (9), Laurie Topp (32) and Cecil Wise (2). The latter was the first player for the club to win an England cap.

Extra time

In all, taking account of incomplete records for competitions in the club's first quarter-century, Hendon have been involved in more than 100 matches going to extra time. The club's records show 42 wins, 40 draws and 23 defeats in extra-time. However, especially in the era before floodlights, a few matches were abandoned in extra-time, some before the extra 30 minutes kicked-off. Eighteen of the 40 draws went to penalty shoot-outs.

It is believed that the club's first ever experience of extra-time was on 2 October 1920 when Hampstead Town lost an FA Amateur Cup tie against Uxbridge Town. George Blackburn, Cecil Burrage and Cecil Wise were all on target as the Town finished the 90 minutes all-square. Sadly, it was the home team which scored the only goal of the additional 30 minutes and Hampstead went out 4–3. The club's first extra-time victory came on 15 January 1938, when Golders Green beat Barking 2–1 at Claremont Road in the Amateur Cup, the Green's goalscorers being Ron Graves and Freddie Boston.

Here are my four favourite Hendon extra-time matches – none of which were finals, all in different competitions. The first was a Middlesex Senior Cup quarter-final replay replay over Harrow Borough on 9 April 1987. A month earlier Harrow had won a replay 2–1, but the match was declared void after they had been incorrectly allowed by the County FA to field two ineligible players. Borough came out all guns blazing and raced into a 3–0 half-time lead, which should have been four, but for a missed penalty. As the teams came out for the second half, Hendon fans gave the team a hero's welcome, which prompted full-back Alan Roughan to say to striker Colin Tate something along the lines of "Let do something special for the fans." It took 22 seconds for Tate to make it 3–1. Within five minutes, Neil Wolstenholme had cut the deficit to one and, by the hour mark, Iain Dowie had made it 3–3. Then a floodlight went out and referee David Elleray decided the other three pylons gave off enough light to continue. There were no goals until 17 seconds into the second period of extra-time when Tate scored his second. Just before the end, Dermot Drummy completed the amazing 5–3 win.

The Premier Interleague (GMAC) Cup semi-final match at Burton – played on a Sunday after both clubs had been in league action a day earlier – was described by a watching policeman as one of the most violent he had ever seen, with Burton the main offenders. There had been almost 1,500 at Eton Park, but the replay on 29 April 1987, attracted less than 350. After 90 minutes of absorbing football it was 1–1, then Wolstenholme gave Hendon the lead. If Burton had equalised and it finished 2–2, they would have reached the final on away goals but, with five minutes to go, Roger Wade scored to seal Hendon's place in the final.

Fast forward to 14 December 1998 and a much-delayed FA Trophy replay against Rothwell Town at Cecil Street – bad weather and our FA Cup replay with Notts County meant the replay came 23 days after Freddie Hyatt had scored in the 1–1 draw at Claremont Road. The Northants club, known as the Bones, seemed happy to be so robust in the challenge that the Roman remains found in the church a few centuries earlier might have been supplemented by fresher ones hewn from the limbs of Hendon players. However, the worst foul of the night was by Simon Clarke, whose dismissal was not contestable. Rothwell had a lead and seemed comfortable, especially as they had the hill in their favour. But, Junior Lewis equalised with a couple of minutes left. The 10 men not only held on in extra time, but with Lewis and Paul Whitmarsh ever dangerous, it was the former who sprinted down the hill, squared the ball for Whits, who finished from close range.

The victory over Eastbourne Borough in the FA Cup 3rd qualifying round replay at Vale Farm on 9 October 2012 was probably the most dramatic of the four. Not only was it similar to the Rothwell game in that the drama came when Hendon were down to 10 men, but beat a team from a higher league, Conference (now National League) South. The 2–2 draw at Priory Lane had been followed by a very tense. goalless

68

90 minutes at Vale Farm. Darren Lok gave Borough the lead two minutes into extra time and, two minutes later, Scott Cousins saw red for a foul. Four minutes into the second period of extra time, Rhys Paul fouled Michael Murray, who scored from the penalty spot. More penalties seemed certain, until the 119th minute, when Elliott Charles set up Isaiah Rankin, who smashed a brilliant curling drive into the corner.

Nowadays extra-time is a much rarer occurrence as most knock-out competitions have the penalty shoot-outs coming when the scores are level at the end of normal time. Only the FA competitions, Cup, Trophy and Vase, have the provision of 30 extra minutes before the agony of "shots from the penalty mark". It is strange, but games going to extra-time almost always seemed to be ones played on the coldest or wettest of nights, rather than on balmy evenings when extra half-hours outdoors were not unpleasant.

F

The FA Cup

The FA Trophy

Bill Fisher

Finales

Floodlights

Friendlies

A plate given to the club by Port Vale FC to commemorate the FA Cup match between the teams in 1964.

The FA Cup

The FA Cup is the biggest competition that Hendon enter and arguably is the world's most famous club knock-out tournament.

Hampstead Town were members of the London League when they first entered the FA Cup, in the 1912–13 season. Hampstead were drawn away to Maidenhead – before they merged with Maidenhead Norfolkians to form Maidenhead United. This Berkshire club had appeared in the first ever FA Cup competition 41 years early, beating Marlow 2–0 before losing 3–0 to Crystal Palace. Sadly, Hampstead's trip on 28 September 1912 was not a success, Oliver Sumner's goal being insufficient response to Maidenhead's brace. The following season, Hampstead beat Marlow 3–1 and Maidenhead Norfolkians 3–0, before going out 3–1 at home to Southall. In 1914, although the Athenian League suspended operations, most cup competitions continued and Hampstead Town reached the fifth of six qualifying rounds before losing 5–2 to Bromley in a replay.

Fast forward to the post-First World War era and as Golders Green the club made its first appearance in the competition proper. It was in the 1934–35 season and for some reason, the Green only entered at the fourth qualifying round stage, where Ilford were the opposition. Freddie Evans scored in the 1–1 draw at Newbury Park and, five days later, got both in the 2–0 replay victory at Claremont Road. This set up a first round proper tie against Southend United, but Golders Green's run ended emphatically at newly-built Roots Hall. Charlie Drinkwater did score, but the Shrimpers mustered 10. The Green played their final FA Cup tie on 29 October 1938, losing 2–1 to Apsley. In 1939, the FA Cup was cancelled once the Second World War had been declared, and in 1945–46, the Green did not enter the competition.

Pinner were Hendon's first FA Cup opponents, on 7 September 1946, the second competitive fixture in the club's present guise. Hendon won 3–2, but exited at the next round, going down 3–1 to Finchley at Summers Lane. The following season, Hendon, again, opted out of the FA Cup, but enjoyed significantly more success in 1948–49, when the Greens started in the extra preliminary round before recording wins against Welwyn Garden City, Hoddesdon, Town, Finchley, Enfield and Wealdstone before Barnet won a thriller at Underhill 5–4 – Billy Dare and Roy Stroud both scoring twice for Hendon – in the final qualifying round. In 1950, the club's FA Cup run was ended – again at the last qualifying round stage – by Tonbridge, who won a replay 2–1 at Claremont Road after a 3–3 draw in the first game in Kent.

The following season saw Hendon given a bye to the final qualifying run, but the team couldn't take advantage, losing 4–3 to Aylesbury United at Turnfurlong Lane, a match where both teams had to wear change kit after failing to agree on the colours. The Ducks borrowed a local rivals' kit and the Greens wore Aylesbury's second kit – and a painting from a photograph of this match adorned the wall of Aylesbury United's boardroom when they were at Buckingham Road. Hendon's biggest ever crowd at Claremont Road, recorded as 9,000 turned up for the club's second ever appearance in the first round proper, with Northampton Town the visitors. The match ended 0–0 and the Cobblers sneaked a 2–0 replay victory.

Since the 1950s, the club's love affair with the FA Cup has remained pretty constant. There have been 18 further appearances in the first round proper, at least once in every decade, apart from the 2000s. Sadly, the departure of the FA's historian David Barber meant I could not ask him if Hendon's record of 29 consecutive seasons of winning at least one tie – the run ended at Sudbury in September 2015 – was the best for any club in the competition. The two first-game exits in the 1980s came in consecutive seasons, 1984–85 and 1985–86, and Hendon's conquerors – Dunstable 3–1 at Claremont Road in 1984 and Ruislip Manor 1–0 at Grosvenor Vale a year later – both ceased playing – the new Dunstable Town team reformed after a four-year hiatus.

Every win is fantastic, especially in the competition proper, but maybe my favourite FA Cup qualifying competition win dates back to 1981–82, a second qualifying round tie against Banbury United. A 2–2 draw at Claremont Road was most notable for Paul Currie's 55-yard strike for our opener. The replay did not look promising when Banbury took a 2–0 lead with 72 minutes on the clock, but Hendon quickly pulled back the two goals, thanks to Kevin Folan and Bobby Gough. With eight minutes to go, Banbury regained the lead, only for Dermot Drummy to lash home a 35-yarder in the last two minutes. Extra time could not separate the teams until the final minute when, at a Hendon corner, the ball bounced around until Anthony Bennett almost lifted the net off its moorings when he lashed the ball home from a yard out. Simultaneously it was ugly and beautiful in equal measures.

Looking at the FA Cup competition proper, in all, the club has made 21 first-round appearances, and reached the third round once, in 1973–74. Overall, the club has played in every round from extra preliminary and preliminary, through qualifying – first to sixth – to first, second and third proper, and faced teams beginning with every letter except I, J, Q, X and Z – we played Valley Sports Rugby in 1988.

In 1955, having played in the FA Amateur Cup final in the spring, we received a bye into the first round proper, where we were pitted against Birmingham League club Halesowen Town, in the West Midlands. The fans arrived at the Yelz's ground to find sheep and cows grazing on the pitch. It was 2–2 at half-time, Colin Edwards and Jackie Rawlings scoring, but Miles Spector and Colin Edwards grabbed second

half goals as Hendon won 4–2. There was more travelling in the second round, where at St James's Park, Exeter, the Grecians won 6–2.

Hendon were regulars in the first round in the 1960s and 70s, but it was not until 1975 that we finally beat Football League opposition. Two seasons earlier, the Greens made national headlines when drawing 1–1 at St James' Park, Newcastle, Pat Howard scoring for the Magpies and Rod Haider equalising. For many years, the Claremont Road clubhouse had a blown-up photograph of Haider's goal, taken by the *Sunday Express*. Hendon should have had a penalty in the dying seconds for a foul on Keiran Somers, but it wasn't given. United won the third round replay 4–0 at Watford, in front of an afternoon crowd of 15,000, and went on to reach the final, where Liverpool beat them 3–0. What might have been (1) …

In 1975, Hendon beat Canterbury City 1–0 in the fourth qualifying round and drew Division Four leaders Reading at Claremont Road. The only goal came just before half-time, a Dave Metchick free-kick was flicked on by John Baker and Alan Phillips scored what proved to be the game's only goal from close range. Only four players appeared in the Newcastle and Reading ties: Haider, Gary Hand, Baker and Phillips. Swindon Town won in the next round, courtesy of a penalty from David Moss after Dave Yerby had handled on the goal-line. Yerby received a yellow card from the referee, who waved away protests that goalkeeper Malcolm Dalrymple had been fouled as he tried to reach the corner.

Hendon have twice reached the first round proper in four consecutive seasons, latterly, and improbably, in the 1990s. The highlight of the 1996 run was a third qualifying round win at Dover, given they were mid-table in the – then one-division – Conference and Hendon were bottom of the Isthmian Premier. Paul Kelly scored the only goal, mainly because the match officials missed his push on the Dover centre-half as they chased a through ball. After winning a replay against Hastings Town, Hendon travelled to Cardiff City in the first round but lost 2–0.

Twelve months later, given a bye to the fourth qualifying round, Hendon won 2–0 away to St Albans City thanks to a pair of Colin Simpson goals and he equalised twice in the first round tie at home to Leyton Orient, which we drew 2–2. The replay at Brisbane Road was won 1–0, Junior Lewis scoring and both Freddie Hyatt and Gary McCann were involved in the build up. Cardiff beat Hendon 3–1 in the next round and Notts County won a first round replay the following year.

One of my favourite FA Cup runs was in 1999, when – undeservedly – we lost 2–0 at Blackpool in the second round proper. In the first round, we had beaten Bath City 2–0 at Twerton Park, thus inflicting a first defeat of the season on the Romans. Much to the referee's dismay, the two captains kissed affectionately in the centre circle before the game, but they were brothers, Bath's Colin and Hendon's Paul Towler. After 88 minutes it was still goalless, then Dominic Gentle scored with a diving header from a Jason McKoy cross. In stoppage time, Gentle set up substitute Bontcho Guentchev for number two. In round three Blackpool drew Arsenal away. What might have been (2) …

Since then, Hendon have enjoyed only two first round appearances, a 3–2 defeat at Chelmsford City and a loss to Aldershot that might have been a third League scalp. If Elliott Brathwaite's header, early in the second half, had added to Dean Cracknell's wonder-strike in the first half, it is unlikely the Shots would have hit back. Instead Danny Hylton scored twice and the Greens lost 2–1. What might have been (3) …

(Programme; Plymouth Argyle 1 Hendon 0 FA Cup First Round 1972)

The FA Trophy

For a club which had appeared in five FA Amateur Cup finals and two other semi-finals in the previous 23 seasons, Hendon's record in what is the senior knock-out competition in non-league football is, to use a euphemism, disappointing. The Greens have never even reached the quarter-finals and have just three visits to the last 16 to show for 45 seasons of effort. The 2017–18 run to the competition proper is only the second in the past 12 years.

But let's go back to the club's first entry, in 1974–75. It was the first season of the "open" era and the FA Amateur Cup had been consigned to history. The FA Trophy was not brand new, having first seen the light in the 1969–70 season. In the first qualifying round, tie number one was an international clash between Abergavenny Thursdays and Bath City; the Romans came out on top 3–2. Bath then beat Bedworth and Frome to reach the third round, where Barnet won 4–3 at Twerton Park. The Bees lost 1–0 to Macclesfield Town in the semi-final, and the Silkmen lifted the Trophy after beating Telford United 2–0 at Wembley.

There were 294 entrants in the 1974–75 competition and Hendon were given a bye to the third qualifying round, where they were handed an away tie against Cambridge City. On 30 November 1974, goals from John Field and Rod Haider were enough to give the Greens a 2–1 victory. In the next round the Greens entertained Hillingdon Borough, runners-up to Telford in 1971, but after a 2–2 draw at Claremont Road, lost 3–1 at Falling Lane. Only four Rothman's – hard to imagine a league sponsored by a tobacco company – Isthmian League teams made to the last 32, Dagenham, Enfield, Ilford and Leatherhead, with the Daggers being the only one to reach even the quarter-finals. Two seasons later, Hendon reached the last 16, seeing off Maidstone United, Bishop's Stortford and Waterlooville, the latter two away from home, and a third straight road trip saw us go down to Dorset for a third round tie against Weymouth. A late equaliser gave Hendon great hope of a quarter-final tie at home to Altrincham, but, on a foggy night in Cricklewood, the Terras raced into a 3–0 lead before winning 5–1.

The following season Hendon made it to the last 16 again, having won 2–0 at Romford – then playing at Victoria Road, Dagenham – and 4–0 at home to Falmouth on a Tuesday night. It was a very strange programme which was published for the tie against Bedford Town (managed by Barry Fry) because they had beaten Hednesford Town only a couple of days earlier in a second round second replay. Bedford got a 1–1 draw at Claremont Road and with a quarter-final home game against Leatherhead the carrot for the replay, Hendon came up on the wrong end of a 2–1 scoreline.

First-game exits followed for the next three seasons but Hendon made the last 32 in 1981–82, this after beating Barnet 2–1 on a frozen Claremont Road pitch and Taunton Town 5–1 on QPR's Omniturf. A trip to Witton Albion in Northwich was their reward and a goal from former Walton & Hersham striker Russ Perkins saw a 1–0 defeat.

For first part of the 1980s, Hendon did little, though they did get to the last 32 in 1988, losing a replay at Barrow. Hendon were victims of quite a few upsets in the next few years, but in 1998–99 reached the last 16 for the third time, winning a replay away to Rothwell Town and away ties against Worthing and Chesham United. The draw could not have been tougher, a trip to the holders and Conference champions elect, Cheltenham Town. Both teams were short of key players and the Robins were comfortable 3–0 winners. The following season Hendon went out one round earlier, 4–1 away to Forest Green Rovers. In 2004–05, the Greens enjoyed victories over AFC Wimbledon, 3–0, and Taunton Town, before losing to Slough Town. Since then, the best run was in 2011–12 when Hendon overcame Cray Wanderers, Bideford and Oxford City, but were upset 2–1 at home by Whitstable Town. Hendon did something in 2017–18 they had never previously achieved, winning four ties. The record-setter was 2–1 victory against National League South Bath City, but it was followed, four weeks later, by a 3–0 defeat away to National League Sutton United.

Overall, Hendon's FA Trophy record 1974 to 2019 is: played: 116, won: 49, drawn: 22, lost: 45, goals for: 170, goals against: 158. We have had two second replays, losing to Slough Town in 1976 and beating Thame United in 1996; two replays went to penalties, Slough being beaten in 2017 and Kettering Town beating the Greens in December 2003.

Finales

Finales are the last games of a season. These aren't necessarily cup finals, but they were all competitive matches. The 16 April 2016 season-ender was actually almost two months earlier than the club's latest finish to a season and a month and a day ahead of the 2015 finale. The 1946–47 season, the first as Hendon was very strange. On Saturday 14 June 1947, one week after both the final of the Middlesex Charity Cup – our third consecutive win, this time 5–0 over Southall at Highbury, thanks to a Bill Reay hat-trick and Roy Stroud double – and the start of the England versus South Africa Test match cricket series, Hendon completed their Athenian League campaign with the championship on the line, but only for our visitors to Claremont Road, Barnet. Trailing Sutton United by two points, it was two for a win in those days, the Bees' goal average already better than the Us – 1.89 to 1.59 – but they had to win the game to clinch the title. Despite a goal from Reay, Barnet netted five in reply and took the title for a third time. It had been a terrible winter, with many matches postponed.

The only other June fixture Hendon have played was on 2 June 1988, the opening day of the first Test match between England and the West Indies. This was the Russell Grant Middlesex Charity Cup final, and the venue was Wembley Stadium, with Wembley FC the Greens' opponents. The Lions' 15-man squad included five former Greens in Adrian Smith, Paul Bhatia, Dereck Brown, Sylvester Williams and Henry Pacquette, but Hendon could boast Iain Dowie, Alan Campbell, Phil Gridelet and Dermot Drummy, to name but four. There were 3,715 in the Stadium to watch the game and they saw the Greens score in each half, through Drummy and Dowie to win 2–0.

There has to be mention, however painful, of the finale of the 2014–15 season, when everything conspired to deny Hendon promotion through the Ryman League play-offs. Margate won 1–0 in a controversial game, this after finishing 10 points worse off than Hendon. Many Hendon fans would have put the 2014–15 season as the club's greatest ever had promotion been achieved, but 50 years earlier Hendon had already beaten Arsenal 4–3 in the London Challenge Cup and won both the FA Amateur Cup and Isthmian League titles before our finale. It came on Saturday 8 May 1965, in the Middlesex Senior Cup final at Enfield, a repeat of the Amateur Cup semi-final against Finchley. A goal four minutes into the second half, scored by Peter

Slade, was enough to give Hendon a 1–0 victory and thus complete a treble.

Margate featured in another famously miserable finale, the conclusion to the 2005–06 season, when first goals by Jeff Campbell and Ricci Crace at Hartsdown Park, should have been added to by Blaise O'Brien. He missed the easiest of sitters and we collapsed to lose 4–2. We would have been relegated, but for the misfortune of another club. Last game safety has been achieved three times, in 1986, 2017 and 2019, but in 1995 and 1996 we managed it in the penultimate and pre-penultimate games, respectively. That 1986 fixture was on 29 April, when we took a 10-game unbeaten League run to Wexham Park, Slough, still needing three points for absolute safety. On a memorable night, Roger Wade, Andy O'Brien, Tony Gibson and Mick Kiely scored in a 4–1 victory.

In 2017, there was a bizarre twist to the game as major road traffic accident delayed the two assistant referees. The referee was advised to start the game at 3.00pm using spectators who were qualified referees as his assistants, but he refused on the grounds that it would put unbearable pressure on fans should there be a contentious decision. The match finally kicked off more than 80 minutes after all the other games in the division, and although they trailed to a fifth-minute goal from Mo Bettamer, approaching half time at Silver Jubilee Park, it seemed that a defeat would not matter as another result was in Hendon's favour. That game turned around and the Greens players trooped off the pitch in the relegation zone. Very early in the second half, Casey Maclaren scored an equaliser to get the point Hendon needed to stay up though, as it happened, the team who fell into the bottom four – Harrow Borough – received a reprieve.

In 2018–19, Hendon went from second in the table in December to the Evo Stik Southern Premier Division South relegation battle in late April. On an incredibly nervous afternoon, the reality was that defeat for Hendon, at home to Swindon Supermarine, almost certainly would have consigned them to Step 4 in 2019–20. However, Shaquille Hippolyte-Patrick scored after five minutes and it proved to be the only goal of the game, enough to see the Greens finish 16th. Such was the congestion in the division that 14th-placed Wimborne Town finished only three points ahead of relegated Basingstoke Town in 20th place.

Golders Green had a memorable finale to the last wartime season, 1944–45. The Green played a number of cup competitions, and in the week of VE Day (Victory in Europe), Golders Green defeated Wealdstone 3–2 in the Middlesex Red Cross Cup semi-final – this was the renamed Middlesex Charity Cup. Eleven days later, we played our Claremont Road tenants Tufnell Park in the final, not at our home ground, but at Wembley Stadium. Doubles from both George Bucci and Alan Cochrane were enough to give the Green a 4–1 victory.

The last end-of-season game I will mention was the club's final fixture as members of the Athenian League. Hampstead Town had joined the competition in 1914 – a season abandoned after three games because of the outbreak of the First World War – and almost 49 years later Hendon ended its Athenian days by entertaining Grays Athletic. It was a meaningless fixture with Hendon in mid-table and Grays near the bottom. David Swain scored three times, Fred Pudney twice and David Bell once in a 6–3 victory.

Bill Fisher

Bill Fisher, one of the all-time greats of the club, was an outstanding player for 20-odd years, and then was manager, assistant boss, coach, reserve team manager and a Committee man until his premature death in late 1978.

He was 19 years old when he joined Golders Green in 1941 from junior side Deerfield. He soon established himself in the first team during the unofficial war-time competitions, and was an ever-present in both the 1941–42 and 1942–43 seasons, completing 100 consecutive appearances at Clapton in February 1944. In all, Bill went on to make 176 consecutive appearances, by which time the Second World War was over. In recognition of this amazing run, he was presented with a gold watch by the club. Bill played in almost every defensive position (there were right and left full-backs, right-, left and centre-halves), and also had a season at inside forward (in either the number eight or number 10 shirt). This versatility was the reason, many Hendon supporters believe, Bill did not receive a call-up to play for the England amateur team – the preference at the time being for single-position players rather than "utility" players. A loyal servant to Golders Green and Hendon, Bill's career appearance mark is almost certainly the club record, despite playing three seasons of wartime matches. The Hendon FC website gives Bill's career figure as 719 first-team matches, including four seasons during World War Two, but other records suggest the figure is closer to 800.

Bill played at Wembley on three occasions, first in the Middlesex Red Cross Cup against Tufnell Park in 1945, and in the FA Amateur Cup finals of both 1955 and 1960, collecting a winner's medal from the latter match, by which time he was 38 years old. Winning at Wembley against Kingstonian in 1960 was probably the pinnacle of his playing career, but Bill had enjoyed numerous cup successes earlier in his career. In all, he also played in three losing London Senior Cup finals, five Middlesex Senior Cup finals (winning once), four Middlesex Charity Cup finals, of which three were victorious. As well as helping Hendon to win two Athenian League championship sides, there were three war-time cup finals in 1945 and he was also in the Hendon team which won the first ever cup tie scheduled to be played under floodlights in 1951.

Although he didn't earn England or Great Britain Olympic recognition, Bill did receive representative honours, playing for the England "B" team against the Army in 1954, and also played for Middlesex, London, and the Athenian League. His seven appearances for the latter included a tour of the Far East.

In the 1959–60 he was made reserve team captain and coach before winning back his first-team place. In fact, he went on to be named the Athenian League's player of the year at the end of that season. On Saturday 28 April 1962, he made his final competitive first-team appearance for Hendon, a 3–1 home defeat against Sutton United. Bill continued to serve the club in various roles off the pitch after hanging up his boots, taking over as first team coach in 1962–63.

He became manager for the 1965–66 and 1966–67 seasons, taking Hendon to an Amateur Cup final and semi-final, before returning to run the reserve team. After spells as assistant manager to both John Evans and Jimmy Quail, in 1974 Bill became first team manager again, and it was under his direction that Hendon achieved their first FA Cup victory over a Football League team with a 1–0 victory over Reading.

In 1976, when Jimmy Quail took over as manager, Bill went onto the club committee, and became the club's public relations officer. However, on Tuesday and Thursday nights he could still be found on the pitch helping with training. He also did some scouting for Arsenal, and was involved with a Sunday team, Sparrowhawk FC. On Thursday 2 November 1978, Bill died of a heart attack at the young age of 56.

Two days later, the shocked team went out of the FA Cup against Hitchin Town – a match that would, in today's football, have been postponed as the club grieved. The club set up a memorial fund for his family, and played a match against Wimbledon FC at Claremont Road on 4 December 1978. As the match programme said: "Bill will always be remembered, not only by those of us connected with Hendon, but by his many friends and colleagues in the game for his great sense of loyalty and warm personality, he truly was football's 'Mr Nice Guy'."

Floodlights

Hendon have an illustrious – pun intended – history with floodlights. Until the 1950s and 1960s, every club suffered abandonments when gloomy autumn and winter weather brought twilight and night earlier than expected and would fall foul of the gloaming, especially cup-ties where extra-time was a factor. So, apart from the installation of all-weather pitches, the last new feature of football grounds was the advent of floodlighting. As permanent features, they first appeared in the early 1950s and Hendon were at the forefront. When Wembley Stadium first installed their lights, the Greens were invited to play a practice match between the first and second teams to test them out.

The first English club to install permanent lighting was Arsenal and they played a friendly on Wednesday 19 September 1951, against the touring Hapoel Tel Aviv from Israel. In fact, their great manager of the 1930s, Herbert Chapman had installed lights at the Gunners' training ground after playing a friendly in Belgium. Hapoel were duly dazzled by Arsenal and lost 6–1. Three weeks later, on Monday 8 October, Highbury staged the first-ever competitive floodlit cup-tie – the first competitive fixture in England had been at The Dell, a week earlier, when Southampton Reserves hosted Tottenham Hotspur Reserves. Hendon were the visitors to Highbury for a London Challenge Cup tie. Sadly, most statisticians now ignore this fixture, and the Saints' one, and claim the second ever game under lights was another Arsenal friendly, against Glasgow Rangers, which attracted a 61,000 crowd.

Arsenal's line-up for this London Challenge Cup tie contained eight players who would make more than 1,300 combined first team appearances: Jack Kelsey, Don Roper, Joe Wade, Len Wills, Bill Healey, John Chenhall, Ryan, Colin Grimshaw, Reg Lewis, Arthur Shaw, James Robertson; Hendon's line-up was near to full strength, with one of finest half-back lines in amateur football: Laurie Topp, Dexter Adams and Bill Fisher. The full XI was: Reg Ivey, Pat Lynch, Micky Lane, Laurie Topp, Dexter Adams, Bill Fisher, Roy Evans, Arthur Phebey, Roy Stroud, Pat Austin, Bob Avis. It wasn't the Gunners' night because they lost both Grimshaw and Shaw to injury, so finished with nine men. And with two minutes remaining, Stroud crossed for Phebey to score the only goal.

Fast forward to 1962, and Claremont Road added floodlights, one of the first clubs to do this outside of the professional game. The lights, which cost £5,000 to install, were certainly impressive and could be seen from a long way away. Claremont Road was the first ground in non-league football to have the four corner pylons, and they were among the most powerful at the club's level, with the light being only slightly less than that of Crystal Palace's. The pylons would be around for more than 50 years, sadly standing as a stark reminder for half a dozen years after Hendon had left the ground.

The club's official opening night was a friendly against Wolverhampton Wanderers and the Wolves sent along their full first team, which included Ron Flowers, Peter Broadbent and Alan Hinton – all England internationals. Hinton had just been called up by Alf Ramsey and made his debut in England's first-ever European Championship match. Another star was as former Aston Villa legend Peter McParland.

Left: one of the Claremont Road floodlights. (Photo: Peter Lush)

The cream of the Amateur game, Hendon were no match for the team which would finish fifth in the Football League that season, and Wolves put on a great show, winning 7–1. Bill Fisher made his final appearance for Hendon that night, the 42-year-old coming on as a substitute for David Hogwood. It was be four more years before subs were permitted in competitive matches.

Night matches at Claremont Road were very special and even with 500 to 600 fans there was a great atmosphere. Maybe it was not strange in retrospect, but when it rained at night the atmosphere was even better – the reason being that fans would congregate under the covered terrace down the side and the noise reverberated in a way only a roof allows. One of those special nights was the FA Cup fourth qualifying round replay against Barnet in 1973–74, when a Roger Connell hat-trick sent the Greens into the competition proper and, eventually the match with Newcastle United.

In 1971, the Claremont Road floodlights were refurbished and this gave the Greens the chance to host another high-profile opponent for the official switch-on, Luton Town. As part of the agreement when he

81

moved there, it gave Hendon fans another chance to watch former winger Peter Anderson in action, albeit for the Hatters. The lights, as well as being very bright were also very reliable and I can recall only one complete failure. That was a pre-season friendly against Birmingham City in August 1981 – Hendon were trailing 1–0 and as fans trooped out of the ground, Tony Wood played "Blinded by the Light" over the tannoy. In the latter years of the club's time at Claremont Road, the cost of replacing lights was high, to say nothing of difficult given the height of the bank, so many matches were played with one or two bulbs dark; nonetheless the quality of illumination was still far above the requirements of the league.

There is still nothing like a big game on a cold evening under floodlights. It's part of what football fandom is all about.

Friendlies

Hendon have played friendlies against both international – i.e. not from the British Isles – and domestic opposition, either on tour or as hosts. The Barassi Cup and other international tournaments were not counted as friendlies.

Looking at the club's international matches, as Hampstead Town, Golders Green and Hendon, the club has played 26 friendlies against clubs from around Europe, the Middle and Far East, only four of which were at Claremont Road. However, probably the highest-profile opponent Hendon played – at least since becoming Hendon – was Torino, at Claremont Road, on 18 September 1971.

The reason for the fixture was a combination of circumstances. Because of the team's success in the FA Cup in previous years, Hendon had been given a bye through to the fourth qualifying round and only a handful of Isthmian League clubs were not involved in the first qualifying round that day. Torino, meanwhile, had played and beaten Limerick 1–0 in the European Cup-winners' Cup in Ireland three days earlier and moved on to London to prepare for the second leg of the Anglo-Italian Cup against Tottenham Hotspur on 22 September. The Anglo-Italian Cup that year was a two-legged contest between the winners of the English and Italian League Cup the previous season (for the record, Spurs, having won 1–0 in Italy went on to win the second leg 2–0 for a 3–0 aggregate triumph).

Torino wanted to give their players match practice, so visited Claremont Road for a friendly. In the first half, the Italians played mainly squad players and were 1–0 down to a John Connell goal. A defeat, even in a friendly, would have been hugely embarrassing, so Torino sent on most of their first-choice players, who turned things on the second half, scoring three times without reply to win 3–1.

The highest-profile opponent played when the club was Hampstead Town was before the First World War, in September 1913. This was, on paper, a complete mismatch because Town were London League champions while Red Star St-Ouen had been runners-up in France's national cup and had several full internationals. Making things even harder for Hampstead was that their players had played twice the previous day and then travelled to Paris.

Town won 3–1 in an FA Cup tie at Marlow with two goals from Arthur Humphreys and one from Oscar James, and a second team beat Old Islington 3–2 in a home League game. George Hyde with two, and R Barratt – his debut and one of two career matches, scored the goals.

Le Red Star Amical, as they were officially known, not Etoile Rouge, had been was founded by, among others, a young Jules Rimet and would go on to win France's Coupe Nationale five times. Their stadium would be used for the 1924 Olympic Games and, 74 years later, a World Cup warm-up game between Brazil and not-so-mighty Andorra, which Brazil won 3–0. A crowd of 2,000 watched Red Star score four first-half goals times against Hampstead and one more after the half-time break to win 5–0.

Town undertook an Easter 1925 tour of Belgium. On Good Friday, 10 April, before crossing the Channel, Hampstead defeated Dover United, 4–0. On the Sunday, Hampstead crushed Stade de Français 6–1 with goals from Ken Seabrooks with three, Freddie Young and Cecil Wise with two. It certainly was a high-profile match, because there were 20,000 fans in the stadium. The following day – it must have been Easter Monday – Wise scored the only goal against Royal FC Liegeois, but it was not all good news because another Hampstead Town squad lost 5–0 to Southall in the club's first Middlesex Senior Cup Final.

The club continued to undertake occasional end-of-season international tours and, in 1966, visited Madeira, where they played two of the island's biggest clubs Nacional and Maritimo – Portugal's island clubs were ineligible for the national league until the 1970s. Visiting the island simultaneously were Liverpool, celebrating their seventh League title and there are photos of the two squads sunbathing on the beach – though some Reds were engaged with England before the World Cup. Dave Swain scored twice in a 3–2 defeat against Nacional, while David Hyde and Swain, two, netted in a 3–1 win over Maritimo.

Hendon's first home game against international opposition, excluding an International Challenge Cup game against Boulogne in March 1912, result not known, was in 1947, a 3–2 victory over Dutch club Utrecht; Pat Austin, Bill Reay and Roy Stroud scored. Fast forward 40 seasons, and Hendon entertained Swedish third-tier club Gotesburg Fotballforening – the fourth club in the country's second city, behind IFK, GAIS and Orgryte (OIS) – and Hendon won 8–1 on 16 March 1978.

The goals came from Bobby Southam with two, Glen Swaby, Alan Hall, Steve Jefferies with three, and Tony Field. The most recent international friendly was a home game against Kuwaiti club Al-Jahra on 7 October 1991, but there is no record of the scorer in the Greens' 1–0 win.

Looking at some friendlies against British opposition, friendlies include practice matches, but invitation trophies, such as the Eastbourne Charity Cup, Arbiter Cup and Alaway Brothers Trophy are covered separately.

Sadly, there are dozens of friendlies for which there are no records, but the club's first friendly we know about came in its first season, on 13 March 1909, when Christ Church Hampstead played and beat Hendon Crescent 6–0. Six months later, Zephyr Athletic were beaten 5–1, the first recorded pre-season friendly in club history. Hampstead Town's first away friendly was on 3 December 1910 at Hyde & Kingsbury, and Town won that game 2–0. The club suffered its first two defeats against Queens Park Rangers XIs in 1911–12. No date is known for Hampstead's home game, which ended 3–1 – Harry Hyde was Hampstead's scorer – but on 16 March – a day when Hampstead also drew 2–2 away to Star United, QPR won 6–1 at home, George Hyde scoring. This was not the club's first game against Football League opposition because QPR were still in the Southern League and went on to win the title for the second time at the end of that season.

Hampstead did not play Football League opposition until after the First World War, on 7 February 1920, when Arsenal won 3–1 in Cricklewood, with J Croal getting Town's goal. However, QPR, Millwall and Watford all sent teams to Farm Avenue in the first three months of 1920 – prior to becoming founder members of Football League Division Three South that summer – and all left victorious. A year later, on 19 March 1921, Hampstead won 2–1 against West Ham United Reserves, with Cecil Wise and Cyril Burrage on target.

Moving forward to the Hendon era provides the biggest wins in friendlies and there are a few Hendon fans who were in Wales on 11 August 1991 for the 11–0 victory against Bargoed Rangers, whose team included the son of our former, sadly-departed Secretary, Dave Stanley. Hendon's scorers that morning were Kevin Quinn with a hat-trick, doubles for Trevor Keen and Marc Das, and the other goals came from Mark Xavier, Uche Egbe, Chris Harwood and Kevin Fowler. On 2 August 2008, Hendon – knowing they would soon become their tenants – abused their landlords-to-be Wembley, beating them 10–1 with nine different goalscorers: Rob Ursell with two, Sam Byfield, Lubo Guentchev, Dave Diedhiou, Charlie Mapes, Casey Maclaren, Mark Kirby, Marc Leach and Brian Haule.

Although I did not see the 9–0 victory over Frigidaire in 1969, I was at Claremont Road for the only time Hendon conceded nine in a friendly and nine in a home game. It was on 9 August 1984, when Watford visited. Three months earlier, they had lost in the FA Cup final against Everton. This was not a full-strength first team but a very strong squad, including future Hendon manager Neil Price, who had played in the 2–0 defeat to Everton at Wembley. Taking the Hornets team that night was John Ward and his pre-match team-talk was something along the lines that this was their most important match ever because if they didn't perform well, they would be out of the club.

Gary Allen, Derek Williams and Manny Lomotey all scored for Hendon – and the Greens had a penalty saved too – but Watford scored nine, with Jimmy Gilligan, Steve Sims, Ian Richardson and Martin Allen amongst the scorers. The 1962 game that launched our floodlights against Wolves was one of three occasions we conceded seven in a friendly, and the other two were back in the Hampstead Town days, 7–4 against Clapton Orient in 1927 and 7–0 against Tottenham Hotspur in 1929, the biggest ever margin of defeat at Claremont Road.

Golders Green's biggest friendly wins were 7–0 against Epsom & Ewell in December 1945, and 6–2 against Golders Green Past in 1938; the Green beat Barnet 6–3 in 1935. The Army Wanderers beat the Green 6–1 at Claremont Road in April 1938, a few weeks after teams from Chelsea, Tottenham Hotspur and Fulham had come for friendlies and left after 1–0 (George Bucci), 1–0 (Billy Breagan) and 4–1 (own goal, Bucci, Breagan and Derek Walker) defeats.

The club has enjoyed much success in friendlies at Silver Jubilee Park since the installation of the 3G pitch, most notably a 9–1 preseason triumph over co-tenants, Edgware Town in July 2018, an 8–1 victory over the same opponents back in January 2014 and the 6–0 defeat of Harrow Borough a month later. For the record, the last home friendly at Claremont Road was on 24 July 2008, when James Bent scored for Hendon in a 4–1 reverse against Stevenage Borough.

G

Golders Green

Phil Gridelet

Grounds the club has used

Boncho Guentchev

Lubomir Guentchev

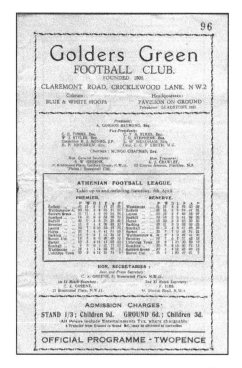

Golders Green programme (courtesy Kim Parker).

Golders Green

Between 1933 and 1946, the club was called Golders Green, but it was very nearly never so. Hampstead had moved into Claremont Road in 1926 and when, in 1933, the club decided to change its name, the preferred one was Hendon, the borough in which the club played. Hendon became part of the London Borough of Barnet in 1965. Hendon, however, was not available as the old club, one which 50 years earlier had played an FA Cup quarter-final tie at home to the holders, the Old Etonians, losing 4–2 at Brampton Grove, were just about still going. Hampstead had met Hendon in two friendlies in spring 1932. The local council was very keen for the club to become Hendon Borough, but Hampstead members were unhappy. Instead, they opted for Golders Green, the borough ward just to the north of the ground.

Golders Green began life with a pair of Athenian League fixtures against the powerful Walthamstow Avenue. Both games ended in defeat, 2–1 at Claremont Road, with Charlie Drinkwater scoring Golders Green's first goal, and 1–0 at Green Pond Road. Isthmian League Oxford City ended the Green's interest in the FA Cup at the first hurdle, winning 4–3 at the White Horse Ground. The first win as Golders Green came on 23 September, 2–0 at home to Uxbridge Town. After losing four of their first five Athenian League matches, Golders Green turned things around and lost only four of the last 21. They eventually finished third in the League, behind champions Avenue and Romford. This was the club's highest finish as Golders Green. They enjoyed a first-ever victory in the Middlesex Senior Cup, defeating Park Royal 2–0 in the final, courtesy of an own goal and one from Freddie Evans.

The following season was the most successful, at least in terms of the FA Cup as the Green reached the first round proper for the first time, albeit losing 10–1 away to Southend United in November 1934. League form was, to be kind, inconsistent, and Golders Green finished the campaign sixth in the table, even though six points behind champions Barking was much closer than the 11 they had trailed Walthamstow in 1933–34. In the 1935–36 season, Golders Green reached the FA Amateur Cup third round, where they lost 4–2 to ICI Alkali – the last 16 matched Hampstead Town's best, in 1926. Golders Green repeated the feat three years later, again losing 4–2, this time away to Sutton United. In other cup competitions, the Green made it to both the London Senior and Middlesex Charity Cup finals. They won the latter 2–0 against London Caledonians, with Bert Broadis and Mike Fallon on the scoresheet on 4 May 1936. However, they lost the former 1–0 to Walthamstow Avenue five days later.

A momentous decision was made at Golders Green's 1938 Annual General Meeting. The club's colours changed from blue to green, and it was as the green-clad club that they won a second Middlesex Senior Cup. Wealdstone had beaten the Green 4–0 in the 1938 Middlesex Charity Cup final, but 12 months on, the score-line was reversed. In fact, Golders Green led 4–0 after 39 minutes, with Fred Boston, Les Ellison, Bob Thomas and Broadis scoring.

The Second World War ended official competitive football for the next six seasons, but, just after VE Day, Golders Green played at Wembley Stadium, in the Middlesex Red Cross Cup Final, as the Charity Cup had been temporarily renamed. Green's opponents were their tenants, Tufnell Park, and it finished 4–1 to the landlords, with doubles from Mac Cochrane and George Bucci.

After the 1945–46, the club voted again to change the name. Hendon was now available – it had been as early as 1934, but two name changes in consecutive seasons would have lacked credibility. Once more, the local council pressed for Hendon Borough, but the club captain told the AGM that "Hendon has a snappy sound to it", and the vote to be Hendon was carried. An attempt by supporters to return to the blue colours was rejected, citing the costs of changing, especially with wartime rationing and austerity still in force.

One effect of the name change was the amendment of the nickname. Having been the Green of Golders Green, the Dons of Hendon, in green, became that, or the (pluralised) Greens. Overall, Golders Green's Athenian League record was:

Played: 184	Goals for: 446
Won: 77	Goals against: 408
Drawn: 33	Points: 187.
Lost: 74	

(Programme: The last Golders Green match, the Middlesex Charity Cup Final at Brentford FC's Griffin Park on 11 May 1946)

Phil Gridelet

Phil Gridelet was Hendon's first England non-league international. Few players make their senior debut, let alone a club debut in a cup final, but that was the first of countless achievements by Phil Gridelet. A former Watford junior, Phil, like his Princess Park FC team-mates Steve Newing and Danny Worley, graduated from Hendon's midweek youth team into the first eleven. The date was Tuesday 7 May 1985, and it was the early in the Middlesex Charity Cup Final when John Palmer collided with a Feltham player and went off with a broken nose. On came Phil, one week after celebrating his 18th birthday.

The injury to Palmer caused a reshuffle in Hendon's formation and Phil was used as a midfielder, as opposed to defender where he spent most of his first spell. His talent had been clear to see and his hair-trigger temperament had certainly been calmed down. But his talent to wind up opponents remained throughout his career and in the second half of the game, he wound up one of the Feltham players so much that he exacted revenge on the next green shirt he encountered; Paul Robinson was led from the field with a nose broken by a savage elbow, spotted the by the linesman, and the offender was sent off. Carl Zacchau of Yeovil, on the opening day of the 1986–87 season, in front of more than 1,600 home fans, lasted only 23 minutes before he was dismissed for retaliating to something committed by Phil – and, seven months later, the Dane was still bitter about it!

That was jumping the gun by a season, because Phil was one of the few consistent shining lights in the Hendon team which battled against relegation in 1985–86. Phil apart, another central defender, Andy O'Brien, and striker Colin Tate were the only two others of the 40-odd players used who appeared in more than 26 League matches that season, indicative of a team that is struggling. He scored his first goal in September, the second in a 2–2 draw with Worthing at Claremont Road, but he managed only eight in more than 250 starts in his career. Stopping the other team scoring, now that was a different story and Phil was one of the best. He and O'Brien were superb is stopping Les Ferdinand when Southall were beaten in the Middlesex Senior Cup final on Easter Monday 1986.

Hendon's 1986–87 season was the longest the club endured with 75 matches – including 33 cup ties. Phil played in 30 of them, bettered only by Dave Root's 31, a tribute to his strength and stamina. He also got his nickname in the first pre-season friendly when a referee at South Bank booked him but wrote down Gripper – then a character in the children's television series *Grange Hill.*

Phil's biggest attributes were his speed, strength and ability to read a situation quickly. Although he would make his name in the Football League as a midfielder, Ted Hardy couldn't find a better sweeper than Phil. The best examples of his talents came as he turned defence into attack single-handedly. Two runs he made stick in my mind: the first was against Worthing, on a desperately foul afternoon in quagmire conditions. He ran from inside his own penalty area and struck an unstoppable drive from the "D" of the Worthing penalty area. An offside flag ruled out the goal, but the home goalkeeper turned around and said, "That was a travesty. I will never be beaten by a better goal!" The next came in the FA Trophy at Fareham; again it was a lung-bursting run from his own box, but this time after the goalkeeper had saved Phil's shot, Iain Dowie scored the goal, taking the ball off Phil's toe.

In 1988–89, Phil received a call-up to play for England and made two appearances, the first in Italy, then at Kidderminster against Wales. After the end of the season, when he won the Supporters Association Player of the Year award, he moved on to Barnet – he had a trial at Nottingham Forest where Brian Clough was manager, before enjoying a long career in the Football League. He played for Barnsley, Rotherham and Southend before moving to Woking in 1998. Phil returned to play for Hendon under Frank Murphy in 2000. He was by now a veteran midfielder and still hard man to get the better of, if not to out-run. Phil this had the unique experience of playing in Hendon's longest, 1986–87, and shortest seasons – 2000–01 ended with two league matches unplayed.

He subsequently played for Bishop's Stortford and Harrow Borough, and was a coach at Harrow and then at Hayes, who were in Conference South at the time.

Grounds the club has used

Throughout the last almost 60 years Hendon have hosted matches at grounds other their designated home venue – or indeed as visitors to opponents who have moved their fixture. None of the club's recent homes, Silver Jubilee Park, Vale Farm or Earlsmead are included. This is by no means a complete list and, just as the ground-share homes are excluded, the same is applied for many of our opponents of recent times – a list which includes Cray Wanderers, Maidstone United, Wealdstone, Staines Town, Enfield, Kingstonian, Grays Athletic, London Bari and Enfield Town.

The most recent example of playing a match at a ground other than Hendon's or the opponents' was on 17 February 2014 when, uniquely, a Middlesex Senior Cup quarter-final against Staines Town at Wheatsheaf Stadium was called off not by anyone involved in football, but by the Environment Agency. The pitch was literally flooded, as was most of the local area and surrounding villages. Give the Middlesex FA full credit, they arranged for one venue to stage three of the quarter-final games on the same pitch on consecutive nights. The upshot was that Hendon met Staines on a Monday night at the 3G pitch just outside what is now Hayes & Yeading United's home. There were 39 people at the match, which saw the Greens come from 2–0 down to beat Conference South Staines 3–2, with Michael Murray, Jefferson Louis and Anthony Thomas netting after Max Worsfold and Louie-Rae Beadle had netted two for the Massive.

In addition to matches at Wembley and Harrow in 2008–09, Hendon had to play Ryman League games at both Northwood, against Harrow Borough, and Staines, against Canvey Island. Borough were crushed 7–0, and even James Burgess got on the scoresheet – his first goal, other than in penalty shoot-outs, in his 231st Hendon appearance – while the Gulls found the western side of the Thames unwelcoming as they went down 2–0.

Claremont Road was used as a ground-switch venue on a few occasions, mainly for Middlesex and/or London Senior Cup ties. Staines – when Wheatsheaf Stadium was being redeveloped and their temporary Chertsey home was not in Middlesex – Hanwell Town, Brimsdown Rovers and North Greenford United all switched games, and Hendon were victorious every time. When Enfield (now Enfield 1893) were homeless, they played a few games at Claremont Road, but this was when neither St Albans nor Boreham Wood's homes were free and the Greens were not the opposition.

However, on Monday 13 March 1989, Hendon suffered one of their most ignominious defeats, worse than the Middlesex Cup exit at Hanworth Villa and London Cup defeat at Brimsdown, losing to Southwark Borough – a club which played senior football for only five seasons, the first four of which were as Southwark Sports – whose regular home did not have floodlights. They played at Salter Road, the home of then rising Fisher Athletic. There were at least three divisions between Isthmian Premier Hendon and Spartan League Premier Southwark, but the Greens, who included first-team regulars such as Erskine Smart, Mark Furneaux, Martin Duffield, Phil Gridelet, Neil Henry, Steve Scott, Colin Tate and Gary Keen, who all made at least 90 appearances, lost to a solitary goal in extra-time.

As visitors, Hendon have played Isthmian League matches away to Barking at both Lynn Road, Ilford FC – this was a huge disappointment for me because it would have been our final game at Vicarage Fields and it was a ground which I never visited – on 27 December 1975, a 2–1 win thanks to goals from Eggie James and Bobby Childs, and Lea Bridge Road, Leyton FC. The latter was a truly dire final-game goalless draw, memorable for Billy Stagg attempting to put a penalty kick into orbit rather than the roof of the net. However, the boot was on the other foot when Hendon won an Isthmian League Cup tie 5–3 against Leytonstone & Ilford at the Blues' Mayesbrook Park home. I remember this bitterly cold night, just before Christmas 1986, a game in which Andy O'Brien, Colin Tate and Richard Bradford scored in the 90 minutes and Tate and Roger Wade settled the tie in the additional – and unwanted – extra 30.

91

Hendon versus Maidstone United in April 2015 at Harrow Borough's Earlsmead ground. (Photo: Derek Beech Photography)

Left: Programme from Hendon versus Woking in the FA Cup at Wembley FC's Vale Farm.

Other cup ties the club decided to switch were a Middlesex Charity Cup tie against Yeading in January 1993, which Hendon lost 2–0 at The Warren and a League Cup tie against Aldershot Town in February 2002, with the same result. The consolation from the game at the Rec was that the attendance was 584, a few times more than would have braved the wilds of Cricklewood.

Going back in time, Hendon have also moved one home FA Amateur Cup and FA Trophy tie apiece to venues less than a half-mile apart in the London W12 postcode. On 11 February 1961, defending FA Amateur Cup-holders Hendon moved their home second round tie against Walthamstow Avenue to White City. At a stadium that hosted the London Olympic Games in 1908 and a FIFA World Cup 1966 match, the baton was passed because not only did the Avenue win 2–0, they went on to defeat West Auckland Town in the final at the 1948 Olympic Games venue, Wembley Stadium.

Fast forward to 21 January 1982, and bitter winter cold snap left most grounds unplayable, Claremont Road included, so Hendon, with a little help from the Currie brothers, Tony and Paul, moved the game to Queens Park Rangers FC's Loftus Road, where Tony was starring. My instinct at the time was that Taunton Town had even less chance than normal in this FA Trophy when Paul ended up with the keys to the Rs' boot room and appropriately-shod, Hendon won 5–1, with goals from Pat Morrisey, Peter Anderson, Martin Sperrin, Dermot Drummy and Bobby Gough.

Bontcho Guentchev

Few players have made as big an impact on Hendon FC starting as few matches as Bontcho Guentchev. On paper, his statistics don't suggest he was anything more than an ageing former professional star playing out the end of his career; the reality could not be more different. Talk to any Hendon player who was coming through the ranks in the late 1990s and appeared with him and there is almost hero worship, because Bontcho left such a massive impression on them, not just with his achievements, but with his personality.

The story started with a summer's afternoon in the Hendon FC offices at Claremont Road in 1999, when a representative of Bontcho Guentchev approached club secretary Graham Etchell. It is not unusual for players and/or their agents to make such an approach, though normally their tales of stardom in this country or the other and their international experience belong in novels. Not with Bontcho: he did win the Bulgarian League title with Etur, he did play in a World Cup semi-final: Bulgaria versus Italy, 1994, replacing Hristo Stoichkov after 78 minutes, he did play in the Portuguese top division for Sporting Lisbon and he also played in England for Ipswich Town and Luton Town.

Why Hendon? The answer was simple, when people say they 'live down the road', it can be a couple of miles; in Bontcho's case is was a few hundred yards, on Claremont Road, where he had moved on joining Luton. He had moved back to Bulgaria, but his two children, Lubomir and Iavor, and wife Sylvia, stayed in England with the boys at a Premiership club's academy, and Bontcho missed them.

Nine months after scoring for CSKA Sofia in the UEFA Cup against Atletico Madrid, Bontcho made his Isthmian League debut, away to Slough Town, a 1–1 draw memorable for a 'Freddie Hyatt special' free-kick. His home debut came a week later at home to Canvey Island and Bontcho celebrated it with an overhead scissors kick after five minutes. The keeper never moved as the ball flew into the roof of the net.

The Greens reached the FA Cup second round proper in 1999–2000, and Bontcho was named as a substitute in every tie until the 2–0 defeat at Blackpool. He came off the bench three times, most effectively when he scored the second goal as Hendon ended Bath City's record as the last unbeaten team that season in English senior football. At Bloomfield Road, a match the Greens were within an inch or so of winning, Bontcho started and hit the underside of the crossbar with an effort that would have gone down as one of the most spectacular goals in FA Cup history, then saw Tony Caig make a miraculous save from another thundering volley.

A year later, Bontcho played 45 minutes in goal when Richard Wilmot broke his arm – he played for 15 minutes knowing the seriousness of the injury – after half an hour at Carshalton. In the dressing room, Bontcho told manager Frank Murphy "I played in goal in Bulgaria," so he was given the gloves instead of the regular stand-in keeper Simon Clarke. Trailing 1–0 Bontcho was brilliant marshalling the defence, though his chest control, turn and dribble past a Robins forward was pure show-boating. Nonetheless the Greens came back to win a memorable game 2–1. The 2000–01 season was not a happy one as the weather and Claremont Road pitch ensured we played only 40 of 42 matches. Bontcho put his hand up more than most in that crazy spell, starting nine of 15 matches in 33 days and making four substitute appearances – he scored five goals too.

After a spell at Carshalton, Bontcho played with London Bulgaria before returning to Hendon in 2006 as player-coach under Gary McCann. He made 11 appearances in 2006–07, aged 42 and scored his final goal in a 2–1 Middlesex Senior Cup defeat against Hayes at Claremont Road, the club's final County Cup tie at its old home. He did have the rare experience of playing with both his sons – though there were never three Guentchevs on the pitch at the same time in a competitive match. Work commitments meant he spent much of the following season back in Bulgaria. The family returned to Bulgaria, with Iavor and Lubomir now playing for Bontcho's old club Etur. However, Lubomir at least is back in England, and was one of the former Hendon players who won the FA Vase in 2019 for Dave Anderson's Chertsey Town side.

Lubomir Guentchev

Lubomir Guentchev was one of the reasons his father Bontcho played for Hendon. A few weeks after scoring for CSKA Sofia against Atletico Madrid in the 1998–99 UEFA Cup, Bontcho decided to return to Cricklewood, where his wife Sophia and sons Iavor and Lubo lived, as the boys were at a Premier League football club's academy. Lubo went to Ipswich Town to be part of their academy, and made three appearances out on loan at Lowestoft Town as a teenager. It didn't work out for him in Suffolk, or at FC Union in Berlin, so he returned to London, where he became a graphic design student.

The third Guentchev to make his debut – Iavor played in the last match of the previous season – Lubo's first Hendon game was as a substitute on the opening day of the 2007–08 season a goalless draw at Heybridge Swifts. A free-spirited footballer, the strict rigours of the Isthmian League meant he would often be used a substitute – indeed more than one-third of his career 166 appearances would be off the bench. But Lubo at full tilt was a joy to watch. A will-o-the-wisp midfielder, in days gone by he would have been an out-and-out winger, Lubo could beat defenders inside or outside, and he had a knack for spectacular goals.

Bontcho was back at Hendon as a player-coach, so most team-sheets contained at least one member of the Guentchev family during the 2007–08 season. The three never actually played a competitive match together, but it could not have been closer. In the Hendon versus Chelmsford City match on 12 April 2008, Kezie Ibe was in the Clarets' line-up, Lubo started in the Greens' 2–1 victory, and Iavor replaced Ben Hudell for the final 15 minutes. As the game moved into stoppage time, Bontcho stood on the touchline waiting for the ball to go out of play. It didn't and the final whistle went before Bontcho made what would have been his only appearance of the season.

The following season must have been frustrating for Lubo because although he appeared in 31 League matches, he was a substitute 21 times and only 19 of his 44 appearances came as a starter. It was also Lubo's least prolific season in terms of goalscoring, netting just three times. It should have been four goals, however, because he should also have had the honour of scoring Hendon's last ever goal at Claremont

Road. He applied the final touch to a Dave Diedhiou cross in the game against Wealdstone on 20 September 2008, but an errant assistant referee's flag – Lubo had been three or four yards behind the crosser when the ball was played across the six yard box – ruled out the goal. Hendon ended the 2008–09 campaign in the London Senior Cup final against Croydon Athletic at Kingsmeadow Stadium, and although he didn't get on during the 120 minutes, Lubo still picked up a winners medal after the Greens won 3–1 on penalties.

Fast forward 12 months and Lubo scored what was probably his finest Hendon goal in the season-ending 3–2 victory over AFC Hornchurch at Vale Farm. His lob from an acute angled sailed 15–20 feet over Darren Behcet's head, bounced on the goal line and rose into the roof of the net. It was an outrageous piece of skill. And it wasn't the first time Lubo had picked on AFC Hornchurch because, in the reverse fixture at Bridge Avenue, he had scored a spectacular hat-trick in a pulsating 4–4 draw. The goal at Vale Farm – in a 3–2 victory – was his ninth goal of the season, but he appeared in less than two-thirds of Hendon's matches and had a strike-rate better than one-in-four.

Lubo would have bettered his career best marks for Hendon if he had stayed for the whole of the 2010–11 season. Matching his career highs of 44 appearances and nine goals, Lowestoft Town signed him just before the transfer deadline in late March. Lubo's final Hendon game was away at Folkestone Invicta, when he replaced Diedhiou for the final 20-odd minutes. It should also be noted that he came on with Hendon trailing 1–0, but he and Darren Ambrose made a massive difference as the Greens rallied to win 2–1. It also says an awful lot for Lubo that, despite having already signed for the Trawlerboys, he still went down to Thamesmead when Hendon won a London Senior Cup later in the week tie to say goodbye to his former team-mates. Lubo spent just over a year in Suffolk before returning home to Bulgaria. A six year spell in Bulgarian football followed, before, now approaching the veteran stage, he joined Dave Anderson at Chertsey Town, winning the FA Vase in May 2019.

H

Rod Haider

Hampstead Town and Hampstead

Gary Hand

Ted Hardy

Harrow Borough

Hayes FC

David Hogwood

Freddie Hyatt

David Hyde

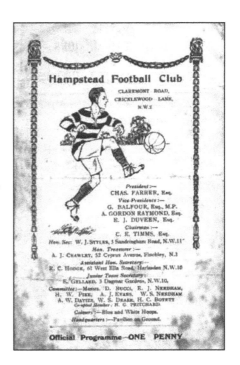

Left: Hampstead FC programme. (Courtesy Kim Parker).

Rod Haider

The word legend is overused in football parlance but, in the case of Rod Haider, it is a massive understatement. Rod has a place in England football history as he won 65 England Amateur international caps, and as that tier of football ended in 1974, no one will pass his total. Second on the list is another Hendon legend, John Swannell with 60.

Rod joined Hendon from Kingstonian – much to their disappointment – in 1967, having already won 10 England Amateur caps. A tireless worker in midfield, he had the uncanny ability to time his runs into the penalty area to finish off attacks with a goal.

His debut came in the opening game of the 1967–68 season, a 5–0 victory over Dulwich Hamlet at Champion Hill, and his first goal came three days later, in a 5–2 defeat of Walthamstow Avenue at Claremont Road.

However, Rod's debut season was his equally-least productive in terms of goals for Hendon. He appeared in 34 League matches and nine cup ties and scored eight goals – the only one of his 12 campaigns in which he failed to register in a knock-out fixture. For the first four seasons, as Hendon slipped from highest echelon of the Isthmian League, Rod was one of the most consistent performers. He had the happy knack of avoiding serious injury and never missed more than half a dozen league matches in any season until he left the club – aged almost 37 – in November 1979.

The first half of the 1970s was Rod's greatest spell. The club captain, he had the honour of leading Hendon out at Wembley Stadium for the 1972 FA Amateur Cup final against Enfield. The Greens scored midway through the first half and, after soaking up huge pressure, sealed the 2–0 win in the last couple of minutes. It was Rod who paraded the Amateur Cup to the Hendon faithful for the third and final time. In 58 League and cup appearances, he scored an astonishing 23 goals – one almost every two-and-a-half games.

`Five months later, it was off to Italy as Hendon represented England in the Barassi Cup – dubbed the European Amateur Championship, though it was an Anglo-Italian challenge – and a 1–1 draw against Unione Valdinvole gave Hendon a 3–1 aggregate victory. Rod had scored Hendon's second goal at Claremont Road. Once again, there was Haider lifting a trophy aloft. The Greens enjoyed a very special campaign, winning the Isthmian League championship after an unbeaten run that stretched 38 matches from 8 August to 17 April.

Rod's busiest season was in 1973–74 and he, once again, hit the national headlines. This time it was in the FA Cup because, Hendon reached the third round proper. There, the Greens were drawn away to Newcastle United and, after conceding a goal to Pat Howard just before half-time, Rod was on the end of a free-kick move to make it 1–1. He nearly grabbed a second late on, but the Magpies held on and won the replay 4–0. Hendon's campaign was arduous in the extreme as a nine-match FA Amateur Cup run ended with a third-round second replay exit at the hands of Leatherhead.

Rod missed only one of 67 matches that season – of which 16 came in 39 days from 9 April 1974. At the end of that season, most of the team moved elsewhere, but Rod stayed loyal to the Club where he had enjoyed so much success. He turned down numerous offers to go elsewhere – he had been offered pro terms earlier in his career – and indeed missed only three matches in the five seasons from 1974–75. His ability to score key goals had been shown in 1969 as he netted the only goal of the London Senior Cup final, and eight years later, as he repeated the feat in the League Cup final against Barking.

In 1979, Rod was appointed player-manager, a role he took on reluctantly and it was not a huge success. He stopped playing for Hendon in November that year and a little later, was sacked as manager. It was the signal for Rod to move on to pastures new and he had spells as a player and coach at both Harrow Borough and Hayes, before playing veterans football for Corinthian Casuals, finally retiring aged 57.

In all he made a remarkable 696 appearances for Hendon, scored 165 goals and won every trophy it was possible for the club to win in his era apart from the FA Cup or FA Trophy.

One of the road signs on the small housing estate built on the site of the Claremont Road ground. Along with the one for John Swannell, it is the only reminder that football was played there. (Photo: Peter Lush)

Hampstead Town and Hampstead

The club first played as Christ Church Hampstead, but it became Hampstead Town after one season and played under the banner of Hampstead Town or Hampstead for almost a quarter of a century, 1909 to 1933, though four seasons were lost to the First World War. Hampstead Town's first recorded fixtures were in September, a friendly against Zephyr Athletic, which they won 5–1. The Finchley & District League Division Two season kicked off on the last day of the month, with a goalless draw against Totteridge. Things were made harder for Town because Bramleigh and North Islington both pulled out of the League, costing the team eight points from four wins against them, compared to nearest rivals Totteridge, who lost only four points. Hampstead won the Division Two title on the final day of the season, crushing Caledonian Old Boys 12–0. Totteridge had to beat Edgware Athletic, third in the table, by more than 12 goals to be champions; instead they lost 1–0 so Town were champions by two points.

The first record of a home ground came in 1910, when the National Athletic Ground in Kensal Green was used – it may have been used in the previous season. As well as the Finchley & District League Division One, Hampstead Town also played in the Willesden and London Leagues, and they won the top division of the Finchley competition. A year later the Willesden League was won, this time after a play-off against Deerfield Social.

For the 1912–13 season, Hampstead Town had another new home, this one theirs, and it was much closer to home. What is now Farm Avenue goes off Cricklewood Lane towards Fortune Green and is in today's London Borough of Barnet, but then the Borough of Hendon. The Avenue Ground was at the Cricklewood Lane end, so less than a mile from Claremont Road in a direct line. It took a lot of work, but the ground gave Hampstead a huge boost and they won both the Middlesex and London Leagues that season, repeating successes the following year, albeit in the London League Amateur Division.

Town moved up to the Athenian League for 1914, only for the outbreak of the First World War to curtail their involvement after three games until 1919. Town did make their FA Cup debut in 1914–15 and made it to the fifth (of six) qualifying rounds before losing to Bromley. For the record Hampstead Town's first FA Cup tie was a preliminary walkover at home to Sutton Court, and the club also got a bye in the second qualifying round.

As members of the Athenian League, neither Hampstead Town nor Hampstead finished top or bottom, but there was one penultimate place and two runners-up places, strangely all coming as Hampstead, 13th in 1926–27 and second in 1928–29 and 1932–33.

Hampstead Town team in Paris in 1913 (Courtesy Kim Parker)

Hampstead Town 1919–20 (Courtesy Kim Parker)

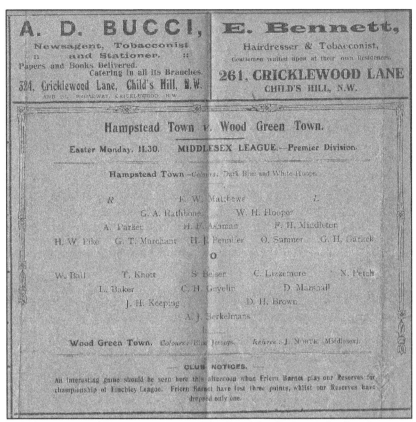

Hampstead Town v. Wood Green Town.

Easter Monday, 11.30.   MIDDLESEX LEAGUE.—Premier Division.

Hampstead Town—Colours: Dark Blue and White Hoops.

R   F. W. Matthews   L.

G. A. Rathbone   W. H. Hooper

A. Parker   H. P. Ashman   F. H. Middleton

H. W. Pike   G. T. Marchant   H. J. Penniler   O. Sumner   G. H. Garrick

O

W. Ball   T. Knott   S. Belser   C. Lizzemore   N. Fetch

L. Baker   C. H. Gevelin   D. Marshall

J. H. Keeping   D. H. Brown

A. J. Berkelmans

Wood Green Town.   Colours: Blue Jerseys.   Referee: J. North (Middlesex).

CLUB NOTICES.

An interesting game should be seen here this afternoon when Friern Barnet play our Reserves for championship of Finchley League. Friern Barnet have lost three points, whilst our Reserves have dropped only one.

1913 Hampstead Town programme. The Bucci family (top left advert) were great supporters of the club. 'Chummy' Parker, Kim Parker's grandfather, is at right half for Hampstead Town.

The first of the two runners-up finishes were the meat in a sandwich of two other bottom-four placings. But, as well as the name amendment in 1926, 18 September that year was another landmark, because it saw the first match for the club at their new home, Claremont Road. The move from the Avenue Ground was pretty much forced on the club after the building of houses and widening of Hendon Way cut into the available space for the football ground. Hampstead were fortunate that Clitterhouse Farm had gone bust a few months earlier and the land was available. For 82 years and nine days, Claremont Road would be the club's home – and where so many glorious achievements were celebrated.

When it came to cup competitions, League Cups did not exist, so as well as the FA Cup and Amateur Cup, the big competitions were the county cups. Hampstead Town and Hampstead both won the Middlesex Charity Cup, in 1922 and 1927, respectively – Hampstead were also

102

beaten in the 1931 Final, 3–2 by Wealdstone at Finchley. As for the Middlesex Senior Cup, there were two final appearances, again once each in the two guises, in 1924–25 for Town – Southall were 5–0 winners at Griffin Park against a weak team, with the first team on tour – and 1930–31 for Hampstead, Hayes winning 4–1 at Wealdstone. The story of the name change to Golders Green is covered elsewhere, but to cut a long story short, the name Hendon was unavailable because that club, although struggling for survival, was still in existence. Hendon Borough as a suggestion was rejected, so the club plumped for Golders Green, a name the club kept for just 13 years, until 1946. The Municipal Borough of Hendon lasted from 1932 to 1965, when it was amalgamated into the London Borough of Barnet; Claremont Road from 1926 to 2008, but this club, Christ Church Hampstead, Hampstead Town, Hampstead, Golders Green and now Hendon lives and fights on.

Gary Hand

Gary Hand is second on the appearances table for Hendon in the Isthmian League era. He left Watford when his apprenticeship ended and joined Hendon at the start of the 1971–72 season. He made his debut in the number 11 shirt for the Greens' second Isthmian League game, away at Loakes Park, Wycombe, where Wanderers triumphed 1–0. Apart from an unused substitute appearance, in the 1–0 win over Walton & Hersham a week later, that was the last Gary was seen in a first-team shirt until 27 December, when he was in his familiar left-back role for the visit of Enfield. Roy Butler's goal gave Hendon all three points.

From that point on, Gary was almost an ever-present – he missed just one match, the day before the first leg of the Middlesex Senior Cup Final against Hampton. Gary's first season was certainly memorable and he finished it as the owner of winners' medals from the FA Amateur Cup and Middlesex Senior Cup and a London Senior Cup runners-up medal.

Hendon manager John Evans and his successor Jimmy Quail put together one of the most dominant and stingiest defences ever seen in the Isthmian League: John Swannell in goal, behind right-back Tony Jennings, centre-backs Alan Phillips and Peter Deadman and Gary at left-back. The quintet had been together in the Amateur Cup Final victory over Enfield at Wembley and all five made at least 52 appearances the following season as Hendon won the Isthmian League with a record of 34 wins and six draws in 42 matches.

The Greens conceded only 18 League goals all season and eight in the 34 games between 22 August and 17 April. Hendon astonishingly did not concede a single League goal from a corner all season, and did not taste defeat until the 39th League game, when runners-up Walton & Hersham won 2–1 at Claremont Road. The Greens' total of 74 points would equate today to 108 with three for win, which came into effect the following season. Gary was selected for the England Amateur international squad, but did not win a cap.

In 1973–74, Hendon enjoyed their best ever FA Cup run, reaching the third round proper. The Greens held Newcastle United to a 1–1 draw at St James's Park, but lost the replay at Vicarage Road, Watford, 4–0. Gary would, in today's football, not have seen out the replay as his spectacular save gave the Magpies a penalty from which they made it 3–0. As he was being booked, the referee said to Gary, "Good save!" In the League, the departure of Jennings, Phil Fry and Derek Baker, plus terrible fixture congestion brought on by cup success and a multitude of Amateur Cup replays, meant Hendon finished runners-up, two points behind champions Wycombe. And Gary enjoyed more FA Cup success the following season, with Wycombe, having left Claremont Road in the summer of 1974.

It was only a one-year hiatus, however, as Gary was back in green and white in 1975. And he would enjoy further FA Cup glory as Hendon recorded their first-ever victory over a Football League club in the competition, beating Reading 1–0 before succumbing to a late Swindon Town goal in round two. Gary finished the season with the first of three Middlesex Charity Cup winner's medals, to go with his earlier hat-trick of Middlesex Senior successes.

A year later, Gary added a second Charity Cup winner's medal and one from the Isthmian League Cup, as Barking were beaten 1–0 at Earlsmead. Three weeks before the Barking game, Gary had celebrated his first Hendon goal – a chip over 6 feet 8 inches Staines Town goalkeeper Kelvin Hopkins; it came in his 254th first-team appearance – rather making a mockery of the line in the 1972 Amateur Cup Final programme, "watch out for his left foot"!

If one word summed up Gary's Hendon career, consistency would be it. He was close to an ever-present every season from 1975–76 until 1981–82, when the club encountered its first big financial problem. New manager Dave Mawson did things on the cheap and used mainly youngsters, but it didn't work and Gary returned to Hendon in February, in the role as player-manager, assisted by his former boss, Jimmy Quail. Work commitments meant he had to give up after seeing Hendon achieve safety, but he returned in the summer of 1985.

It proved to be a most unhappy time in charge as the Greens were bottom of the table when he was relieved of his duties and replaced by Ted Hardy. It wasn't quite the end, however, as Gary returned in the early 2000s, managing the under-18s midweek team and then the reserves.

Ted Hardy

Ted Hardy merits inclusion in this book as a manager only, without having played for Hendon. His managerial career saw him in charge of, among others, Leyton, Bishop's Stortford, Dagenham, Leytonstone & Ilford and Enfield before he was appointed Hendon manager just before Christmas in 1985, succeeding Gary Hand. The Greens were languishing at or near the bottom of the Isthmian League table and had suffered some crushing defeats, most notably 5–3 away to Epsom & Ewell, having led 3–0 early, and 4–0 away to Windsor & Eton. The defence was leaky, the midfield lacked bite and the forwards were lightweight.

Hardy's reputation as a no-nonsense manager was already the stuff of legend, having won the Isthmian League title with Enfield and the FA Amateur Cup with Bishop's Stortford – one of his four appearances as a manager in the final. Used to almost unbroken success and wealthy clubs, a battle at the foot of the table for a club with significantly fewer resources was a very different challenge.

It quickly became clear to Ted that the team needed the injection of both quality and experience, though few of the players recruited were hardened battlers against relegation. The return of goalkeeper Mark Broughton was important as was the arrival of Roger Wade, who marked his New Year's Day debut with the goal that brought a point against Bishop's Stortford. A couple of weeks later, Ted was forced to make more changes after a pitiful 3–0 defeat against Kingstonian at Richmond Road, a match which marked the arrival of Micky Kiely, to partner Colin Tate in attack, and veteran left-back John Knapman.

Two weeks later, there were three more arrivals, Derek Brown and Dave Clark from Dartford and Tony Gibson – a key member of the Enfield squad which had dominated non-league football for almost a decade. Of all the players to represent Hendon, few have been as uncompromising and – there is no nice way of putting it – efficiently violent as Gibson. What he brought, however, was not only a winning mentality, but a midfield presence that allowed Knapman to move to left back and a certainty that the younger Hendon players weren't going to be bullied. In the trio's second match, a 2–0 victory at Worthing, Hendon had a new face in the dugout, albeit for only this game – John Still.

Things got worse before they got better and the nadir was reached on 23 March 1986, a 5–0 drubbing at Farnborough, which left Hendon eight points behind 20th-placed Epsom & Ewell, having played nine more matches. It would be the Greens' final defeat of the season as Ted engineered a miraculous turnaround. With free-spirited midfielder Steve Parsons on board for a few weeks, Hendon suddenly were dangerous opponents and five wins and five draws – plus victory in the

Middlesex Senior Cup Final – meant the Greens had their fate in their own hands when they travelled to Slough Town for the last game of the season. Three key results were a come-from-behind 3–3 draw at Wokingham and a quick-fire League double over fellow strugglers Billericay Town, 4–1 away and 4–2 at home. At Wexham Park, Wade – looking suspiciously offside – scored early with a 30-yard chip, Broughton produced a wonder save to keep the lead at half-time and Andy O'Brien, Kiely and Gibson added further goals to seal a 4–1 win and safety was assured.

One of Ted's strengths was his ability to organise his teams. They may not have been the prettiest to watch, but they were remorseless, efficient and uncompromising. A team that let Hendon play usually found themselves outsmarted and outplayed; a team that wanted to mix it up, got more than they bargained for and usual lost both the battles and the war. A final finishing place of fourth in 1986–87 would have been better with less success in cup competitions, but the Greens lost in the finals of both the AC Delco (Isthmian League) and GMAC (Premier Inter-League) Cups. The quarter-final replay replay (sic) against Harrow Borough – 5–3, having been 3–0 down at half-time – and the two games with Burton Albion stand out as especially memorable. The draw in Staffordshire on a Sunday afternoon came a day after a 3–1 win over Croydon at Claremont Road.

Sadly, it all fell apart early the following season. A shock FA Cup exit against Hertford Town in late September resulted in Ted's resignation. His long-time assistant Micky Janes took over as manager and he led the team out at Wembley in June 1988, mainly with the players Ted had brought to the club or nurtured.

Ted stayed in football until March 1999, when approaching 70 years old, he finished his fourth spell at Victoria Road, having become the oldest man to lead out a team in a Wembley cup final in 1998.

Harrow Borough

There is the only club that Hendon has played annually for the past 40 years – actually 41 years – and that is the club's near neighbours, former landlords and good friends, Harrow Borough.

Like Hendon, Harrow have had more than a couple of names. They began life as Roxonian before becoming Harrow Town and Town were the opposition the first four times the teams met. In 1953, Hendon won an FA Cup tie 3–2, with Charlie Nock getting a double and John Core the other. In Middlesex Senior Cup ties, in 1962, 1965 and 1967, Hendon dominated, beating Town 4–2, 8–0 and 7–0 respectively, Danny Lakey bagging hat-tricks in the last two encounters. The first meeting against Harrow Borough was another Middlesex Senior Cup tie, three days before Christmas 1973, two weeks before our trip to Newcastle. Derek Baker, Rod Haider with two, and John Baker were the Greens' marksmen in a 4–1 victory.

Borough caused more problems at Earlsmead the following season, forcing a 0–0 draw, which was abandoned after 90 minutes because of floodlight problems. The replay went Hendon's way, 3–1, thanks to a John Field double and another from Steve Jefferies. The Greens continued to dominate the rivalry, winning two Middlesex Charity Cup ties – the second, in 1979, was the final – and an Isthmian League Cup tie, before League meetings began.

Since Boxing Day 1979, Hendon and Harrow have met every season in the Isthmian League, but it was not until September 1982, at the 19th time of asking that Borough (or Town) tasted victory. It ended 3–1 at Earlsmead, with Des Dennis getting Hendon's goal. Harrow then enjoyed the upper hand, especially in the league over the next few years, but one of Hendon's most remarkable victories came in this period, a controversial Middlesex Senior Cup quarter-final replay replay.

The first replay, on 17 February 1987 was ruled void because Borough had been incorrectly informed about player eligibility by a County official, so the tie was replayed rather than forfeited. When, on 9 April, they finally got back to action, Borough raced into a 3–0 lead and missed a first half-penalty. The Hendon fightback was astonishing as Colin Tate scored 22 seconds into the second half and Neil Wolstenholme and Iain Dowie levelled matters within 20 minutes. Then a floodlight pylon went out, but referee David Elleray said the three floodlights were good enough to continue. There were no more goals until the second period of extra time, when Tate, 17 seconds after the resumption, and Dermot Drummy ensured a 5–3 Hendon victory.

The rivalry with Harrow has, in the main, been very good natured and a lot of this has to do with the two clubs being quite similar in that, for long spells, the teams were fighting to stay clear of the danger area more than chasing title glory. Between them, the teams have managed just three play-off appearances. They have also had a number of player and management links; Bob Dowie and Dave Anderson have managed both teams. More often than not, at least one of the teams has fielded a team with at least a couple of former players from the other team.

In recent times, Harrow were very kind to Hendon, acting as landlords for three seasons until Hendon were able to secure Silver Jubilee Park and the ground was brought up to the required standard.

In all, Hendon have faced Harrow Borough on 109 occasions in competitive fixtures, plus four recorded friendlies and four against Harrow Town (all four won by Hendon with a goal difference of 22–4). Hendon won the only FA Cup and FA Trophy meetings (two in the Cup, one in the Trophy), but have lost three of four Isthmian League Cup ties. In the London Senior Cup, both teams have won twice, Borough in 2018, and they also won the only Premier Inter-League Cup meeting. In the three Middlesex Charity Cup contests, two of which were pre-season group games, Hendon had a win and a draw, and, as mentioned earlier, won the 1979 final, 3–1 thanks to goals by Haider, Graham Stewart and Roy Butler. In 19 Middlesex Senior Cup meetings, including those against Town, Hendon lead 14 to 3 in wins – including the void match, which counts as a competitive fixture – and there were four draws, the last of which Hendon won 2–1 in one of the worst penalty shoot-outs in football history; three successful kicks – one wind assisted – were matched by three footballs fired out of the ground.

Hendon's cumulative cup record against the three incarnations of Harrow is: Played 38, Won 25, Drawn 4, Lost 9, Goals for 90 and Goals against 46. That leaves the Isthmian and Southern League fixtures and Hendon's record is: Played 79, Won 32, Drawn 22, Lost 25, Goals for 141, Goals against 115. The reason for the odd number is because the second fixture of 2000–01 was not played. Entering the 2019–20 season, Hendon hold the clear lead in all 117 competitive fixtures, with 57 wins against 34 defeats and 26 draws, with a goal difference of 231 to 161.

Hayes FC

Hayes FC were county rivals in the Athenian and Isthmian Leagues for more than 50 seasons, although the club ceased to exist when it merged with Yeading in 2007 to form Hayes & Yeading United.

Like Hendon, Hayes began life with an entirely different name, Botwell Mission, hence the nickname of Missioners, which lasted throughout their existence. The similarity between the clubs' early years is great: both were formed in the first decade of the last century; enjoyed success in local leagues; won county cup competitions and changed names between the two World Wars.

The first meeting was on 18 October 1919, an FA Amateur Cup tie at Farm Avenue. It was a very close affair, ending 4–3 to Hampstead Town, with goals from Eric Wright, W. Bush, Bill Little and Dennis Bullough. The teams met in early May in each of the next two seasons, in the final of the Middlesex Charity Cup. On 7 May 1921, the Missioners won 3–1 at Brentford's Griffin Park. F Packham scored for Hampstead Town. On 13 May 1922, at the same venue, Town got revenge, winning 2–1, with goals from S Howard and H White. Botwell Mission became Hayes in 1929, before which there were regular cup meetings, including an FA Cup tie at Claremont Road. On 21 September 1929, Hampstead defeated Hayes 2–0, thanks to goals from Stan Moore and Harry Shearcroft.

The clubs met in the Athenian League every season after Hayes joined in 1930 – the Second World War excepted – from 1930 until November 1962, a 2–0 Hendon home victory with Peter Flann and Miles Spector on target, after which the Greens entered the Isthmian League. Hayes followed Hendon in 1971 and the first Isthmian meeting was at Claremont Road in March 1972, when Tony Jennings's goal gave the Greens a 1–0 victory. The clubs had annual Isthmian League meetings until 1995–96, when the Missioners won the title and were promoted to the Conference, where they stayed until 2002.

There were only five more meetings between the clubs, four League fixtures – two won by Hendon, one by Hayes and the other a draw – and a Middlesex Senior Cup semi-final at Claremont Road on 14 March 2007, the last-ever meeting. The Greens were in an exhausting run of games and could not quite overcome their Conference South rivals, going down 2–1, a freakish own goal making it 2–0 before Bontcho Guentchev pulled a goal back in the final 10 minutes, his last goal for the club.

There have been a number of memorable meetings between the clubs, with possibly the most famous – or infamous – being the FA Trophy tie at Claremont Road on 3 December 1988. Tempestuous does not come close to describing a match, which saw a cynical challenge from behind by Reg Leather on Duncan Hardy in the opening seconds, a foul that today would have been an instant red card, but then earned the defender a lecture. More fouls followed before Hardy took matters into his own hands and both players were cautioned.

What happened next made the lead story on national radio 30 minutes later. Another bad challenge by Leather caused Hardy to snap. The Hendon player got up angry and was punched unconscious with a single blow from the centre-back. Iain Dowie and Lee Payne – both of whom would enjoy long Football League careers – were the only two players not involved in the 19-man brawl which followed. When the dust had settled, Hardy, who had come around but was still groggy, Steve Scott and Alan Campbell of Hendon and Leather and Paul Hyde, the goalkeeper, were dismissed. Eight versus nine left plenty of space on the pitch and the match ended 3–3. Hendon won a very tame replay three days later 2–0.

In 2001–02, Hendon produced a stunning display to win a Middlesex Senior Cup quarter-final at Church Road – where they would also win the final. The Missioners were in the one-division Conference while the Greens were hardly pulling up trees in the Ryman League. An own goal and efforts from Eugene Ofori, Martin Randall, Ricci Crace and Steve Forbes saw Hendon win 5–1.

The rivalry came to an end when Hayes FC and Yeading FC merged in 2007. In 2011, Hayes' Church Road ground, together with the huge car park at the front and clubhouse to the side, was sold off. As for the ground, much as with their near neighbours Southall, the grandstand was small in comparison to the rest of the surroundings – the record attendance (as with Hendon, it was in 1951) was more than 15,000. The stand did, however, have a capacity of 500.

Amazingly, given the clubs' proximity to each other, the only friendly between them was in August 1998, when former Missioner Andy Cox scored for the Greens in a 2–1 defeat at Claremont Road (it probably had something to do with the fact that the clubs met in the League every season and also were regular cup-tie rivals. Proof of this is the fact that the clubs met 20 times each in the Middlesex Senior and Charity Cups, six times in Charity Cup finals – Hendon's record is two wins, four defeats – and twice in the Senior Cup, both Hendon losses. This is Hendon's record of League matches between the clubs: P108, W50, D27, L31, Goals for 197, Goals against 158. In cup ties, Hendon again hold sway, winning 28 of 56 ties, drawing seven and losing 21, while enjoying a goal difference of 116–94. So, in 164 competitive matches, Hendon's record is:

Won 78
Drawn 34
Lost 52
For 313 goals
Against 252 goals.

David Hogwood

David Hogwood was a loyal servant and one of the few to play for and manage Hendon. He was part of the great teams of the 1960s and won pretty much every medal there was to win as a Hendon player. Signed as an 18-year-old from Wembley – where he had made his debut aged 16 – David's first games came as a left-back at the start of the 1962–63 season, and he went on to play 38 times in that weather-accursed campaign. By the start of the 1963–64 season, Hendon's first in the Isthmian League, David had shifted from left-back to right-back, but he played in only 23 League matches as the Greens finished runners-up behind champions Wimbledon.

The following season was possibly the greatest in Hendon's history, completing the treble of Isthmian League, FA Amateur Cup and Middlesex Senior Cup. David was a near ever-present, playing in 38 of 39 League matches and all 19 cup ties, including the famous 4–3 defeat of Arsenal at Highbury in the London Challenge Cup. In the League play-off final, David's performance was highlighted in the press for the way he played England international winger Terry Howard out of the game.

An utterly dependable full-back, quick across the ground, good in the tackle and blessed with exceptional positional sense, David was one of the first names on the managers' team-sheets for the next five seasons. In this period he missed only seven league matches and passed 50 appearances five times in six seasons. He missed out on the half-century in 1967–68, when Hendon's cup form deserted them and there were no knock-out runs to enjoy.

After back-to-back Wembley appearances in the Amateur Cup, David almost scored the goal that would have made it a hat-trick. In the first semi-final against Skelmersdale United, at the Baseball Ground in Derby, his shot in the dying minutes beat the opposing goalkeeper all ends up, but the ball went just the wrong side of the post. The match ended goalless but, after a 2–2 draw in the first replay at St Andrews, Birmingham, Skelmersdale prevailed 3–1 at The Hawthorns.

For a player who averaged a goal every 18 matches in his Hendon career – pretty good for a full-back who would not have been a set-piece target – it is amazing that it took him more than 200 games to open his Hendon account. That goal came in the 13th match of the 1966–67 season, the last goal in a 3–1 victory away to Oxford City, his 201st first-team appearance. He added another five in the next 41 games that season It certainly helped that he became the club's penalty-taker and he rarely missed from 12 yards. This was despite regularly using the same kick – a dummy and shot into the bottom corner.

In 1966–67, David earned the first two of his seven England amateur international caps. He later represented Great Britain in Olympic Games qualifying matches and when Great Britain played West Germany at Claremont Road, David, along with John Swannell, Roy Sleap and Rod Haider had the honour of playing for Great Britain on their home ground. England lost the match, conceding the only goal, but they won the tie 2–1 on aggregate. Sadly, Great Britain didn't make it to the Mexico City Olympic Games in 1968, being knocked out by Spain. David also played for Middlesex and the Isthmian League. He worked for the Post Office as a telephone engineer, and represented the Post Office at an international tournament.

Although Hendon's level of success dipped in the late 1960s, they could rely on David for top performances. This dip in success level needs to be put into some perspective, however, because not once in David's eight Isthmian League seasons, up to 1970–71, did the Greens finish outside of the top six; in the 40 years since 1974, the Greens have finished fifth or better on only seven occasions!

David left Hendon after the 1970–71 season, joining St Albans. However, as many have found out, Hendon was in their blood and following the departure of David's successor at right-back, Tony

Jennings, he returned to Claremont Road where he made four appearances at the end of the 1973–74 season. After two appearances, with injuries taking their toll, David retired as player, having made 440 appearances and scored 24 goals, and became assistant manager. In December 1977, he succeeded Jimmy Quail as caretaker-manager, only losing the temporary tag after three months. The club, however, was struggling to compete against clubs more prepared to spend big money and David lasted less than a year in charge.

Freddie Hyatt

Freddie Hyatt was both a member of the club's management team, but also graced the green (blue) and white shirt as an outstanding midfield player. When Frank Murphy was looking for one or two final additions to his squad for the 1997–98 season, he chose a kindred soul: fantastic footballer, heavy smoker, free spirit on-and-off the pitch. For proof of this, look at the official team picture before the 1997 Leyton Orient tie. Welcome Freddie Hyatt, who filled all three criteria. Freddie had won an Isthmian League winner's medal with Hayes in 1995–96 and left the Missioners and Conference football to play for Frank at Claremont Road. He had previously played for Wokingham Town, for whom he won a runners-up medal against Hendon in the 1994 Full Members' Cup Final, and Burnham.

Freddie signed on 16 August 1997; the day Hendon kicked off the season with a 2–1 victory over St Albans City. Three days later, he was on the bench for a salutary night in Kent as Gravesend & Northfleet scored three times in five minutes just before half-time, on their way to a 4–0 trouncing. Freddie came on for Paul Kelly long after the Greens had gone into damage-limitation mode.

Playing in the centre of midfield, he could spray the ball around the pitch effortlessly and set up chances from open play or set-pieces. His talent on the ball had made him a fan's favourite where he had played – except where lung-bursting work-rate and effort were considered more important than good, solid, fundamental basic passing, together with more than a little flair.

Hendon fans were given a special taste on one of the greatest nights in the club's history – 25 November 1997 – when Leyton Orient's colours were lowered at Brisbane Road in that famous FA Cup first round replay. Freddie's part in the goal was an outrageous piece of skill. He flicked the ball over his marker, turned, ran onto the ball and sprayed the ball out to the right wing, where John-Simon White was raiding. He crossed – and the rest is history. Thanks, Junior!

Freddie's goals came in three categories: penalties, stunning or vitally important – and sometimes in two or more of those categories.

112

His finest goal came in March 1998, and it is one he never tires of repeating. Hendon were leading Sutton 2–1 midway through the second half and were coasting, even if the scoreline didn't suggest it. Sutton's goalkeeper ran to the edge of his penalty to clear some danger, but his clearance landed some distance short of half-way. Freddie called off a team-mate as the ball bounced towards him, then volleyed it into the roof of the net from the half-way line. It was aimed; it was intended and it was inspired: typical Freddie Hyatt.

Hendon finished the season with the Full Member's Cup as Basingstoke were beaten 4–1 at Chesham United's ground. Freddie won his second Full Member's winner's medal 12 months later as Worthing were downed 1–0 at Sutton United's gander Green Lane, and that completed a cup double for the season as he had won the Middlesex Senior Cup final – against Wembley at Enfield – with an audacious chip – in a penalty shoot-out. It was the decisive penalty, so there hadn't been any pressure to make sure he hit the target.

Fast forward to 1999–2000, Freddie's last playing season with the club, and injuries hampered his progress. He scored three times in cup competitions, in consecutive weeks, to open the scoring in victories over Blakenall (FA Cup third qualifying), Slough (FA Trophy) and Margate (the only goal of a very tight FA Cup last qualifying round match) and all were powerfully struck free-kicks. Only the Margate goalkeeper even touched the ball.

Like all great showmen, Freddie made sure his last Hendon appearance was more than memorable. Thirty minutes into the season-ending game away to Heybridge Swifts – 10 minutes after his penalty had opened the scoring – Freddie ran towards Mark Cranfield, flicked the ball up with his heel, sending it high over the full-back. Before he could react, Freddie had run past him, trapping the ball before it bounced, then set off for goal, only for his effort to be smothered by the home goalkeeper. Mr Murphy's reaction? "If he had scored that, I would have taken him off the field and told him to retire, because he'll never beat that!" Spoken by a showman, who appreciated the talent of a showman.

Freddie played for a few other clubs before retiring. But he returned to Hendon in February 2006, to become Gary McCann's right-hand man – their friendship long pre-dated their Hendon careers – a role he has held ever since, for 12 years at Hendon and subsequently with Gary at Hampton & Richmond.

David Hyde

David Hyde is the last of the four players to have netted 100 goals in their Hendon career and the single-season goalscoring record-holder. He joined Hendon at the start of the 1963–64 season, leaving Enfield along with Roy Sleap and Jimmy Quail. He had the attributes for a forward: strength, pace and one of the most powerful shots in football. He was also a good crosser of the ball and created almost as many goals as he scored. His debut came in the opening league game victory over Clapton and he netted his first goals – a double – on the Tuesday night when Ilford were beaten 7–1. Hendon were scoring goals for fun at the start of their Isthmian life and Dulwich Hamlet were the most harshly treated, conceding 19. David scored three as the Greens triumphed 10–1 at Claremont Road on the second Saturday, although he was outdone by four-goal Gerry O'Rourke. But in the return at Champion Hill, on the Saturday after Christmas, he got five in a 9–1 victory.

Almost uniquely that season, in the Isthmian League Hendon scored everything from nil to 10, but didn't win a game 1–0. It was a nearly season, with only the London Senior Cup won – Enfield beaten 1–0 in the final thanks to another O'Rourke goal – but the Greens were runners-up behind Wimbledon. In all David played in all but four matches and scored 37 goals – two fewer than O'Rourke.

However, great the 2014–15 season will end up for Hendon, it won't match 1964–65. The Greens won the Isthmian League championship – after a play-off against Enfield – the Amateur Cup – the era's equivalent of the FA Trophy – the Middlesex Senior Cup, reached the FA Cup first round proper and beat Arsenal in the London Challenge Cup.

David was at the centre of all the big events for Hendon. His club-record – one that will probably never be beaten – 59 goals, in 54 appearances, included a hat-trick in that memorable 4–3 win at Highbury, the only goal in a 2–1 loss to Port Vale at Vale Park in the FA Cup, two goals in the Amateur Cup Final and the first in the play-off at Dulwich's Champion Hill. Only in the Middlesex Senior Cup final did he miss out – Peter Slade got the only goal – but David grabbed four in an 8–0 win over Hounslow and both in the 2–1 defeat of Enfield in earlier rounds. The eye-catching totals earned David international recognition. He won four England Amateur caps and marked his debut against Wales with four goals.

Neither David, nor Hendon, could match their feats in 1965–66, though things started brightly for both player and team: he netted a hat-trick in the 8–3 opening game victory over Clapton and scored in seven of the first nine Isthmian League matches; the Greens won the first eight but then were held to a 1–1 draw by Wycombe Wanderers.

It should be noted that Hendon, as well as playing on every Saturday and in midweek, added two prestigious friendlies to their schedule – an August Bank Holiday game against Whitley Bay for the Will Mather Cup and a game against the England Amateur XI. Maybe the stress of so many games caused Hendon to lose form, but it didn't help that David missed around one-third of the remaining 29 league matches. The Greens finished runners-up in the Isthmian League, two points behind champions Leytonstone. Their only consolation was being the top scorers in the division with 111 goals. After his flying start to the campaign, David's contribution was 'only' 10 in his last 20 League matches – overall he netted 22 times in 40 appearances. He did play in the Amateur Cup final at Wembley in April 1966, but Hendon were beaten 3–1 by Wealdstone. Future Hendon star Bobby Childs netted twice, the Greens' goal came from centre-half Geoff Riddy. One of the cup-ties David missed was the Middlesex Senior Cup semi-final replay against Wealdstone.

At the end of the season, after 118 goals in 140 games for the club, David turned professional and signed for Wimbledon, who had joined the Southern League after winning the 1964 Isthmian League championship. He then moved to Brentwood Town, but returned to Claremont Road in April 1969 playing for the 1965 Amateur Cup winning-team against the then current squad. Later that year, now with Cambridge City, he played against the Greens in an FA Cup fourth qualifying round tie, but could not score as Hendon triumphed 1–0 at Claremont Road.

I

Illnesses and Injuries

Internationals – England

Isthmian League

Isthmian League Cup

Below: The programme from the
2015 Isthmian League Cup Final.
Right: The teams from the Clapton
versus Hendon match on 24 August
1963, the club's first Isthmian
League fixture.

Illnesses and Injuries

Illnesses and injuries are the bane of all footballers' careers. Illnesses are unfortunate and often sudden, but few could be as difficult as the one Hendon suffered in March 2003. Winger Kieran Gallagher was named in the starting line-up for a match against Grays Athletic, but shortly before the match started feeling unwell with what he thought was a migraine. It soon became obvious that it was far more serious that a migraine and he spent the next few days in Barnet Hospital being treated for meningitis. Thankfully for everyone concerned, Kieran made a full recovery and although his season was over, he did return to play for Hendon briefly at the start of the 2005–06 season.

A few years before him, another player missed significant time following something that happened in the dressing room. It was the opening day of the 1999–2000 season and we were about to face Aldershot Town when full-back Matt Howard suffered burns to his foot when the urn for players and management staff's tea and coffee was accidentally dislodged from the table. The boiling water splashed over his feet and he missed many weeks while the injury healed.

Our former manager Gary McCann was no stranger to the treatment table, the result of a knee injury he suffered playing for the Greens against Harrow Borough in April 2000. Although the injury did not actually end his career, he made only 24 appearances over the next four seasons before hanging up his gloves. Very bravely, or insanely, in July 2001, just a few weeks after major knee surgery, he helped out new manager Dave Anderson by playing a friendly against Southend United and further damaged the joint.

If Gary was insanely brave in 2001, then fellow goalkeeper Richard Wilmot was insane (he admits it, too) when, in November 2000, he played for 15 minutes with a broken arm. Richard was in the last game of a three-month loan spell, when he dived at the feet of Jamie Pace and got a kick on the arm. He knew the severity of the damage, but kept it from the physio and team-mates until half-time, when he admitted he had to go to hospital – where the break was confirmed. He did rejoin the Greens at the end of that mad season, carrying another injury and there was a match at Gravesend where the crocked Wilmot played 45 minutes before being replaced by the equally hobbled McCann.

One former recent player stands out as a victim of terrible injury misfortune is Elliott Brathwaite, who had a third knee reconstruction, two of which happened after he joined the Greens. Elliott made his debut in August 2011 – a 1–0 win over Concord Rangers – but suffered a reaction to the previous knee reconstruction, which came while he was with Hampton & Richmond Borough, and needed surgery on damaged knee cartilage. He reappeared in September 2012, playing well in a 3–0 FA Cup defeat of Lewes. The following morning, his car aquaplaned on the M25 and the vehicle ended up – a complete write-off – in a ditch. Accident investigators could not believe Elliott had suffered only minor concussion and whiplash injuries.

After a few weeks out, he came back, but his season ended in March, when his knee gave way again, leading to another reconstruction. He finally returned to action just over year later. Elliott showed his true quality in 2014–15 when, partnering Charlie Goode, he proved himself to be probably the best central defender in the league. Sadly, Elliott suffered a third cruciate knee injury in the 2015–16 season and ultimately had to retire from football.

The most freakish injury any Hendon player has suffered may well be the triple fracture of a leg, which befell Lee O'Leary, against Horsham at Worthing on 21 March 2009. With 10 minutes to go Lee jumped for a ball with Mark Knee and they clashed heads. Lee was knocked instantly unconscious which meant he could not brace himself on landing. He came too almost as soon as he landed and fans in attendance could not understand how a clash of heads could lead such a serious leg injury.

To finish, here are two odd injuries suffered by Hendon players in the FA Cup. In November 1973, Roger Connell had just completed a hat-trick to set up the Greens' 3–0 fourth qualifying round replay defeat of Barnet, when he put himself out for two months by stepping on the ball and breaking his ankle.

Finally, second substitute Michael Peacock – who had replaced first substitute Aaron Morgan – had been on the pitch for barely two minutes of a third round qualifying tie at Whitehawk in October 2010, when he bent down to pick up the ball to take a throw-in. His back went into spasm, he collapsed and had to be stretchered off the field, to be replaced by third substitute Danny Dyer.

Internationals – England

This piece refers to the numerous players who have appeared for Hendon and represented England. This list specifically excludes amateur and semi-professional (England C) and profession-based teams, such as the Armed Forces, emergency services, Post Office, Civil Service, etc.

To start with, a few players who appeared for Hendon have also played in full internationals for England. The most recent of these was Peter Taylor, the club's player-manager from June to December 1993. He is also the only Hendon player to have managed the national team too, taking charge of a friendly against Italy as caretaker coach in 2002, when he appointed David Beckham as captain. Almost a decade earlier, the Greens were graced with the presence of Tony Currie, one of England's finest midfielders. His best days coincided with Don Revie's reign as manager, so being a classy footballer meant he didn't get much of a look-in.

During the Second World War, local Hendon man Leslie Compton made a few appearances for Golders Green, having started at the club as a youngster. His professional career, like his brother Denis's, was spent exclusively at Arsenal and, at 38 years and 64 days, Leslie, against Wales in November 1950, remains England's oldest ever debutant. Denis may have played in junior teams, but never in the Golders Green or Hampstead first team. His only England football appearances were in unofficial wartime games.

Before the Comptons was a man who became, in 1936, the last amateur footballer to win full England honours: Bernard Joy. His was an amazing career because he was registered to play for Casuals, Southend United, Fulham and Hampstead and Golders Green in the time he made his two appearances for us. Although an Arsenal player in May 1936, he was officially listed as a Casuals player for the game against Belgium.

One player who nearly made the list is Peter Simpson, a Greens player in 1979. The former Gunner was called into a number of Alf Ramsey's squads, but never was selected to win a cap.

In the last 10 years, on Hendon's books were two players in a more recent England team: Sam Murphy and Charlie Kuehn were both members of the England 6-a-side team coached by former Hendon player and coach Scott Cousins whilst they were still with the club. The squad Cousins put together included a number of others who had played for the Greens, most notably Dale Binns, Craig Carby (Vargas) and Lubomir Guentchev.

Going back through time, many Hendon players could point to England selection at junior levels, normally in their days at professional clubs, but Steve Newing was a registered Hendon player when earning the last of his England Schoolboys caps. Another former player who deserves special mention is striker Ben Odeje, who, according to the Football Association's statistics was the first black player ever to represent England. He was a schoolboy in North London when he appeared for England, but his Hendon career was short, just three matches in the 1974–75 season, twice as a substitute – both defeats – and a start in the 8 February 1975 Isthmian League win over Bromley.

The Greens' most recent international was a member of the 2018–19 squad and he was selected for the England schoolboys team. Shaquille Hippolyte-Patrick came through Hertfordshire Schools and earned a national trial. He impressed those watching and was selected for the England Under-18 Schools team, the one for players not contracted to Football League clubs. Shaq played on more than one occasion, but his county coach at the time cannot recall how many times or the opposition.

Hendon have, however, fielded many England internationals whose main sport was cricket. Part of the reason for this was that cricketers would keep themselves fit by playing football during the offseason – they also had to find employment from late September to March. Most notable were Fred Titmus, Micky Stewart and Mike Gatting, the second of whom was later England coach and selector and the last-named was also captain. Gatting, a striker whose brother Steve chose football over cricket, played only 14 times for the Greens, all before he turned 20. I recall an evening reserve match against Kingstonian – during an England tour of India – when the Ks goalkeeper was one of Gatting's rivals for a place in the middle of the England batting order, the late Graham Roope. During the second half, the pair almost collided with each other and had a good laugh about it. My reaction was that a collision between the pair of them might have disastrous consequences for England's hopes in the summer's upcoming Ashes test series. One more former Hendon player who merits a mention played only in amateur internationals for England, but he did play county cricket for Middlesex as well as being a very successful stockbroker. William (Tagge) Webster, in retirement, was not only The Football Association's Finance Committee chairman 1974–86, but was President of the Marylebone Cricket Club for the year 1977–78.

Mark Ramprakash was another cricketer who had a run-out for the Greens (no pun intended). His was memorable for the wrong reasons as, in an Under-18s cup-tie against St Albans at Claremont Road, he was subjected to what he claimed was racial abuse, complained to the referee, who ignored him, so he took matters into his own hands. The three-match ban he was handed was served long before he again laced on football boots.

In 1994, one of the players Mick Browne had on trial in preseason was Nko Ekoku, brother of rugby league star Abi and footballer Efan. He was a true athlete, having been good enough to represent England in the discus. Browne didn't rate him very highly, but he did spend a number of years playing in the Conference and for other clubs in the Isthmian League.

Isthmian League

The Isthmian League was the league in which Hendon played from 1963 to 2018, thanks to sponsorship known for many years as the Ryman League and, at the time of writing, the Bostik League.

First, what does isthmian actually mean? An isthmus is a narrow strip of land in Greece separating two larger land masses with water on both sides. As with the Spartan, Hellenic, Delphian, Corinthian, Nemean and Athenian Leagues, the Isthmian name was taken from Greece and the Isthmus of Corinth in southern Greece was famous for ancient games not dissimilar to the Olympic Games.

The Isthmian League began life in 1905 with six clubs. From the original six founding members, three can point to modern-day status in senior football, Clapton and Ilford – the latter having reformed in the 1980s – now play in the Essex Senior League (Step 5) and Casuals, who merged with Corinthians in the 1930s, are in Bostik League (Step 3).

Although Clapton were the only club to play in every Isthmian season until the 2005 centenary, they left in 2006. Dulwich Hamlet holds the record for longest continuous membership, from 1907 to 2018, when they were promoted to the National League South. They also had the most consecutive years in the top division, 58 three more than Hendon.

Hendon joined the Isthmian League in 1963, 50 years after the club, as Hampstead Town, had first applied to play in the competition. Rejected in 1913, before the club joined the Athenian League – Hampstead did not receive a single vote in favour – there were further unsuccessful applications in 1921, 1929, 1930 – the club was the only team applying, but lost out to existing members Tufnell Park and Leytonstone – 1931, 1932 and 1934, as Golders Green. Isthmian League football almost came to Claremont Road in 1939, but Tufnell Park, who were ground-sharing were away for the only round of fixtures before the outbreak of the Second World War and the subsequent suspension of the Isthmian League. Golders Green did not reapply for the League again but, in 1963, Hendon did and were successful.

It would be fair to say Hendon made an immediate impact. On 24 August 1963, the Greens' Isthmian debut was a 2–1 win at Clapton, Peter Slade and Tony Knox scoring. A trip to Ilford, the following Tuesday, ended 7–1, Gerry O'Rourke bagging a hat-trick, before the first home game, with Dulwich the visitors. It finished 10–1, still Hendon's biggest Isthmian League home win, with O'Rourke grabbing four goals and David Hyde three. The return, on 28 December, resulted in a 9–1 win at the old Champion Hill ground, where Hyde scored five times. During that season, Hendon registered everything from nil to 10 goals, a unique achievement.

Hendon finished runners-up in their debut season, beaten only by Wimbledon, who then joined the Southern League. In 1964–65, Hendon won the title, beating Enfield 4–1 in a play-off at the Greens' happy hunting ground, Champion Hill. For the next decade, Hendon would be one of the strongest teams in the Isthmian League, never finishing outside the top six until the 1974–75 season, the first in the post-amateur era. There was one other championship to celebrate, in 1972–73, when Hendon did not lose a league game until 17 April 1973, their 39th of the League's first 42-match schedule. A runners-up spot in 1974 was not repeated for 42 years, the miraculous 2014–15 season, when the Greens finished three points behind champions Maidstone United, but lost out in such disappointing circumstances to Margate in the play-off final.

In 2017–18, Hendon finished third, with 85 points from 46 games. Hendon faced Dulwich Hamlet in the play-off Final at Hamlet's temporary home at Tooting & Mitcham, having beaten Folkestone Invicta 4–0 at SJP in the semi-final. A dramatic game in front of a 3,321 crowd ended 1–1, and the Greens missed out on promotion through losing the penalty shoot-out 4–3.

Those intervening years should not be glossed over as there were a few top six finishes in those times, including third place in 2002–03, fourth place in 1976–77, 1986–87 and 2003–04 and fifth in 1997–98. The first time Hendon finished in the bottom third of the table – 15th or lower – was in 1984–85, by which time the competition had grown from 20 clubs in one division to more than 80 clubs in four divisions. That season was the start of a period of sustained mediocrity. Apart from 1986–87, Hendon did not finish better than 10th until the Frank Murphy squad of 1997–98, and in 1985–86 secured safety in the final game. In 1994–95, it was in the penultimate match and one game earlier a season later.

It is a matter of fact and pride that Hendon have never played in a division lower than the highest one of the Isthmian or now Southern Leagues, but the reality, being in the third tier of non-league football, is that the Greens are now two tiers lower than the club was in 1978, before the start of what is now the National League. And, in 2005–06, when Hendon sank to its lowest finishing position of 19th – a position Hendon held in 1985–86 and 2015–16 (though five teams were below Hendon in that season) – the club was only saved from relegation by the financial misfortune of another club.

Isthmian League Cup

Hendon have won this competition twice and lost in another final. The Greens' history in the Southern League Cup is brief as it consists of a single evening at Imber Court, Metropolitan Police, ending in a 1–0 defeat.

The Isthmian League had been in operation for almost 70 years before there was a cup competition exclusively for its senior clubs. In the first season, 1974–75, entry was limited to Division Two (second tier) clubs and was called the Subsidiary Cup. The following year, participation was voluntary and Hendon – among others – opted not to enter. In 1976–77 League Cup entry was mandatory and the Greens went all the way to win the trophy. The club's first ever Isthmian League Cup tie was on 26 October 1976, at home to Wokingham Town (posters for the game called them Workingham) and John Butterfield, two, Alan Campbell, Rod Haider and George Brooks were on target in a 5–1 win. It was almost five months before Hendon returned to action in the competition and a George Brooks double sealed a 2–0 defeat of Slough Town. A week later, the team reached the last eight, defeating Sutton United 3–2 after extra time at Gander Green Lane – Hendon did not win an Isthmian League game away to Sutton between 1975 and 1993 – they did spend five years in Conference – but did win two cup-ties there.

A 2–0 quarter-final win at Woking set up a semi-final tie with Staines Town at Claremont Road, and Hendon cruised to a 5–0 win. Barking were the club's final opponents, with the game at Harrow Borough's Earlsmead ground. It was an utterly one-sided game with Malcolm Dalrymple, Hendon's goalkeeping hero. He saved a Laurie Abrahams penalty and the Blues had a goal disallowed, but Rod Haider's eighth minute goal was enough for the Greens to take the trophy.

Hendon did reach the 1984–85 quarter-final, but went two better in 1986–87, a cup run most memorable for the 2–0 away victory against Yeovil Town in the semi-final, the second goal coming when the Glovers' goalkeeper stumbled on the Huish slope and dropped the ball over the goal line as he fell. The final, at Stag Meadow, Windsor, was controversial. Hendon lost 3–2 to Bognor Regis Town. With the score at 2–2 a shot from Dermot Drummy was "saved" by Bognor goalkeeper Alistair Sperring half a yard behind the line – it would have been his hat-trick – but the linesman didn't award a goal. Instead, Bognor broke straight to the other end and Russell Burtenshaw scored the winner.

Another long barren period followed, though four matches stand out; Mark Xavier bagged four goals in a 6–4 extra time win at Chalfont St Peter in 1991; Hendon crushed Hertford Town 7–0 in September 1992 and also inflicted the second-ever competitive defeat on Aldershot Town that November; and there was an 8–1 demolition of Staines at Chertsey when centre-half Richard Nugent scored four times as an emergency centre-forward. Hendon did reach the semi-final in 2002–03, which included a 5–2 extra-time victory over Wingate & Finchley when Rob Haworth was awarded a hat-trick, though he did not get the final touch on any of his three "goals". His reward was a child's size 3 football. In the semi-final, Canvey Island won their home leg 4–2 in a pulsating tie, and had enough in hand to hold on for a 2–2 draw at Claremont Road.

The feast or famine formula has followed Hendon in the competition. For most of Gary McCann's spell early exits were commonplace, but there was a surprise win against AFC Wimbledon at Kingsmeadow in 2005, when Blaise O'Brien scored the only goal. But then, in 2014–15, Hendon won the trophy – sponsored in that year by Robert Dyas – for the second time. What was most notable was that, to reach the final, the Greens beat the teams which finished, first, third, sixth, seventh, 12th and 15th in the Premier Division – the hardest run any cup-winners have had in the competition's 40-plus years. The run started with Hendon going 3–0 down inside half an hour at Wingate & Finchley, but Max McCann, a Sam Murphy penalty, Leon Smith and an Olu Sogbanmu own goal gave the Greens a 4–3 victory. Enfield Town and Hampton & Richmond Borough were then beaten 1–0, Maidstone United 2–0 and Margate 2–1 in the semi-final.

The final itself provided a magnificent night's entertainment at Whyteleafe as the Greens recorded a 3–2 victory over Grays Athletic. Andre Da Costa with a double, and Kezie Ibe were the marksmen. Hendon never trailed, but Ben McNamara was outstanding in goal and Da Costa scored two magnificent goals. There was a dramatic twist when Sean Cronin scored in stoppage time to make it 3–2, but Hendon held on to win – as the headline said, "Hendon take home the hardware!"

In 42 Isthmian League Cup seasons, Hendon have met 64 opponents and the club's overall record is P109, W59, D14, L36, Goals for 225, Goals against 163. If the penalty shoot-outs are included as results, there would be 60 wins against 10 draws and 39 defeats.

Hendon went to extra time 24 times, winning 10, drawing 10 and losing four, but have lost three out of four penalty shoot-outs. The Greens' biggest wins were 8–1 at Staines, 1997 and 7–0 at home to Hertford, 1993; the worst defeats were 3–0 at Tilbury in 1991 (on the day Barnet Council closed Claremont Road over unpaid bills) and 6–3 at home to Leatherhead in 2005 – a goal just before full--time was up, followed by three more in the first six minutes of extra time.

J

Jamaica, Caribbean and CONCACAF

Tony Jennings

The letter 'J'

Jamaica, Caribbean and CONCACAF

Five Hendon players have represented Caribbean countries (make that CONCACAF region as it affects Caribbean, Central and South American nations) at full international level, two were, technically, current internationals and one other who previously had played in the World Cup finals.

That latter man was Frank Sinclair, who played at France 98 for Jamaica in the Reggae Boyz' finals debut. The early records of the club are incomplete in terms of line-ups, making exact statistical pronouncements impossible. Nonetheless, it is quite possible that Frank Sinclair was the oldest player to make his Hendon debut in our Isthmian League era. Born on 3 December 1971, he was three weeks short of his 40th birthday when making his Hendon debut, a 1–0 win over Canvey Island at Vale Farm. A stomach upset prevented him playing for the Greens on his 40th birthday, a 1–1 draw with Aveley. Born on the same day 32 years earlier, his nearest challenger in my memory is Roger Day, but he was 58 days younger than Frank when he made his bow in a 7–0 FA Cup win at Buckingham.

Frank enjoyed a long career at the highest level of English football, mainly at Chelsea and Leicester City, the latter where he was a team-mate of our player-coach at the time Junior Lewis. The Greens were struggling with a long injury list and Junior persuaded Frank to join the club, this after leaving Wrexham the previous summer. If Frank wasn't the oldest debutant, he certainly travelled the most to play for us. He lived just outside of Bolton and travelled more than 200 miles each way for home games – and in midweek went by train. His last game in his 30s was a 29 November game at AFC Hornchurch, a match Hendon won 1–0. I travelled back to central London with him on the District Line as he raced to catch the last train from Euston – it left just before midnight. Frank played 28 times for Jamaica and scored one goal, and that was 18 more appearances than he managed for Hendon.

Another Hendon player who represented Jamaica internationally did so only at youth level. A product of our youth system in the mid-1990s, Pat Sappleton played for Alan Rolnick's teams in the Southern Counties Youth League and Harrow Youth League as well as Jamaica's youth teams. He was six months and nine days past his 18th birthday when he made his debut in what was effectively a reserve team which played in an Isthmian League Full Members Cup tie at Harlow Town. Boosted by Bontcho Guentchev and Marvyn Watson, Hendon defeated Harlow's full-strength first team thanks to goals from Ike Obiji and Watson. A similarity with his Jamaican compatriot Sinclair, Sappleton played only 10 times for Hendon before playing for several Ryman League clubs.

126

Pat's brother Ricky – also a Jamaican Under-20 international – scored goals in the Ryman League for Billericay Town.

A player who made one full international appearance for a Caribbean island and later played for Hendon was Jefferson Louis. Maybe professional football's most travelled man, he denied the accuracy of his Wikipedia entry which listed 43 moves – including loan deals – but he didn't say if it was too many or too few. A career goalscorer, he appeared against Hendon for two teams in 2018–19, Farnborough and Chesham United – in the New Year's Day game witht Generals, the then 39-year-old was marked by a man five years and 18 days his senior, Scott McGleish. Jefferson's most successful spell at any club in terms of goals per game was at Hendon, where he mustered 26 goals in just 33 appearances before joining Margate. He subsequently joined Wealdstone – only the second club for which he made 50 League appearances in one uninterrupted spell – his 50-plus for Oxford United 2002–04 included loan spells at Woking and Gravesend & Northfleet. Early in his career, Jefferson made a solitary international appearance for Dominica.

Otis Roberts is another former international who turned out for Hendon. His time at Hendon was brief but, then again, so was his international career – just two appearances for Grenada in 2000, whilst he was a Harrow Borough player. The midfielder, uncle of Jason Roberts MBE, made his Hendon debut in a goalless draw at Thurrock and he went on to play eight times for the Greens during the chaotic end to the 2000–01 season. Other famous sportsmen related to Otis and Jason are Cyrille, Dave and John Regis. Cyrille, who, like Jason left Hayes for the professional game, went on to play five times for England and sadly died in January 2018; Dave and Jason were both at Barnet in 1990; John, meanwhile, was a world class sprinter, multiple Olympic and World Championships medallist, and his British 200m record, set in 1994, remains unbroken.

On 18 September 2011, Elliott Charles played his second international for Grenada in a 2–1 FIFA World Cup 2014 qualifying round defeat against St Vincent & Grenadines. Eight days later, he made his Hendon debut, scoring in a 2–0 Ryman League victory at Wealdstone. He went on to make 48 appearances across four spells with the Greens, scoring 16 goals. Yet to turn 30 at the end of 2019, his career was rather derailed by a succession of knee injuries, and his time at Hendon in 2018–19 comprised two games and a goal.

Striker Marcel Barrington played a few times for Guyana and one of his appearances came while he was at Hendon. On 25 March 2017, he played in the Greens' 4–0 victory at AFC Sudbury, a result that went a long way towards their successful battle against relegation. Three days later, he was in South America, representing his country in a friendly against Martinique. Marcel's time with the Greens was quite brief, just 21 games at the end of the 2016–17 season and he scored four times.

Tony Jennings

Tony Jennings is one of the very few players to have won both FA Amateur Cup and FA Trophy winners medals. His career was one of the most decorated in non-league football. Not only did he win the Amateur Cup with Hendon, he was captain of Enfield and England Non-League (now England 'C'). He was still only 20 years old when he arrived at Hendon in the summer of 1971, joining the club from Leytonstone. Brought in to replace a combination of Mickey Cooper and Dave Hogwood, both Claremont Road stalwarts, Tony was a tough-tackling right-back. Not tall, even for those days, he was defensively very sound and linked well with Bobby Childs in front of him. John Evans built his teams from the back and the quartet of Jennings, Gary Hand, Alan Phillips and Peter Deadman – in front of John Swannell – was, for almost three seasons, one of the most dominant defences in non-league history. Tony's debut came on the opening day of the 1971–72 season, a 1–1 draw away to Sutton United. Tony made a total 57 appearances during the campaign and played in every one of the Greens' 22 cup-ties. Although there was no FA Cup glory, a fourth-qualifying round replay exit against Barnet, in the other three competitions, Hendon went all the way – and met Enfield in the latter stages too.

In the Middlesex Senior Cup, it was the semi-final, and Tony scored his first cup goal for the Greens against the Es, in a 2–0 victory – his first two goals had come in a 4–0 win over Corinthian–Casuals in October and the only goal to beat Hayes in March. Hendon's cup success came at the expense of the Isthmian League and in the three months, December to February, inclusive, the Greens played only twice in the league – a win and a draw against Enfield. In April 1972, Tony lined up against the Es at Wembley Stadium in the Amateur Cup Final, and ended up with a winners' medal after a 2–0 victory. There was another winners' gong in the Middlesex Senior Cup – a two legged victory over Hampton – but Enfield avenged their Amateur Cup by beating the Greens in the London Senior Cup Final.

The following season, Hendon dominated the Isthmian League in a way that few teams have ever done. It took until the 39th match for the Greens' colours to be lowered, by which time the championship had long been decided. Take out the first game and the last five, and Hendon's Isthmian League record was played 36, won 32, drew 4, but maybe even more astonishing was the defence's achievement of conceding only 18 goals in 42 games – none from corner kicks. The cornerstone of John Evans and Jimmy Quail's teams – Quail replaced the Bogota-bound Evans in the new year – was continuity. Tony was one of 10 players who missed 10 League games or fewer in the season; he missed four games. Tony collected three winner's medals: the League, Middlesex Senior Cup and the Barassi Cup, the Anglo-Italian Amateur Cup-winners Cup. The first match was at Claremont Road, and the Greens won 2–0. In the return in Italy, Hendon achieved a 1–1 draw to claim the Cup 3–1 on aggregate.

Tony was called up for the England Amateur squad in the final season of the amateur game, where he was joined by team-mates Swannell, Deadman and captain Rod Haider.

Hendon enjoyed their best-ever FA Cup run, reaching the third round proper. Tony's free-kick, midway through the second half, was headed on by John Baker and knocked into the net by Haider as Hendon achieved a 1–1 draw away to Newcastle United. The replay was lost 4–0. Favourites to retain their league title when the season started, the cup success played its part in the second-place finish, as did the mid-March departure to Enfield of Derek Baker, Phil Fry and Tony. The Greens ended up runners up by two points behind Wycombe, who beat them 2–0 at Loakes Park on 30 April, when there were still seven league matches left.

At Southbury Road, Tony's career thrived. He was England semi-professional captain for a dozen matches and he won just about every medal imaginable, including in 1982 when he lifted the FA Trophy. After retiring as a player, Tony spent a few months as Hendon coach, but living out in the wilds of Essex, the commute was too much for him. He did, however, become the first man to captain and coach the Non-League team and also was manager of Dagenham. As England Non-League manager, Tony gave Hendon defender Phil Gridelet his first international caps. Tony died in 2015, aged 64, following a long illness.

The letter 'J'

This piece covers all the clubs containing the letter 'J' that the club has played. In the club's 111 years, and more than 6,350 matches, there have only been five competitive fixtures against teams containing a "J" and a similar number of friendlies. There will be no fans reading this book who attended the first four of the five competitive games.

Amazingly, those four matches were in all the club's inaugural season, 1908–09, and the first of Christ Church Hampstead's opponents were Johnsons Athletic. My best research has come up blank as I tried to find who Johnsons were, but my best guess is that they were a works team. Thanks, however, to Peter Lush, in our club history book, the final Finchley & District League Division Three table is reproduced, even if a significant number of results are lost in the mists of time. According to the results that are definitely known, the opening league fixture was on 21 November 1908, and this was a goalless encounter at home to

Caledonian Old Boys. Two weeks later, on 5 December, Christ Church Hampstead's first away Finchley & District League match was away to Johnsons Athletic and they became the first team Christ Church Hampstead defeated, the game ending 2–0. In March 1909, the return, at home resulted in a 3–0 victory. None of the goal scorers for the whole of the season are known, which is a real shame, especially as the man who netted the opening goal at Johnsons also has the honour of having scored the club's first ever competitive goal.

By a strange coincidence, another Christ Church Hampstead opponent in that inaugural season was St John's Friern Barnet. The away game on 16 January was a 4–1 win, but the home fixture is one of those for which no result was known. Given that St John's finished bottom of the table with only four wins and Christ Church Hampstead lost twice, other than to Priory Athletic in February 1909, Christ Church Hampstead probably won the return. As Christ Church Hampstead went on to win the Division 3 title, and thus gained promotion, it was the only time the club encountered either Johnsons or St John's.

More than one hundred years passed before the club, now Hendon, played another competitive fixture against a team with a 'J'. On 1 October 2011, Hendon made the short trip north to Oxhey Jets to play the Molten Spartan South Midlands League club in an FA Cup second round qualifying tie. The Greens were prohibitive favourites to reach the next round, but it was not plain sailing, despite Elliott Charles giving the Greens a first-half lead. Former Hendon man Lewis Putnam fired an equaliser early in the second half, but Greg Ngoyi grabbed what turned out to be the winner just before the hour mark.

Of the friendlies, none of the opponents play on the English mainland and four came while Hampstead Town, Hampstead and Golders Green made Easter tours, something unimaginable in modern football. In 1923, Hampstead sailed to Jersey for two games on Jersey and one on Guernsey. The first game, on Good Friday was against the Jersey Amalgamated and it ended in a 1–1 draw, Travis Day scoring for Town. A day later, the opposition was a Jersey Island XI, and they were not able to stop high-scoring Hampstead, who scored six times, through F Butler, Lewis Smith, Cecil Wise, Day and a double from Freddie Young. Our hosts did score three in reply making an excellent afternoon's entertainment. On Easter Monday we played, and defeated a Guernsey Island XI 4–3.

Six years later, Guernsey provided the opposition for two Easter friendlies before Hampstead sailed across to Jersey for a game against the Island XI. This time the game ended 3–0 to Hampstead, with Harry Vanner, Harry Shearcroft and A Potter getting the goals. Then, in 1937, again over Easter, Golders Green made the trip to the Channel Islands, stopping off first with a pair of friendlies against Guernsey Island XIs before meeting a Jersey Island XI on Easter Monday. Joe Bloxham and E Soden – who had scored in the 1–0 win over Guernsey two days earlier – were the Green's marksmen in a 2–2 draw.

In 2018, it was announced that Jersey will follow Guernsey and play in the English football pyramid. Playing as the Jersey Bulls, they will be members of the Combined Counties League Division 1, step six of the English game. As with Guernsey, members of the Bostik (Isthmian) League Division South East in 2019, for the purposes of regionalisation, Jersey will be considered a club based at Gatwick Airport – the landing point for planes from the Channel Islands.

The only home friendly or – more likely – behind-closed-doors practice match which was played at Claremont Road came on 7 October 1991, when our visitors were from Kuwait. The match against Al-Jahra ended 1–0 to Hendon, but there are no more details on the club's exhaustively-researched website. Hendon were due to play Jersey in a late-season friendly at Claremont Road about 15 years ago, but bad weather forced the match to be postponed a day before it was due to be played.

K

Kingsbury

Kingstonian

Knock-out competitions

Kingsbury

This piece is on a club and a place, Kingsbury Town FC and Kingsbury's Silver Jubilee Park (SJP), now Hendon's current home.

Hendon and Hampstead Town played teams with the name Kingsbury, although there seems to be no link between Hyde & Kingsbury, a club Town met mainly before the First World War, and Kingsbury Town, the now defunct club which occupied SJP for four decades in more recent times. The Willesden & District League was one of dozens of local leagues in and around London, and Hampstead Town spent a couple of years in it, at the same time as the club went through the three divisions of the Finchley & District League in its first three seasons.

Hampstead Town's first meeting with Hyde & Kingsbury was on 19 November 1910, winning 1–0 at home. A fortnight later, in an away game, the Town were victorious 2–0, but the scorers of the goals in both games are unknown. The clubs met again in the following season, winning 4–1 at home on 25 January 1912, when the Hampstead goal scorers were Herbert Pike, Harry Hyde, Alfred Tomkins and Clive Bowden. There is, unfortunately, no record of the return fixture. It was almost nine years before the clubs met again, in a New Year's Day friendly at Farm Avenue. The result was a 3–1 defeat, Cecil Wise scored for Town. However, in September 1921, the teams were back at Farm Avenue for an FA Amateur Cup tie, and it was Hampstead who triumphed, 6–2, thanks to a hat-trick from Reg Kirby, a double from C Vance and one from Wise. As Hyde & Kingsbury sank away, a new club, playing at Silver Jubilee Park sprang up. Formed as Davis Sports in 1919, they became Kingsbury in 1923, but there was no official meeting – competitive or friendly – before the 1960s.

Hendon's first match against Kingsbury Town was a Claremont Road friendly, played on Thursday 28 April 1966. Over the next 40 years, there were six competitive fixtures and three more friendlies. Laurie Churchill scored all three Greens goals that day in a 3–1 victory. Although throughout Kingsbury's history, Hendon were the higher ranked club, it was they who had better head-to-head figures in competitive games, 3–2, with one draw. That draw was the first cup meeting, on Saturday 11 August 1979, when the Middlesex Charity Cup was a pre-season round-robin event. Hendon's team included Micky Cooper, Gary Hand, Peter Deadman, Rod Haider and Roy Butler, who combined for almost 2,500 appearances, and Alan Roughan, Jim Hendrick and Mick Garrini, who all were around the 100-game mark. It finished 2–2, with Butler and Garrini scoring. The next meeting was also in the Charity Cup, this time a knock-out match, but also at Silver Jubilee Park in March 1986. Derek Brown scored the Greens' goal, but

133

it was Kingsbury who won 3–1 after extra time. Nine months later, in the Middlesex Senior Cup, Mick Kiely scored the only goal in a victory at Claremont Road.

There was one meeting in the Isthmian League Cup, in November 1987, a bitterly cold night when Hendon were off colour and Kingsbury really up for the game. Despite a late equaliser from Dermot Drummy, extra-time again proved the Greens' undoing, this time 2–1. Hendon's last cup encounter was back in the Middlesex Senior Cup, almost 14 years later, and at Silver Jubilee Park. Hendon ran Kingsbury off their feet, with Byron Bubb was outstanding in a 5–0 win and he scored a fabulous goal – Eugene Ofori, Davis Haule, Dale Binns and Paul Fewings got the others – and the Greens went on to win the Cup on Easter Monday 2002.

Hendon came out on top in two friendlies. Joe Gallen was the headline scorer in a 7–1 victory at Silver Jubilee Park in 1997. He scored three, while Tony Kelly with 2, Curtis Warmington and Tony Lynch were also on target. In between, in March 1983, Des Dennis, Adrian Smith and Barry Henley scored in a 3–0 victory. The last meeting, like the three previous friendlies, was at SJP and it was Kingsbury who prevailed 1–0 in August 2005.

At the end of that season, Kingsbury merged with London Tigers, were briefly Kingsbury London Tigers, and, in that first season, they split games between Silver Jubilee Park and the old Viking Sports Greenford ground on the A40 – the latter having problems with the playing surface. KLT survived for five seasons – the last four of which were almost exclusively based at Greenford – before the FA granted the club's wish to drop Kingsbury.

As for Silver Jubilee Park, it lay essentially fallow for most of a decade. The purchase of the ground by Robert Morris and his partners, the laying of the 3G pitch, renovating of facilities and arrival of first Edgware Town, then Hendon, has seen everything change. The footprint of Silver Jubilee Park may remain as it has more than half a century, but it is now a modern stadium, hosting many community activities, thanks to Rob's leadership, imagination and inspiration.

The stadium may not be in the London Borough of Barnet, but Brent's border is almost directly behind the main stand and powerful clearances that clear the clubhouse or dressing rooms area will frequently leave Brent and land in Barnet. It is possible to walk from the A5 Edgware Road to the ground, but after Goldsmith Avenue, the path from the entry to West Hendon Playing Fields disappears at about half-way and then there is a tramp across often boggy turf to the gap in the hedge at the top of SJP. This is the borough boundary and a matter of a few steps into the London Borough of Brent, the entrance to SJP is welcoming.

Silver Jubilee Park

Top: Panoramic view of the ground, middle: the café & shop, bottom: the main stand (Photos: Peter Lush)

Top: The ground's two teams; middle: the McCann stand, with goalkeeper Chris Grace saving a penalty against Dorchester Town; bottom left: the club's Middlesex heritage; bottom right: a gentle reminder. (Photos: Peter Lush)

Kingstonian

One of our longest-lasting rivalries is with Kingstonian. In July 2016, I received an email from Kingstonian's programme editor asking me for my memories of Hendon's clashes with the Ks as it was, he thought, the 100th competitive meeting between the clubs. It gave me no pleasure to create extra work for him, but, as statistics are dear to me, the facts ruined an otherwise good story.

According to my records, taken from the Hendon FC website, as Hendon we had met Kingstonian 100 times going into the 2016–17 season, 82 times in the Isthmian League and 18 times in a multitude of cup-ties. What our good friends had not realised was that in the 1920s, Hampstead Town and Hampstead had played Kingstonian in the Athenian League twice a season from February 1920 until April 1929, 10 seasons, 20 meetings. Whereas Hendon's applications to join the Isthmian League always were rebuffed, Kingstonian were invited to join the League for the 1929–30 season.

In 1919, Kingstonian were in their first season in that guise, the result of a merger between Old Kingstonians – who had been elected to the Athenian League that year – and Kingston Town. The first two meetings, in early 1920, ended in 2–2 draws, but Ks just shaded the remainder of the fixtures, winning nine times to Hendon's eight with a solitary draw. They also won the Athenian League twice, in 1924 and 1926, and were runner-up in 1927. Hampstead's best in that decade was runner-up, in 1929.

From 1930 until 1963, when Hendon finally joined the Isthmian League, there were only two meetings, both in the Amateur Cup and both ending in 2–1 victories for the Greens. Bill Reay and Les Fontana scored in January 1948 and Terry Howard and Laurie Topp did so in 1960. This latter contest remains the biggest one we have played because it was at Wembley for the FA Amateur Cup. It was, to put it mildly, dramatic. Johnny Whing scored for Kingstonian just before half-time and they had another effort ruled out for a foul on Greens' goalkeeper Peter Shearing, all this after Hendon had dominated the opening 45 minutes without scoring. It seemed as if the Ks' resistance would bring them the trophy as the match moved into the closing minutes – the story goes that red ribbons were already being tied on the cup – but then it all turned around. In the 87th minute, Laurie Topp – arguably the finest player in the club's history – smashed an equaliser from 20 yards. Two minutes later, Miles Spector set up Terry Howard for the winner, although Hendon had to survive an effort from Oakes which hit a post.

League meetings resumed in 1963, when we joined the Isthmian League, and the Ks won the first meeting on 20 December, 1–0, but

Hendon gained revenge six days later, when they travelled to Richmond Road and returned with two points thanks to a 4–0 win. Peter Slade grabbed a hat-trick and Jimmy Quail got the other goal.

Returning to cup ties, the teams have met 18 times in all, twice in the Amateur Cup, twice in the Premier Inter-League (also the GMAC), twice in the Isthmian League Cup, once each in the FA Cup and FA Trophy and 10 times in the London Senior Cup. In 2012, there was a clash in the London Senior Cup Final, at a rain-soaked Imber Court, the home of Metropolitan Police FC. Hendon came out victorious 2–0, thanks to goals from Darren Currie and Jack Mazzone. In 2015–16, Kingstonian won a penalty shoot-out in the League Cup to avenge a 1–0 Hendon win in 2003, while Hendon won the only FA Cup tie, 2–1, and Ks the only FA Trophy meeting, 4–2; these games were five weeks apart in autumn 2009.

Since I started watching Hendon, Kingstonian have lost the use of two home grounds and been in groundshare arrangements at three clubs. Since the mid-1980s: Hendon have visited Richmond Road, then Hampton's The Beveree, Kingsmeadow (a ground built for them but taken over by AFC Wimbledon), and Fetcham Grove, Leatherhead FC, a one-season deal in 2017–18. From summer 2018, Kingstonian played at Corinthian–Casuals FC, in Tolworth, but Hendon have yet to have an away game against Ks at this ground.

Hendon just about hold the upper hand in League encounters, claiming five more victories than Kingstonian. However, when it comes to goals, it is the Ks who have the advantage, having enjoyed a 7–2 victory in 1927, 7–0 (at the Beveree, Hampton FC) in 1989 and 5–0 in 1991. In the Athenian League Hampstead twice mustered five goals, winning 5–2 in 1921 and 5–3 in 1926. Hendon's biggest margin of victory was 6–1 in a London Senior Cup tie at Claremont Road, on Saturday 26 October 1974 … three days later, a League game at Claremont Road ended 2–1 to the Ks. These are the full statistics for Athenian and Isthmian League matches: P104, W43, D23, L38, Goals for 138, Goals against 143. In cup ties, Hendon have been far more successful, winning 12 of 18 ties, with two matches drawn and one lost, during which time the Greens netted 41 times and conceded 25. As for the overall record's Hendon's totals stand at: P122, W55, D25, L42, GF179, GA168.

Knock-out competitions

This piece looks at other knock-out cup competitions, in reality the Isthmian League Full Members Cup and the Premier Inter-League Cup.

The Full Members Cup ran for 11 seasons, with a multitude of sponsors, and Hendon's record of three competition wins is the best. A supplementary league cup, only the top two divisions participated, the lower divisions playing for the Associate Members trophy. From 1988–89 to 1992–93, Hendon's best achievement was the last eight, but in 1993–94, the team went all the way. With turmoil off the field, player-manager Bob Dowie oversaw the campaign, which ended in the final at Marlow FC. With future Hendon star and assistant manager Freddie Hyatt pulling the strings in midfield, Wokingham Town were the opposition, but Hendon triumphed 2–1. Tommy Mason's first-half penalty and Mark Hill – with his only Hendon goal – book-ending Elliott Pearce's equaliser.

Most notable in the next three, barren, years was a 4–3 defeat against St Albans City in 1995 when teenager Keith Dowson scored a hat-trick, but never played for Hendon again. There is, however, a back story to this. Dowson – who had been very close to breaking into Charlton Athletic's Premier League squad – suffered an ankle injury soon after his third goal and by the time he had returned to fitness, interim manager Ray Brandon (Mick Browne's successor) had been replaced by Neil Price and Michael Banton and Mark Dawber were the front two of choice.

It was a different matter under Frank Murphy as the Greens lifted the trophy in back-to-back seasons, 1997–98 and 1998–99. In the first of those seasons, the final was played at Chesham and Ian Mancey gave Basingstoke a 1–0 half-time lead. The second half was utterly dominated by the Greens, who eventually equalised through Tony Kelly. Junior Lewis, Curtis Warmington, with a spectacularly powerful header, and Michael Banton added goals as the Greens ran out 4–1 winners. In their six matches in 1997–98, Hendon scored 19 goals; in five games in the Greens' successful defence, they scored just eight times. In a 2–0 last-16 win at Canvey Island, Simon Clarke, after colliding with the home goalkeeper, was told not to kick his cousin – only then did the Hendon man realise that the Gulls' keeper was his cousin, Mel Capelton. Both Chesham United and Worthing had the chance to avenge earlier FA Trophy defeats, but both failed, the latter doing so in a turgid final at Sutton, where Matt Maran's early goal was enough for Hendon.

Hendon's last ever match in the competition was a second-round tie at a frozen Scraley Road, Heybridge, where the Greens led 4–1 at half-time, but lost 6–5 after extra-time, Bontcho Guentchev being denied a last-gasp equaliser. The pitch was so treacherous the referee admitted he would not have allowed a penalty shoot-out.

The other cup competition was the Premier Inter-League Cup, known first as the GMAC (General Motors Acceptance Corporation – a subsidiary of the motor manufacturer and Conference sponsor) Cup in 1986–87. It was open to teams, in the top division of the Isthmian, Southern and Northern Premier Leagues and the Conference, whose teams entered after one round. The full tale of the Greens' run to the 1987 final is in the entry Premier Inter-League Cup.

The semi-final involved a trip to Northern Premier League Burton Albion on Sunday 26 April, both teams having played home league games a day earlier. It was one of the most violent matches I can recall, although somehow the referee kept all 22 players on the pitch. A crowd of 1,439 required a significant police presence and the atmosphere on the terraces was intimidating. After the final whistle I chatted to an Inspector who was policing the end at which Hendon fans stood; he told me he would have sent off five players, four from Burton and Alan Campbell.

Ted Hardy's Hendon thrived on these occasions and kept their discipline well in a 1–1 draw. Three days later Hendon won a pulsating replay at Claremont Road, 3–1 after extra time, Dermot Drummy, Neil Wolstenholme and Roger Wade scoring.

Sadly, the final was a one-sided affair, Hendon having lost a coin-toss for hosting the final – Aston Villa and Manchester City's grounds had been mooted for the venue. The toss was held with the Kettering Town official in the Conference League's offices and the Hendon official being on the phone. The programme for the game showed Kettering's substitute being Frank Murphy, but he had played for Corby in an earlier round and was ineligible. However, the Poppies did have former £1.4 million transfer man Steve Daley in their line-up and they won 4–1, the Hendon goal being a Drummy cross deflected into his own net by a defender.

However, once entry became voluntary, the Premier Inter-League Cup rather withered on the vine and Hendon played in only two of the other four competitions, reaching the last 32 in 1990–91, going out to Carshalton Athletic. The competition may have had a better chance of continuing if clubs had been given the option of entering or not a couple of months into the season, when they would have a better idea of their prospects and cup schedules.

L

Danny Lakey

Junior Lewis

London Challenge Cup

London's (other) professional clubs

London Senior Cup

A remarkable 4–0 win for Hendon against a professional club.

Danny Lakey

Danny Lakey made a big impression during a little more than three years with the Greens. He joined Hendon in the summer of 1964, prior to the Greens' second season in the Isthmian League. Described as a robust winger, he was much more than the typical playmaking wide-man who created goals rather than scoring them. A return of 55 goals from 125 matches would, in the present era, be a more than acceptable total for the leading goalscorer, especially the 30 goals in 49 appearances in 1964–65. There is a strong case to say that Danny was the missing link in the Hendon team, the final key component that turned a very good team into a Championship winner. In his three seasons at Claremont Road, Hendon played in the FA Amateur Cup semi-final each year.

The 1964–65 season was barely under way when Danny made his debut. Hendon had won three and drawn one of the opening four league games, and beaten Leyton in the FA Cup, when Danny played in a 2–2 home draw against Kingstonian, David Hyde grabbing both goals. The crowd at Claremont Road that Tuesday night – 8 September – was 1,861, almost 500 fewer than had watched the local derby against Enfield a week earlier, but still what proved to be Hendon's third-highest in the league that season.

Danny's first Hendon goal came in the win away to Hitchin Town a week after his debut. It was the start of a run of scoring nine goals in as many matches – he got a double in the FA Cup defeat of Ford United, but didn't score in the 3–1 London Challenge Cup victory over Enfield, although he made the second goal. That set up maybe the greatest performance in the club's history, the 4–3 win over Arsenal in the latter competition. After a hat-trick from a young John Radford, Danny reduced the arrears before a Hyde hat-trick won the game for the Greens at Highbury.

If Arsenal's defence couldn't cope with Danny and the Hendon attack, what chance did the Isthmian League or lesser amateur clubs have? The Greens amassed 192 goals in all competitions – scoring everything from nil to nine – and finished with a treble of Middlesex Senior Cup, Isthmian League title and Amateur Cup. The league was won in a play-off against Enfield at Dulwich Hamlet and Danny scored the last goal in a 4–1 win. He was one of five Hendon players to be selected for the Isthmian League representative team that season.

Hendon couldn't repeat the Amateur Cup success in 1965–66, losing 3–1 to Wealdstone at Wembley, and a large part of the reason for that was the long injury list. In particular, Jimmy Quail suffered a terrible broken leg in the quarter-final victory over Wycombe Wanderers. Danny also caught the injury bug and didn't play between 15 January and 19

April, four days before the Amateur Cup Final, for which he wasn't selected. All-in-all he played in just 28 out of 53 games, but still contributed nine goals.

The crowded end-of-season season schedule saw 10 league games, the Amateur Cup Final, two Middlesex Senior Cup ties – also against Wealdstone – the Wycombe Hospitals Cup and a friendly in 41 days. The title decider came on 3 May when Danny and Hendon couldn't break down the Leytonstone defence and the goalless draw eventually proved enough for the Granleigh Road club to take the title by two points – it was two for a win in those days – so a Hendon win would have left both teams on 60 points.

Although Danny enjoyed much better fitness in 1966–67, Hendon were not as strong as they had been in the two previous seasons. Danny missed only a dozen of 57 games and netted 16 times to finish joint-second on the scoring charts with Dave Swain, 14 behind Tony Harding. The Greens finished in fifth place, but the goals for column showed only 64, down from 111 the season before. His absence in the second replay of the Amateur Cup semi-final, a 3–1 loss to Skelmersdale, certainly didn't help Hendon's cause.

All good things must come to an end and it was clear early in the 1967–68 season that Danny was no longer a regular first choice. A move to Kent made playing for Hendon difficult, and he made only three first-team appearances, one of which was a London Challenge Cup tie against West Ham United at Upton Park. The Hammers won 1–0. Danny joined Ramsgate in December 1967, but made one final appearance for Hendon. On 13 April 1969, there was a special challenge match between Hendon of 1968–69 and the all-conquering 1964–65 team. John Swannell and Dave Hogwood were eligible for both squads, but elected to join Danny, now with Maidstone United, in the 1964-65 squad, who won 3–1.

Junior Lewis

Junior Lewis was involved with Hendon both as a player and player-coach. He was one of the most passionate players to appear for Hendon in the 1990s. He is also the only man to have played in the top nine tiers of the English football pyramid. Junior played briefly in the Football League with Fulham in the early 1990s before joining Dover Athletic, managed by Peter Taylor in 1995. After a shot spell at Hayes, he joined Hendon, making his debut on 21 September 1996, a 3–1 win, in which he scored the first goal.

Neil Price's team struggled to put together a string of results in the League, but had much more success in the FA Cup – after escaping against Fisher in the second qualifying round. Junior returned to The

Crabble in the third qualifying round where a Paul Kelly goal gave Hendon a shock win over Conference club Dover, and played his part in the victory over Hastings Town in the final qualifying round. The 2–0 win in the replay at Claremont Road gave Hendon a tie against former FA Cup winners (albeit 70 years earlier) Cardiff City, where the Bluebirds triumphed 2–0. A few weeks after Price departed, Frank Murphy was appointed and he engineered the Greens' escape form relegation

The following season, Junior and Hendon enjoyed even greater success, once more in the FA Cup. A first round proper tie at home to Leyton Orient attracted great interest and two Colin Simpson equalisers forced a replay at the Matchroom Stadium (Brisbane Road). There, on 25 November 1997, the current Hendon management team of Gary McCann, Freddie Hyatt and Junior combined for the Greens' winning goal – the decisive cross coming from John Simon White. It was only Hendon's second ever FA Cup victory over a Football League club, first away from Claremont Road, and the second half was broadcast live on BBC 5 Live, with John Murray commentating. Cardiff ended the Cup run 3–1 in the next round.

But Junior was given a new strike partner straight after the Leyton Orient victory in the shape of Paul Whitmarsh. Simpson left to join Leyton Orient, a transfer that Junior took personally as he considered himself – justifiably, it must be said – a far better footballer. He told some Hendon youngsters in 2008, "When Simpson joined Orient I wasn't jealous, I was angry because I knew I was a better player, but I was even more determined to get back into the Football League. I knew I could play in the League."

Whitmarsh and Lewis formed a lethal partnership in the second half of the 1997–98 season, which culminated in a 13-match unbeaten run, including a thumping 4–1 demolition of Basingstoke Town in the Full Members Cup final at Chesham United's ground. The run of nine wins and two draws to end the campaign saw Hendon finish in fifth place, one of the best placings in a quarter of a century. Junior finished the season with 22 goals in just 41 appearances, and the Greens' stunning end-of-season form made them title favourites for 1998–99.

It must be said that the campaign was more than a little disappointing. There was another FA Cup first round appearance and Junior was nearly a hero again against Notts County when he twice came within inches of scoring in the first game at Claremont Road – the replay, after a postponement, was lost 3–0. The Ryman League form, however, was inconsistent at best, mainly because all the goals scored by Lewis and Whitmarsh were more than cancelled out by less-than-stellar defending. Junior scored 28 goals in 55 appearances, but was eclipsed by his strike-partner who grabbed 42 in 53 appearances.

144

Whitmarsh excepted, only once since 1967–68 – Tony Bass, with 30 in 1972–73 – had a Hendon player scored more than Junior's 28 goals in a season.

That saw the end of Junior's first spell at Hendon as Peter Taylor gave him a chance at Gillingham. All in all, Junior played more than 200 matches for Gillingham, Leicester, Brighton, Swindon, Hull and Brentford. A close of friend of Del Deanus, Junior then played in non league football for Del and Steve Newing at Edgware Town and Welwyn, helping with Del's care when he was diagnosed with MND and arranging fund-raising events. He returned to Hendon in 2011, mainly on the coaching side, though Junior did pass the 150-appearance mark with eight games off the bench.

In June 2014, Junior was appointed as coach at Leeds United, working with Dave Hockaday, s surprising appointment as the club's manager. They were only there for 70 days before Hockaday was sacked by the club's owner. Junior also left. He subsequently coached Canvey Island before joining Barnet, where he is now working with Darren Currie, another former Hendon player.

London Challenge Cup

Hendon entered the London Challenge Cup only a few times and never came close to winning it, but were involved in some famous and historic contests.

Hendon began life in 1908 as Christ Church Hendon; that same year the London Challenge Cup was also launched. Its final season was 1973–74, coincidentally also the last one of the amateur era. Entry into the competition for London's Football League clubs was compulsory at various times, though from the 1930s, reserve and or youth teams were routinely selected, while amateur and semi-professional clubs competed by invitation. For the amateur clubs, the semi-finalists in the London Senior Cup were invited to play in the next season's London Challenge Cup. In all, as Hampstead Town, Golders Green and Hendon, the club played 44 London Challenge Cup matches, between 1921 and 1972. The first match was on 9 September 1921, when Hampstead Town entertained Tufnell Park at Farm Avenue and goals from H White and Cecil Wise sealed a 2–0 victory. Charlton Athletic were in their first season in Division Three South when, on 21 September, Town visited The Valley for the club's first competitive match against Football League opposition. The match ended in a 1–1 draw, Reg Kirby netting the Town's goal. Hampstead Town withdrew from the replay, which was arranged for a midweek Thursday afternoon, because they already had a match on the Monday afternoon that week and therefore could not raise a team, as the players would have had to take a second afternoon off work. Three were also committed to a representative match on the Wednesday afternoon.

Neither Hampstead nor Golders Green enjoyed significant success in entries in 1922 and 1936, respectively, but Hendon returned to the London Challenge Cup in 1950. We recorded our first victory over League opposition when, after beating Walthamstow Avenue 3–1 – a fine result in itself – Millwall were crushed 4–0 at The Den, with goals from Bob Avis, Johnny Westmore, a double, and Roy Stroud. In the next round, Charlton won a replay 1–0 after a goalless draw. The following season, on 8 October 1951, English football history was made with the first senior competitive match played under floodlights. This match, Arsenal versus Hendon, was covered in the A–Z piece on floodlights, but Hendon overcame an injury-weakened Gunners at Highbury, Arthur Phebey getting the only goal. Two weeks later, Phebey again scored the only goal, this time beating West United at Upton Park. Charlton ended Hendon's run, once more needing two goes to achieve it, Johnny Westmore scoring in a 1–1 draw at Claremont Road before a 2–1 loss at The Valley, with Roy Shea on target.

Having beaten Arsenal and West Ham, Hendon found it harder against Tottenham Hotspur and Chelsea. In 1952, Stroud and Dexter Adams netted against Spurs, but it ended 3–2 to the visitors at Claremont Road. At Stamford Bridge, the Football League champions won 6–3 in 1955, Graeme Cunningham, Dave Roden and Guy Holden getting Hendon's goals. In October 1959, West Ham avenged their defeat eight years earlier, winning 2–0 at Upton Park.

Hendon's victory over Arsenal at Highbury on 8 October 1964 – also covered in greater detail elsewhere – remains one of the club's most famous results. John Radford had scored a quick-fire hat-trick to put the Gunners apparently in control, but his feat was matched by David Hyde, this after Danny Lakey had reduced the arrears, and it gave the Greens a 4–3 win at Highbury. This Arsenal team contained two full internationals, Eddie Magill and Ian Ure, and every other player went on to make at least 100 Football League appearances, many being part of the 1971 Arsenal "Double" team.

Hendon weren't invited to the 1965–66 or 1966-67 competitions, but in 1967, the Greens won 1–0 at Walthamstow – thanks to a Tony Harding goal – to earn a trip to Upton Park, where a young West Ham side won 1–0. In 1969, the Greens defeated Barnet 2–0 at Underhill and then entertained Millwall. John Baker and Rod Haider netted for Hendon, but the Lions earned a 2–2 draw and, a week later, won the replay 2–0. Our last match in the competition in its original format was in September 1972, when Barnet were the visitors to Claremont Road.

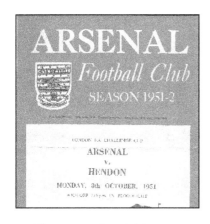

Hendon's only defeat to non-league opposition before January 1973 came in this game, a 2–0 Bees win with Lou Adams scoring both goals.

The competition returned in the 1990s, though it was not the same as its predecessor. From the 1990–91 season, the London Football Association rebranded and split the Senior Cup, with the clubs highest in the pyramid playing for the Challenge Cup instead. As Hendon's county affiliation is with the Middlesex FA, the club's entry into the London Senior or Challenge Cup was not compulsory and the Greens played in only four of the 10 seasons. It was hardly a huge success. The only two wins Hendon enjoyed were against Bromley, 2–0, and Croydon 5–1. A 4–3 defeat at Barking came about after losing two players to injuryl, but there weren't the same excuses for the 4–1 loss at Kingsbury or 3–1 reverse at Uxbridge. Hendon's final game in the London Challenge Cup – unless it is revived again – was in February 1999, when the Greens entertained Welling United and lost 3–0.

London's (other) professional clubs

Arsenal, Leyton Orient and Queen's Park Rangers have articles of their own in this book; this piece looks at the links Hendon have had with the 10 other professional clubs in London. Watford are a Hertfordshire club and are not included here. Also, we mainly look at players who have joined professional clubs from Hendon, not players who spent time at a professional club in the schoolboy or youth set-ups before joining Hendon.

Brentford are the first club alphabetically, and Hendon – under all the club's names – have played 10 matches at Griffin Park. The most significant games were two Amateur Cup semi-finals. In 1960, Enfield were beaten 2–0. Laurie Topp scored in the first half, and Brian Figg added a second on 51 minutes. At Wembley, Hendon beat Kingstonian 2–1 to win the Cup for the first time.

The second semi-final was 12 years later. Wycombe Wanderers were Hendon's opponents in the club's first Amateur Cup semi-final since 1967. Hendon supporters were massively outnumbered in the 9,210 crowd. Johnny Baker put Hendon ahead on 14 minutes, but then Wycombe equalised early in the second half. With 16 minutes left, Peter Deadman scored the winner with a spectacular long-range shot. It took

147

Hendon to Wembley, to win the Cup for the third – and final – time. Peter played 552 games for Hendon, scoring 15 goals. This was undoubtedly both the best and most important.

Between the Wars, Griffin Park was a regular venue for Middlesex Senior and Middlesex Charity Cup finals. Hampstead Town's first appearance in a Middlesex Senior Cup Final was in 1925, against Southall at Griffin Park. They had to field a reserve team, because the first team were on an Easter tour in Belgium. Southall won 5–0. In the Middlesex Charity Cup, the club played seven finals at Griffin Park between 1921 and 1946. The 1946 game, a 3–2 win against Southall, was the last game as Golders Green FC. The only other win at Griffin Park had been in 1921, when Botwell Mission (who subsequently became Hayes FC) were beaten 2–1.

Hendon played a pre-season friendly against a Brentford XI in July 2010, losing 1–0 at Vale Farm. On the players front, Bob Thomas signed for Brentford from Golders Green in 1939. Billy Dare joined Hendon from Kingsbury Town in September 1948. However, he was already on Brentford's books as an amateur, and turned pro with them in December. He went on to play 222 first team games for the Bees, scoring 64 goals, before joining West Ham United in 1955.

The club has played **Charlton Athletic** five times, all in the London Challenge Cup. In 1921, Hampstead Town drew 1–1 at The Valley, but had to withdraw from the replay as the club was unable to field a team for a second midweek afternoon match in the week it had to be played. In 1950, having beaten Millwall, Hendon drew 0–0 with Charlton in the semi-final, and then lost the replay ay The Valley 1–0. It was a similar story in 1951. A 1–1 draw at Claremont Road was followed by a 2–1 loss at the Valley, after extra time.

Hendon have only played **Chelsea** once in an official fixture. In 1955, a Monday afternoon match at Stamford Bridge saw the Blues win 6–3 in the London Challenge Cup. Chelsea were 4–1 up at half-time, and included famous amateur players Jim Lewis and Seamus O'Connell in their team. Hendon's goals came from Roden, Holden and Cunningham.

In the spring of 1938, Chelsea's 'A' team were beaten 1–0 in a friendly. In the autumn of 1962, Hendon played a series of friendlies to mark the installation of the club's floodlights. Chelsea won 6–1 in front of a 2,000 crowd. In pre-season friendlies, Hendon lost 3–2 in August 1986 and won 2–0 in July 1994. Chelsea also sent an under-21 team, coached by Dermot Drummy, to play Hendon at Earlsmead in August 2013. A 361 crowd saw the Blues win comfortably 2–0. Dermot Drummy is one connection between the clubs. Another is Ted Drake, who was Hendon's coach from 1946 to 1947. He then managed Reading before moving to Stamford Bridge to become Chelsea's manager in June 1952. He led the club to their first League Championship in 1955.

A third link between the clubs is Miles Spector. He played for Chelsea's first team while a schoolboy at Hendon County Grammar School. He decided to go to university rather than turn professional, and joined Hendon in 1955, where he stayed until 1963. He is fondly remembered by supporters of both clubs.

Hendon have few links with **Crystal Palace**. In 1951, the Amateur Cup semi-final replay was played at Selhurst Park; a disappointing 3–2 defeat. In the mid-1960s, Jimmy Quail played some reserve team games for Crystal Palace, but never played for the first team.

Although they are no longer in the Football League, Hendon did play **Dagenham & Redbridge** once when they were members. It was in the London Senior Cup and the Greens triumphed 2–1 in December 2005. The goals came from Jeff Campbell – a New Zealand full international who joined from then Isthmian League AFC Wimbledon – and Jimmy Froud, his only Hendon goal, and the Greens went on to reach the final, losing 3–2 to Fisher Athletic. The best Dagger (as a League club) to play for Hendon was Darren Currie, who combined his duties as D&R assistant manager with stellar performances in midfield while the club was playing at Vale Farm.

Hendon have played **Fulham** three times. In March 1938, their 'A' (third) team lost 4–1 in a friendly at Claremont Road. Thirty years later, in July 1968, the Cottagers were beaten 4–0 at Claremont Road in a pre-season friendly. Defender Ray Poole played up front and scored a hat-trick. Six of the Fulham team had first team experience, but the *Hendon Times* report said they were "very mediocre". In 1998, Fulham returned for another pre-season match, and won 4–3.

Hendon have played **Millwall** three times, all in the London Challenge Cup. In 1950, Hendon won 4–0 at The Den. In 1969, the teams drew 2–2 at Claremont Road before Millwall won the replay 2–0.

In 1955, Hendon played their second Amateur Cup semi-final at White Hart Lane. Hounslow were beaten 2–1 to secure a place in the Final against Bishop Auckland. In 1952, **Tottenham Hotspur** had visited Claremont Road in the London Challenge Cup and won 3–2. It was not their first visit to the ground. In 1938, Golders Green played a series of friendlies against London professional clubs' 'A' teams, and Spurs lost one of these games 1–0. In 1980, Spurs won a pre-season friendly 1–0, and in 1992 won a similar match 3–0 at Claremont Road. In 1928, Jimmy Smy turned professional with Tottenham from Hampstead. In the 1950s, Dexter Adams played for Spurs reserve team as an amateur.

Hendon have stronger links with **West Ham United**. The clubs met three times in the London Challenge Cup at Upton Park. In 1951, after knocking out Arsenal, Hendon won 1–0 at Upton Park. In 1959, the Hammers took revenge with a 2–0 win, and in 1967 won 1–0.

On the playing side, Roy Stroud played as an amateur for West Ham's first team before turning professional in November 1953. He played first team football for West Ham, but left in 1957 to play in the Southern League with Chelmsford. In 1960, goalkeeper Peter Shearing moved from Hendon to West Ham after playing against Kingstonian in the Amateur Cup Final. He never quite made it at Upton Park, but went on to have a successful professional career.

Hendon played Wimbledon FC many times when both teams had amateur status in the 1950s and 1960s. The Dons did make one appearance at Claremont Road as a League club, playing in the Bill Fisher Memorial Match in December 1978, a month after the legendary clubman had died. The match ended 1–1, George Brooks getting Hendon's goal. When **AFC Wimbledon** was formed following the original club's move to Milton Keynes, the teams again met as the new club worked its way up the pyramid to regain Football League membership. Since then, the teams met in the London Senior Cup semi-final at Kingsmeadow in April 2012. Hendon won 2–1 in front of a 611 crowd. The previous season, Hendon had won 3–2 in the London Senior Cup semi-final, but AFC Wimbledon were in the Conference Premier that season, on their way to promotion back to the Football League. It was still a notable victory. Two former MK Dons players have appeared for the Greens. First was Sam Page, a centre-half who was booed mercilessly by AFC Dons fans. The other is currently Hendon's longest serving player Luke Tingey, who started the 2019–20 season, his fifth at Hendon, having made 156 appearances and scoring five goals.

London Senior Cup

The club first entered the London Senior Cup in 1912, Hampstead Town's inaugural season with senior status. They played in the Middlesex and London Leagues and, for the first time, entered the FA Cup, FA Amateur Cup, Middlesex Senior Cup, Middlesex Charity Cup and London Senior Cup. In fact, we have played in more editions of only the FA Cup and Middlesex Senior Cup than the London Senior.

The Hendon club which folded in the 1930s was London FA-affiliated, but Hampstead Town were affiliated to Middlesex from the club's earliest days and thus were not compelled to enter any London competition. There were spells when Hendon did not enter, most recently the early 2000s, partly because at that time disciplinary proceedings for "naughty" players resulted in bans counted in weeks rather than matches – and London ties did not count in any suspensions being served. This change in regulation was the result of clubs becoming very clever in scheduling county ties to clear suspensions (in the 1980s, until the weather intervened, Phil Gridelet would have completed a three-match ban on a Tuesday – League match – Wednesday – London Senior Cup – and Thursday – Middlesex Senior Cup – of the same week).

Given the club's strength in the first 30 years as Hendon, when it was victorious in three of the five FA Amateur Cup finals in which it appeared, only two wins from six London Senior Cup final appearances – with a much smaller and rather less competitive fields – was hardly a great return. Compare that to the 13 seasons under Gary McCann's management – seven finals, three wins and four defeats – and Hendon's record has become significantly better, albeit in not such a strong field.

Golders Green reached one London Senior Cup Final, in 1935–36, but were beaten 1–0 by Walthamstow Avenue, after overcoming Leavesden, Clapton, Finchley and Ilford. The final was at Lynn Road, Ilford, and the Green were desperately unlucky to lose, having lost Tommy Evans to an injury very early in the game. There were no substitutes in those days, so the Green had to play with 10 men – Evans tried to continue but could barely walk out on the wing – and they almost held out for a replay, but EC Collins won the game with a header in the last minute of extra time.

Hendon lost three finals at Highbury in the 1950s: 4–3 to Bromley in 1951, Roy Evans scoring a hat-trick in the losing cause; 3–2 to the Avenue, again, in 1955, this time after conceding two early goals; and in 1959, when Tooting & Mitcham led 2–0 and 3–1 before winning 5–2. It was a happier story in the 1960s as Hendon finally won the London Senior Cup in 1964. The Greens had just lost 4–1 to Enfield to close out their debut Isthmian League season – as runners-up behind Wimbledon

151

when they met the Es four days later in the final. Gerry O'Rourke, Hendon's scorer in the league game, got the only goal, set up by Jimmy Quail and David Hyde.

Five years later, at Barnet FC's Underhill, in front of a crowd of 1,014, the Greens overcame Dagenham 1–0 with Rod Haider getting the only goal early in the second half. In 1972, Hendon defeated Enfield in both the FA Amateur Cup and Middlesex Senior Cup, but in the London Senior, it was the Es who triumphed, 2–0, at Wealdstone's Lower Mead.

It was 34 years before Hendon returned to the London Senior Cup final. The 2005–06 Ryman League campaign had been very difficult and relegation was a possibility when the Greens met Fisher Athletic at Tooting & Mitcham's Imperial Fields. The Fish were on their way to promotion to the Conference through the Isthmian League play-offs and had a high-priced talented team. They had already knocked Hendon out of the FA Trophy and Isthmian League Cup and raced into a 3–0 lead before late goals from Marc Leach and Mark Cooper gave Fisher a late fright. Two years later, Tooting held on for a controversial 3–2 victory – Danny Dyer and Brian Haule, a penalty, getting Hendon's goals – but the Terrors were the better team.

Forty years after beating Dagenham, Hendon won their third London Senior Cup at Kingsmeadow Stadium. Croydon Athletic provided the opposition and goalkeeper William Viner was Hendon's hero, saving three penalties in a shoot-out after efforts from James Bent and Glenn Garner had been matched by Sam Clayton and Richard Blackwell. Dyer, Leach and Bent netted Hendon's three attempts while the Rams were successful with only the second of their four attempts. Another defeat followed in 2011, a 3–1 reverse against Wingate & Finchley after Greg Ngoyi had given the Greens an early lead at Tooting.

The best win of Hendon's three recent successes was the 2–0 victory over Kingstonian at Imber Court in 2012. Darren Currie and Jack Mazzone scored. A 3–2 win over Tooting in 2015, also at the Metropolitan Police's home saw Hendon equalise late through Aaron Morgan to force extra time. Morgan and Kezie Ibe made it 3–1 before the Terrors got a late consolation. In May 2016, a fourth Hendon versus Tooting London Senior Cup final, and third in eight seasons at Imber Court, saw the Terrors control the game and run out 2–0 winners.

M

Casey Maclaren

Kevin Maclaren

Managers

Gary McCann

Middlesex Charity Cup

Middlesex Senior Cup

Middlesex Wanderers

Casey Maclaren

Casey Maclaren played 358 games for Hendon, scoring 51 goals, in 11 seasons at the club. He left in June 2018 to join Gary McCann at Hampton & Richmond.

During his Hendon career, he had to endure a huge amount of time on the sidelines and should have made more than 400 appearances, but back, knee and muscle problems have kept him out of one-third of all matches. Casey's bravery in overcoming these setbacks, together with this loyalty and willingness to help the team where ever it is needed are just two of the most laudable of his attributes.

Casey joined Hendon in the summer of 2007, aged 20, after he had been released by AFC Wimbledon. He was an unused substitute in the opening game of the season, but made his first-team debut three days later, a 2–1 home victory against Leyton, albeit as a stoppage time substitute for Brian Haule. Casey made his first start at Earlsmead on August Bank Holiday Monday, another 2–1 win against Harrow Borough.

It would be wrong to say that Casey's versatility hurt him, but as he was comfortable at full-back, centre-back and in midfield – his attacking days were in front of him –it did mean he didn't have one position. As a right-back, he opened his Hendon scoring account, netting the first in a 2–0 victory over Horsham at Claremont Road in mid-November, the goal coming as he anticipated a deflection and was athletic enough to apply the *coup de grâce*. Two weeks later, at an almost waterlogged Folkestone Invicta, midfielder Casey opened the scoring in a 4–0 win, scoring with a 20-yard strike. Although he appeared in only two-thirds of the matches in 2007–08, he still managed to register six goals – a more than acceptable strike rate of one in six. Towards the end of the season, however, Casey began to experience back trouble and he missed the London Senior Cup final defeat against Tooting & Mitcham United at Imber Court. He had more than played his part in earlier rounds scoring against both Corinthian–Casuals and Leyton. Away from football, Casey attracted national attention by becoming the youngest-ever holder of a taxi-driver's green badge, receiving it on his 21st birthday, the youngest possible age.

The 2008–09 season was one of huge frustration for Casey as he was limited to just nine appearances, only six of which were starts. A multitude of tests failed to discover the cause of back problems. There was a reward for him at the end of the season as he was on the substitutes' bench for the London Senior Cup final against Croydon Athletic at Kingsmeadow. Although he didn't come on, he did receive a winner's medal after the Greens triumphed in the penalty shoot-out following a 2–2 draw.

At the start of the following season, Casey gutted it out and he scored one of the most important goals in his Hendon career when he equalised against Kingstonian in the FA Cup, a match the Greens won 2–1 and they went on to reach the last qualifying round. It was Casey's most prolific season for Hendon and a total of 10 goals was a laudable return, as he played in defence, midfield and – on a couple of occasions – lone striker and he missed only one League game all campaign. His willingness to take on that attacking role summed up Casey's dedication to the club and the cause. Twelve months later, Casey was a key member of the squad which reached the first round proper and it was his goal that sealed victory over the Metropolitan Police at Imber Court in a fourth qualifying round replay. He played the full 90 minutes in the 3–2 loss at Chelmsford City.

Unfortunately, the 2011–12 season was another injury-ravaged one for Casey as he suffered a serious knee injury in the FA Cup defeat at Luton Town. He did make it back for the end of the season and collected a second London Senior Cup winner's medal, this time playing the full 90 minutes in the 2–0 defeat of Kingstonian at Imber Court. The following season, Casey again played in the FA Cup first round proper, being part of the team which was so unlucky to lose 2–1 at Aldershot.

Over the years, Casey continued to fulfil a variety of roles in the team, and it is hard to say which is his best. He could also score important goals. In 2015, he scored in the League play-off semi-final against the Metropolitan Police to help Hendon secure a place in the final. Two years later, at the other end of the table, he scored against Staines on the last day of the season to secure the point that kept the club in the top flight of the Isthmian League.

In his time with Hendon, he won the London Senior Cup three times and the Middlesex Senior Cup once. He was one of only two players to feature in both the 2014–15 and 2017–18 league play-off finals; Ollie Sprague was the other one (Dave Diedhiou was an unused substitute in the second match).

Kevin Maclaren

Kevin became the second member of the Maclaren family to join Hendon in the summer of 2008, a year after older brother Casey had arrived. A third brother, Conor, played in pre-season in 2010. The teenager arrived from Walton Casuals and made his debut on the opening day of the 2008–09 season, a 3–0 defeat of Dartford and it was a foul on him that led to the opening goal. Brian Haule scored from the resultant free-kick.

Whereas Casey is a capable full-back, accomplished central defender, very good midfielder and a willing, if occasional striker, Kevin

155

is very definitely a central midfielder. He is the ball-winning player who loves a tackle and then to play a short pass to a team-mate with greater flair. That is not to say that Kevin is only a negative player – he is easily the best player Hendon have had in the heart of midfield for many years. He has a talent for striking long-range efforts and can float dangerous crosses into the penalty area with either a rolling ball or from a set-piece. The goal statistics of the two brothers tell their own story: Casey has scored 40 times in 276 appearances, with 10 in two different seasons, Kevin has netted just eight in 282 matches, and never managed more than two goals in a single season.

In years gone by, players such as Kevin were fairly commonplace and every successful team had a combative player protecting the defence from in front. To those players, modern football is for wimps as it frowns on tackles; it is not quite true, but any sort of mistimed challenge will result in a card, normally yellow, but sometimes red. For Kevin, the fine line between firm-but-fair and foul and dangerous has been crossed too often though, in most cases, it has been the result of a tiny misjudgement not malice. Referees in the 2010s, however, frequently consider them to be the same when it comes to issuing punishments. It would certainly be fair to say that Kevin is the sort of player you want on your side rather than against you because of all that he brings to a game.

Kevin's first Hendon season was one of transition as the club left Claremont Road and had a largely nomadic campaign, a contributory factor in the Greens' lowly finish, 16th, only nine points clear of relegation. He made 40 appearances – pretty much his average through his first seven seasons – and scored once, an absolute screamer in a 3–1 April win over Horsham. A week later, he was collecting his first winner's medal, the London Senior Cup after Croydon Athletic had been beaten on penalties in the final at Kingsmeadow. Things were better the following year as Hendon rose to a comfortable mid-table 10th place, only eight points short of the play-offs. Kevin made 43 appearances overall, and the magic goal, also against Horsham at Vale Farm, involved neat skill before a clever finish.

In 2010–11 Kevin made his first appearance in the FA Cup proper as part of the team which was beaten 3–2 against Chelmsford City. A combination of injuries and suspensions meant it was an overall frustrating season for Kevin who missed the London Senior Cup final defeat against Wingate & Finchley at Imperial Fields, Tooting. His presence in the heart of the midfield was sorely missed, as the conditions favoured rolled-up-sleeves midfielders rather than slick passers. A year later, Hendon were back in the Final, winning 2–0 against Kingstonian at Imber Court. However, Kevin missed out having suffered a bad head injury in the semi-final victory over AFC Wimbledon.

There has never been any question of Kevin's commitment to the Hendon cause, proof of which are the fact that he and Casey shared a house near Leatherhead and both have turned down more lucrative offers to play closer to home. He is a natural leader and manager Gary McCann had very few reservations when appointing Kevin as team captain in succession to Scott Cousins in the summer of 2013. The added responsibility has calmed him down without diminishing his competitiveness.

But this will-to-win has cost him a lot of playing time. In 2014–15, Kevin appeared in only 35 of 65 matches, more than one-third of the games he missed being down to a recurring muscle injury. He was, however, back for the end of season run and thus had the honour of lifting two cups, the Isthmian League Cup after the victory over Grays Athletic at Whyteleafe and the London Senior Cup, when Tooting were downed at Imber Court. Sadly, circumstances beyond his and Hendon's control meant there wasn't a third winner's medal to treasure in the Isthmian League Premier Division Play-off final.

An off the field incident saw Kevin banned for the whole of the 2015–16 season, which was seen as very harsh by many fans. He started playing again for Hendon, but – given his disciplinary record – on the basis that a further sending off for violent conduct would mean that the club would release him. This happened in January 2017, and he continued his career elsewhere. He was part of the Chertsey Town team that won the FA Vase under Dave Anderson's management in 2019.

Managers

Given the responsibility that managers now enjoy, it is hard to believe that it was not until the 1950s that managers actually selected teams. They may well have been a part of a club's selection committee, but they didn't have the only say. Once the coaches or trainers had the autonomy of team selection as well as the tactical side and keeping players fit, managers became ever-more important and – dare I say it – easier to replace when things go wrong.

The first notable man in that role at Hendon was Ted Drake, formerly the Arsenal centre-forward, but he left after one season to become manager of Reading. Fast forward to when the Greens joined the Isthmian League in 1963, when there was another big-name appointment. Ron Burgess, a Welsh international who had been captain of Tottenham Hotspur when they won the Football League title in 1951, brought a new style and great success to Hendon, winning the League, Amateur Cup and Middlesex Senior Cup in 1965.

Having won pretty much all there was to win in two seasons, Burgess moved on – to Fulham – and Hendon went back to the tried and tested policy of appointing from within as Bill Fisher took over. Bill could not replicate Ronnie's success and, after three seasons, he stepped aside to become reserve team boss and Ron Patterson came in for the 1968–69 season. Patterson's only link with Hendon had been as a player for Northampton when the Claremont Road record attendance of 9,000 was set in 1952, but he had moved to London and, in his only full season, the Greens won the London Senior Cup for the second time. In October 1969, Ron announced he would be moving on as his job had changed though he did stay on for a few months. Bill Fisher took interim charge to the end of the season.

Taking over for the new season, 1970–71, was former Barking player-manager John Evans, who had previously played for the Greens. This was an inspired choice, because Evans led Hendon to victory in the FA Amateur Cup against Enfield in April 1972, and was also in charge for a large part of the 1972–73 campaign when Hendon went undefeated for 38 matches on their way to the title. Ever the innovator, John departed for pastures new, very new, as he became coach of Santa Fe FC in Bogota, Colombia. He brought in Jimmy Quail, who, in 1974, achieved the unique feat of taking the Greens into the last 64 of the FA Cup, and the memorable pair of ties against Newcastle United in the third round. The 1–1 draw at St James's Park could not be repeated in the replay as the Magpies won 4–0 at Watford FC.

The end of the amateur era in 1974 saw huge changes at Claremont Road with only two players from the Newcastle match starting on the opening day of the "open" era and the ever-reliable Bill Fisher succeeded the departing Jimmy Quail. On 22 November 1975, Bill did something no Hendon manager had done before and that was to beat a Football League team in the FA Cup. Hendon's 1–0 defeat of Reading earned a second-round tie at home to Swindon Town, which also ended 1–0, but it was the visitors who would play – and lose to – Isthmian rivals Tooting & Mitcham United in round three. The next decade was not one of consistency and the managerial merry-go-round included Dave Hogwood, Quail, again, Rod Haider – whose dismissal as manager signalled the end of his Hendon playing career – and Evans, again. In 1981, an "outsider", Ken Payne, formerly of Wealdstone, became manager and he put together a much stronger team than for many seasons. The costs, however, were too steep and after going out of the FA Trophy, the team was broken up and Payne departed, with his successor being the youth team manager Dave Mawson. He lasted less than a year with Gary Hand completing the season as player-manager, assisted by Quail.

Roy Ruffell, once of Hayes, had one season, 1983–84 and he was succeeded by Eddie Presland, who had played for West Ham United and Crystal Palace, and been the manager of Wealdstone, Dagenham and Dulwich Hamlet. However, he was dismissed in January 1985, with Hand returning. This time Gary started the following campaign but in November he was let go with Hendon in deep relegation trouble.

Veteran non-league manager Ted Hardy saved the Greens from the drop, had a great season in 1986–87, but left in September 1987 and was replaced by his assistant Micky Janes. He took Hendon to Wembley to win the Middlesex Charity Cup, but in 1990, Alan Randall – another former Hendon player and whose son has been a coach in the Silver Jubilee Park youth set-up – came in for an unsuccessful stint. By the time Victor Green had taken over the club in late 1991, Gwyn Walters was in charge and he lasted until the summer of 1992. With Green as chairman, two big names took over the hot seat.

First was Barrie Williams, the man who led Sutton United to Isthmian League success and victory over FA Cup-holders Coventry City, but he left in February 1993 and his assistant Bobby Makin took over. Makin was informed he would have no role at the club in 1993–94 and if we wanted to leave before the final game of the season he could and Green himself would manage the team. Makin managed the team to a 3-1 defeat at Carshalton. Peter Taylor, the former Crystal Palace, Tottenham Hotspur and England winger, turned down the chance to be Glenn Hoddle's number two days after taking the Hendon job, but left in December 1993, to take charge of his home-town team, Southend United. Bob Dowie, his captain and centre-half finished the season as player manager, after Terry Harris, three games, and former West Ham full-back Paul Brush, 45 minutes on the evening of Thursday 30 December.

Stability came in March 1997, this after both Micky Browne, 1994–95, and Neil Price, 1995–97, had recorded identical 59-point records – 14 wins, 17 draws 23 defeats in 54 league matches. Ray Brandon and Andy O'Brien were interim bosses before Frank Murphy became manager in March 1997. He would be in charge for more than four seasons – then the longest unbroken spell of any Hendon manager. Under Frank, the Greens won their second-ever FA Cup tie against Football League opposition, the 1–0 defeat of Leyton Orient on 25 November 1997, a team which contained Gary McCann, Freddie Hyatt and the goal scorer and future coach Junior Lewis. Frank brought style and panache to the club, and no little talent. Hendon finished that campaign with a magnificent flourish, ending up in fifth place and winning the Isthmian League Full Members Cup. Twelve months on, the Full Members Cup was retained and the Greens also claimed their first Middlesex Senior Cup for 13 seasons. Hendon also reached the FA Cup second round for the second time in three years in 1999, losing unluckily to Blackpool.

Frank left in the summer of 2001 and his replacement was Dave Anderson, previously the assistant manager. He had a very different style and mentality about football, but his results were statistically much better, with a third-place finish in 2003 and fourth in 2004. He also enjoyed a hat-trick of Middlesex Senior Cup wins in his three seasons in charge. In May 2004, Hendon took the difficult decision to decline promotion to the newly-formed Conference South Division, by which time Dave had already decided to move to AFC Wimbledon; no less than 13 players and coaching staff members followed him.

New boss Tony Choules was faced with a complete rebuilding project, but his time at Claremont Road was brief and he resigned in October, with his assistant Gary Farrell taking over the reins. Off-field issues didn't help Farrell, but his team was in decline and suffered some hugely embarrassing defeats before he was relieved of his duties after a London Senior Cup exit away to Fisher Athletic in January 2005. His replacement was Gary McCann, in his first job as manager of an adult team. McCann's playing career had been curtailed after a terrible injury suffered playing for the Greens and a few comebacks tries were unsuccessful.

Gary's immediate task was to stop the rot and pull Hendon clear of relegation. He had 16 matches to save the Greens and seven wins, six draws and three defeats later, it was mission accomplished. The least said about the end of the 2005–06 season, the better and Hendon were only reprieved from relegation because of another club's financial woes. What followed in the next campaign was a target for results, based on beating the bottom third of the division, splitting results with the middle third and scrapping for morsels from the top seven. "The McCann Plan" could not have worked better, as matches against clubs finishing positions 1–7 elicited 7 points, those ending between 8th and 15th (Hendon were 14th) brought 15 points and the Greens feasted on those between 16th and 22nd with 32 points, 18 of which came against the bottom three in the table.

Saturday 15 December 2008 was a special day in Hendon history as the Greens travelled to Leyton and set a new club Isthmian League record with an 11–1 victory. It also took them to the top of the table. It was the high point of the season, though the Greens did lose in both the Middlesex and London Senior Cups. By now, Gary's management team was very settled, with his assistant Freddie Hyatt and Sports Therapist Mark Findley alongside him in the dugout. The miracles Gary had worked in keeping Hendon competitive became even tougher to achieve as the Greens were made homeless in September 2008. What followed was some years of struggle, but two FA Cup first round appearances and three London Senior Cup victories, including an almost perfect 2–0 demolition of Kingstonian in April 2012.

What followed in 2014–15 was the stuff of dreams. Hendon enjoyed their longest ever unbeaten run, 26 matches from the end of January to mid-May. The Greens finished three points behind champions Maidstone, but there was misery in the Play-off final as Margate took the second place in Conference South. Hendon were hampered because the final was delayed almost two weeks, two players could not cancel or delay their holidays and there was an unjust red card early in the first half. However, Hendon could also reflect on winning the Isthmian League Cup and the London Senior Cup. Gary was in charge when Hendon found a new home, Silver Jubilee Park, and achieved relegation safety on the final day of 2016–17. The following season was one of ultimate misery as Gary took Hendon to the play-off Final in the league, but the Greens lost to Dulwich Hamlet on penalties. That summer, The Football Association switched Hendon to the Southern League Premier Division South, McCann, after 13 years and three months, left the club to join Hampton & Richmond, and Jimmy Gray came in. He had to build a completely new squad but, after early success, a long losing run followed, but a last-day victory over Swindon Supermarine ensured relegation was, once again, avoided.

Gary McCann

Gary McCann made a huge contribution to Hendon as a player and then became the club's most long-serving manager. He joined Hendon on Easter Monday, 31 March 1997, signing in time to make his debut that afternoon against Aylesbury United. It was a tough first game for the former Sutton and Dulwich keeper, and the relegation-threatened Greens ended up on the wrong end of a 3–0 scoreline.

Gary more than played his part in the team's subsequent escape from the drop, especially in the return victory over Aylesbury at Buckingham Road and then at Top Field, Hitchin. Before the latter game kicked-off, Gary looked a picture in the programme of the Hitchin penalty taker scoring from the spot with a shot towards the goalkeeper's left upright. That nugget of information was stored in his memory bank. After Junior Lewis and Richard Nugent had given Hendon a 2–1 lead, in the final seconds of stoppage time, the Greens conceded a penalty. Up stepped the same kicker, he went the same way and looked on in dismay as Gary pushed away the ball with the game's final touch. Other results that day confirmed Hendon's safety.

The following season was probably Gary's best at Hendon. It certainly held his proudest moments, two outstanding displays in the FA Cup first round proper matches against Leyton Orient.

Gary speaking at a presentation evening at Claremont Road. (Photo: Peter Lush)

The Os' top-scorer that season, Carl Griffiths, is probably still wondering how he didn't score in either game. Gary missed only six matches in the 1997–98 season, and ended it with his first winner's medal at Hendon. He played his part in the 4–1 second-half demolition of Basingstoke Town at Chesham in the Full Member's Cup Final.

By modern standards, Gary was not tall for a goalkeeper, but had every other attribute: great reflexes, an almost elastic reach, safe hands, excellent positional strength and an ability to organise defenders in front of him. He enjoyed another run to the FA Cup first round proper the following season, and added to his medal tally with a second Full Member's Cup gong and one from the Middlesex Senior Cup. A goalkeeper is often the hero of a penalty shoot-out, but they are not often among the first five to take spot-kicks. At Enfield, after a 2–2 draw against Wembley, Gary stepped up and blasted his spot-kick ... somewhere towards Brimsdown! Another of Gary's strongest suits, however, was his concentration, because he didn't let his miss affect him and he ensured that Avi Schwarz's failure in sudden-death gave Freddie Hyatt the chance to win the Cup for Hendon, which he did.

A third consecutive FA Cup first round appearance with Hendon followed in 1999–2000 and Gary was outstanding as Bath City's unbeaten run ended in a 2–0 defeat at Twerton Park. It was the same score in the second round, but Blackpool were more than a little fortunate to sneak past the Greens, denying Gary and the team the chance to take on Arsenal at Highbury in the third round. Tuesday 18 April 2000 is, no doubt, excruciatingly etched into Gary's mind. It was on that night that his career was effectively ended. He suffered a terrible knee injury, involving a reconstruction operation, the effects of which haunt him to this day. His next Hendon game was on 30 December that year, on a frozen tundra at Heybridge Swifts in an utterly insane 6–5 extra-time defeat in the Full Members Cup. It probably wasn't the ideal surface on which to make a comeback, but he managed 21 appearances in the second half of the season, knowing there would be another visit to the surgeon at the end of the campaign.

Just 10 weeks later, to help out Dave Anderson as he built his new squad following Frank Murphy's May 2001 departure, Gary played in a pre-season friendly against Southend United at Claremont Road. It was far too soon and his knee couldn't cope. Over the next two seasons, a number of attempted comebacks failed and he made just 12 appearances before deciding to retire. Nonetheless, as an unused substitute, he picked up Middlesex Senior Cup winners' medals in 2002 and 2003. There was one more game to help out Anderson, a 2–0 victory away to Bedford Town on 20 September 2003, his 196th match for Hendon.

But it was not the end of Gary's love affair with Hendon and, on 2 February 2005, he was back, as manager. His time in charge at the club covered the departure from Claremont Road in 2008, with home games being played at a variety of grounds, two ground-shares and the move into SJP. Despite working at times on very limited budget, he guided the team to two Isthmian League Play-Off finals, two appearances in the first round of the FA Cup, winning the London Senior Cup three times and being runners-up on four occasions; winning the Isthmian League Cup in 2014–15 and winning the Middlesex Senior Cup in 2017–18 and being runners-up in 2008–09. He was given a testimonial by the club in 2015, when Hendon beat a QPR XI 4–3. He left in the summer of 2018 to join Hampton and Richmond.

Middlesex Charity Cup

The Middlesex Charity Cup is the second of the two senior cup competitions run by the Middlesex County FA. However, unlike the Middlesex Senior Cup, on two occasions we have played the Final at Wembley Stadium. The two matches could hardly have come in more different circumstances and – technically – they were not the same competition.

Golders Green FC was in its penultimate campaign under that name when it made its first official visit to Wembley. The club had been there before, playing a friendly when the stadium was being tested out, but the Middlesex FA decided to hold its 1944–45 Red Cross Cup Final at the venue. Previously the Charity Cup, it would revert to its better-known name once the Second World War was over. On 10 March 1945, Golders Green beat another Green, Wood Green Town, 8–0, with Mervyn Griffiths grabbing a hat-trick. A month later, in the quarter-final, Finchley played out a 0–0 draw at Claremont Road, before falling 3–0 to the Green at Summers Lane. That set up a semi-final against Wealdstone on 5 May, when Griffiths, R Halton and Alan Cochrane were on target as Golders Green won 3–2. The following week's *Hendon Times* headline was: "WE WIN! WE WIN!! WE WIN!!!". I am sure that this was our local paper's reaction to the victory at Lower Mead, though the end of the hostilities in Europe might have occupied their minds a little more. The final on 16 May, was the most local of derbies, given that Tufnell Park were Golders Green's Claremont Road tenants.

The final was the last of three for the Green in 1944–45, Barnet having won the Herts & Middlesex League Cup 3–2 and Southall the Middlesex Senior Cup 3–1. There was no mistake at Wembley as George Bucci and Cochrane were in unstoppable form. In the 15th minute, Roy Stroud fed Griffiths, who set up Cochrane for the opening goal. Five minutes later, Griffiths and Cochrane combined and it was Bucci who made it 2–0. Bucci grabbed his second goal three minutes into the second half, heading home a Stroud cross. Although Tufnell Park pulled a goal back after 75 minutes, Cochrane sealed the victory with his second goal, five minutes from time, set up by the excellent Griffiths.

Fast forward to the 1987–88 season, when the Middlesex Charity Cup was sponsored by Middlesex non-league doyen Russell Grant – better known as a television astrologer. He arranged for the final of the Charity Cup to be at Wembley Stadium, as part of a Middlesex Football Festival. The date was Thursday 2 June 1988, the opening day of the first cricket Test match of the summer, England versus West Indies. I took a day off work to watch the morning and afternoon sessions with friends in a pub before we made our way to the stadium. To reach the final, Hendon had beaten Haringey Borough 3–0 with two goals from Iain Dowie and one from Neil Wolstenholme and Hayes 1–0, Dowie scoring again, in the quarter-final. The semi-final against Finchley at Claremont Road was close until the Finches' centre-half Rory Gleeson broke his arm when landing badly in the penalty area. Dermot Drummy's opener was cancelled out by a goal from Jason Dale before Wolstenholme and Dowie, with two, finished off the troubled Finchley.

Wembley FC were Hendon's final opponents, this after they had gone to Griffin Park, Brentford and come through in a 2–1 upset. Three players stood out for Wembley at Griffin Park, all former Hendon men, Henry Pacquette, Dereck Brown and Sylvester Williams – two others, Adrian Smith and Paul Bhatia also played. Browne worked as a Number 7 bus driver at the time and could not get away to train with the Lions, but he still started in the final while Williams and Pacquette were given places only the bench. Hendon's only selection issue was giving Colin Tate the start at Mick Kiely's expense and Dave Robotham was preferred as a substitute ahead of Steve Shea. Hendon fans made up the majority of the 3,715 crowd and serenaded the Wembley fans with "You're supposed to be at home." The surroundings, more imposing than Vale Farm, and Hendon did enough to stop Wembley.

The programmes from the 1945 and 1988 Finals.

Hendon forced four corners in the first six minutes and opened the scoring in the 19th minute when Phil Gridelet sent Dermot Drummy clear and his cross was turned into the net by Dowie. Brown caused Hendon a few problems, but Dave Root was equal to everything that came his way. Then, with four minutes remaining, Drummy broke clear and shot past Jeff Fanner to seal the 2–0 win. It would be Hendon's last match at the old Wembley stadium and for veterans Alan Campbell and Roger Wade, glory under the Twin Towers was especially sweet.

Looking overall at our participation in the Middlesex FA's second most important competition, our record as Hampstead Town, Golders Green and Hendon is very good, winning it 14 times in the seasons between 1912–13 and 1992–93. Hampstead Town stepped up to senior status in 1912, allowing the club to enter not only the FA Cup and FA Amateur Cup, but also the London Senior, Middlesex Senior and Middlesex Charity Cups. Their first match in the Middlesex Charity Cup was on 26 October 1912, a 5–1 victory over Polytechnic FC, with Harry Pride bagging a hat-trick. The club made an immediate impression, reaching the Final – its first as a senior club, but Uxbridge Town prevailed 2–1, with Ollie Sumner scoring Town's goal. It was not until 1922 that the Town won the Cup for the first time, avenging previous season's 3–1 loss to Botwell Mission (later Hayes FC) with a 2–1 victory, the goals coming from S. Howard and H. White. Hampstead reached three more finals in the 1920s, losing twice to the Missioners but in 1927, Hampstead shared the trophy with Barnet after a 3–3 draw in the final, Harry Shearcroft, G. H. Smith and George Howell scoring.

165

It was as Golders Green, in 1936, that the Middlesex Charity Cup was won outright for a second time. In the final against London Caledonians, Bert Broadis and Mike Fallon were the scorers in a 2–0 victory. As outlined above, the Charity Cup was renamed the Red Cross Cup during the War years, when, in 1945, the Green beat Tufnell Park at Wembley Stadium. The last match played by Golders Green was the 1946 Middlesex Charity Cup Final, a 3–2 victory over Southall at Brentford's Griffin Park. Mervyn Griffiths with two and Ron Mitchell were the Green's scorers. Hendon completed the club's hat-trick of successes with a comprehensive 5–0 victory over Southall at a ground the club always enjoyed success – Arsenal's Highbury Stadium. Due to the bad winter, the match was played as late as 7 June 1947 and a small crowd watched Bill Reay net a hat-trick and Roy Stroud a double. Stroud was Hendon's hero 11 months later, as the club won its fourth consecutive Charity Cup. In a very close final against Hayes, Mac Cochrane gave the Greens a lead, only for the Missioners to take a 2–1 lead, before Bob Avis levelled matters. Dominant in extra-time, it was Stroud who scored the winner.

Hendon were winners twice in the 1950s, in 1954 and 1957. John Core got the only goal of the former Final, netting in extra time after a goalless 90 minutes against Southall at Hayes. It was a dramatic affair with goalkeeper Don Archer suffering an eye injury early in the second half, forcing Colin Edwards to take the gloves, and Ron Stanton also getting hurt. With no substitutes in those days, the injured players remained on the pitch, but were little more than passengers. Three years later, Southall again provided the opposition, and it was the Greens who again triumphed after extra time. Jimmy Quail opened the scoring, Roy Thomas made it 2–2 in the second half and Tommy Lawrence and Miles Spector netted in the extra 30 minutes.

The 1960s was a barren Charity Cup decade for Hendon, but the club was frying much bigger fish in that era. Three victories in four seasons 1976–79 signalled a return to the Greens' domination. At home in both games in 1976, the Greens needed extra-time in the semi-final – Mike Gatting netted a 118th-minute winner against Finchley – and in the final against Wembley, with Tony Field curling home a free-kick. Uxbridge were beaten 2–0, also at Claremont Road in 1977, thanks to goals from Alan Campbell and Rod Haider. The victory over Harrow Borough in 1979 was much more comprehensive, 3–1 at Earlsmead, with Haider, Graeme Stewart and Roy Butler netting for the Greens.

Hendon's victory in the 1984–85 final, 5–1 at home to Feltham was notable for the debut of Phil Gridelet and that two Hendon players suffered broken noses in challenges. An early replacement for John Palmer, Gridelet so needled the Feltham team that Kelvin McDonough was dismissed for ending Paul Robinson's involvement, an offence seen

166

by a linesman. Martin Coates, two, Gary Allen, George Duck and Bob O'Leary scored the Hendon goals, Mike Strzadala having pulled a goal back soon after McDonough's expulsion.

The last victory was the one at Wembley in 1988, and the Greens entered the competition only five times more. The final match, against Yeading in 1992–93, saw Hendon cede home advantage and lose 2–0 at The Warren. It was a disappointing end to an 80-year involvement in the competition.

Hendon's results in the final (Hendon scores first):

Season	Opponents	Score	Venue
1912–13	Uxbridge	1–2	Staines
1920–21	Botwell Mission	1–3	Brentford FC
1921–22	Botwell Mission	2–1	Brentford FC
1925–26	Botwell Mission	3–4	Southall FC
1926–27	Barnet[†]	3–3	Brentford FC
1928–29	Botwell Mission*	0–1	Brentford FC
1929–30	Wealdstone	1–3 (aet)	Brentford FC
1930–31	Wealdstone	2–3	Finchley FC
1932–33	Hayes	2–3	Wealdstone FC
1933–34	Hayes	1–2	Brentford FC
1935–36	London Caledonian	2–0	Finchley FC
1937–38	Wealdstone	0–4	A
1939–40	Wealdstone	1–4	A
1944–45	Tufnell Park	4–1	Wembley Stadium
1945–46	Southall**	3–2	Brentford FC
1946–47	Southall	5–0	Arsenal FC
1947–48	Hayes	3–2	Wealdstone FC
1952–53	Hounslow	1–2	Hayes FC
1953–54	Southall	1–0	Hayes FC
1956–57	Southall	4–2 (aet)	Hayes FC
1957–58	Finchley	1–2	H
1975–76	Wembley	1–0 (aet)	H
1976–77	Uxbridge	2–0	H
1977–78	Hillingdon Borough	0–1	A
1978–79	Harrow Borough	3–1	A
1981–82	Uxbridge	1–2	A
1984–85	Feltham	5–1	H
1987–88	Wembley	2–0	Wembley Stadium

[†] Cup shared after match was drawn
* Botwell Mission FC became Hayes FC in 1929
** Last match as Golders Green FC

Middlesex Senior Cup

The Middlesex Senior Cup is the competition the club has entered and won more than any other. Needless to say (but I'll do it anyway), there have been many memorable moments and matches over the years.

Hampstead Town gained senior status in 1912, a season after they had entered the London and Middlesex Leagues. As well as the Amateur and FA Cups, Town entered both the London and Middlesex County senior competitions – they lost their first tie in the FA, Amateur and London Senior Cups – but there was success in the Middlesex Charity Cup before, on 16 November 1912, Wood Green provided Hampstead with their first Senior Cup opposition. Henry Pennifer scored twice, Oscar Sumner and Harry Pride were all on target as Hampstead won 4–1. Two months later, 2nd Battalion Grenadier Guards ended Town's interest 2–1, with G Heeley on the mark for Hampstead.

In 1925, Hampstead reached the Middlesex Senior Cup final for the first of 28 times. The club was unfortunate that they had already agreed to undertake an international tour to Belgium over the Easter period and almost all the first team was out of the country when Southall won 5–0 at Brentford's Griffin Park. In 1931, Hayes were Hampstead's Final opponents, at Wealdstone, and the Missioners – Amateur Cup finalists – won 4–1 with Bill Morton scoring the Hampstead goal. At the third time of asking, in 1934, Golders Green won the Middlesex Senior Cup, the victory coming against Park Royal at Brentford. An own goal and one from Freddie Evans gave the Green a 2–0 victory. In 1939, Green won the Cup for a second time, crushing Wealdstone 4 –0 at Summers Lane, Finchley FC. Jock Ellison, Fred Boston, Bob Thomas and Billy Breagan were the men on target.

Photo: A souvenir of the 1964–65 season.
(Photo: Peter Lush)

There was one more Final before Golders Green became Hendon, a wartime appearance in 1945 against Southall at Wealdstone, when Mac Cochrane's goal was topped by a trio from Southall.

Two years later, in 1947, Hendon lost the Senior Cup Final at Tottenham's White Hart Lane stadium, going down to a solitary goal from Enfield. From the mid-1950s, Hendon played in five finals in six seasons, winning in 1956 – beating Wembley 2–1 at Wealdstone, Dave Roden and Jeff Darey scoring – 1958 with Jimmy Quail, two, Tommy Lawrence and Miles Spector netting in a 4–0 defeat of Enfield at Finchley and 1960 Enfield being beaten 2–1, both scored by Jimmy Quail, also at Finchley. On their way to losing 1–0 to Hounslow Town at Wealdstone in 1957, Hendon set a club record by routing Wingate 13–1 at Claremont Road, with Miles Spector's four goals trumped by five from Tommy Lawrence. Jackie Rawlings with two, Douglas Orr and Peter Terry got the others.

Hendon, the dominant amateur club in the country in 1964–65, completed their Isthmian League, Amateur Cup and Middlesex Senior Cup treble with a 1–0 victory at Finchley, thanks to a Peter Slade goal. Two years later, the County Cup final had become a two-legged affair and Hendon overcame Enfield 3–2 on aggregate, the Claremont Road second leg ending 2–0, with Danny Lakey and Tony Harding the marksmen. The Middlesex Senior Cup final record for consecutive appearances is five, and Hendon's achievement of the feat came between 1971 and 1975, starting with a two-legged loss to Enfield in 1971, 0–1 and 0–2, and ending with a 1–0 replay defeat at the hands of Staines Town at Wealdstone. In 1972, John Connell and John Baker in the first leg, Bobby Childs, Rod Haider and Tony Bass were the scorers as Hendon beat Hampton 2–1 and 3–0. Twelve months later, Bass, Fred Pudney and Childs won a replay 3–0 against Enfield after 1–1 and 2–2 draws. Edgware Town made it to the 1974 Middlesex Final, and Hendon made it three in a row, winning 3–1 and 1–0. In those three winning two-legged finals, and five players appeared in all seven matches, John Baker, Peter Deadman, Rod Haider, Alan Phillips and John Swannell, while Gary Hand played in six. In the ensuing 25 years, only Colin Tate's extra-time double to see off Southall 2–0 at Southbury Road, Enfield in 1986, was enough for Hendon to win the Cup.

However, in January 1978, Hendon produced an amazing comeback to defeat Hampton 4–3 at Claremont Road. The Greens had been a model of inconsistency, following six defeats and two draws in eight matches with four straight wins, when the Beavers visited Hendon. With 10 minutes left, it was 3–1 to Hampton, but George Brooks, scorer of Hendon's first goal, was bundled over in the box. "Because I am smaller than most, I get knocked over more easily," he admitted after the game, and Tony Field converted from 12 yards.

Hampton panicked and Hendon struck twice more, through Field, again, and Alan Campbell to win 4–3. The run ended in the final at Summers Lane, Finchley, where Enfield triumphed 2–0.

There was no trophy at the end of the 1986–87 Middlesex Senior Cup campaign, either, but the quarter-final saga with Harrow Borough was very special. After a mundane goalless draw at Claremont Road on 3 February 1987, the tie went to a replay, played two weeks later at Earlsmead. After 90 minutes, the score was 1–1, Dermot Drummy scored for the Greens. Borough scored in extra time to set up a last-four tie against Hayes. However, in the intervening two weeks, Borough signed two players from Wales and the club checked with the County FA to see if they were eligible. Incorrectly, Borough were told both were eligible, though the rules said otherwise. Hendon appealed and the match was declared void but, because Harrow had been permitted to play the players by a County FA official, a replay was ordered. Harrow appealed and eventually lost, by which time six weeks had passed. A new date was set, Tuesday 7 April, but the match was postponed because of a waterlogged pitch and it was rearranged for two days later – with the semi-final being on the Saturday afternoon.

As Harrow seethed, they made Hendon pay and raced into a 3–0 half-time lead – Steve Emmanuel, Matt Loddy and Lawrence Holmes on target – it should have been four, but Mark Adams failed to convert a penalty. As the Hendon team came out for the second half, Greens fans were singing and cheering their heroes and Alan Roughan and Colin Tate felt even more honour-bound to give it a real go. Twenty-two seconds later, Roughan sent Tate through to make it 3–1 and the fightback was on. Neil Wolstenholme added a second a few minutes later and, within 15 minutes of the restart it was 3–3 thanks to Iain Dowie. Then a floodlight pylon went dark, but referee David Elleray was happy there was enough light to continue. There were no more goals until 37 seconds into the second period of extra-time, when Hendon took the lead through Drummy; Tate added another in the last couple of minutes to complete a 5–3 win. Forty-two hours later, the exhausted Greens lost 3–0 to Hayes.

In 1999, Hendon defeated Wembley in the Final at Southbury Road, Enfield FC. The match went to penalties and Gary McCann, after missing with his attempt – the ball was retrieved from outside the ground – produced a brilliant save to deny Avi Schwarz and Freddie Hyatt chipped the ball over the diving Keita Karamoko for the decisive spot-kick.

The 2001–02 Cup run, the first under Dave Anderson, was both exciting and prolific. The run began with a 5–0 demolition of Kingsbury Town at their Silver Jubilee Park home, Dale Binns and Byron Bubb being irrepressible attacking down the flanks. Both scored, as did Eugene Ofori, Davis Haule and Paul Fewings. In the next round, Staines

170

were beaten 5–0 at Claremont Road – the match had to be moved to Hendon – with Binns and Bubb on target again, and Ross Pickett, two, and Phil Ruggles also scoring.

But the best performance was the quarter-final hammering of Hayes at Church Road. The Conference club was not quite at full strength, but the Greens triumphed 5–1, with Ian Hodges (own goal), Ofori, Martin Randall, Ricci Crace and Steve Forbes Hendon's marksmen. In the semi-final, Steve Butler's goal gave Hendon a 1–0 win over Enfield Town. The final, at Hayes, saw Northwood give Hendon problems, but Randall bagged a double and Crace and Binns added two more as the Greens triumphed 4–2 after extra time. It was the start of a run of three consecutive victories in Middlesex Senior Cup, Hendon beating Enfield Town 2–0 (Crace and Ofori scoring) at Northwood in 2003 and Uxbridge 3–1, after extra time, at Yeading, with Randall and Dave Hunt getting the decisive goals in the additional 30 minutes after Ofori's second half opener. Six players, Binns, Butler, Mark Cooper, Crace, Ofori and Randall played in all three of the finals.

Since then, Hendon have played in only three more finals, going down 3–0 to Hampton & Richmond Borough at Uxbridge in 2007 and 2–0 to Brook House at Northwood two years later. The Greens' most recent Senior Cup success, however, came in 2017–18, when Staines Town were beaten 5–4 in a penalty shoot-out after a goalless 90 minutes at Uxbridge FC's Honeycroft ground. Tom Lovelock saved decisive penalty from Elliot Buchanan after the first nine had been converted. Both the quarter-final and semi-final results stood out. Spelthorne Sports were routed 9–1 at Silver Jubilee Park with on-loan striker Joe White (from Dagenham & Redbridge) equalling the club record with five goals (Ashley Nathaniel-George grabbed a hat-trick and Liam Gordon got the other). In the last four, also at SJP, Hendon achieved their most recent victory over Football League opposition as Barnet were beaten 2–0 thanks to efforts from Harly Wise and Harold Joseph.

All in all, the club has started 296 Middlesex Senior Cup ties (against 56 opponents) in the 101 competitions since 1912. Two matches, however, were declared void because of inadvertent breaches of rules (the Harrow match, above, and a game against Southall which was decided in extra time, but the rules demanded a replay after a drawn 90 minutes) and five matches were abandoned, three after the 90 minutes were up (they, like the void games, count as completed fixtures). Hendon's overall record is:

Played 294   Lost 84
Won 169   For 668 goals
Drawn 38   Against 385 goals.

Seven of the draws went to penalty shoot-outs, of which Hendon won five and lost two and 27 matches ended all square after 90 minutes, including void and abandoned matches.

Middlesex Wanderers

Middlesex Wanderers developed in the Richmond area in the early twentieth century. Founded in 1905, and becoming Middlesex Wanderers in 1912. The club promoted football through international tours. It was founded by the Alaway Brothers, and later played for the Brothers Alaway Memorial Trophy. The club still exists today, although the nature of it has changed slightly, and it is now involved in veterans football as well as tours.

Hendon have links with the club in two ways. More than 50 Hendon players have played for Middlesex Wanderers at football, and Arthur Phebey was involved in a cricket tour to the Channel Islands in 1947. Hendon have also played the Wanderers three times for the Brothers Alaway Memorial Trophy. On 29 August 1960, the Wanderers won 2–1, on 23 November 1965 the teams drew 4–4, and on 18 March 1984, the Wanderers won 5–2.

The club grew from its original Richmond base, and from 1912 selected players from Middlesex. The first Hampstead Town player selected for the Wanderers was a C. Jones who was involved in a tour to France in April 1912. He also captained the Wanderers in 1914 on a tour to the Netherlands. Arthur Humphreys was also selected in 1912, along with a William Guscott, who the Wanderers club history says also played for Hampstead Town. Most of the players in the 1912 touring party played for more senior clubs than Hampstead Town. And at this time, and until 1974, when amateur status was abolished, only amateur players were selected. In November 1913, a Walter Guscott toured the Netherlands, along with C. Jones, who was now playing for the Civil Service FC. Establishing club affiliations for players at this time is difficult, and some of these players are not listed on the Hendon FC website.

After the First World War, when Hampstead Town joined the Athenian League, the club's players were selected by the Wanderers more regularly. Harold Pease played for them between 1922 and 1932, and was captain of a tour to the Channel Islands in April 1927. A.T. Anderson was also in that squad along with players from Tottenham Hotspur and the Stock Exchange. Cecil Wise, Hampstead's first England international, does not seem to have played for the club, nor does

Freddie Evans. Indeed, very few Hampstead or Golders Green players were selected by the Wanderers in the 1930s. Their club history does say that F. Swan toured the Netherlands as a Golders Green player, but he is not mentioned on the Hendon FC website. Gradually the Wanderers widened their base for selection of players, with those from the north of England now involved.

As Hendon's status grew after the Second World War, so more of the club's players represented the Wanderers. Roy Stroud toured the Netherlands in May 1949, and Laurie Topp visited the same country five months later. Most of the club's leading players from the 1950s and 1960s played for Middlesex Wanderers. The Wanderers club history says that nine of the team that won the Amateur Cup in 1972 had played for Middlesex Wanderers. John Swannell captained three Wanderers tours, and was their "Wanderer of the Year" in 1968.

After the game went open in 1974, the Wanderers decided to change their selection policy, and pick players from any club. The number of Hendon players involved fell, although Dermot Drummy was selected in 1981, and Barry Blackman in 1993. Another problem for the Wanderers was that if players were under contract to their club, they had to be given permission to tour, which was not an issue in the amateur era.

One reason that some of the top amateurs of the post-war period up to 1974 did not turn professional was the opportunity for international tours that the semi-professional game did not offer. Many players enjoyed trips abroad with the Middlesex Wanderers set up, and the club also played a positive role in promoting football around the world. The most Hendon players on any tour was four. In 1964, Gerry O'Rourke, John Swannell, Jimmy Quail and Roy Sleap toured Iceland, along with Bobby Cantwell who was on the verge of joining Hendon. The club was a significant part of the development and history of amateur football in Britain and Hendon players were involved from 1912 to 1993.

N

New Grounds

Newcastle United

Northern awaydays

New Grounds

There are two types of new ground to football fans – to state the obvious – those a supporter has never previously visited and those which are either opening for the first time or have been completely redeveloped on an adjacent site.

On 29 July 2016, Hendon became the first team to play at the redeveloped Hayes & Yeading United ground on Beaconsfield Road, which was the former home of Yeading before they merged with Hayes in 2007. To get to that stage had been a tale of woe for H&YU fans because after leaving their Church Road ground, formerly of Hayes, they became homeless for a number of seasons. Their groundshare was anything but local, with first Woking and then Maidenhead United their landlords.

When Hendon arrived at the new stadium last July, it was immediately clear that not all was ready for football at their level. Hendon won 2–0, but the result was secondary for the hosts. After a few games, the club's safety licence was withdrawn and they spent most of 2016–17 playing elsewhere, including one game at Silver Jubilee Park and others at Uxbridge and Beaconsfield.

IN 2014, Hendon were the second team to visit Barnet for a friendly – it was at The Hive due to heavy rain leaving Harrow Borough's pitch too wet to be risked for a pre-season fixture. The Hive was a magnificent place to visit and Hendon did have a slight delay because, during the second half, there was a sharp shower at one end of the pitch as the sprinklers suddenly came to life. They left goalkeeper Mike McEntegart a rather forlorn and soggy figure. For the record, Barnet, just relegated from League Two and managed by Edgar Davids, who was not at the match, won 4–1 with Anthony Thomas getting the Greens' goal.

The last club Hendon visited who opened their ground for our visit in a competitive match was back on 3 October 1992, Dulwich Hamlet at the new Champion Hill. Hendon had the honour of scoring the first ever goal at the ground, Gary Donnellan smashing a 20-yarder into the bottom corner. Lionel Best ruined the Greens' day and made Hamlet's with an inspired second half display which led to Dulwich winning 2–1.

In 2017–18, in Bostik League games, Hendon visited two new grounds. The club has never played Brightlingsea, even in a friendly, so the visit to the Taydal Stadium was a first and a late missed penalty meant it was a losing one. The other new venue was the home of Dorking Wanderers – the one at Westhumble. This was a much happier trip, resulting in a 3–0 win despite finishing with 10 men.

There is a nice story about Brightlingsea's ground. In 2014, still playing at step 5, Regent reached the last 32 of the FA Vase and even

175

though the game against Bodmin was in doubt because of bad weather, club officials bought a new stand for the match (more importantly, the stand was needed for the club to climb to step 4). The only slight problem was that the stand was on the Isle of Wight and club officials travelled across the Solent, put in on a low loader, sailed back to the mainland, drove home to Essex and, working through the night erected at their ground. There efforts were rewarded as a council official ruled the stand safe and the referee passed the pitch fit. Regent responded by winning 3–1, but they then lost Dunston UTS in the last 16. Brightlingsea went on to win their division and in 2017, won promotion from Ryman League Division One North.

The move to the Southern League in 2018 resulted in a large number of grounds being visited for the first time. Of the other 21 teams in the Premier Division South, the Greens paid their first visit to 11 of them: Weymouth (at Bob Lucas Stadium, having previously played twice at the Recreation ground), Poole Town, Kings Langley, Hartley Wintney, Swindon Supermarine, Beaconsfield Town (for a competitive senior fixture), Wimborne Town, Walton Casuals, Tiverton Town, Gosport Borough and Frome Town. The trips to both Merthyr Town and Salisbury were to grounds we had played before, but the clubs we met were new incarnations of what had been Methyr Tydfil and Salisbury City (some people mused that Merthyr could have simply added Town to their old name, but were unaware that the translation of Merthyr Tudful – to give its Welsh language spelling – is actually Merthyr Town!). In addition, in the FA Cup we visited both Lancing and Chippenham Town for the first time.

The 2019–20 Southern League Premier Division South comprised another five venues never previously visited for competitive fixtures, if Hayes & Yeading United's home is considered new: Blackfield & Langley, Hayes & Yeading United, Truro City, Weston-Super-Mare and Yate Town. As a comparison, when Hendon joined the Isthmian League from the Athenian League in 1963, the only two teams, out of 19, that had not been visited for competitive fixtures were Woking and Wycombe Wanderers – and the Greens had played friendlies at Loakes Park. Of course, it did help that many of the clubs had also been members of the Athenian League in the past. At the same time, those two clubs Maidstone United and Oxford City, were easily the longest League trips Hendon undertook – far cries from Truro, Tiverton, Taunton, Dorchester and Merthyr in the far-flung Southern League.

Newcastle United

The biggest match in Hendon's history was the 1974 FA Cup third round tie against Newcastle United. The Greens certainly didn't have the most taxing of paths to the last 64 of the 1973–74 FA Cup, receiving byes before beating Southern League Barnet in the fourth qualifying round and Merthyr Tydfil in the second round proper. In between, fellow Isthmians Leytonstone were downed in round one. The tie with Barnet needed a replay after a 2–2 draw at Underhill and, second time around, Roger Connell bagged a hat-trick before stepping on the ball and breaking his ankle. Leytonstone came to Claremont Road having already played six matches since the first qualifying round, but their run ended as the Greens came away with another 3–0 success, John Baker and Keiron Somers with two, getting the goals.

Hendon's reward was a trip to the Welsh valleys where Merthyr Tydfil awaited. Former Leeds United legend and Wales international John Charles – one of the finest players of his era – was in the Martyrs' squad, but Somers, John Baker and, maybe appropriately, Welsh international Alan Phillips all scored as Hendon advanced 3–0. When Hendon revisited Penydaren Park to take on Merthyr Town in early 2019, members of their board recalled the game with both fondness and disappointment, one saying, "We were professional and Hendon were amateur so we thought it would be an easy win for us. But we were wrong and you completely outplayed us."

The draw was made as the coaches were heading back towards the border and the drivers deserve some credit for keeping their vehicles on the road when Newcastle United came out of the draw immediately before Hendon. The game was to be played at St James' Park on 5 January 1974. There was drama as the players left Claremont Road, the day before the game, when it was realised that a players had forgotten his contact lenses. That was sorted out and the Hendon team was John Swannell, Tony Jennings, Gary Hand, Peter Deadman, Alan Phillips, Rod Haider, Derek Baker, Bobby Childs, John Baker, Keiron Somers and Phil Fry, with Mickey Cooper the substitute (only one in those days).

In front of a crowd of 31,606 – the biggest ever for a Hendon match in England not at Wembley – Tommy Craig hit the Hendon bar early in the game, and Hendon's best first half chance fell to Fry, who was thwarted by a brilliant Liam McFaul save. Just before the break, a long throw-in from Malcolm McDonald was converted by centre-half Pat Howard. Hendon felt it was a soft goal.

Midway through the second half, Hendon, having weathered strong Newcastle pressure, found themselves back on level terms. Just like the Magpies' goal, it was a set move: Jennings curled in a free-kick, John Baker headed the ball on and Haider, arriving late, swept the ball into the net. Late in the game, another set move saw Derek Baker denied by McFaul, but the plan was for the ball to reach Haider, who felt he would certainly have scored.

The replay kicked off at 1.45pm at Watford's Vicarage Road ground. This was during a power crisis and electricity cuts, so the floodlighting could not be used – Hendon, later in the season, borrowed a generator to play midweek matches. Even though the game was played on a Wednesday afternoon in the working week – one day after Barnet schools went back after the Christmas holidays – the crowd was around 15,000. Tommy Cassidy replaced Jimmy Smith for Newcastle, and he made a big difference, while the only Hendon change was fit-again Roger Connell replacing Mickey Cooper on the bench.

Newcastle got the early goal they craved as a pass from midfield released the pacey Malcolm McDonald. The linesman's flag went up, but against John Tudor, not McDonald and after "Supermac" had fired past John Swannell, the referee allowed the goal to stand, much to Hendon's chagrin. Early in the second half, Somers had a good chance to equalise, but he put his header from a Bobby Childs corner over the bar. Having escaped the scare, Newcastle soon put the game beyond Hendon's reach. Terry Hibbett scored with a powerful long-range drive and, five minutes later, Gary Hand made a spectacular save to earn himself a booking – the story goes that the referee complimented him on the save as he took his name. It was in the days before cards and dismissals for professional fouls. Terry McDermott converted the penalty and, with 12 minutes to go, John Tudor, considered by Peter Deadman to have been far more of a handful than McDonald, scored a fourth goal.

Hendon went on to win the Middlesex Senior Cup, but went out in the third round of the FA Amateur Cup, despite playing nine ties against Harwich & Parkestone, Tilbury and Leatherhead. The FA Cup and Amateur Cup runs and the power crisis combined to leave Hendon with massive fixture congestion. In the end it was just too much for the Greens to overcome and they finished a couple of points behind champions Wycombe Wanderers. It would be 41 years before Hendon finished as high as second again.

Newcastle, meanwhile, breathed a huge sigh of relief that they didn't suffer a second exit in three seasons against Non-League opposition having lost to Hereford United in 1972. In fact, they played another eight matches in an FA Cup run that ended in a 3–0 defeat against Liverpool in the Wembley Final. Scunthorpe United were despatched after a replay, West Bromwich Albion at the first attempt and then, controversially, Nottingham Forest in the quarter-final. The first match, at St James' Park was delayed by a major pitch invasion and the FA ordered the match to replayed at neutral Goodison Park, Everton, a match that ended in a goalless draw. The replay was also at Goodison and Newcastle won it 1–0 and the semi-final 2–0 against Burnley (at Sheffield Wednesday) before being dismantled by Bill Shankly's Reds.

Northern awaydays

The cut-off point for this piece on the club's matches in the north is 180 miles from London, essentially anywhere in Cheshire, Lancashire, Yorkshire and further north, so Lincolnshire, Staffordshire, Nottinghamshire and Derbyshire are not included. The other criterion is that it has to be a competitive game, including the Will Mather Cup.

The first northern trip was by Hampstead Town in 1926 for an FA Amateur Cup third round (last 16) tie to take on Ferryhill Athletic at their Darlington Road ground. Hampstead were brushed aside clinically by Ferryhill, who won 4–0 before losing to St Albans City in the quarter-final. Sadly, the club left Ferryhill and went out of business in 2006. Golders Green never made a northern trip, but Hendon made the club's second trip to the north-east in 1949, another last-16 game in the Amateur Cup, this time away to Billingham Synthonia. Roy Stroud did score for the Greens, but Billingham got two goals. In their only quarter-final, Synthonia (synthetic ammonia, as manufactured in the town by its largest employer, Imperial Chemical Industries – ICI) entertained Romford and the Essex team prevailed 2–1. The Greens continued to struggle on their longest travels, losing again in 1952, this time in an FA Amateur Cup second round replay against Bishop Auckland. The first game at Claremont Road ended 1–1, Stroud again scoring for Hendon, but the return ended 5–1 to the Bishops, despite Dexter Adams's goal.

A northern victory was finally achieved at Hallam in 1959, when Roy Thomas scored the only goal in Yorkshire. Twelve months later, Hendon visited the first world champions, West Auckland Town in the Amateur Cup quarter-final, and came away with a 1–1 draw, Terry Howard scoring. This was the year when Hendon won the Cup for the first time and Miles Spector and Brian Figg booked the Greens' semi-final berth.

For more than a decade in the 1960s and 70s the club had a good relationship with Whitley Bay, though they were probably sick at the sight of Hendon. In an Amateur Cup quarter-final at Hillheads Park in 1965, Peter Slade and a David Hyde double gave the Greens a 3–1 victory. Both teams reached the last four in 1966, and when they were paired together, the venue chosen was Roker Park, Sunderland. Roy Sleap and Geoff Riddy got the goals to seal a 2–1 Hendon victory and third FA Amateur Cup final appearance. Hendon also met Whitley Bay for the Will Mather Cup five times, three times at Claremont Road, all Hendon wins, and twice in the north-east. On the first of these, Bay won 2–0, but Hendon won what remains the most recent encounter, 3–1 in 1983, with Dermot Drummy, Billy Macmillan and Stan Alexander scoring. The players were in such a hurry to spend the night on the town that they left the trophy on a settee in the bar. Luckily, a couple

179

of Hendon fans – I was one of them – spotted it and we carried the trophy back through the town to the team's hotel.

In 1969, Hendon thought the hard part was done with a 1–1 draw at North Shields, but Bobby Wilson's goal was the Greens' only one of the tie because the replay ended 2–0. A year later Hendon were involved in a saga with Evenwood Town which took four Saturdays to resolve. The first trip to the north-east ended in an abandonment because of fog, the freezing variety. Some Hendon fans still recall the Evenwood goalkeeper being unaware the match had been suspended.

A week later, frost caused a postponement even before the supporters had left NW2. John Baker got our goal in the match a week later, but it ended 1–1. In the replay, Hendon were unforgiving hosts, as Bobby Wilson, Rod Haider, Peter Anderson and Paul Collett all scored in a 4–2 win. Blyth Spartans ended the Greens' run as Amateur Cup holders in 1973, when they won 1–0 at Claremont Road, this after Tony Bass had earned the Greens a 1–1 draw in what proved to be Hendon's final northern trip in the Amateur Cup.

Newcastle apart, our only Lancashire trip in the FA Cup was in November 1999, when Hendon were far the better team against Blackpool, but went down 2–0. The club has made three northern trips in the FA Trophy, losing 1–0 away to Witton Albion in 1982, and falling to a late own goal to lose 2–1 in a replay at Barrow in 1988, Iain Dowie having scored at Claremont Road, and Alan Campbell netting at Holker Street. The club's last trip north came in 2003, to Belle Vue, the – very brief – home of Wakefield & Emley FC. Hendon fans were allowed to watch the first half from an executive box behind the posts (sorry, goal) at the famous rugby league ground. Hendon were dragged into a battle which ended 10 (for the Greens) against nine, but without goals. The replay ended 1–0 to the Yorkshiremen. The club's record in 18 competitive matches in the north – including the Evenwood abandonment – is: four wins, six draws, seven defeats, 14 goals scored and 25 conceded.

O

Andy O'Brien

Eugene Ofori

The Olympic Games

Leyton Orient

Internationals – Other

Oxford

Andy O'Brien

Andy O'Brien gave long and distinguished service to Hendon. He had three spells at the club, first as a youngster, then as a veteran coming back twice to help out his old club at a time of need. He joined Hendon as an 18-year-old and played in the reserves in the first part of the season before making his debut four days after the Greens had lost to Wycombe Wanderers in an FA Cup first round replay. Ken Payne's team was made up of vastly experienced players at various levels – Fred Smart, Gary Hand, Peter Deadman, Pat Morrisey, Bobby Gough, Paul Currie – and youngsters – Anthony Bennett, O'Brien, Dermot Drummy, Alan Cosby and Tom Murphy. Only mid-20s Kevin Folan didn't fit into either category. It was a losing start for Andy, a 1–0 reverse at Colston Avenue, but he got another chance when replacing the injured Bennett for a New Year's fixture against Harrow Borough, a 2–0 Greens victory.

When (high-priced) senior players were released in February 1982, a number of younger ones were given the chance to shine. None took the opportunity more successfully than Andy. He scored his first Hendon goal in just his fourth appearance, a Middlesex Senior Cup win at Southall. He became a cornerstone at the heart of an inexperienced Hendon defence managed by Dave Mawson, then Gary Hand in 1982–83, missing just four League games all season. Andy's performances earned him the first of three Supporters Association Player of the Year awards. This era was notable for Hendon changing managers on an almost annual basis and the 1983–84 man in charge was Roy Ruffell, who knew a good thing when he saw it – and that included Andy in the No.5 shirt. What was more remarkable was that Andy was studying at Nottingham University and he commuted from the north Midlands to play for the Greens.

This dedication no doubt played a part in Andy winning his second Supporters Association Player of the Year award in 1985, a season which saw the Greens struggle to avoid relegation under first Eddie Presland, then Gary Hand. Hendon won the Middlesex Charity Cup, beating Feltham in the final at Claremont Road and Andy collected his first cup-winners' medal. This time Gary was able to continue as manager in 1985–86, but it was not a happy time and relegation would have been a certainty, if he had stayed beyond December. Instead Ted Hardy engineered a miraculous recover, and Andy more than played his part, contributing goals in massive victories at Worthing (when John Still had a game on the coaching staff), Billericay and Slough. He collected a second – and last cup-winner's medal when Southall were beaten 2–0 in the Middlesex Senior Cup final.

In 1986–87, Andy's chances were limited and after 14 appearances, he left, joining Wembley early in 1987. It was almost exactly three years before Andy returned to Claremont Road, and his second debut came in the FA Trophy, a 2–1 defeat at Wivenhoe Town. He slotted straight back into the Hendon defence, normally at centre-half, and started 83 of the next 86 games (for which he was eligible) in the following 16 months, including all 61 in the 1990–91 season. Off the field, things were going rapidly downhill for Hendon, but Andy had already left the club for a second time – and this time he was away for four seasons.

By the time Andy returned in 1995, Mick Browne was starting his second season as manager, the second year of the club's ownership by Ivor Arbiter and the Arbiter Group. Andy was signed to help out with the reserves, but still be available for first team duty. As it turned out, once Neil Price had taken over in December 1995, Andy would be a regular and he played in 37 League and cup games during a campaign which once again saw a battle against relegation.

Andy was promoted to reserve team manager for the 1995–96 season, but when Price left Hendon in mid-February, Andy was made first-team player manager. His debut in dugout was a 2–1 defeat of Kingstonian at Claremont Road – a Price-less victory according to the local press – but he would be in charge for only a couple more matches before Frank Murphy took over. Andy made a handful of appearances in the season, but that ended his first-team career. Overall, he made 370 appearances, scoring 26 goals.

Since retiring Andy moved back to the Midlands, though is frequently down in London on family matters – his brother used to be the postman at Claremont Road – and watches the occasional Hendon match, when he will reminisce with fans who fondly remember cheering on a dedicated and loyal Hendon man.

Eugene Ofori

Dave Anderson was not at the game when Eugene Ofori made his first Hendon appearance, in a friendly at Claremont Road against Yeading in August 2001. Assistant manager Jon Turner, the former Yeading boss, took one look at the stocky striker, who had played in the Ghanaian top division as well as trialling with Watford, and nicknamed him "Yeboah", because of the physical similarities between Ghanaian compatriots Ofori and Tony Yeboah, then one of the most exciting strikers in the Premier League. He had also won under-21 honours for Ghana.

Eugene's debut was brief – and as a substitute – and he did not actually appear in a competitive match until late September, coming off the bench late in a 3–1 defeat against Canvey Island. For a player who scored a goal every 2.76 appearances, it is surprising that he failed to register until his 10th game, a Middlesex Senior Cup tie at Kingsbury

Town. Eugene also finished the season with an eight-game goalless run. He was used strangely in the campaign, coming off the bench 13 times in 28 League matches, but starting 11 of 12 cup-ties. But it was a successful season for Hendon in that there was silverware at the end of it in the shape of the Middlesex Senior Cup – Anderson's teams won the trophy in all three seasons he was Hendon manager. The first final was a thriller against Northwood, at Church Road, Hayes, and the Greens won 4–2 after extra-time. The following season, capped by a Middlesex Senior Cup victory over Enfield Town at Northwood, in which Eugene scored the decisive second goal just before half-time ,followed a similar pattern to 2001–02, because while Eugene was an almost ever-present in cup-ties – starting 13 times in 15 appearances – but 15 of his 35 League games were as a substitute. More importantly, he was a big contributor of goals, grabbing 17, four behind top-scorer Ricci Crace.

The best of Eugene's four seasons at Claremont Road was in 2003–04, when he averaged a goal every other game and appeared in 54 of the Greens' 57 games. He netted seven times in eight cup starts but more laudably managed 20 in the Ryman League, always a benchmark for a striker, irrespective of a season being 38, 42 or 46 matches. Eugene was again on target in the Middlesex Senior Cup final, grabbing the first goal in the 3–1 extra-time victory over Uxbridge at Yeading. In a spell of eight games from the first weekend of February to the first weekend in March, he scored eight times, helping Hendon to an unbeaten run of 16 matches. Hendon fans recognised Eugene's contributions and he was the easy winner of the Supporters Association's player of the year award. The Greens would have finished second if they had done better in their final four matches as they slipped from second to fourth in the table, but part of the dip in form could be attributed to the rumours surrounding the regarding Anderson's future – he would join AFC Wimbledon – and the promotion to the newly-formed Conference South.

It was all change in 2004–05 as 13 members of the Hendon playing and management staff moved to Kingsmeadow. More importantly the club decided not to take their place in the new second tier of Non-league football and had to find a new manager from outside, something that had not happened since March 1997. Tony Choules, from Northwood, was selected to take charge of team affairs and Eugene was one of the few players to remain loyal to Hendon. Although the season started well, things fell apart after the embarrassing FA Cup defeat at Stevenage Borough and Choules' immediate departure. Choules' assistant, Gary Farrell was the new manager and he oversaw a catastrophic January which saw exits from four cup competitions and 32 goals conceded. Farrell was sacked after three months as the Greens lurched towards relegation – they had been top of the table in September. Gary McCann became the third manager of the season on and he steadied the ship, seeing Hendon safely avoid relegation. Only goalkeeper Dave King and centre-back René Street made more than Eugene's 47 appearances, but Ofori's 14 goals were a distinct drop from the previous season. Hendon opened the 2005–06 season with a trip to Braintree Town. The Iron wasted little time in putting in an approach to sign Eugene, and his final Hendon goals before moving to Essex came in his penultimate appearance – a double in a famous 5–4 win at Wealdstone. He subsequently played for Chesham United and Northwood after his time at Braintree.

The Olympic Games

When there was much debate about a Great Britain football team playing in the London Olympic Games in 2012, it was generally forgotten that in the era of amateur football, a Great Britain team regularly entered the competition.

Hendon's first link with the Olympic team was in 1936. Bernard Joy, who played for the Casuals, and was the last amateur to captain the full England team, captained the team in their two matches in the Berlin Olympics. He had played twice for Hampstead and Golders Green. His son Chris played for Hendon in the 1960s.

In 1948, the Olympics was staged in London. Jack Rawlings, then playing for Enfield, played in the bronze medal play-off match. He later joined Hendon in 1955, and enjoyed three successful seasons at Claremont Road.

The next tournament was in 1952, in Helsinki. Laurie Topp played for Great Britain in their preliminary round 5–3 defeat to Luxembourg. Most of the players were from Isthmian League clubs, Finchley's George Robb was the only other Athenian League player. The players attended the opening ceremony which was staged after their only match. They had been surprised by the quality of the Luxembourg team.

For the 1956 tournament in Melbourne, Great Britain played qualifying matches against Bulgaria. Eric Beardsley played in the first match, a 2–0 defeat in Sofia. Laurie Topp returned to the team for the second match, a 3–3 draw at Wembley. However, various withdrawals from the tournament saw Great Britain take part. Mike Pinner, who played for Hendon in the early 1960s, played in the qualifying matches, but missed the main tournament through injury. Laurie Topp captained the team in a 9–0 win against Thailand, and a 6–1 defeat against Bulgaria. Dexter Adams was also in the squad, but was injured and flew home.

The 1960 Olympics was played in Rome. Again, there was a qualifying competition. Mike Pinner played in goal, and a young Ropy Sleap, then with Barnet, played in all four qualifying matches against The Republic of Ireland and the Netherlands. They were both in the squad for the finals, along with Hendon winger Terry Howard. The Great Britain team had their best results in an Olympic finals, losing 4–3 to Brazil, holding hosts Italy to a 2–2 draw and beating Formosa 3–2, with Howard making his debut. This was the last time until 2012 that a Great Britain team appeared in the finals.

The 1964 Games were in Tokyo. Great Britain beat Iceland 10–0 on aggregate, but then lost 5–3 over two matches to Greece. Jimmy Quail had been a reserve for the two matches against Iceland, but played against Greece at Stamford Bridge and in the second leg in Athens. Other players with Hendon connections included Enfield's Tommy Lawrence and Wealdstone's John Ashworth.

For the 1968 qualifying competition, Hendon had their biggest representation when John Swannell, David Hogwood, Roy Sleap and Rod Haider all played against West Germany, with the second leg at Claremont Road. A 2–0 win in Augsburg followed by a 1–0 defeat in the home match saw Great Britain through. Derek Gamblin, who later joined Hendon, also played, and Peter Deadman, then with Bakring, was a substitute. Swannell and Sleap both played against Spain in the next round, with Haider coming off the bench in the second match at White City. Great Britain lost 1–0 on aggregate.

In the spring of 1971, Great Britain faced Bulgaria – again – in the qualifying matches. In the first match at Wembley, in front of a 2,200 crowd, they won 1–0 with John Swannell in goal, Rod Haider in midfield and Peter Deadman on the bench. This was a remarkable result against a strong Bulgarian side. Paul Clements, who has played for Hendon in 1967 before moving to Skelmersdale, played in the second leg along with Swannell and Haider. Reality returned for Great Britain with a 5–0 defeat in front of 30,000 fans in Sofia.

The end of 'amateur' status in football in Great Britain meant that there were no further entries into the Olympics until 2012, when the team was made up mainly of under-23 professional players.

(Information from *GB United?* By Steve Menary)

Leyton Orient

One of the greatest nights in Hendon's history was Tuesday 25 November 1997, when the Greens beat Leyton Orient, in an FA Cup first round replay. A bye into the fourth qualifying round in 1997 gave the Greens only one team to beat to reach the competition proper for a second straight season. Two goals from Colin Simpson at Clarence

Park were enough for Hendon to defeat St Albans City 2–1 – until a few years ago, no team other than Hendon had ever beaten the Saints at Clarence Park in the last qualifying round. The draw, made live on television, barely half an hour after the final whistle, elicited massive cheers from the Hendon fans in the bar and a sickened silence from the hosts: "Hendon will play Leyton Orient."

The mind games began immediately, with Os chairman Barry Hearn offering Hendon money to switch the tie to Brisbane Road, promising a crowd in excess of 5,000; Hendon refused. An early kick-off on 15 November – it was an international weekend – did not stop 2,241 fans coming to Claremont Road. Hendon's line-up was, Gary McCann, John-Simon White, Simon Clarke, Paul Kelly, Richard Nugent, Steve Bateman, Steve Heard, Freddy Hyatt, Colin Simpson, Tony Kelly and Junior Lewis. On the bench were Matt Howard (who replaced Tony Kelly after an hour), Tony Lynch (on for Simpson after 81 minutes), and the unused Nas Bashir, Greg Tello – who later played for Leyton Orient in an international friendly against Wales at Brisbane Road – and goalkeeper Andy Lomas.

Carl Griffiths gave Orient a fourth-minute lead, which they held without too much difficulty until the 25th minute, when a clearance from former Hayes goalkeeper Paul Hyde was blocked by the thigh of Simpson and the ball looped into the net for the equaliser. Mark Smith restored the visitors' lead before half-time, but in the 55th minute, Simpson got in front of former Hendon defender Simon Clark and his header eluded Hyde before ending up in the net. It stayed 2–2, meaning the Greens got their game, albeit 10 days later, at the Matchroom Stadium, then the name of the Os' Brisbane Road ground.

More mind games came just before the replay. Orient boss Tommy Taylor put in a bid to sign Simpson, clearly trying to turn the striker's head. Simpson had only recently joined Hendon and was not under contract, but wanted to be part of the Greens' FA Cup run, so the offer was declined. There was an understanding it would be revisited once Hendon's FA Cup run was at an end. For the replay, Howard replaced Nugent in the starting line-up and Michael Banton, Curtis Warmington and Keiran Gallagher were named on the bench – the first two were used, but Gallagher, Lynch and Lomas did not play.

The Greens' hero at Brisbane Road was Gary McCann; the goalkeeper made a number of outstanding saves. It certainly helped Hendon's cause that Carl Griffiths, normally so prolific in taking chances, failed to do so when a number of clear-cut openings came his way. That said, it was not one-way traffic and the most inventive player on the pitch was Freddie Hyatt.   Then, with 18 minutes to go and the game still in a goalless deadlock, Hendon's former long-serving manager and his assistant combined in the set-up of Hendon's winner.

Left: The teams from the match programme.

McCann was quickly out to gather an overhit through ball and he immediately rolled it to Simon Clarke. Hyatt received Clarke's pass, produced an outrageous flick to lift the ball over Joe Baker, ran around the bemused midfielder and instantly sent a pass out to the right wing. John-Simon White raced onto the ball advanced to the middle of the Orient half – still out wide – and curled a cross into the penalty area. Simon Clark was the last defender, but he was not quick enough to reach the ball. Junior Lewis was ... and his flying header gave Hyde no chance of making a save.

I looked at my watch and there were 18 minutes to go, but time seemed to stand still and referee Martin Bodenham played about six hours of additional time – or so it seemed – but there was no way the Hendon defence was going to give up their advantage. The final whistle blew and the hundreds of Hendon fans, as well as all the players and Frank Murphy's management team went very noisily berserk.

Sitting in the press box, I was not allowed to cheer, until the Orient media manager congratulated me and said it was fine if I celebrated. I don't know how I had stayed calm and mainly quiet, but I did ... until I let out a whoop of joy that almost lifted the roof off the stand. Orient's fans did not take the result well, with loud chants demanding the removal of Taylor. I had to stay focused on my job as Hendon press officer and sort out Frank Murphy's side of the press conference, but I was aware that I was in an almost dreamlike trance. Asked to described my emotions by the editor of *The Kilburn Times*, who was also at the match, I described it as being in a state of "catatonic euphoria and wearing a beatific grin". He told me afterwards that he had never even seen catatonic euphoria written down – or beatific grin for that matter – but also admitted that it had been a pretty accurate assessment.

Three days later, I was still on a high from the result, but Hendon were brought down to earth by Carshalton Athletic on the Saturday – Paul Whitmarsh made his Greens' debut off the bench– losing 3–1. Hendon's Wembley dreams ended at Cardiff on 6 December and Simpson duly joined the Os, but nothing can away the glorious memories of that night in East London.

Internationals – Other

This piece covers full internationals who have represented countries other than England and also played for Hendon. I realise there have been many more than the ones below, including players for Wales, Scotland and Northern Ireland, as well as Great Britain in the Olympics, but these have interesting side stories to their international careers. There are many more players from the Caribbean and other CONCACAF nations in the piece about Jamaicans, but Hendon have two players who were or would be full internationals from the region.

In addition to Elliott Charles, two other Grenadian full internationals have appeared for Hendon, the Bubb brothers. Byron actually played, in a friendly, for a Hendon team in the Harrow Youth League, when he was 13 or 14. Millwall signed him and he played eight times in the Football League before returning to the Greens, aged 19, in 2001, under Dave Anderson. His free-kick to score against Enfield at Boreham Wood that season is still the most remarkable strike I have ever witnessed. The ball almost literally turning right before ending up in the side-netting just inside the far post – something he had promised captain Jon-Barrie Bates he would do as they stood over the set-piece. Byron returned to Hendon in 2005, and again in 2011–12, where he played alongside brother Bradley. The younger brother was only 16 when he made his Hendon debut at the end of the 2004–05 season and he moved on after half a dozen appearances the following season. Bradley also has played in the Football League.

There were a few games in the 1993–94 season, when Hendon played three full internationals in the same team. England's Peter Taylor was joined by Anthony Sibanda and Tommy Mason. Sibanda, a striker, played only 26 times for the Greens – he scored three goals – and that was 25 more matches than he played as a full international. However, one game for Zimbabwe was enough for him to make this list. Mason, was a dyed-in-the-wool Londoner, but the left-back played club football in New Zealand and, given the chance to represent the All Whites, he did so and ended up playing eight times. The club's most recent New Zealand international was a Kiwi who lived in Childs Hill, Jeff Campbell. He joined Hendon from AFC Wimbledon in September 2005 and played the rest of that season, making his debut in an FA Cup tie at home to Metropolitan Police. He returned home after the end of the season and played in the early years of the Australian 'A' League for Auckland. In all, he played 16 times for New Zealand, including twice in qualifying for the 2010 FIFA World Cup, but did not make the squad for the tournament in South Africa.

The two FIFA confederations which are the most fertile for internationals playing at Hendon's level are two of those mentioned so far, Africa and CONCACAF (Confederation of North, Central American and Caribbean Association Football). One of the strangest of those was Bajan international Yusuf Bangura, who played a couple of times for the Barbados nation before joining the Greens in the summer of 2004. Yusuf's international career would have been longer if he had been prepared to pay his own fare – and I think lodgings, too – to play in a tournament in the Caribbean. It was more than he could afford and he felt he should not have needed to pay to represent his country.

One African player who got away, as it were, was Charlie Ntamark, who was rejected by Hendon, then Boreham Wood a week later, after trials in reserve teams. Cameroon thought him good enough to play 31 times for them, winning an Africa Cup of Nations winners medal in 1988, and he also made more than 300 appearances for Walsall.

In 2018, the Confederation of International Football Associations held their world cup in England. CONIFA represents those regions and the odd nation that does not have membership of FIFA. The CONIFA World Football Cup was a joyous celebration and one former Hendon players appeared.

Aryan Tajbakhsh, who played twice for Hendon in September 2015, appeared for the Somali diaspora in England, known as Barawa. He was sent off for fighting after the conclusion of Barawa's second group match – disciplinary issues are not a new experience for him – he was at the centre of Enfield Town (and Hendon's) play-off delay in 2015 and, six months later, he saw red seven minutes into his Hendon debut. Amazingly, Tajbakhsh spent parts of two seasons at League Two Crawley Town and made more than 20 League appearances.

The last player to be mentioned is one of only two men to appear in the Isthmian League and a FIFA World Cup semi-final – Bobby Moore didn't play for Oxford City when he was their manager in 1980. Paul Parker played in the 1990 World Cup and made a handful of appearances for Heybridge Swifts, but Bulgarian legend Bontcho Guentchev, a semi-finalist in 1994, spent a number of seasons as a Hendon player.

Bontcho joined Hendon from CSKA Sofia in 1999, nine months after scoring in the UEFA Cup against Atletico Madrid. Missing his family in London, including his sons and future Hendon players Lubo and Iavor, Bontcho returned to his house a couple of hundred yards from Claremont Road.

He scored 11 times in 72 appearances between 1999 and 2001, then returned as player-coach in 2006, making another 11 appearances and scoring once.

Oxford

The club's matches against clubs from Oxford, mainly Oxford City, have a long history. On 3 May 1919, Hampstead Town made the relatively long trip to Oxford for a friendly against City. Oxford City had been Isthmian League members since 1908, and would have been considered strong opposition for the Town, so it was a good result to get a 2–2 draw.

Eighteen months later came the first competitive match between the clubs, in the FA Cup fourth of six qualifying rounds. This wasn't quite new territory for Hampstead as they had lost to Gnome Athletic after a replay at the same stage in 1919. Once again, there was no fifth round qualifying game for Hampstead as Oxford won 3–0 at home. Hampstead finally got the better of City almost nine years later, at Claremont Road in a second round qualifying tie. It ended 2–1 with the goals coming from Freddie Sherman and Stan Moore.

A year later, and one round further into the competition and Hampstead again came out on top, this time 3–1, with Moore, Vic Gardner and Freddie Evans on target. Amazingly, Golders Green were drawn against Oxford again in 1933, a third meeting in five years. Despite a double from Ronnie Rowe and another from Charlie Drinkwater, the Green lost 4–3 in Oxford. The last meeting before the Second World War was a March 1938 friendly in Oxford, and a hat-trick from John Lammie secured a 3–2 win.

It was almost 20 years before the next match, a friendly in April 1957 which ended 3–1 to Hendon at Claremont Road, with John Rawlings, Tommy Lawrence and Miles Spector getting the home goals.

League meetings began in 1963 and, over the next 17 seasons, there were regular home and away contests. Hendon were one of the strongest clubs in the Isthmian League, while Oxford were perennial strugglers – they have never won the Isthmian League's top division title. Nonetheless the first Isthmian game ended with Oxford City 3–0 home winners, and they shared the points in a 2–2 draw in the return. The following season, a 1–1 draw at Oxford was followed by a 7–1 Hendon win, with David Hyde bagging a hat-trick, Jimmy Quail, two, and there were one each for John Evans and Danny Lakey. Hendon then completed the double over Oxford in 1965–66, and won 3–1 in Oxford the following season, this after being held to a goalless stalemate at Claremont Road. But it wasn't the last meeting between the clubs; the only Amateur Cup tie – in the last eight – ended 4–3 to the Greens, Tony Harding with two goals, Roy Sleap and Lakey the men on target.

Hendon dominated most of the next 10 fixtures, but a day before the first leg of the Middlesex Senior Cup final against Hampton in May 1972, Hendon visited Oxford with a team none of whom played a day later. The team still contained Arthur Paisley, David Poole, Micky Cannon, John Wilson, Roy Butler, Newton Ashman and manager John Evans, with Mickey Cooper on the bench, but we suffered a worst-ever – in the rivalry – 4–0 defeat. In March 1980, Terry Glynn scored in a 1–0 Hendon win at Oxford which turned out to be the last meeting for a while. Oxford endured 15 turbulent years before the Isthmian League rivalry resumed. A goal from Jimmy Bolton and crazily misplaced back-header from a defender gave Hendon a 2–0 win in October 1996, a result avenged in March 1997.

Hendon managed to avoid relegation that season, but a Hendon double helped to ensure that City dropped down to Division One. Since then, there has been only one further meeting between Hendon and City, in November 2013, when Carl McCluskey and Anthony Thomas were on target at Earlsmead as Hendon won a first-ever FA Trophy tie against the then Conference North members 2–1.

Hendon have also played Oxford United when they were Southern League members in 1960, a year before they joined the Football League. They had changed their name from Headington to Oxford at the start of that season. Hendon fought to a 2–2 in the FA Cup first round proper at Claremont Road. Miles Spector and Brian Figg scored, but the replay went Oxford's way 3–2 at the Manor Ground, despite goals from Terry Howard and Jimmy Quail. Ten years later, Hendon and Oxford United clashed in a friendly at Claremont Road which ended in a 2–2 draw.

There was also a friendly at Claremont Road in 1957, against Oxford University, and this also ended with four goals equally shared. Finally, the Oxford link should mention the 1951 Amateur Cup semi-final against Pegasus, the combined Oxford and Cambridge University team. A missed penalty in injury time meant Pegasus escaped with a 1–1 draw and they reached the final with a 3–2 win in the replay. Eleven years later, in Pegasus's penultimate season, Hendon drew 0–0 away and scored a 6–1 victory in the replay with David Bell and Miles Spector both grabbing hat-tricks.

P

James Parker

Alan Phillips

Play-offs

Postponements

Premier Inter-League Cup

James Parker

James Parker left the club in 2012, after almost seven years at Hendon. His arrival at the club barely merited a mention. He was a few weeks short of his 19th birthday, and joined the club from Bishop's Stortford. As a 17-year-old, he had been a Stortford substitute in their 6–0 FA Cup first round proper defeat away to Football League club Mansfield Town in November 2003.

His Hendon debut was also unsuccessful. James found himself at left-back against a Fisher Athletic team which went on to win the London Senior Cup. Hendon were 4–0 down at half-time, after which Fisher got bored and the Greens scored a couple of second-half goals. It was an important night in club history because, after this debacle, Gary Farrell and his coaching staff were sacked. Gary McCann, Andy Pape and Gary Anderson came in and their first game was a 2–1 win over Cheshunt, with Dave Sargent – whose late arrival had given James his debut – scoring both goals in his Hendon swan-song.

James was an ever-present for the rest of the season, and his place in McCann's improved defence certainly helped to turn around what had seemed a certain drift to relegation under Farrell. The following season, James suffered a career-threatening injury at Bromley near the end of the campaign. Still on crutches, James did receive the Supporters Association Player of the Year Award, scant consolation for an injury which left him with a permanent weakness in his ankles.

His ability to read a game made James ideal as either a central defender or a full-back, while his solid, dependable tackling meant he frequently averted danger, even before most people saw it develop. Of course, he didn't get forward very often and didn't break his goal scoring duck until he had made more than 80 appearances – heading home a Marc Leach corner – and he finished his Hendon career with just seven. In his early years at Hendon, James was a student, training to become a teacher. His intelligence, combined with good communication skills, made him ideal captaincy material and it was not long before he took this role.

If, off the field, things were very difficult, on it there was much positivity, and in 2007–08, Hendon had the first of a number of jousts to enter the play-offs, eventually coming up just short. James played in 48 matches, his best total for the Greens, having passed the 100-game mark early in the campaign. He was part of the team that lost, controversially, to Tooting & Mitcham United in the London Senior Cup Final. The Centenary season, of course, was marked by the departure from Claremont Road, and Hendon struggled for most of the first half of 2008–09 before turning things around. Although there was disappointment in the Middlesex Senior Cup, Hendon got it right against

Croydon Athletic in the London Senior Cup Final at Kingsmeadow, winning on penalties. It was James's first cup medal as a Hendon player.

Solid and dependable, James was still a regular and made his 200th appearance in January 2010, in a season which saw the Greens finish a laudable 10th in the Ryman League Premier Division. The next season saw Hendon end an 11-year wait for an FA Cup first-round appearance, and James led out the side at Melbourne Stadium against Chelmsford City. The Conference South team won 3–2, but the injury-ravaged Greens were far from disgraced. And there was another London Senior Cup Final appearance, albeit another defeat, to Wingate & Finchley at Tooting & Mitcham's Imperial Fields. James now had two runners-up medals to go with a winners' one.

The following season, he levelled his London Senior Cup Final medal count at 2–2, though the Final was a match James was lucky to be allowed to finish at his manager's terms. Hendon were strolling to a 2–0 victory over Kingstonian at rain-lashed Imber Court, when James received his second yellow card of the match. The referee, somehow, managed to confuse James's Number 2 shirt with that of Carl McCluskey – Number 12, who had been on the pitch for barely a minute. Gary McCann immediately substituted James and when he asked his manager why he had been taken off, Gary whispered, "How many yellows did you want?"

James finished the season on 295 appearances, but only made five more in 2012–13, so did reach the 300 mark. He left the club after a defeat away to East Thurrock United. Having been promoted to House Master at his school, he could no longer devote the necessary time to football and effectively retired from the senior game aged only 26.

Alan Phillips

Alan Phillips is one of only two Hendon players to score the winning goal for the club in FA Cup ties against Football League clubs.

On 22 November 1975, he added his name to the pantheon of Hendon greats. It was his header, from a Dave Metchick free-kick, past Reading goalkeeper Steve Death, that gave the Greens a 1–0 win, the club's first ever FA Cup victory against Football League opposition. But that is getting ahead of ourselves, because it came in Alan's second spell, and the last of his four seasons at Claremont Road. Alan first joined Hendon from Isthmian League rivals Tooting & Mitcham United at the start of the 1971–72 season. At 25 years old, he was an experienced player, with four Wales Amateur international caps to his name – earning two each at Tooting and Barry Town. Alan was a clever centre-half, not particularly robust in build, but good enough to keep taller players quiet in an era when challenges were distinctly more physical and referees more lenient.

In Alan's first season, Hendon finished nine points behind champions Wycombe Wanderers, but they did beat them 2–1 in a memorable FA Amateur Cup semi-final. In the final, Hendon met Middlesex rivals Enfield at Wembley. Alan, and the rest of the Hendon defence, were magnificent as they kept Enfield out as the Greens won 2–0. It was not Alan's only winner's medal that season, as he also played in Hendon's Middlesex Senior Cup triumph against Hampton – and Enfield denied him and the Greens a treble by winning the London Senior Cup final. Alan, who worked for Heinz, had his football exploits publicised in an illustrated feature in the company magazine.

Hendon's defence in 1972–73 was arguably the meanest in Isthmian League history and it was the Greens' proud boast that none of the 18 goals they conceded in 42 league matches came from a corner. Hendon raced to the championship and did not lose a league game until 17 April 1973, ending a run of 13 straight league wins which had begun on 25 November and had seen just two goals conceded. Stability was key and between goalkeeper John Swannell, the regular back four of Alan, Tony Jennings, Gary Hand and Peter Deadman and the two central midfielders, Phil Fry and Rod Haider, just three cup-ties were missed between them. Many more league games were missed, but clashes with internationals made that inevitable. Alan won his last two Wales Amateur caps during his first two Hendon seasons, including one in 1972–73 – as an aside, Wales's final ever amateur international came on 23 February 1974, the day Hendon entertained Leatherhead in the Amateur Cup and while Alan put club ahead of country, future Hendon manager Gwyn Walters, then at Barking, did play in the game. Hendon won two other trophies that season: in October, as the Amateur Cup winners, they played Italian side Unione, for the Barassi Cup and won 3–1 on aggregate; then, in May, retained the Middlesex Senior Cup, beating Enfield in the final.

Alan missed only one of 67 matches in 1973–74, the season in which Hendon hit the national headlines by holding Newcastle United to a 1–1 draw in the FA Cup third round. In the previous round, Alan was on the scoresheet in his homeland when Hendon won 3–0 at Merthyr Tydfil. Only a crazy run-in to end the season – Hendon had played nine FA Amateur Cup ties, but drew six of them – saw the Greens end up two points behind champions Wycombe. More importantly, it was the end of the amateur era, and while clubs such as Wycombe and Enfield spent heavily on players, Hendon were more frugal – the upshot of which was wholesale departures, Alan included, from Claremont Road.

A move to Wycombe brought Alan more FA Cup glory as the Chairboys held top-division Middlesbrough – managed by World Cup winner Jack Charlton – to a goalless draw before losing the replay 1–0 on their sloping Loakes Park pitch. A year later, Alan was back at Hendon and the Greens reached the FA Cup second round, where Swindon won 1–0 at Claremont Road thanks to a late penalty. In the previous round, Hendon had been drawn at home to Reading. The Biscuitmen – as they were known in those days – were riding high at the top of the old Fourth Division, but Hendon matched them in every department and Alan's headed goal proved to be the only one of the match.

The Greens finished the season in sixth place, with Alan having played in all 42 matches – he missed just one cup-tie – and added the Middlesex Charity Cup to his already large collection of medals. He scored the last of his 11 Hendon goals in his penultimate appearance for the Greens, the consolation in a 3–1 defeat at Woking.

Play-offs

For Hendon fans, play-offs have been both a source of joy and frustration. Let me start by saying that the events of 2014–15 and 2017–18 in no way coloured my judgement of the play-off system – quite simply it rewards mediocrity. In other sports – especially in the USA, where the five major team sports all play unbalanced schedules, it is a competitive necessity. Here, rugby league has an unbalanced schedule, with either 23 games or more home than away, while rugby union's top clubs meet when some are more severely hit by international call-ups than others. Football doesn't satisfy any criteria for the need for play-off, other than money.

By most criteria of that time, there should not have been an Isthmian League play-off in April 1965. Admittedly, Hendon and Enfield finished on the same number of points, but Enfield won 29 Isthmian League matches and Hendon 28; the Es' goal average was 2.80, more than 10 percent better than Hendon's 2.51. Goal difference didn't come into effect until 1973–74, but Hendon's 74 was better than Enfield's 63. A little known fact from the game, however, was that if it had ended level, then the title would have gone to Enfield.

The match on 29 April 1965 remains the only Isthmian League championship decider which was an actual play-off – though the fixture list has occasionally pitted the first and second placed teams in their season-ender. Fans from the two north London clubs traipsed down to Dulwich Hamlet's Champion Hill on a Friday night, on the eve of the FA Cup Final and in front of a crowd of 4,900, Hendon prevailed 4–1. The Greens never trailed, taking the lead after 20 minutes through David Hyde, who collected Peter Slade's pass, went past Alf D'Arcy and slotted the ball past Mark Mitchell.

Slade was the centre of the key action as he hit the crossbar with an effort before half-time and extended Hendon's lead after 57 minutes. When Roy Drake made it 3–0, the title was definitely on its way to Claremont Road and although McDonnell did pull a goal back, Danny Lakey round off the scoring in the dying minutes.

Hendon's next play-off game was not until 2015 and, after finishing runners-up behind Maidstone United, the margin was three points and Maidstone had a vastly superior goal difference, the Greens had to wait to find out who their opponents would be. The long-running appeal of Enfield Town against a three-point deduction because of the ineligibility of Aryan Tajbakhsh – coincidentally a 1–0 victory over Hendon in early January – was only resolved a week after the play-offs were due to be completed.

Quite simply, the Football Association took an age to make their decision, forcing the Isthmian League board to confirm the points deduction – then there was the appeals process.

The upshot was that on Thursday 14 May, 19 days after the season's end and 10 after the original date for the play-off final, Hendon entertained Metropolitan Police, who had taken Enfield Town's place. After Andre Da Costa had smashed a free kick against the underside of the crossbar, the Blues took a surprise lead when Charlie Collins converted a penalty. Hendon's equaliser came 13 minutes before half-time when Casey Maclaren turned in a vicious, swirling corner from Sam Murphy. Two minutes into the second half, Hendon got the winner, Da Costa scoring with a screamer from open play, a curling dipping strike that gave Steve Searle no chance. Metropolitan Police's hopes of getting back into the game were pretty much brought to an end when Rob Bartley was dismissed with 15 minutes to go and they finished with nine men after Searle saw red for a deliberate handball to deny Murphy a third goal.

Four days later, wealthy Margate – whose owner had paid for a couple of players to return from holiday, something the Greens could not afford with Elliott Brathwaite and Sam Murphy – came to Harrow and returned to Kent as members of the National League South following a controversial afternoon. Ryan Moss was probably lucky to receive only a yellow card for a scything challenge from behind on Ollie Sprague, but, in the 18th minute, Aaron Morgan saw red for what, on appeal, the FA deemed not to merit even a caution. Six minutes before the break, Moss scored and it proved to be the only goal of the game. In truth, the 10 of Hendon rarely threatened the Margate goal, but the sense of injustice at all that happened is still raw with many.

Three years later, Hendon were back in the playoffs. This time, Hendon had finished third, behind champions Billericay Town and runners-up Dulwich Hamlet. The two Bostik League – the Evo Stik brand had replaced Ryman for 2017–18 – teams had met twice and Josh Walker's stoppage-time, only-goal winner at Champion Hill was countered at Silver Jubilee Park by Rickie Hayles' equally late Hamlet equaliser to make it 3–3. The upshot was Hendon entertained Folkestone Invicta and absolutely routed the Kent club 4–0 and Dulwich just got the better of Leiston.

Temporarily homeless, and sharing with Tooting & Mitcham United, Dulwich were narrow favourites to make it into Vanarama National League South, but the real shame was that weather conditions ruined what might have been a truly outstanding game between two teams who had the ultimate respect for each other and who played at a high tempo offering great entertainment to fans. The temperature, in the shade, was around 34°C (93°F) and the pitch offered no shade. Incredibly, 3,321 fans crammed into Imperial Fields – a ground record – and they witnessed Ashley Nathaniel-George give Hendon the lead after 36 minutes, but Gavin Tomlin equalised early in the second half. The match was still watchable, but the heat sapped the energy of both teams and the tension was almost paralysing, so neither could force enough pressure for a winner. Extra-time could not separate the teams and the penalty shoot-out went Dulwich's way, 4–3. Four days later, Hendon were moved to the Evo Stik Southern Premier Division South; not long after that Gary McCann and his management team took over at Hampton & Richmond Borough and Jimmy Gray oversaw a brand new challenge in 2018–19.

Can the play-offs be made fairer? I'm not sure. Home advantage really isn't sufficient a reward for the higher placed team in a playoff, especially when there is a large points difference – it was 10 in both 2015 and 2018. It might be better if teams from the division above were involved, or maybe the lower-placed team has to win in 90 minutes and/or there is a goals for points benefit too.

Postponements

There have been some strange postponements involving Hendon over the past 30-odd years. Saturday 6 September 1997 was a lovely sunny day, the weather had been good and there were no problems with amenities at Claremont Road. Uxbridge were our scheduled opponents in the Suburban League, but four days before the game we told them there was no way the match could be played. League officials ordered that it should go ahead, so the club rang the FA for guidance. That day, 6 September 1997, was Diana Princess of Wales's funeral and the FA backed us to the hilt, especially as every senior league had moved their fixtures and no football was played in the country. There was no security risk about the game, mainly because it would have been almost impossible for anyone to drive to the ground any time between noon and 4pm because the three main roads surrounding the ground were closed for the funeral cortege.

Nothing is more frustrating, for visiting fans in particular, is to turn up and find the game called off less than an hour before kick-off. Hendon travelled to play Notts County in 1998 for an FA Cup First Round replay and an uneventful journey from north-west London suddenly became an issue when supporters entered Nottingham. A fog descended over the river Trent and inside Meadow Lane only half the pitch was visible. My problem was that I had a 1,500-word report to send to the *Kilburn Times* by first thing Wednesday morning. When I notified the sports editor of the postponement, he told me he still wanted the 1,500 words with the same deadline. I thus wrote 1,500 words about nothing – just try it – and I even provided the headline, Hendon haven't the foggiest, one of my finest headlines.

Three weeks earlier, the boot had been on the other foot, when Bath City travelled to Claremont Road, only to find that the pitch was unplayable. Knowing Bath were travelling on the morning of the game, we arranged for a very early inspection – inconvenient for the groundsmen, club and inspecting officials. At the time, the pitch was playable, but the weather forecast was dire, from around 11am. The rain arrived on time and left water inches below the surface. When the match referee arrived, he took two steps onto pitch, wrote off a pair of shoes and postponed the game. Bath's chairman arrived at around 2.15pm and furiously accused Hendon of deliberately bringing his club down to London and calling off the game, knowing Bath had two players unavailable in midweek. Secretary Graham Etchell said little, but invited the chairman to test the pitch himself ... two steps on the pitch, and another pair of written off shoes later, he was full of apologies and muttered something about the nature of the storm – and, yes, it was that bad.

But Bath's travails were less than Yeovil Town's in the spring of 1987. This was the second leg of an AC Delco (Isthmian League Cup) semi-final, which Hendon led 2–0 after a superb win at the Huish. Once again, very heavy rain meant that Yeovil turned up and were leaving at 7.45pm after referee David Keen had tried and failed to get a ball to roll across the sodden surface. The Yeovil coach broke down at Staples Corner and was stuck there for many hours. The team reached

Somerset at around 3am, by which time they knew they would make the journey again later that day! When manager Gerry Gow told his players, goalkeeper Dave Walter said, "Sorry, boss, I can't do it. It's lambing season." Walter was a farmer in Cornwall and had a three-hour journey for home games. Yeovil's second-string keeper, a student, was unavailable and the third-choice custodian conceded twice as Hendon reached the final 4–1 on aggregate.

Some call-offs just can't be predicted. Even all-weather pitches can be beaten by the weather – remember Hendon's abandonment against Billericay in January 2017 when the Greens led 2–0 – but the club were even more unfortunate a couple of months earlier when an electrical fault caused a Middlesex Senior Cup tie against Northwood to be postponed. In January 2002, the referee – with the floodlights on – noticed glass glistening in sand spread on the pitch before an FA Trophy replay against Cambridge City. How it got into sand, which was stored outside the ground, is unknown, but it couldn't be seen in daylight or when the sand was spread on the pitch. The club didn't play a home game for a month as the shards were carefully harvested.

Lastly, and back to the weather, there is the tale of Hendon's FA Cup marathon with Dagenham & Redbridge in 2000. Saturday 28 October, Monday 30 October, Wednesday 1 November, Monday 6 November and Wednesday 8 November all recorded "match postponed" from Hendon. Sadly, on Tuesday 14 November it was Hendon 1, Dagenham & Redbridge 3. How badly damaged was the pitch? Between that night and 24 February 2001, Hendon played just one Ryman League home fixture.

Technically, the farcical events surrounding the delayed Ryman League Premier Division playoffs in 2015, were not postponements. The slow-moving FA Disciplinary procedure, League ratifications and subsequent appeals meant the game against Enfield Town was never called off – and when the semi-final was eventually played Metropolitan Police had been promoted to fifth place.

However, in 2018–19, Hendon's FA Cup second round qualifying tie was called off – and, once again, the opponents were not the originally scheduled one as Phoenix Sports were removed from the competition for playing a suspended player (it should have been an open and shut case, but the FA's arcane disciplinary process made it a bigger issue).

The decision, made less than 48 hours before the scheduled game, meant Hendon were without a fixture on the Saturday and they had exited the London Senior Cup in the midweek, when they and Harrow Borough could have played on the Saturday with both at full strength.

Premier Inter-League Cup

The Premier Inter-League Cup, first known as the GMAC Cup, was one of the shortest-lived national competitions the club ever entered.

The Alliance Premier League was set up in 1979, and used that name until 1986, when General Motors became sponsors. The league became the Football Conference, officially the GM Vauxhall Conference. General Motors decided to create and sponsor a 'rival' to the FA Trophy, but limited entry only to the Conference and the top division of each of the Isthmian, Southern and Northern Premier Leagues, thus 88 clubs, as opposed to the Trophy's 150-plus (from the Isthmian and Southern lower divisions, Northern League and other clubs a step lower). The Premier Inter-League Cup sponsor was GM's financial arm, General Motors Acceptance Corporation – GMAC.

To get from 88 to 64 clubs, the 22 GMVC clubs received byes, as did the top six finishers in the three other leagues in 1985–86, leaving a first round of 24 ties. A competition rule was that if match ended all-square after 90 minutes, there would be a replay; if it was again level after 90 minutes, the higher-scoring away team would go through on away goals. If both 90 minutes ended with the same score there would be extra-time after which, because of the away-goals rule, only a goalless 30 minutes would lead to a shoot-out.

Hendon were drawn away to Hayes on 21 October 1986. A sparse crowd, on a foul night, watched Colin Tate and Neil Wolstenholme score in the Greens' 2–1 victory. Hendon then had a home tie against Kingstonian, which the Greens won 3–1, with Glenn Bickles, Iain Dowie and Wolstenholme on target. Two games in and Hendon were in the last 32, only one round short of the Greens' best-ever FA Trophy performance. The club's third round opponents were the fearsome Fisher Athletic, who won the Southern League that season. Hendon were distinct underdogs when the sides met at Claremont Road on 27 November. An excellent match was decided by Dermot Drummy's solitary goal in the last couple of minutes. The reason I have special cause to remember the date was that I was cheering on two fronts, 4,000 miles apart. My American Football team the Green Bay Packers beat the Detroit Lions on a Walter Stanley punt return at almost exactly the same time as Drummy was winning the tie for Hendon. I was listening to the NFL on my radio while watching at Claremont Road!

It was almost three months before we returned to GMAC action, a very tough last-16 game away to Conference club Dagenham. The Daggers were flying high in the Conference and their home form was very good. Nonetheless, Hendon achieved a very creditable 1–1 draw and followed it up by winning 2–1 in the replay, with goals from Dowie, who scored who had scored at Victoria Road, and Danny Worley.

Most Hendon fans feared the worst when Conference newcomers Sutton were the team's quarter-final opponents, especially at Gander Green Lane, where Hendon had not won a league game since November 1975. This remains one of my favourite Hendon wins, 2–0, with goals from Roger Wade and Drummy booking a last-four place. At this time the talk was of the final being played at a Football League ground, with Manchester City and Aston Villa thought most likely. First Hendon had to get past FA Trophy finalists Burton Albion and that game was set for Sunday 26 April. Both teams were exhausted having played on the Saturday, but Hendon had to travel to Staffordshire.

There was a crowd approaching 1,500 with a hostile atmosphere and significant violence, almost all on the pitch, thanks to a large police presence. The result was probably the one both clubs dreaded the most, a draw, Drummy scoring in the 1–1 stalemate, but it was a superb Hendon performance. Iain Dowie was unavailable due to his degree final exams. As mentioned in the Knock-out Cups piece, the Sergeant in charge, himself a referee, would have dismissed four Brewers and Alan Campbell, but one particular challenge from Bob Gauden on Campbell nearly resulted in an arrest "but I would have feared for my safety if I had done that," he told me as we left the ground

The replay, three days later at Claremont Road was a magical night. It was 1–1 after 90 minutes, Drummy – who else – scoring. In extra time, if there were no more goals it would be a penalty shoot-out, otherwise Hendon had to win because a 2–2 would have been to Burton's advantage. The first 15 minutes were goalless, then Wolstenholme put Hendon in front, followed a couple of minutes later by a Wade effort. There was no comeback.

Sadly, the competition had gone on too long for Football League clubs to be interested in hosting the final, so a coin-toss, with Hendon officials connected by phone only, was held and Kettering Town won it. Hendon were always struggling and although a Drummy cross was deflected into the net, Kettering ran out deserved 3–1 winners.

Maybe it was Hendon's early exit from the 1987–88 edition, followed by two seasons of taking the chance not to enter, but the PILC did rather lose its cachet and became "just another cup" but with the possibility of some horrendously long midweek trips. The Greens returned to play in the 1990–91 tournament, beating Leyton Wingate 3–1 in a replay after a 2–2 draw, Uche Egbe scoring three goals in the two matches, then Kingstonian 2–1 with Paul Shirt and Laurence Holmes – the other scorers in the two Leyton Wingate games – netting at Claremont Road. The final game for Hendon was on the fourth anniversary of the memorable night against Fisher Athletic, and it ended in a 3–0 home defeat against Carshalton Athletic. Interestingly, Dave Root was the only Hendon player to appear in both matches.

Jimmy Quail

Queens Park Rangers

Hendon v Queens Park Rangers XI

Tuesday 28 July, 2015   Kick Off 7.30pm

Hendon	Queens Park Rangers
Belal AITE-OUAKRIM	Joe LUMLEY
Mahrez BETTACHE	Aaron LENNOX
Elliott BRATHWAITE	Harly WISE
Andre Da COSTA	Frankie SUTHERLAND
Dave DIEDHIOU	Michael PETRASSO
James FISHER	Aaron MITCHELL
Sam FLEGG	Ben PATTIE
Kezie IBE	Max EHMER
Mark KIRBY	Cole KPEKAWA
Max McCANN	Coll DONALDSON
Melvin MINTER	Darnell FURLONG
Aaron MORGAN	Jordan GIBBONS
Sam MURPHY	Bruno ANDRADE
Lee O'LEARY	Brandon COMLEY
Chris SEEBY	
Scott SHULTON	
Leon SMITH	
Oliver SPRAGUE	
Tony TAGGART	
Joe WRIGHT	

The squads from the Hendon versus QPR XI match in 2015.

Jimmy Quail

Jimmy Quail was one of the finest players to grace the Isthmian League when Hendon entered the competition in 1963. He had already spent seven seasons with the Greens – before moving round the North Circular for a couple of years at Enfield. In modern football, he would probably be either a striker or attacking midfielder, in the mould of Zinedine Zidane.

His family had moved from Bambridge, Northern Ireland before he was old enough for school, living in Harlesden. He wrote to the club in 1953 to ask for a trial and was taken on, but did not become a regular Hendon first-teamer at Claremont Road until 1956.

Jimmy played in the 1960 FA Amateur Cup winning team, and was rewarded with a place in the British squad for the 1960 Rome Olympic Games, but didn't get a game. He did, however, earn the first of his two Northern Ireland amateur international caps and, in November 1960, also came very close to selection for the full Northern Ireland team. In a scenario that wouldn't have happened today, Jimmy played in an FA Cup replay against Oxford United instead of representing Northern Ireland against Scotland at Hampden Park in a Home Nations Championship match. Quail scored Hendon's second goal in a 3–2 defeat.

After two years at Enfield, Jimmy returned to Claremont Road for the start of the Greens' venture into the Isthmian League – was now the number one amateur competition in the south of England, and Hendon were among the very best. The Greens finished runners-up behind Wimbledon in 1963–64, but the following season was the greatest in club history.

With Jimmy pulling the strings, Hendon won the League and Amateur Cup. But there was an earlier highlight, in the London FA Challenge Cup, a competition for London Football League clubs and two invited amateur teams – the finalists of the previous season's London Senior Cup. Hendon were drawn away to Arsenal, who filled the team with a number of players who would become household names. Ian Ure, a recent big-money transfer, was at centre-half, Bob Wilson was in goal, Jon Sammels played in midfield and John Radford led the attack. Radford scored a hat-trick, but Danny Lakey and David Hyde, also a hat-trick, ensured Hendon advanced.

Jimmy and Hendon returned to Highbury for the Amateur Cup semi-final, and Quail set up David Hyde for the first goal in a 4–1 Hendon victory over near-neighbours Finchley. On 24 April 1965, Jimmy scored at Wembley in the Greens' 3–1 victory over Whitby Town and, six days later, was in the Hendon team at Champion Hill, Dulwich, as Enfield were crushed 4–1 in the only championship play-off in Isthmian League history.

On 26 February 1966, playing against Wycombe Wanderers in the Amateur Cup quarter-final, Jimmy suffered a double break to his leg. Without Quail, Hendon reached the final but succumbed to Wealdstone. Jimmy did return the following season but, by his own admission, was not the same player. He returned to Enfield for a brief spell, then joined Walton & Hersham, but he retired after one season.

In November 1972, Jimmy was contacted by former Hendon team-mate John Evans, who had managed Hendon to victory in the Amateur and Barassi Cups that year. Evans was leaving to manage in Colombia, and Jimmy was invited to take over as boss. His first game back (Evans remained in charge for a few more weeks) could hardly have been tougher, an FA Cup first round proper tie against Plymouth Argyle. Hendon came within a few seconds of forcing a replay, losing 1–0.

Quail finished what Evans had started, a dominant season, unbeaten in the first 39 Isthmian League games and champions by Easter. The following season saw Hendon's best FA Cup run, reaching the third round proper, where Newcastle won a replay at Vicarage Road after a 1–1 draw at St James's Park. Eventually the Greens finished runners-up behind Wycombe in the race for the title, after which football lost its amateur-professional distinction, and Hendon slipped out of the elite. Jimmy had already decided to resign at the end of the season because of work commitments.

Jimmy returned to manage the club for 18 months in 1976, leaving at Christmas 1977, and then again in 1982, when he worked with Gary Hand, who was officially the manager. They kept Hendon in the Premier Division, but Gary's work commitments meant he (and Jimmy) left at end of the 1982–83 season. Although Gary returned in 1985, Jimmy has had no involvement with football management since then.

Overall, Jimmy played 383 games for the club, scoring 174 goals. He still attends matches at SJP occasionally.

Queen's Park Rangers

Queen's Park Rangers are probably – behind Barnet at The Hive – the second most local club to Hendon Football Club. Arsenal may have been closer when the club was based at Claremont Road, but at Silver Jubilee Park, Loftus Road probably shades it.

What is certain, however, is while the club's links with the Gunners has been predominantly a football union, Hendon have far greater in common with the Rs. After all, the club has never used any Arsenal ground for our home games, but three of QPR's homes have been used for Hendon matches.

The link goes back to Hampstead's first few seasons, when played at National Athletic Ground, Kensal Rise, which had been QPR's home in two short spells, 1899 to 1901 and 1902 to 1904. The grounds have long disappeared, but one of the entrances to the long walkway to the main stadium is now 80 College Road, NW10, another was by the side of Kensal Rise Station. This was Hampstead's home until the club moved to the Avenue Ground, by what is now Farm Avenue, NW2, and close to Brondesbury Cricket Club, in 1912.

The second former – and also future – QPR ground Hendon used was the famous White City Stadium, venue of the 1908 Olympic Games and one 1966 FIFA World Cup tie. QPR had spent two seasons at White City, 1931 to 1933 and were back there in 1962 for another season as a short-lived alternative to Loftus Road. Hendon played Walthamstow Avenue at White City on 11 February 1961, in the FA Amateur Cup; the Avenue won 2–0. The match was moved because the Claremont Road pitch was unfit.

Almost 20 years later, Hendon were forced to find another pitch after a prolonged spell of bad weather for an FA Trophy tie and QPR came to the club's aid. Thanks to one of the QPR stars of the time, Tony Currie, his brother Paul – father of Darren – somehow found himself with keys to the QPR boot-room, a huge benefit because Hendon played Taunton Town on Loftus Road when the pitch was Astroturf – actually Omniturf, but that is being picky. QPR staged a double header that day and those who watched Barnet and AP Leamington play out an awful goalless draw a couple of hours earlier feared that Hendon and Taunton would not be able to cope with the difficult surface. Thanks to the Curries, Hendon's footwear was the appropriate for the "plastic" and the Greens ran out 5–1 winners with Bobby Gough, Martin Sperrin, Dermot Drummy, Pat Morrissey and Peter Anderson scoring.

Hendon's football links with QPR are much harder to find. Some players went from Hendon to play for the Rs or vice versa, including Iain Dowie in 1998 and Tony Currie played five times for Hendon in 1985–86, after leaving full-time professional football. Of course, there have been dozens of players who learned their trade at QPR before dropping into Non-League football and playing for Hendon. These include Martin Duffield, a former England Youth international, who had one first-team game for the Rs and 188 appearances for the Greens in two spells between 1988 and 1996.

QPR are one of only three London full-time professional clubs Hendon have never met in a competitive fixture – Crystal Palace and Fulham are the others – though the Greens have played at Selhurst Park – the 3–2 FA Amateur Cup semi-final replay defeat against Pegasus in March 1951. The clubs have met in eight friendlies, including a game in July 2015 to mark Gary McCann's Testimonial. Hendon won

4–3. In July 2016, Hendon again scored four times, but former Hendon loanee Brandon Adams, back at his parent club netted for the Rs in a 5–4 Greens defeat. Prior to these two matches, in 2010, Hendon ended a 38-year gap between fixtures against QPR with a 4–2 win at Vale Farm.

Hampstead Town and Golders Green played four friendlies against QPR, two in 1911–12, 6–1 and 3–1 defeats, and 3–2 losses in 1920 and 1931. The other match, the only one between 1931 and 2010, was on 26 February 1972 and, without it, this piece may never have been written. The reason is that it was my first Hendon game since 1967; I had fallen out of love with professional football and Hendon was my local club. QPR were in Division Two – they won their place back in the top flight a year later – but they sent a strong squad with a few players boasting first-team experience. They were no match for the Greens, who went on to win the Amateur Cup two months later. Johnny Baker opened the scoring and second half goals from John Connell and Rod Haider, both substitutes, sealed a 3–0 win. I remember Connell and Baker both wearing the number 9 shirt – little and big Number 9s as I called them – and the giant Tony Bass also playing. This, I thought, was real football, with real players, real fans, a real stadium and people seemed to matter; I was hooked.

R

Representative games

Reserve teams

Geoff Riddy

Dave Root

Rugby League

Hendon Reserves programme from 1955, with Jimmy Quail playing.

Representative games

Hendon have played 32 matches against what can be considered representative teams, though many can be discounted, such as against Guernsey and Jersey selections. A similar case can be made for games against the Armed Forces or educational establishment XIs, Loughborough Colleges and Oxford University, and the International Club.

The really grey area surrounds Pegasus, the only one of the representative teams Hendon played in competitive matches. Pegasus was one of the most successful amateur teams in England in its 15- year existence from 1948 until 1963. Made up of the best footballers who were attending or had attended Oxford or Cambridge Universities, the Pegs, as they were known, won two FA Amateur Cups, beating Hendon in a replayed semi-final, then Bishop Auckland in 1951, and Harwich & Parkestone 6–0 in 1953 – both times in front of Wembley final crowds of 100,000.

Hendon's semi-final defeat at Highbury was galling. Hendon were awarded a late penalty, when Roger Avis was tripped, but – this is an often-told tale –goalkeeper B.R. Brown saved Dexter Adams's attempt. In the replay at Selhurst Park, Roy Stroud and Avis gave the Greens the lead twice, but Tony Pawson and a late double from John Dutchman – on 84 and 90 minutes – gave Pegasus a 3–2 win. (See programme above)

Pawson played county cricket for Kent, was one of the world's finest fly-fishermen, he was world champion in 1984, was *The Observer's* long-time cricket correspondent and was in the 1952 British Olympic Football squad. Dutchman played as an amateur for Leeds United and Queens Park in Scotland and later won two England Amateur caps. Also in that team was Donald Carr, another county cricketer and later a top cricket administrator. Hendon's other Amateur Cup meetings with Pegasus were in 1962, when after a goalless draw, the Greens won the replay 6–1 with both David Bell and Miles Spector scoring hat-tricks. By then the club was in decline.

Another series of matches which merit special mention were the ones in 1953, 1956, 1961, 1965 and 1973, against League select squads – Athenian for the first three and Isthmian for the other two – because these were part of the rewards for winning the previous season's league title. Although they were friendlies, there was honour to be gained from them and Hendon's record was actually very good, winning three out of five and drawing another. Roy Stroud and John Core scored in the 1953 game, which ended 2–2; three years later, Johnny Darey and Eric Beardsley, with two, helped Hendon to a 3–0 win. In 1961, Miles Spector got a hat-trick and Ken Aldridge and Bell also netted in a 5–1 victory. The Isthmian League XI – containing future Hendon men Rod Haider and John Ashworth – lost 3–2 to Hendon in 1965, for whom Danny Lakey and Roy Drake, two, scored. However, in 1973, Peter Deadman's goal came in a 2–1 defeat. There was one other match against a League representative team, celebrating the club's 75th season; it came on 22 February 1984 and Peter Stapleton, Andy O'Brien and Steve Hudson scored in a 3–1 Hendon victory.

In 1951, Hendon had a short tour to Hong Kong and beat a Hong Kong Selection 2–0, thanks to goals from Laurie Topp and Roy Evans, and two days later played out a 2–2 draw with a Selection, Stroud and Avis scoring. The Greens' preparation was hardly ideal for a long flight – 12 matches in 17 days including a Middlesex Charity Cup semi-final and the London Senior Cup Final, both defeats, the latter a day before departure.

A much higher profile opponent was the famous Middlesex Wanderers team – they provided a squad close to the quality of the England Amateur team. These games were great entertainment and were played for the Alaway Brothers Memorial Trophy. Selection for the Wanderers was a great honour, not quite as prestigious as an international appearance, but highly valued in any case. In 1960, Jimmy Quail's goal was not enough as the Wanderers won 2–1, but there was a 4–4 draw in 1965, when David Hyde, John Evans and Roy Drake, two, were the marksmen. In 1984, in another game celebrating Hendon's 75th anniversary the Greens were well beaten 5–2, despite goals from Stewart Mitchell and Alan Anderson. For further information about the Wanderers – who still tour and whose veterans team competes for the Isthmian League Veterans Cup – see the feature on the club.

Two other matches which quasi-representative were in 1938 and 1969, both fund-raisers for the club and the opposition was Golders Green Past and the 1965 Amateur Cup winners. Given that Golders Green's first season had been 1933, after the name change, and the Amateur Cup win was only four years earlier, these games were not very competitive, but welcoming back the 1965 side was memorable.

In 1965 Hendon played a friendly against the England Amateur XI as a preparation for an international tournament. Keith Mills scored a hat-trick in a 3–2 win against a team which contained two Greens, John Swannell and David Hogwood, and a future Hendon player, Tony

Harding. Former Hendon star Terry Howard played for both the England and Isthmian League teams in 1965.

Reserve teams

A reserve team is something which some managers consider to be essential to the overall club, others useful if available and the rest a waste of the first-team budget.

Running a reserve team at Hendon has been impossible since 2008 because in a ground-sharing situation, pitch availability is an insurmountable issue, especially when the competition is a Saturday league. This explains why, with an additional nod to youth development, the Greens have run midweek youth sides at various age groups including in 2018–19, an Under-23s squad, an age group which permitted a number of first-teamers the chance to get match action.

Since I started watching the Greens, the club has played in the Isthmian League Reserve section, Essex & Herts Border Combination, Suburban League and Capital League. The very first time I went to Claremont Road, in the mid-1960s, was for a reserve fixture against Tooting & Mitcham United. Hendon won 1–0 and Tooting missed a penalty kicking towards the car park goal. In the club's first six seasons in the Isthmian League the record in the Reserve section was – with one exception – very good, second, first, 12th, third, second and first. Hendon followed that up, in 1969–70, by finishing bottom after which the club dropped out of the competition, which was a year before Reserve League was cancelled.

Fast forward to the late 1970s and Hendon joined the Essex & Herts Border Combination – even though Hendon was in neither Essex nor Hertfordshire, but it was not too much of stretch to say the club was on the Hertfordshire border given that the northern end of the London Borough of Barnet is actually in the county. The first manager in Essex & Herts was former reserve player George Rocknean – he made 16 first-team appearances across five seasons in three separate spells. His assistant was Fred Hilling, who was a semi-regular first-teamer with 20 appearances in 1962–63, and eventually played 29 games in five seasons.

They produced a very strong team with some excellent players, including Jock McGleish, who stepped up to become a first-team regular. Another of his players was a former Chelsea junior, whose career was derailed by his father. Charlie Richardson was an immensely talented midfielder, but his father was the infamous south London gangster, also Charlie Richardson. Charlie Senior absconded from prison in the time Charlie Junior was playing for Hendon's reserves. One unusually warm April night Charlie Junior was playing for us, watched by two large gentlemen in overcoats, who walked around the Claremont Road ground looking in all the places someone hiding might be. After the game, as the two gentlemen drank their lemonades, Charlie Junior walked into the bar and said to them, "Sorry gents, dad's not here tonight," or something along those lines. The two police officers left almost immediately.

Hendon won the League and the League Cup under George and Fred and they also discovered John Barnes. John was playing for Sudbury Court and he almost single-handedly beat the Greens in a Middlesex Cup tie. The manager came back to the bar at Claremont Road and said, "I have just seen a future England player. His name is J. Barnes and he is very special. He scored a magical goal; bosh, bosh, bosh, ping."

The next league Hendon joined was the Suburban League and the team did not fare anything like as well until 1992–93, when it won the North Division without losing a game. It was an outstanding achievement by Dave Finn, the manager, but in 1993–94, Hendon went without a reserve team, a decision made by incoming manager Peter Taylor, so the supporters never got the chance to see what those players could do in the top flight. We were back a couple of years later, but in the top division, the team was often in relegation dogfights.

One battle went right down to the wire and Hendon picked up a key point in a game against Dulwich Hamlet. Playing at sweeper was Bontcho Guentchev and in midfield in front of him was Ricardo Alves, a Brazilian midfielder, whose football was better than his English. Leading the line for the Hamlet was Dean Green and he scored a hat-trick. A 50-yard pass from Guentchev to Alves cut the deficit and two other Guentchev goals sealed the draw. The second was a 25-yard free-kick which Guentchev placed into the roof of the net with exquisite precision. Hamlet were managed by Ossie Bayram, a regular thorn in Hendon sides in his playing days. He named himself and his son, also Ossie, on the bench and junior entered the fray midway through the second half. Fifteen minutes later, the boss tried to come on, but was stopped by the assistant referee, who called over the referee and said, "He has told me his name is Ossie Bayram, but he has already come on." The referee responded, "Yes I know," called over Junior and said to his assistant, "Ossie Junior and Ossie Senior."

The last league Hendon's reserves played in was the Capital League, once of a very high standard with many Football League second teams participating. Hendon spent only a couple of seasons in the competition and the club's last year in the Capital League was in 2005–06, when the reserves finished fifth in the table.

213

Geoff Riddy

Geoff Riddy made his debut for Hendon in an Athenian League match at home to Finchley just before Christmas 1961. He came through the reserves as a centre-half and spent most of his first three seasons in that role, and mainly as squad player.

After making 16 appearances in his debut season, he was rarely seen the following campaign, starting just twice. It does need to be said that Geoff's appearance total would probably have been many more if modern rules about substitutes were in place, but he left the Greens before even a single substitute was permissible. Geoff was a centre-half when Hendon made their Isthmian League debut, the 2–1 victory at Clapton on 24 August 1963, but apart from an FA Cup appearance in September, he saw no first team action until the Greens lost 3–2 at Wealdstone in the Middlesex Senior Cup in late January 1964. It would be another month before he returned – a 2–0 League victory at Bromley – but he then missed only three matches in the last two months of the season.

On 25 April 1964, the Greens won their first London Senior Cup and Geoff picked up a winner's medal after a superb defensive performance had helped Hendon defeat Enfield 1–0 at Wealdstone's Lower Mead ground. The following season was Hendon's finest and Geoff played a full part in it. Now the first-choice centre-half, he missed only a handful of games as Hendon won the Isthmian League, FA Amateur Cup and Middlesex Senior Cup. He played in the three "finals", Amateur Cup, League playoff and County Cup as Whitby Town, Enfield and Finchley, respectively, were all beaten. He also scored his first goals for Hendon, breaking his duck with a double in the famous 9–2 defeat of Wycombe Wanderers in December 1964. Earlier in the season, he had been charged with keeping John Radford quiet in the London Challenge Cup, but it didn't work out too well – at least in the early going as Radford claimed a hat-trick in the first 18 minute – but with David Hyde, three, and Danny Lakey replying as Hendon beat Arsenal 4–3, still one of the club's finest ever results.

Geoff scored in the second game of the 1965–66 season, but his most important ones for Hendon came at the other end of the season, the opening goal of the FA Amateur Cup semi-final against Whitley Bay at Sunderland's Roker Park and the opener of the final too, against Wealdstone at Wembley. Sadly for the Greens, the Stones replied with three goals to deny the Hendon the honour of successfully defending the trophy.

A week later, also against Wealdstone, this time in the Middlesex Senior Cup semi-final at Church Road, Hayes, Geoff made his 129th and final appearance. He suffered a serious ankle injury in the match which ended in a 2–2 draw, and he was absent for the remaining fixtures of the campaign and the tour to Madeira after the League fixtures had been completed. In the summer of 1966, Hendon, fearing that Geoff's injury might signal the end of his career, signed the Wealdstone centre-half John Ashworth. Riddy was determined to return to fitness and senior football too. Not unreasonably for a player who had earned Isthmian League representative honours the previous season, he opted for first team football and went in the opposite direction to Ashworth, joining Wealdstone.

Dave Root

Dave Root gave many years of fine service in the club's tradition of outstanding goalkeepers. He joined Hendon from Walthamstow Avenue in the summer of 1986. In the late 1970s, Dave had the misfortune of being the second-best goalkeeper in Barking's youth team – but he was behind Kevin Hitchcock, who went onto enjoy a long career as a full-time professional. Although Kevin was the regular first-team and youth-team keeper, Dave made 16 appearances for Barking in 1982–83 and, by the time he moved with his family to run a guest house in Cornwall in 1985, he had played 97 times for the Blues. Dave turned out a few times for Launceston Town, but returned to London and signed for the Avenue in 1985–86.

Mark Broughton, a Hendon hero in the 1985–86 relegation battle, returned to Derbyshire, so Ted Hardy was looking for a new goalkeeper, and he chose Root. Dave made his debut in a 2–1 defeat at Yeovil. It was the busiest season in the club's history as the first-team played in 76 matches and Dave set a club record, one which will, almost certainly, never be beaten, starting 31 cup ties in the campaign – if Hendon were to win every cup competition they enter next season (including the FA Cup), they would play a total of 33 ties.

Dave had all the attributes to be a goalkeeper, height, speed, agility and safe hands – until he became a courier van driver, he was a chandelier repairer. Hardy and Hendon were happy to ignore his one weakness – he was a very poor kicker – and Dave quickly became a fans' favourite. Although bad games were rare, Dave had a very disappointing AC Delco (Isthmian League) Cup Final, against Bognor Regis Town at Windsor. The Greens lost 3–2 and Root was the scapegoat.

The upshot was that, for the start of the 1987–88 season, John Jacobs was between the sticks; it was a short-lived and unsuccessful experiment – Jacobs' last eight matches saw him concede at least two a game and 20 in total – and at the end of October – albeit after Hardy had resigned to be replaced by his number two Micky Janes – Dave was back in the number one shirt to stay. He played in all but two of the remaining 42 League and cup matches, including the Middlesex Charity Cup Final against Wembley FC at Wembley Stadium. Root's first visit to Wembley had come a few weeks earlier, as a fan, for the FA Trophy final, and he spent much of the afternoon walking around the stadium, open-mouthed in awe at the surroundings.

A strange statistic regarding Dave's career is that in eight seasons, excluding the third of a season he missed in 1986–87, and 442 overall appearances, Dave was never an ever-present, although he did play at least 50 matches in every campaign and missed no more than four league games in each season. This is even more remarkable given the state of flux at the club; managers came and went, budgets were cut regularly and the dressing room door frequently resembled a turnstile. But through all this, Dave was 'Mr Dependable'. Other clubs were very keen to sign him and one prospective buyer walked away when the league's transfer tribunal came up with a valuation far higher than both clubs rated him.

When Victor Green became chairman at the end of 1991, Hendon went on another wild ride, with rapid turnover everywhere at the club – well, everywhere except in the number one shirt. At the season's end, Dave became one of an elite group of Hendon players to be awarded the Supporters Association Player-of-the-Year trophy for the third time – he had won two and four years earlier. The following spring, as a way of persuading him to stay for an eighth season, Dave was awarded a testimonial season.

The 1993–94 season started very brightly and ended in chaos despite Hendon picking up silverware at the end of the season, in the Full Members Cup. With a very bleak future – the club's survival was confirmed only 24 hours before new season's start – all but two players on the books in 1993–94 departed, Dave included. He spent a number of years at Kingstonian before joining Boreham Wood. Sadly, some fans never forgave him for moving on and publicly vilified him at every opportunity. A loyal club servant – and thoroughly decent bloke – he deserved a much better reaction than that.

Rugby league

Claremont Road staged many different football matches over the years. But on occasions other sports were played there as well. Gaelic Football was played at the ground, and also rugby league.

Professional club rugby league was played for a brief period in the 1930s in London. The sport then returned to the capital when Fulham RLFC was formed, based at Craven Cottage. By 1989, the team had split from the football club, and were playing at the Chiswick Polytechnic

Stadium, which did not have floodlights. The club played in the Lancashire Cup, a midweek competition, and after winning at Workington in the first round were drawn against the mighty Wigan. Even if the game had been scheduled for a Sunday there would have been a case for moving it to a more developed stadium. As it was, Fulham RLFC needed a ground with floodlights, which the Polytechnic Stadium lacked.

In those days, before rugby union went 'open' in August 1995, professional rugby league could not be played at a rugby union club ground. So clubs such as Harlequins or Rosslyn Park missed out on seeing Wigan –and Fulham – play.

It should be stressed that Wigan were not only a famous team, but were becoming the dominant team in the sport. The team they fielded against Fulham included Henderson Gill, Dean Bell, Shaun Edwards, Bobby Goulding, Andy Platt and Andy Goodway– some of the most famous names in the sport. Fulham's Second Division London-based team faced a side who were the holders of the Challenge Cup, the Regal Trophy and the Lancashire Cup. Almost every player was either an established international, or went to play at international level. On 27 September 1989, a crowd of 3,204, the biggest at Claremont Road for some time, saw Wigan win 34–4, scoring six tries and five goals. Fulham's points came from two goals by Steve Guyett.

In 1993, Fulham, now renamed London Crusaders, moved to the Barnet Copthall Stadium. On 9 January 1994, their home league match against Keighley was planned to be played at Claremont Road. However, the pitch was unfit. Barnet Copthall was waterlogged, and still was the next week, when Dewsbury based amateurs Shaw Cross came to play the Crusaders in the Challenge Cup. A crowd of around 500 saw the Crusaders win 40–14, on a pitch of deep mud in places. Apparently Barnet FC were also keen to stage rugby league matches and build up links with the rugby league club. The next round of the Challenge Cup was also staged at Claremont Road, and Featherstone Rovers beat the Crusaders 28–14 in front of a 1,557 crowd.

Soon after the Shaw Cross match, the club was taken over by the Brisbane Broncos, and became the London Broncos. At the start of the 1994–95 rugby league season, due to the Copthall Stadium being unavailable because the pitch was being reseeded, the club played five Second Division matches at Claremont Road from September to November 1994. Keighley Cougars won the first 30–10, but the Broncos won the next four, beating Batley, Swinton, Bramley and Carlisle. Later in the season, a Challenge Cup match was scheduled to be played at Claremont Road because of an athletics meeting at Copthall. But the pitch was unfit for play, the Broncos – at the last minute – switched it back to Copthall with a 4.30pm kick off.

The Broncos now had plans to develop the club further, and Claremont Road was not big enough for their future. They did not play at Claremont Road again.

S

St Albans City

Semi-finals – FA Amateur Cup

David Shacklock

Roy Sleap

Slough Town

Erskine Smart

Southall

Substitutes

Supporters Association

Sutton United

Dave Swain

St Albans City

St Albans City are a local club that Hendon used to play on a regular basis, but the clubs have not met for 15 years. Saints, whose Clarence Park home is less than 20 miles north of Silver Jubilee Park, were also founded in 1908. They joined the Spartan League where they enjoyed much success before the First World War. They returned to competitive football in 1920, as members of the Athenian League, which was the start of the club's rivalry with them.

Hampstead Town's first match against St Albans was an FA Cup third round qualifying tie on 6 November 1920. A crowd of 3,500 at Clarence Park watched as a double from Cecil Wise gave the visitors a 2–1 victory. The first Athenian League encounter came on 23 April 1921 and a goal from Stan Briscoe earned Town a point at the Avenue Ground. The return, in early May, ended 2–0 to Saints as they went on to win the League title at the first time of asking. St Albans won all three meetings in the following season – and the title again. An FA Cup tie at the Avenue Ground ended in a 4–2 defeat with Wise and E. Wilson netting for Hampstead. Wilson's Town career comprised a Middlesex Charity Cup tie against Wealdstone in 1920 and this FA Cup encounter – and he scored once in both games.

After the 1922–23 season, St Albans moved to the Isthmian League, where they were champions three times in their first five seasons – their only title since then was Isthmian Division 1 in 1985–86. Hampstead and Golders Green met the Saints three times in the 1930s, with one win each in the AFA Senior Cup and the Green taking an FA Cup tie in October 1936. Bert Broadis and Les Green – with a hat-trick – scored in the 4–0 win.

As Hendon, the first game against St Albans was in the 1952–53 FA Cup, a tie the Greens won 3–1 in a replay after 1–1 draw. Roy Stroud scored at Clarence Park while Arthur Phebey grabbed a double and Bob Avis got the other in the replay. There was also a first ever meeting in the Amateur Cup in February 1962, won 3–0 by the Saints at Wealdstone, the Claremont Road pitch being unfit for play.

Regular league encounters resumed in 1963–64, when Hendon joined the Isthmian League. This rivalry lasted until the Saints were relegated in 1974. Hendon had the better of the first five and last two of these 11 seasons and won an FA Cup fourth qualifying round replay at Clarence Park in 1970, an own goal and one from Peter Anderson giving the Greens a 2–1 victory. They weren't the only cup meetings because the Greens won a pair of London Senior Cup ties, 3–0 in 1969 and 4–0 in 1972, and avenged an Amateur Cup loss in 1962 with a 2–0 win at Clarence Park in January 1969. While St Albans were in the

Hendon versus St Albans, April 2004. (Photo: Peter Lush)

lower divisions of the Isthmian League, the clubs met in three pre-season friendlies, Hendon losing in 1975 and drawing in 1977 and 1981.

St Albans returned to the Premier Division in 1986, and in the first few seasons, there was added spice because Iain Dowie had joined Hendon from the Saints that November. Hendon completed league doubles twice in three seasons, after which Saints held sway until 1997–98, during which time the Greens failed score more than twice. It was a different matter in the Full Members Cup as Hendon won 3–0 1989 and 6–1 in 1997 – in between Keith Dowson, in his final Hendon appearance, scored a hat-trick in a 4–3 defeat. In November 1997, we were underdogs for an FA Cup fourth qualifying round tie at Clarence Park, but Colin Simpson grabbed a double as the Greens won 2–1 to earn a tie against Leyton Orient.

A year later Hendon won our only League Cup tie, 4–1, Simpson again amongst the Greens' scorers. Our final meeting was back in April 2004, when Martin Randall's equaliser earned us a 1–1 draw. The Saints, who moved up to Conference South that off-season, won promotion to the Conference Premier two years later, but were relegated in 2007. They dropped into the Southern League in 2011, but gained promotion back to the Conference, now National League, in 2014, since when they have played in the National League South.

In all competitions the clubs have met 83 times, plus three friendlies. Hendon's cup record shows a dominant 12 wins, two draws and only five defeats in 19 games, scoring 43 goals and conceding 20. In 64 league fixtures – Hendon didn't win one until the club's first Isthmian season – the Greens hold the narrowest of edges, 25 wins and 15 draws to 24 defeats, and the 98 goals to 95 advantage held by St Albans can be attributed in part to the most one-sided scoreline in the rivalry, a 6–

0 Saints win in 1922. Thus, excluding the friendlies, Hendon's complete competitive record against St Albans City is P83, W37, D17, L29, Goals for 138, Goals against 118.

Semi-finals – FA Amateur Cup

Many people say that losing a semi-final – especially a major competition – is the most disappointing feeling a player can suffer. The semi-finals in this piece focus exclusively on the FA Amateur Cup, for many years the most important competition open to non-league clubs.

Hendon reached seven Amateur Cup semi-finals and enjoyed success on five of those occasions. In 1951, Hendon played in their first FA Amateur Cup semi-final. They avoided Athenian League champions elect Bromley – the Greens would finish third – and the pre-eminent northern amateur club Bishop Auckland, but drew Pegasus, the combined Oxford and Cambridge University team. The game was played Arsenal's Highbury stadium, so travelling was minimal for Hendon's supporters. The pitch was very muddy and Hendon went ahead with a 25-yard strike from Roy Stroud after 70 minutes, only for John Tanner to level after 86 minutes. Two minutes later, Bob Avis was tripped in the penalty area, but Brown saved Dexter Adams's spot-kick. The replay at Selhurst Park, Crystal Palace FC, saw Hendon lead twice, through Stroud, then Avis, but Tony Pawson made it 1–1 and, in a frantic final six minutes, John Dutchman scored twice to break Hendon's hearts.

Hendon's next Amateur Cup semi-final was in 1955, when the Greens were drawn against Hounslow Town, also of the Athenian League. Bishop Auckland played Wycombe Wanderers in the other tie. Once again, the fans didn't have to leave London because the game was played at Tottenham's White Hart Lane. Eric Parker gave Hendon the lead in the first half, but Hounslow equalised after an hour. There was an air of controversy about the Hendon winner, after 73 minutes, Eric Beardsley's indirect free-kick ending up in the net, but the referee ruled the ball had grazed a Hounslow player. In the final, Hendon lost 2–0 to Bishop Auckland.

Five years later, Hendon were back in the last four, and drew Enfield. Kingstonian beat Crook Town in the other semi-final. The match was played at Brentford and Hendon were fairly comfortable 2–0 winners. Jimmy Quail hit a post after five minutes before Laurie Topp scored a rare goal after 31 minutes. Enfield failed to convert a great chance to level soon after and, in the 51st minute Quail set up Brian Figg for the second goal. In the Final, Hendon scored twice in the last couple of minutes to beat Kingstonian 2–1 to win the Cup for the first time.

Programmes from two Amateur Cup semi-finals at Griffin Park.

It was five more years before Hendon returned to the Amateur Cup semi-final. In 1965 the Greens were handed a local derby against Finchley at Highbury. The Finches rather froze in the semi-final and could not stop David Hyde – but they were in good company that season – as he grabbed a double, the first coming from a Quail free-kick. Early in the second half, Dave Emson scored an own goal and Hyde finished off a move involving Peter Slade and Roy Drake after 63 minutes. With 20 minutes to go Jimmy Cooley reduced the arrears, but Slade completed the 4–1 victory, turning in a cross from Danny Lakey. In the final, Hendon beat Whitby Town, conquerors of Enfield in their semi-final, 3–1.

A year later, Hendon had to travel north for a semi-final, all the way to Roker Park, Sunderland, where Whitley Bay provided the opposition. Wealdstone defeated Alvechurch in the other tie. Although the Greens were injury hit – made worse when John Swannell suffered a back injury five hours before the game, but played anyway – they were too strong for the men from Hillheads Park. Hendon won 2–1 with goals from Geoff Riddy and Roy Sleap before former Hendon star Tony Knox pulled one back. Hendon lost 3–1 to Wealdstone in the final.

A third consecutive semi-final in 1967 saw a dramatic trio of contests against Skelmersdale United. The Cheshire club were the only non-north London team in the last four as Enfield played Walthamstow Avenue in the other tie. Hendon's games were played at the Baseball Ground, Derby, St Andrews, Birmingham and the Hawthorns, West

223

Bromwich and the games ended 0–0, 2–2 and 3–1 to Skelmersdale, respectively. Hendon barely escaped from the first game, though Dave Hogwood nearly won it with a last-minute drive that flew narrowly wide of the post. A week later, the Greens were trailing 1–0 before Quail forced extra time. And, trailing 2–1 at the end of the extra 30 minutes, a speculative ball into the penalty area from Mickey Cooper eluded everyone and ended up in the net. Dave Swain scored at West Brom, but already Hendon were deservedly 2–0 down and conceded a third near the end. The match was covered on the BBC 1 nine o'clock news, showing the status the competition still had. Enfield beat Skem in the final, which went to a replay.

Hendon's last semi-final was in 1972 and, for John Swannell, Rod Haider and Peter Deadman, the 2–1 victory over Wycombe at Griffin Park, Brentford, was one of their most memorable for the club. Wycombe's fans massively outnumbered those from Hendon, but they had little to cheer about when John Baker scored after 14 minutes. Wycombe equalised early in the second half, a goal which infuriated the Hendon players and Deadman took out his frustration with a stunning drive from outside the box to decide the tie. In the final, Hendon beat Enfield 2–0 (the first game I watched at Wembley), thanks to a Mick Smith own goal and a late second from Tony Bass.

David Shacklock

David Shacklock played in Hendon's earliest days in the Isthmian League. His name will not resonate with modern-day Hendon supporters. Indeed, he was not a stand-out player during his seven seasons with the Greens – and he was a first-choice regular in only two of those campaigns. He joined Hendon soon after playing for Cheshunt against the Greens when the Ambers produced a shock 3–2 win in the London Senior Cup in November 1964. He made his debut in in a 2–0 pre-Christmas victory at home to Hitchin Town, playing at right-back where he had been so effective as an opponent. But David's best position was centre-half, and Hendon had Geoff Riddy in that role in the season Hendon completed the double of Isthmian League Champions and Amateur Cup winners. Of course, these were days before substitutes, so David didn't appear at Wembley, or the League Play-off against Enfield at Dulwich Hamlet – or, indeed in the Middlesex Senior Cup Final victory over Finchley – and he made just four appearances, all in the league, during the campaign. However, he did collect three winner's medals as Hendon Reserves swept the Isthmian League Reserve Division – the Greens lost once in the league all season – London Intermediate Cup and Middlesex Intermediate Cup.

The following season, David broke into the first team and finished with 15 appearances, including in the Amateur Cup Final at Wembley, where despite Hendon taking the lead through Riddy, Wealdstone won the trophy 3–1. The Greens also finished runners-up in the Isthmian League, two points behind champions Leytonstone, when there were still two points for a win.

For the 1966–67 season, the Isthmian League allowed substitutes to be named and David was the first Hendon player ever to wear the number 12 shirt – though he was not used, that honour went to Jimmy Quail. The Greens were in a state of transition and finished the season 10 points behind the champions Sutton United, and in fifth place. But this was also the season that David cemented his place in the team, as a centre-half – his best position. Riddy had moved on and he was the natural successor.

The late 1960s was an era when most defenders stuck to their goal-stopping role and David's defensive reliability was further highlighted by the fact that he failed to score a single goal in more than 200 appearances. In 1966–67, David finished joint-top of the appearance-makers with 54, the same as David Hogwood, out of a possible 57. He played in all three matches in the epic and ultimately unsuccessful Amateur Cup semi-final against Skelmersdale, but won a first-team winner's medal for the first time as Hendon beat Enfield 3–2 on aggregate in the Middlesex Senior Cup. In both matches, he played as defensive midfielder, just in front of John Ashworth and Ray Poole.

The following two seasons saw David play a little more than half of Hendon's first-team matches. In the 1967–68 seasons, he was restricted to just 22 games and it was 31 the following campaign. He played in exactly half of the Isthmian League games in 1968–69, but was a regular in cup ties, missing only three of 15. David played in every round of the London Senior Cup as Hendon won the competition for only the second time, beating Dagenham 1–0 in the final, thanks to a Rod Haider goal at Barnet FC's Underhill ground. His best season followed in 1969–70 when David again finished joint-top of the appearance-makers, this time with 57, the same as John Swannell. There was no silverware at the end of the season, and the Greens finished fifth in the Isthmian League, a dozen points behind champions Enfield, but Hendon did take Millwall to a London Challenge Cup replay and reached the second round proper of the FA Cup. David's contribution did not go unnoticed, by Hendon fans at least, because he was named the Supporters Association Player of the Year in 1970.

That summer John Evans arrived as manager and started to rebuild the team. One of those whose chances became more limited was David Shacklock, who played in only 32 matches, including three as a substitute. In the summer of 1971, Alan Phillips was signed to be the centre-half and that was the signal for David to move on, joining Kingstonian.

While David didn't win international honours at Hendon, his daughter Kerry competed at the Barcelona 1992 Olympic Games, finishing sixth in the duet class of the Synchronised Swimming competition.

Roy Sleap

Roy Sleap is one of the few players who won the Athenian League and Isthmian League Championships as well as the Amateur Cup with Hendon.

He joined Hendon in September 1960, after representing Great Britain at the Rome Olympic Games. Although only 19, he had already carved out a big reputation at Barnet, earning England and Great Britain representative honours as a teenager – a rare distinction at the time. Technically Roy was not a Hendon player when appearing twice, in Rome, including against the hosts. He had resigned as a member of Barnet, but had not actually signed for Hendon, even if it was known that was his intention. At Claremont Road, Roy had giant shoes to fill as he was replacing arguably the finest player ever to represent Hendon, Laurie Topp. He made his debut against Grays Athletic, a match the Greens won 3–0. Roy made 20 appearances during the season as Hendon won the Athenian League title by a point from Wealdstone, with Barnet a further two points adrift.

Before the start of the 1961–62 season, Roy – along with Terry Howard and Jimmy Quail – joined Enfield, where they stayed for two seasons and were joined by several other Hendon players. When the Es, Sutton United and Hitchin Town all switched from the Athenian League to the Isthmian, Jimmy and Roy returned to Claremont Road, where they enjoyed great success. Hendon missed out on the title by six points, finishing runners-up behind Wimbledon, while Roy was absent for the London Senior Cup final victory against Enfield having picked up a knee injury. He did earn another England Amateur cap during the season.

The 1964–65 season was the greatest in Hendon history and Roy played a huge part in it, normally at a left-back, though he later became what we now call a midfielder, then a half-back. The Greens won the FA Amateur Cup, 3–1 against Whitby Town, the Isthmian League title in a playoff against Enfield, 4–1 at Dulwich, and the Middlesex Senior Cup, 1–0 over Finchley, in the last three games of the season. There was also the London Challenge Cup victory over Arsenal at Highbury – when Hendon came back from 3–0 down to win 4–2 and a narrow 2–1 FA Cup first round reverse away at Port Vale. Roy – who wore the number 3 shirt in all give of those games – missed just three out of 58 matches in the season, and registered his first Hendon goal, the Greens' only one in a 1–1 draw at Oxford City. He also added to his list of representative honours, playing for England, the FA XI and London teams during the season.

Apart from a return to Wembley in the Amateur Cup final – where Wealdstone beat Hendon 3–1 – it was not a happy cup season for Hendon, and they played only 15 knock-out matches, but Roy played in all but one of the Greens' 53 outings, scoring nine times. Roy was exceptionally strong and would rarely lose a tackle, but could also pass the ball well when necessary, though he would usually feed it to a playmaker in front of him. Over the next three seasons, Hendon's levels of success dipped and the team showed numerous changes. Roy, by now a midfield linchpin, playing alongside Rod Haider, had his most prolific season in 1966–67, scoring 12 times in 51 appearances and he was one of four Hendon players who took to the field at Claremont Road when Great Britain played a 1968 Olympic Games qualifying match against West Germany. Sadly it was the visitors who won 1–0 as Great Britain failed to qualify for the Games in Mexico City. Roy also added to his collection of England Amateur Caps, finishing with 16 in total, the majority while with Hendon.

Roy briefly left Hendon during the 1967–68 season, and made only 37 appearances in all. The following season, Roy moved to Slough Town, but did return to Claremont Road for a special match on 13 April 1969, when the current Hendon team took on the 1965 FA Amateur Cup winners. Amazingly, only four years after the victory at Wembley, just John Swannell and David Hogwood were still at Claremont Road, and the Amateur Cup-winners ran out 3–1 winners. Roy made his final Hendon appearance on the opening day of the 1970–71 season, but was substituted by John Baker in a 3–2 home defeat against Barking. With his chances at Claremont Road extremely limited, Roy returned to Slough, before moving on to Sutton United a few weeks later. He retired as a player at Guildford City, and went into management at Slough, taking the Rebels into the Isthmian top division in his first season, 1973–74. Roy died in October 2005, at the age of 65.

Slough Town

Hendon has played Slough in 61 competitive fixtures, most of which were as Slough Town. There have been FA Trophy meetings in four different seasons, the Rebels holding a 2–1 edge with four draws – including the last of which, in 2017–18, Hendon won after a penalty shoot-out. The clubs have also met on two very famous occasions in the Isthmian League. The Greens' first encounter with Slough Town was a 1951 FA Amateur Cup tie, which Hendon won 3–2, thanks to goals from Bob Avis, Roy Stroud and Roy Evans. The clubs met again in the competition in 1971, losing a replay 3–1.

In between there were two FA Cup matches, one win each, in 1964 – 3–1 to Hendon – and 1968 – 2–1 to Slough. In October 1932, what proved to be Hampstead's last FA Cup tie (Golders Green made its debut in 1933) was a 2–1 defeat against Slough at Claremont Road, Ronnie Rowe scoring for Hampstead. Slough would have a very confused couple of decades with the names Slough Centre, Slough United and, from 1947, Slough Town being used. Golders Green met Slough United in a wartime Herts & Middlesex League Cup fixture in 1945, winning 1–0 thanks to a goal from C. Fair.

The first of 23 seasons of Isthmian League meetings was in April 1975, a 3–2 victory with goals from John Field, Bobby Childs and Bobby Southam; Hendon completed the double over the Rebels, thanks to Eggie James and Southam, in a match played at Wokingham Town as Slough were building Wexham Park having left the Dolphin Ground a year earlier. In 1975–76, the teams met in the FA Trophy and played out a 2–2 draw at Claremont Road where John Baker netted both Greens goals. The replay at Wexham Park was goalless after extra time, on a bitterly cold night, but it was still warmer than the frozen pitch for the third game, at Wembley FC. The bare facts are that Slough won 1–0, but the drama came when Rebels keeper Paul Barron collided with Eggie James and both players were knocked out. James left the pitch, but Barron stayed on – something modern concussion protocol would not have permitted – as Slough's only substitute was not a goalkeeper. My abiding memory was of the dazed Barron, his head swathed in bandages, attempting to take a goal kick from the angle of the 18-yard-box, proof if more was needed that he was not *compos mentis*.

In 1999, Hendon returned to Wexham Road for an FA Trophy first round tie that was notable for the Rebels having two players sent off in the first half, one desperately unjustly – in fact, the referee recalled it when we spoke about it 10 years later. Freddie Hyatt and Dominic Gentle scored Hendon's two goals in a 2–0 win, but neither team dared make a tackle in the second half. Another FA Trophy meeting was in the January 2005 – Gary Farrell meltdown month – when we went down 4–3 at Stag Meadow, Windsor, where Slough had set up home after leaving Wexham Park. Trailing 2–0 at half-time and lucky it was only two, Hendon twice reduced the arrears after the break, only to concede almost immediately, wasted a penalty, made it 4–3 deep in added time and nearly snatched an undeserved equaliser. The 2017 FA Trophy meeting was memorable as Kezie Ibe scored deep in stoppage time at Silver Jubilee Park to force a replay at the Rebels' new Arbour Park ground. Hendon had to draft in teenage goalkeeper Dan Purdue to replace Tom Lovelock and he had an inspired debut. Dan Uchechi gave Hendon the lead, but veteran Manny Williams forced extra-time with a very late equaliser. The game went to penalties, when Purdue was the hero, making three saves as Hendon won 3–0 in the shootout.

The two memorable League matches were in April 1986 and August 1994. The first came at the end of the Greens' astonishing run to pull out of the relegation zone and they went to Wexham Park needing a win to be sure of safety, though other teams still had games to play. Roger Wade scored early in the first half, and Mark Broughton produced one of the finest saves I have ever seen from a Hendon goalkeeper to keep it at 1–0. Two goals in three minutes from Mick Kiely and Andy O'Brien gave Hendon breathing room until Slough reduced the arrears. Nerves jangling, the game was made safe in the 88th minute with a counter-attack from Danny Worley and Steve Newing and when the ball was played into the penalty area, Tony Gibson netted and hugged me in celebration behind the goal.

Eight years later, on 12 August 1994, the season when kick-ins could replace throw-ins in the Isthmian League, Ivor Arbiter confirmed his takeover of Hendon FC, saving the club from oblivion; a couple of hours after the noon signing deadline for the season – with the League's permission – secretary Graham Etchell registered a team to play in the Isthmian League. A day later, Hendon travelled to Wexham Park to face a Slough team which had just been relegated from the Conference. The Greens had a brand-new team with 13 debutants in the 15, most of whom were stepping up two divisions with manager Mick Browne from Malden Vale. Slough – who would gain promotion at the end of the season – were filled with experienced players and the Hendon fans feared a rout when conceding early. But Uche Egbe equalised and then Steve McKimm gave the Greens the lead with less than 25 minutes played. It didn't last as Slough drew level, but they could not get a winner and that 2–2 draw is, in my opinion given what had gone on in the previous four months, one of Hendon's finest ever results.

Erskine Smart

Erskine Smart was a defender who came through the ranks at Claremont Road in the 1980s. He made a couple of appearances for Hendon at under-18 level, before becoming a regular in the reserve team. In October 1985, manager Gary Hand gave the 21-year-old Erskine his first-team debut in the Isthmian League Cup at Feltham. It was a banana-skin tie against a mid-table Isthmian League Division Two South team at Feltham Arena, a windswept athletics stadium with an Astroturf pitch. Erskine played on the right side of midfield with future Fulham first-teamer Richard Langley behind him. The Greens were

229

struggling near the foot of the table and eventually saw off their hosts 3–1 after extra-time. Erskine scored Hendon's first goal thanks to a spectacular long range strike. His league debut followed week later, but there was little to celebrate as Farnborough Town recorded a 5–1 win at Claremont Road.

Langley soon moved on – to Corinthian–Casuals from where he made the step up to the professional game – and Erskine became the regular right-back. He finished the season with 30 appearances, including the Middlesex Senior Cup Final victory over Southall at Enfield's Southbury Road. He was also right-back the night Hendon achieved Premier Division safety with a 4–1 last game victory away to Slough Town, a night indelibly etched in the memory of every Hendon fan who was at Wexham Park.

Erskine's second goal came in September 1986, in the FA Cup, in very strange circumstances. Banstead Athletic were first qualifying round visitors to Claremont Road when, midway through the first half, Athletic's centre-half was escorted from the pitch, and – in full kit – taken to a waiting car. He wasn't being arrested, but had just been informed that his house was on fire. With no time to prepare a substitute for action, Banstead were down to 10 men as Hendon took a corner, from which Erskine netted. This was Hendon's longest season, comprising 76 matches, and Erskine made 59 appearances, all but one as a starter. He also collected runners-up medals in both the AC Delco (Isthmian League) and GMAC (Premier Inter-League) Cups, after defeats against Bognor Regis Town and Kettering Town, respectively.

The late 1980s were nothing if not eventful for Hendon FC. In 1987–88, Erskine started all 42 Isthmian League, matches. He also played in a number of memorable cup ties that year, including the 4–2 reverse to Reading at Elm Park in the FA Cup first round proper. Six and a half months later, Hendon were at Wembley Stadium, playing in the Russell Grant Middlesex Charity Cup Final, against Wembley FC. Erskine collected his second – and final – winner's medal at Hendon, as the Greens won 2–0 in their last appearance under the Twin Towers.

Erskine was an old-fashioned full-back in that he was a defender first and foremost, though he was more than able to provide width on the overlap. He had great speed, which meant few wingers got past him. His timing and tackling techniques made him one of the best full-backs in the Isthmian League. Erskine missed only four league matches in 1988–89, a season which started brightly and ended with the club in disarray, especially off the field. The following season saw the Greens slide backwards as key players were allowed to leave, mainly to balance the books. Erskine, as one of the most valuable assets was one of the first to go, leaving at the start of December. He went on to play for

Enfield and St Albans, among others and – as recently as spring 2014 – was named by many Saints fans in their all-time team.

After more than six years away from Claremont Road Erskine was one of the first of the myriad signings by Neil Price as he desperately tried to keep Hendon in the Premier Division. His second debut was in a 3–0 home defeat at the hands of Kingstonian, and this second spell, like so many of Price's signings, was brief. Playing now at left-back, instant results were demanded and two draws in five matches was not considered good enough. It says more about Price's panic than anything else that after five games, 31-year-old Erskine was replaced in the number 3 shirt by Michael Gonzague. Overall, Erskine made 231 appearances for the club, scoring three times.

After leaving Hendon for a second time, Erskine moved into coaching and worked at Yeading. In 2010, he ran in the London Marathon and two of those who sponsored him were long-time Hendon team-mates Dave Root and Colin Tate, the latter posting a message on his Just Giving messageboard "Good luck Skinhead. Pace yourself son, and then crash it up the channel!"

Southall

Hendon has met Southall in three different League competitions, as well as in various cup competitions. Southall FC were also briefly known as Southall & Ealing Borough.

The club's history with Southall goes back to 15 March 1913, when Hampstead Town, in its fifth season overall and first in senior football, met Southall in the Middlesex Charity Cup. Oscar Sumner scored in a 1–1 draw and the Town won the replay on Thursday evening, 3 April, 5–0, but there are no details of the scorers. Six months later the clubs were rivals in the FA Cup, but this time Southall came out on top, 3–1, with Bill Hooper scoring Town's goal. A year later, Hampstead Town joined the Athenian League, which was suspended following the outbreak of World War 1, but the club again played Southall in the FA Cup which was played to a conclusion, this time winning 3–1, with Alan Humphreys, George Garlick and Hooper netting.

While Hampstead Town were still a relatively new club, Southall were already more than 40 years old, having been founded in 1871. Members of the Southern League from 1896 to 1905, they had been members of the Great Western League since 1907. Throughout the clubs' rivalry – until the final meeting in 2004 – Hendon's away games were always played at the very strange Western Road ground. The capacity of Western Road was well in excess of 10,000 – they shoe-horned in almost 20,000 for their FA Cup third round tie against Watford in 1936, but there were seats for barely 150 in a stand perched at the top of terracing down one side.

Hampstead Town's first official league match against Southall was, in fact, the club's first league game since the Athenian League was abandoned in September 1914. It was in the short-lived, eight-team United Senior League that ran for the half-season of winter and spring 1919. On 4 January 1919, Hampstead suffered a 5–3 defeat at the Avenue Ground, but took revenge in mid-April with a 2–0 away win. T. Poltock scored in both games, a double in the loss, while Henry Caves and Charlie Allwright got others, the latter at Western Road.

Southall then joined Hampstead in the Athenian League from 1919, but first the teams met for a third time in the FA Cup in that year, when George Blackburn and W. Bush, with two, gave the Town a 3–1 victory. In the League meetings, Hampstead completed a quick-fire double, Blackburn scoring in a 1–0 win at Western Road on Christmas Day and Fred Burrage and John Croal, a 2–1 Boxing Day success at the Avenue Ground. The only FA Amateur Cup meeting came in November 1921 when goals from Reg Kirby and Les Vance were enough for a 2–1 win. Strangely, given the closeness of the two clubs, they would meet only twice more in the FA Cup, both victories for Southall, in 1927, 3–2, and in 1931, 3–0.

By coincidence, not only were Southall Hampstead Town's first post-war opponents in 1919, they were also Golders Green's last Athenian League rivals before the outbreak of the Second World War caused the suspension of that competition in 1939 – a 0–0 draw.

In Hendon's various guises, the club met Southall in every Athenian League season between 1919 and 1963 – a total of 77 matches in 38 seasons. Southall spent 48 mainly mediocre seasons in the Athenian League, the rare exceptions being 1925 FA Amateur Cup runners-up, they lost 2–1 to Clapton at Millwall, league champions in 1927 and runners-up in 1955. In their Athenian days, they also won both the Middlesex Senior and Middlesex Charity Cup on eight occasions, including doubles in 1923 and 1937.

The league rivalry resumed from 1975 to 1978, when they were Southall & Ealing Borough. Hendon were their first Isthmian League top division opponents in August 1975, when Eggie James and Alan Phillips helped earn a 2–2 draw. In the return, Dave Metchick, Rod Haider, Tony Field and John Baker netted in a 4–2 victory. The other four games were split with one win each – a young Alan Devonshire, who went on to play for West Ham United and England, destroyed Hendon in a 3–0 Southall win at Claremont Road in September 1976 – and two draws before Southall were relegated in 1978. In 1986 Hendon won 2–0 in the Middlesex Senior Cup Final at Enfield, a day marked by sunshine, rain, snow, sleet, hail, thunder and a Colin Tate extra-time double to decide it. The last meeting was a Senior Cup semi-final in 2004, a match Hendon won 2–0 at Chesham United's Meadow Park ground thanks to two goals from Eugene Ofori.

Overall the club's record shows 67 wins, 22 draws, 44 defeats in 133 competitive matches. Hendon won and drew two friendlies and lost the voided match in the 1939–40 season. Having won 23 more matches, unsurprisingly Hendon have a large goals advantage too, 281 to 210. The biggest win in the rivalry was Golders Green's 9–0 triumph in the 1932–33 Middlesex Charity Cup, while the biggest defeat was a 7–3 reverse for the Green in February 1935 – Billy Breagan grabbed doubles in both matches.

Having lost their Western Road ground some years ago, Southall disappeared from senior football after pulling out of the Combined Counties League Premier Division in 2005–06. The club was back, in the Spartan South Midlands League Division One, in 2012 and won their first league title in 90 years in 2018, earning promotion via an FA switch to the Combined Counties League Premier Division.

Substitutes

When I first watched football, many decades ago, substitutes were almost unknown. They were not part of the game until the mid-1960s and when England won the World Cup in 1966, the 11 who started were the 11 who finished, unless a player had to go off through injury.

Substitutes were available in some friendly matches – though not the wholesale 11 changes which occur in early pre-season games nowadays – but the first player to be a used substitute for Hendon in an Isthmian League fixture was Jimmy Quail, who replaced Danny Lakey against Wycombe Wanderers at Claremont Road on 3 September 1966. The clubs records show that in the first four league games, Hendon did not use a substitute. I am fairly certain in that 1966–67 season, the rule was that a substitute could only replace an injured player, and none of the replacements managed to score during the season or in 1967–68 for that matter. Welsh international Barrie Davies – who rejoined the club briefly in 1974–75 – was the first replacement to get on the Hendon scoresheet when he replaced Micky Cannon against Oxford City at Claremont Road on 20 August 1968 and netted the opener in a 4–2 victory.

The media's love for alliteration (*mea culpa*) has brought "super-sub" into football-speak and three super-subs stick out in my Hendon memory. Two out of the three went on to start more than 100 games for the Greens, Steve Jefferies and Dale Binns, but both were used as substitutes in more than a quarter of their appearances. The last, Danny Worley, started only 21 of his 61 first-team games. Strangely, all three had occupations in the public sector: Jefferies was a City of London policeman, meaning he was unavailable on the day of the Lord Mayor's Show – normally the day of the FA Cup first round proper; Binns still works for a London borough council and Worley became an RAF airman though tragically, working in the private sector, he was killed in a plane crash in 2000. However, his actions helped to save the lives of his passengers – including F1 motor racing driver David Coulthard.

I thought that Jefferies had limited skill as a player, but was blessed with exceptional pace. His first season was 1974–75, when the club was rebuilding after the team which had played Newcastle broke up. He spent four seasons with the club and only in the third was he used as a shock tactic against tiring defenders; it was also his most prolific as he netted 11 times in 36 appearances, 17 as a sub. Overall, he scored 30 goals in 141 appearances, both starting and off the bench.

Worley joined Hendon in the mid-1980s, when Princes Park FC became the Greens' Under-18 midweek side. His team-mates included Phil Gridelet and Steve Newing, who went on to have long careers, Phil in the professional game and Steve mainly at Edgware Town. Watching Dan was especially exciting for me because I worked with his father at a central London publishing house and he also lived relatively close to me. I got to know Dan quite well and he was a genuinely nice person, someone who seemed surprised that he enjoyed so much success at such a high level of football – one of the finest managers in our level of non-League football, Ted Hardy, thought the world of him.

Some Hendon fans might find it strange that I have put Dale Binns in the list of super-subs, but his record for Hendon shows it is not inappropriate. Dale made his debut as a sub against Boreham Wood at Meadow Park on Easter Saturday, 3 April 1999, aged 17. In his two seasons when Frank Murphy was the manager, Dale came off the bench 43 times and started only 40 games; he netted 20 goals too. With Dave Anderson in charge Dale was in the starting 11 on 73 occasions from 2001 to 2003 and was a used substitute 20 times. In his last season, as he fought a niggly groin injury, Dale was a substitute 20 times in 35 appearances. When he returned, in 2016–17, now aged 35 and a veteran of top-level non-league football, the pace had been replaced by guile, but he appeared only five times, once as a substitute, before recurring injuries caused him to walk away from football. Twenty years after his senior debut, Dale – along with a number of other former Hendon players and off-field staff – enjoyed Wembley glory, winning the FA Vase against Cray Valley Paper Mills.

Early in his only season with Hendon, 2017–18, Josh Walker certainly made an impact in three of the four times he came off the bench. He scored the winner against Dulwich Hamlet barely four minutes after coming on as a sub and at Worthing, Josh needed only five minutes to turn one point into three for the Greens.

Finally, probably the most amazing debut by a Hendon substitute was that of Brian Haule on 14 September 2002, who earned a point for the Greens at Hampton & Richmond Borough, scoring with his first touch in senior football. At the other end of the scale, Aryan Tajbakhsh made his debut as a half-time substitute away to AFC Sudbury, but was sent off after only eight minutes on the pitch as the Greens lost 3–1.

Supporters Association

There is a group of people without whom, Hendon Football Club probably would not exist, the Hendon Football Club Supporters Association. Before I go any further, this is not to ignore the club's current owners, Hendon FC Supporters Trust – without whom the club definitely would not be here and playing at Silver Jubilee Park, now – but the Supporters Association is approaching 90 years old.

The Association was founded in September 1933 when the club had just become Golders Green and the stadium at Claremont Road was only seven years old. I am fairly certain that no founding members are still associated with HFCSA. The first chairman was Mark Rutherford, who held the post for 35 years. His successor was Ernie Webb, followed by Len Burt and then Mike Hogan. At the end of the Supporters Association's 81st season, there had been only four chairmen – at which point Mike retired, being appointed Life President, and Sandra Wood became number five.

I joined the Supporters Association in the early 1970s, mainly because only HFCSA members could travel on the coach to away games. The coach steward? Mike Hogan, of course. When I started watching the Greens, there was a largish structure behind Claremont Road's car park end goal; it was the Supporters Association viewing area, built as a small reward so that the hard-working committee members, having finished their pre-game tasks, could watch games from a reasonable vantage point.

The aim of the HFCSA has always been the same, to support, physically and financially, the football club in whatever ways it can. It is hard to know exactly how much money in donations the Association has passed to the football club over the years, or how much they have spent on stadium upkeep and purchasing other equipment.

I never knew either Mark or Ernie because I joined the HFCSA Committee in the early 1980s, after the latter's passing. Len was not a Hendon man; he came from south-west England and married into the Hendon family because his wife was the sister of long-time committee member Fred Plowman – and they lived on different floors of the same house in West Hampstead when I got to know them.

Len's passion for Hendon FC was boundless and his love for the club, as HFCSA Chairman was all consuming. I remember the bleak night in 1994 when it was announced that he had died – just before a game at Claremont Road – and it was my sad task to write his obituary in the Hendon programme. I cannot recall exactly what I wrote, but I do remember that one consistent theme was that Len would never publicly – or in a meeting – criticise anything the football club did, whether he agreed with it or not. My resignation from the HFCSA Committee came from one of these disagreements. I felt something very wrong had been done by the club, and although Len had agreed with me, when it came to a club meeting, Len could not bring himself to oppose the move. In hindsight – and it took a few years for me to realise this – Len had to SUPPORT the club (the capitals are deliberate).

Mike Hogan has done just about everything for Hendon except being involved in playing, coaching or managing. Bits of the stadium being built, rebuilt, made safe … there was Mike, a carpenter by trade, bending his back and getting the job done. Then when the club decided that the match-day catering at Claremont Road should be taken over by the Supporters Association, Hogey's Tea Bar was created. For decades, Mike preferred the away games to the home ones, simply because he could watch the Greens and not burgers being cooked. Mike retired from work in the mid-2000s and, following the death of his parents – both of whom had previously helped Mike in the tea bar – sold his house a short drive from Claremont Road and moved to Colchester in Essex, a long commute; it's 150 miles and a four-hour round trip to SJP.

The role of chair has passed through a few hands and, in summer 2019, it was John Rock. He succeeded husband and wife Tony and Sandra Wood, two more Hendon fans for whom the football club is in their blood. Sandra's first match was the 1965 Amateur Cup semi-final against Finchley at Highbury – Hendon won 4–1 – and for most of the past 53 seasons she has been a regular. Sandra met Tony, at a Hendon match and for many years, they were accompanied their two daughters Vicky and Sarah. In addition, Sandra's two sisters, Janet and Geraldine were long-time fans, though sadly, Geraldine died early in 2017 – less than a year after her husband Dave, another dyed-in-the-wool, roll-up-the-sleeves supporter. Dave Clarke built the concrete wall that stood in front of the main stand at Claremont Road, but that is was what Hendon fans do. Sandra and Tony will still be found on most matchdays at Silver Jubilee Park running the club shop, in a part of the ground named in honour of Sandra's sister and brother-in-law.

You want a family club? Sandra is proof, but so were Mike, Len and Ernie before her.

Sutton United

Sutton United are one of Hendon's most longstanding rivals. Although there were spells when the two clubs did not meet, the first fixture was in the Athenian League almost 96 years ago, on 28 January 1922, when a double from Reg Kirby and another from Stan Briscoe gave Hampstead Town a 3–1 victory at the Avenue Ground. Sutton got their revenge in the return three months later as they won 4–1, H White netting for Town. With the exception of the Second World War – when the Athenian League was suspended – the clubs met in league action every year for 64 seasons, a run which included both clubs joining the Isthmian League for the 1963–64 season.

Sutton joined the Athenian League in 1921 season and, like Hendon, won the League title on three occasions, in 1928, 1946 and 1958. They were denied a double on goal difference in 1947, when Barnet topped the table. Hendon's Amateur Cup record is better than Sutton's, the men in amber and chocolate reached the final only once in the clubs' Athenian era, and that was in 1962–63, when Eddie Reynolds bagged a four-timer of headers to give Wimbledon a 4–2 victory at Wembley.

Leyton were an integral part of Sutton's two other best runs of this era, both to the quarter-finals; in 1928–29, Sutton were expelled from the competition after beating the Cup-holders, and Leyton triumphed after a replay in 1936–37 – in both cases the Lea Bridge Road club lost in the Final. In their Isthmian days, Sutton reached the 1967–68 semi-final, losing to Leytonstone and the 1968–69 final, going down to North Shields. Sutton have been to Wembley once in the FA Trophy, losing 1–0 to Bishop's Stortford in 1981, but they have also suffered two semi-final reverses, in 1992–93 and 1999–2000, to Wycombe Wanderers and Kingstonian, respectively.

Amazingly, given the clubs have played each other for almost 100 years, there has never been an FA Cup meeting. However, there were three in the Amateur Cup – all in Surrey, once each as Hampstead, Golders Green and Hendon – and four in the FA Trophy the last of which was in January 2018. In the Amateur Cup United won two out of three, and three out of four in the FA Trophy.

Hendon, in the 1965 Amateur Cup, run claimed victory 2–1, with

237

David Hyde and Peter Slade the marksmen. Davis Haule and Ross Pickett were the Greens' goal scorers in a 2–1 FA Trophy success in 2001, a result which came either side of losses in 1996, 3–1 with Dean Murphy netting, 2008 – Harry Hunt scoring in the 2–1 defeat – and 3–0 in 2018. Although Sutton dominated the rivalry in the past 45 years, Hendon won 2–0 at Gander Green Lane in the 1987 GMAC Cup when Roger Wade and Dermot Drummy scored the goals.

A decade earlier, Hendon had surprised United with a 3–2 extra-time victory in the Isthmian League Cup, thanks to goals from Alan Campbell, Tony Field and Bobby Southam. In the London Senior Cup, Hendon have won three of the five ties, in 1925–26, 1945-46 (after a goalless draw) and in 1966–67. Sutton, were victorious in January 1958 and again 20 seasons later.

High-scoring games have been a notable feature of the 147 Athenian and Isthmian League meetings – it's an odd number because, in 2000–01, a late-season fixture pile-up saw the much-postponed Gander Green Lane match being called off for a fourth time on the final day of the season, when Hendon were due to play three times: 08.00 at Sutton, 15.00 at Dulwich – which was played and won 3–0 – and 20.30 at home to Harrow Borough; the Harrow game was called off.

Golders Green actually hold the record for the biggest win of the series, 8–0 in 1935–36, but there are no details available of the game at Claremont Road. A season earlier, the Green had won 7–1 at Claremont Road just six weeks after being on the wrong end of a 6–2 scoreline in Surrey. And the Green, in their last season before the club became Hendon, had the worst pair of results, losing 7–2 at Gander Green Lane in August 1945 and 6–0 at Claremont Road in March 1946.

Hendon have also suffered two other 6–0 home defeats against Sutton, in 1962–63, the pre-penultimate Athenian League match, and in 1991–92, it was the same story. In April 1982, Sutton goalkeeper Dave Collyer, wanting nothing of another home goal in stoppage time, blasted a penalty closer to the West Sutton Station platform than the goal to keep the score at 5–1. Eighteen months later, there was no such mercy. Neil Norman's only Hendon goal and a double from Derek Williams came in a 7–3 rout. However, Hendon fans have very fond memories of the 4–2 win at Claremont Road on 14 March 1998, when Freddie Hyatt smashed one in from the half-way line.

As far as rivalries go, this one is almost even. Sutton hold the narrowest of leads in League encounters, having won 61 to Hendon's 60, with 26 draws. In cup competitions, both clubs have won seven with a solitary draw, so Hendon's complete record against Sutton is:

Played 162	Lost 68
Won 67	Goals for 301
Drawn 27	Goals against 309.

Dave Swain

In modern football, a player scoring a goal every other game would be just about the first name on the team-sheet. Dave Swain joined Hendon from Tooting & Mitcham United in the summer of 1962 and made a scoring debut against Dulwich Hamlet in a London Charity Cup defeat that November. Despite scoring 15 goals in 19 matches that season, 14 in the Athenian League – he was top league scorer and joint-top overall with Miles Spector – he spent the next two campaigns as essentially a reserve. It is perhaps unsurprising, that getting only very occasional first-team outings he was not successful and those two seasons brought a combined seven appearances, and no goals. Playing for the reserves, Dave was prolific and the second string emulated the first squad in 1964–65 by completing a treble of their own, this one the Isthmian League reserve section and London and Middlesex Intermediate Cups. Five of the squad went on to have long careers as first-teamers at Claremont Road: Dave, David Shacklock, Micky Cooper, Fred Pudney and Laurie Churchill.

Of course, it had to be said that Hendon were anything but short of goals, especially in 1964–65's first-team treble season, when Jimmy Quail, Danny Lakey and Peter Slade all amassed at least 30 goals – and David Hyde added another 59 – in all the net bulged 192 times! In 1963–64, the Greens had two men with 21 goals and Hyde and Gerry O'Rourke on 37 and 39, respectively.

Hyde suffered an injury during the 1965–66 season, and this gave Dave Swain his chance. Although he made only 18 appearances in the Isthmian League, Dave still found the target 15 times, and his 18 from 30 games overall was a better strike rate than Hyde's 22 from 40, though far behind Laurie Churchill's 39 from 49. Hendon were, it must be said, still scoring goals for fun and in 1965–66, they notched 168 in 53 matches (3.2 per game). In the 1965–66 Amateur Cup final, it was Swain who wore the No.9 shirt while Hyde wore 11. Despite this, the only Hendon goal came from centre-half Geoff Riddy, and Wealdstone got three to take the trophy.

Hyde then turned professional at Wimbledon – who had joined the Southern League after winning the Isthmian title ahead of Hendon in 1964 – but Dave was not given the centre-forward's role. This went to former Barnet forward Tony Harding, who delivered 30 goals in 45 appearances. Swain made the same number of appearances but his total was only 16, joint second-best with Danny Lakey and one more than Jimmy Quail. Struggling to match his strike rate from previous seasons, Dave scored in the FA Amateur Cup semi-final second replay defeat against Skelmersdale United, but it was his first goal in seven matches, in those days a long drought and, it proved, his last.

239

Dave played in a 1–0 Isthmian League defeat at Barking, but did not play again for the first team, and thus missed out on a Middlesex Senior Cup winner's medal from the 2–0 defeat of Enfield. It seemed clear to Dave that his Hendon opportunities in 1967–68 would be, at best, limited, so he took the decision to seek first-team action elsewhere and, like so many players at the time, if it was not Enfield then it would be Wealdstone. Never a regular, Dave played in only 67 out of 168 League matches in five Hendon seasons – his scoring total of 40 goals was a strike rate of almost 0.6 per game – so it would be fair to say he was never given a real chance to show his talents. He signed for Hendon's local rivals Wealdstone, having started 101 games for Hendon and scored 49 times.

It must be remembered that this was a very different era of football. Players were all amateurs; there was no pyramid so, for them, the single-division Isthmian League was significantly the best available, with the three-division Athenian League a distinctly lesser option. They also were more likely to stay local as significant numbers would have to rely on public transport to get to training and matches – something of an issue in midweek; the other factor was limited use of substitutes: only one could be named and until 1967, they could only be used to replace an injured player.

John Swannell

For older Hendon fans – anyone who can remember the 1973–74 season and earlier – John Swannell was probably the greatest goalkeeper in English amateur football history, and was Hendon's goalkeeper from 1963 to 1974 and briefly in 1980–81.

As a student, John played in two professional matches, both in the early years of the Football League Cup, for Stockport County and Crystal Palace, but was keener to pursue his career in engineering than turning professional. At Corinthian–Casuals, John got a grounding that would hold him in good stead throughout his career. Hendon, amongst other clubs, followed his progress with the Casuals and when they joined the Isthmian League in 1963, John signed up.

By modern standards, John would be considered small for a goalkeeper, and in those days he was merely a little below average in height, but he was well-built and able to look after himself. An outstanding shot-stopper, he was brilliant at organising his defence and rarely got his angles wrong. When it came to the hurly-burly of the six-yard box at set-pieces, John was not afraid to punch and his technique was excellent.

His first season at Claremont Road saw a great challenge for the League title, but Wimbledon pipped the Greens and there was no glory in the FA, Amateur or Middlesex Senior Cups. However, he kept a clean sheet in the London Senior Cup final, a 1–0 victory over Enfield. In 1964–65, Hendon carried all before them, winning the League – with a 4–1 victory over Enfield in a playoff – and the FA Amateur Cup, a 3–1 defeat of Whitby Town at Wembley, and Middlesex Senior Cup. Another highlight came at Highbury when Arsenal were beaten 4–3 in the London Challenge Cup. John was injured during the Amateur Cup run and missed a few matches, but still played 47 times during the season, including all the key finals, and made his England debut.

John's England career was outstanding and his total of 60 caps earned while at Hendon is the all-time one-club record – Rod Haider won 55 while at Hendon, having won 10 with Kingstonian. He also was also first choice for the Great Britain Olympic team in an era when eastern Europe dominated amateur football with their full internationals being eligible as amateurs, usually through serving in the military or police forces. He was one of four Hendon players who played against West Germany in a qualifying round match at Claremont Road in 1967.

Hendon slipped a little from their mid-decade perch as the very best in the Isthmian League in the second half of the 1960s, but were still a strong team. In the 1970s, however, the Greens returned to the top and Swannell played a massive part in the resurgence. After winning a second Amateur Cup in 1972, Hendon's defence in the next two seasons was exceptional. In the 1972–73 season, when the Greens were undefeated until the 39th match, Hendon conceded just 18 goals, none from set-pieces.

In 1973–74, Hendon reached the third round proper of the FA Cup and went out after a replay against finalists-to-be Newcastle United. Multiple cup runs meant the Rothman's Isthmian League campaign took a back-seat. A three-day working week and electricity rationing in February, saw Hendon have a very busy end-of-season schedule. The Greens finished two points behind Wycombe Wanderers in the league, having conceded just 20 goals. So, in 84 League matches over two seasons, Hendon conceded just 38 goals, less than one every two games.

John left Hendon in the summer of 1974 to join Leatherhead and enjoyed another long FA Cup run with the Tanners, reaching the fourth round proper, where First Division hosts Leicester City came back from 2–0 down to win 3–2. After half a dozen seasons at Fetcham Grove, John returned for a last hurrah at Hendon. On Tuesday 16 December 1980, aged 41 (41 days short of his 42nd birthday), John played his last Hendon League match, a 3–2 win over Hitchin Town. In fact, he wasn't finished with football and continued to play, ending with veterans matches, until he was in his mid-50s. He also played cricket at a good club level, and in retirement coached athletics.

241

The two streets at the housing development at Claremont Road were named
after Rod Haider and John Swannell. (Photo: Peter Lush)

T

Colin Tate

Tooting & Mitcham United

Laurie Topp

Colin Tate

Colin Tate scored lots of goals and played a key role in the club during the late 1980s. He appeared for Hendon in seven consecutive seasons, but the reality is that his Greens' career was in two parts and six seasons. He was a much-respected striker when signed by Gary Hand early in the 1985–86 season and made his debut against Epsom & Ewell on 31 August 1985, scoring two goals at West Street as Hendon blew a 3–1 lead to lose 5–3. It was a very difficult season for the Greens and it was not until Ted Hardy arrived as manager just before Christmas that things began to turn around. Colin's goals were a key factor in Hendon's late run, in which the Greens won six and drew five of the last 11 games to avoid the drop in the final game of the season – the famous 4–1 victory at Slough Town. Colin won the Supporters Association Player of the Year award, playing in every League match after joining the Club and finishing the season with 21 goals in 51 appearances. Two of these came when Hendon beat Southall 2–0 after extra time in the Middlesex Senior Cup Final at Enfield.

In the almost interminable season which followed – Hendon played 75 matches in total – Colin suffered a few injuries and, as a result, was able to only match his 51 starts – he also came off the bench twice – from the previous season. He did, however, improve his goal tally by a couple, the last of which was on 25 April 1987. This goal, against Croydon in a 3–1 win at Claremont Road, was followed by a full 90 minutes, 24 hours later, as Hendon drew 1–1 away to Burton Albion. Earlier in April, he had scored twice in one of the most remarkable Hendon victories, coming from 3–0 down at half-time against Harrow Borough in the Middlesex Senior Cup quarter-final to win 5–3 after extra time. He got the ball rolling with the first goal 22 seconds after the resumption. All Hendon had to show for their efforts were runners-up medals in the GMAC (Premier Inter-League) and the AC Delco (Isthmian League) Cups.

Before the start of the following season, Colin left the club, but he still made one appearance – right at the end – on 2 June 1988, when Hendon met Wembley in the Russell Grant Middlesex Charity Cup Final at Wembley Stadium. Some fans felt that the players who had performed all season deserved the glory of a Wembley appearance, but manager Micky Janes went with the players most likely to win the Cup. As it happened, there were two match-winners already in the squad and both Dermot Drummy and Iain Dowie scored in the Greens' 2–0 victory.

Colin's second spell lasted from, effectively 1988 to 1992, as the club went through very difficult financial times. In 1988–89, injuries played a key part in a campaign that fell apart in December. He played in the

Greens' 4–2 FA Cup first round defeat at Reading, but didn't get on the scoresheet, and his strike rate for the season dropped from 1 in 2.5 in his first spell to worse than 1 in 6 in 1989 – but he had not been relied upon as the main goal scorer. Things did get better in 1989–90, when he played the most matches of his Hendon career, with only Dave Root and Greg Zacharia passing his total of 55. Colin was much more of a second striker now, and Uche Egbe and Sean Baker – whose season ended prematurely – both got more than his 13.

Not the tallest of players, nor the most imposing, Colin's game was built around his intelligence – unsurprising for a lawyer – and ability to create openings. He was always a willing runner, though without a breathtaking turn of pace to get him clear of defenders. Nonetheless, he needed constant attention, which gave others around him the chance to shine. His final season with the Greens was in 1991–92 and when the new owner Victor Green started signing high-profile players such as strikers Kurt Davidson and Colin Sowerby, there was nowhere for Colin to play. The final one of Colin's 86 Hendon goals came against Marlow in a 2–1 home defeat and, on 17 March 1992, 32-year-old Colin played his final game for Hendon. At least he went out on a winning note, a 1–0 defeat of Enfield.

Tooting & Mitcham United

Hendon's 4–0 victory at Silver Jubilee Park at the end of September 2017 was the 100th competitive meeting between the clubs, if the 1924 London Senior Cup victory over Mitcham Wanderers is excluded. That game ended 6–0 to Hampstead Town with Ken Seabrook grabbing a double, Cecil Wise one and Freddie Young the last three.

Tooting, previously Tooting Town and Tooting Graveney, merged with Mitcham Wanderers in 1932, and moved into the latter's Sandy Lane ground which had opened in 1922. The United suffix was added three seasons after the merger, while Sandy Lane was the club's home for 80 years. Given a rivalry has stretched back almost a century, it is very surprising that, as London rivals, the clubs have met only 14 times in cup competitions. Nine of these ties – the Mitcham game included – were in the London Senior Cup, one in the London Charity Cup, two in the FA Amateur Cup and one each in the FA Cup and FA Trophy. In FA knock-out games, both teams have two wins, one each in the Amateur Cup. The Charity Cup game was in 1959, at Sandy Lane, and ended 3–1 to Tooting. Terry Howard scored for the Greens. Four London Senior Cup meetings were in finals and the Terrors lifted the trophy at Hendon's expense in 1959 at Highbury, 5–2, Roy Thomas's double being in vain; 2008 – 3–2, Danny Dyer and Brian Haule, a penalty, netting for Hendon; and 2016 – 2–0. The Greens' triumph was 3–2 in

2015, an extra time success, thanks to a double from Aaron Morgan and a third from Kezie Ibe. The last three finals were all at the Metropolitan Police FC's Imber Court.

Tooting joined the Athenian League in 1937 and won the first encounter 3–2 despite goals from Billy Breagan and Fred Boston. Derek Walker scored the only two goals in the Claremont Road return as the Green avenged their earlier defeat. There was a hiatus between 1956 and 1963 as Tooting joined the Isthmian League eight years before Hendon. The Greens won 11 of 26 Athenian League matches.

Tooting have enjoyed some significant FA Cup success, reaching the fourth round proper in 1975–76, this after beating Hendon's second-round conquerors Swindon Town in the last 64. However, their most notable run was probably in 1958–59, when they beat Bournemouth and Northampton before losing to eventual winners Nottingham Forest in a third round replay. The Terrors failed to make a mark in the Amateur Cup, reaching only two quarter-finals and they also made the last eight once each in the Trophy and Vase.

Once the clubs' rivalry had been resumed in the Isthmian League in 1963–64, they were regular opponents for 26 campaigns, until the Terrors were relegated in 1989. It was 20 seasons before they met again in league action, but there was a friendly in 1995 – Hendon's last visit to Sandy Lane – during a heatwave that had turned the grass yellow. The level of smog was such that the light was almost cream-coloured, none of which was an excuse for an awful 2–0 defeat. Hendon won the only FA Cup meeting, 3–0 thanks to Rob Haworth, two, and Paul Yates, in 2002. Three seasons later, Dave Hunt won a London Senior Cup semi-final with a late winner; it was the last time the Terrors played at Claremont Road.

In 2008, Tooting won promotion back to the Isthmian League top flight, but spent only four seasons there, and the Greens won four of eight meetings, with two draws. The first saw a 1–0 defeat at Imperial Fields, when Hendon had no answer to a young flier by the name of Michail Antonio, but as he has become a full England international with West Ham United, Hendon shouldn't feel too bad about it. Tormentor-in-chief in Hendon's other league defeat was Kiernan Hughes-Mason, who bagged a hat-trick as Hendon went down 4–3 in the 2011–12 season opener. The last Hendon hat-trick came in the 2009 London Senior Cup, when Glen Garner was unstoppable in a 4–0 victory.

246

Tooting were relegated in 2011–12, conceding 116 goals and finishing 20 points from safety, in 21st place. The meeting just before Christmas ended in a 3–0 Greens victory, thanks to Elliott Charles, Greg Ngoyi and a Terry Lee Fennessy own goal. The return, on the penultimate Saturday of the campaign, was even more dominant as Scott Shulton scored twice with other goals from Isaiah Rankin, Ngoyi and Carl McCluskey in a 5–0 win. The Terrors returned to the Isthmian League top division in 2017, but were relegated at the end of the campaign. After the 4–0 victory at Silver Jubilee Park, the return on 17 March was played on one of the coldest days the Greens have had a match go ahead. The area surrounding Imperial Fields was covered in snow, but the grandstand and high walls around the ground meant the pitch was almost clear of the white stuff, despite it continuing to fall throughout the game. Goals from Ashley Nathaniel-George and Zak Joseph ensured a 2–0 victory that kept up Hendon's eventually successful challenge for a playoff place.

Hendon had much the better of Isthmian League rivalry, winning 31 out of the 62 matches and it was the same in the few knock-out encounters, the Greens winning seven out 13. The biggest wins were Hampstead's 6–0 rout of Mitcham in the 1924 London Senior Cup and 5–0 as Hendon in 2012, while Tooting beat Golders Green 6–1 in a December 1945 Athenian League game. The Greens' record of matches against Tooting & Mitcham United (excluding Mitcham Wanderers) is:

Played 101   Lost 31
Won 49   Goals for 165
Drawn 21   Goals against 131.

Laurie Topp

Laurie Topp is considered by many followers of amateur football to have been the finest player ever to appear for Hendon. He spent almost all of his career with Golders Green and Hendon. At the end of Peter Lush's biography of Laurie in the club's centenary history book, he summed him up quite simply: "If there ever is a Hendon Football Club 'Hall of Fame', Laurie will be one of the first to be nominated." Much of what appears is taken from the book.

He was born in St Pancras on 11 November 1923, and moved to Edgware before starting school. Although his school was in Harrow, he played for the Hendon Borough schools team as Harrow did not have one at that time. Laurie was one of Hendon's mainstays from the mid 1940s until he retired in 1961. One of the most honoured players of his generation, with two Olympic Games, 32 England caps and many other representative honours, his period at the club saw Hendon become

247

established as one of England's top amateur teams, culminating in the 1960 Amateur Cup final 2–1 triumph against Kingstonian.

He played for Arsenal's junior sides as a youngster, but never turned professional. "I had offers, but I turned them down", he recalled. "I wasn't sure I was quite up to it". Of course, in those days, a player who signed as a professional was disbarred from the amateur game. Also, with the maximum wage in force, there were no fortunes to be made in football.

On leaving school, Laurie's mother found him a job at Desoutters in Colindale. The firm made electrical drills, used for making aircraft during the war. Being in a reserved occupation, Laurie never went into the forces.

He joined Golders Green in 1942. "I played for Davis Sports, [who subsequently helped create Kingsbury Town]. There was a fellow on the committee at Golders Green, Harry Boycott, who worked at Desoutters, and he asked me to go for a trial at the club."

The club's first Wembley appearance, often forgotten, was at the end of the war in the Middlesex Senior Red Cross Charity Cup. Laurie and Bill Fisher were the only players from that team to play in the 1955 and 1960 Amateur Cup finals. Laurie recalled: "I played at Wembley a few times, for England amateurs as well as the cup finals. I suppose I was a bit nervous, you would worry about how you were going to play. When we played Bishop Auckland, that Bob Hardisty was a great player. And in 1960 I scored against Kingstonian."

Goals from Laurie were fairly rare. He played right half – defensive midfield in today's terms. "I was told to defend, or be more attacking, depending on who we were playing. I had to run back if someone beat me and tackle them. I didn't get many goals, the forwards told you to go back if you went up too far."

Laurie has particularly fond memories of Bill Fisher. "He was there when I joined. He looked after me, helped me out, told me what to do – he was right back and I was right half. He was my best mate at the club." He recalled Dexter Adams as a "real terror" at centre half, and Pat Lynch, who joined the club from Tufnell Park after the war as "a hard player. Not many got past him." Roy Stroud was another outstanding player: "you gave him the ball, and no one could catch him."

Getting time off work for football was not usually a problem. "Stan Greene [the club secretary] used to send tickets to the managing director of Desoutters for the big games. That kept them happy. I remember when we won the cup in 1960, I spoke to the managing director as I was going up the steps to the Royal Box."

Descriptions of Laurie written during his playing career show his standing in the game. The programme for a 1953 England amateur international says he was "a tenacious tackler, and great worker and one of the most popular figures in amateur football". Another England amateurs write-up the same year describes him as "a great fetch-and-carry wing-half in the modern style". The 1955 Amateur Cup Final programme said he was "stylish, clean tackling, always smiling", while the 1960 Final programme described him as "a household name in amateur soccer and one of the most respected players".

After retiring as a player in 1961, aged 37, Laurie coached for a short time at Enfield, but felt he "was not cut out to be a coach" and soon lost interest in football. He took up golf, and used to see former Hendon colleague Bob Avis at South Herts Golf Club. He worked at Desoutters until he retired at 65, showing the same loyalty he had shown in football to Hendon. When Peter and I interviewed Laurie for the book, he brought out two black bin bags in which he "stored" his football memorabilia, including caps and medals. He offered us anything we liked from the collection, but we declined to take anything. In January 2017, the club was sad to announce that Laurie, after a long illness, had died aged 93.

Laurie played 503 matches for Hendon, scoring 11 goals (this was an era when the Athenian League never had more than a 30-match season and it was mainly 26). With Golders Green, including two wartime seasons, he made 84 appearances and netted five times. Laurie's final match was the 1960–61 Middlesex Senior Cup Final against Hounslow Town at Hayes FC's Church Road, a match. Hendon lost 3–2. During his Laurie's career at Claremont Road, the club won the Amateur Cup, three Athenian League titles, six Middlesex Charity Cups and three Middlesex Senior Cups.

U

Uxbridge and RAF Uxbridge

Hendon versus Uxbridge in the 2004 Middlesex Senior Cup Final.

The victorious Hendon team with the Cup.
(Photos: Peter Lush)

Uxbridge and RAF Uxbridge

Uxbridge / Uxbridge Town apart, there was little in the way of 'U's to choose from. Hampstead Town or Hampstead met RAF Uxbridge, four times between a 3–2 FA Amateur Cup win in October 1921 and a 5–1 Middlesex Senior Cup success in 1932 – the other two matches were also in the Senior Cup, Town winning 3–0 in March 1925, but losing 2–0 three years later. Only five players whose surnames have the "U" initial played competitively for Hendon prior to this season: Dan Uchechi 33 appearances, 3 goals, John Ugbah, 21, 3 goals, Mehmet Unal 1, Simon Underwood 11, 1 goal, and Rob Ursell 3. United is almost too broad a canvas to paint.

Uxbridge can trace a football history back to the early 1870s. A predecessor of the current club appeared in the second FA Cup competition, but they lost to eventual runners-up, Royal Engineers. A second Uxbridge club also folded, but they had been members of the Southern League second division for five years and lost 2–0 to Middlesbrough in the 1898 FA Amateur Cup final at Crystal Palace. In 1902, a third incarnation entered the West Middlesex League and joined the Great Western Suburban League a year later. It was as member of that competition when Hampstead Town first played them. On 12 April 1913, Uxbridge Town won 2–1 in the Middlesex Charity Cup, Oscar Sumner scoring the Town's goal. Uxbridge joined the Athenian League after the First World War, but were not re-elected to the league – relegated – after one season. Hampstead had won the two meetings 5–0 and 4–0, and Uxbridge spent four seasons in the Great Western Suburban League before returning to the Athenian. After losing four of the first seven League meetings, Hampstead and Golders Green went on to dominate the rivalry, losing only twice in the last 19 league contests, with a draw and two others abandoned – Hampstead and Golders Green respectively had been leading at the curtailment.

In the FA Amateur Cup, Uxbridge Town beat Hampstead Town in 1920, 4–3 after extra time, but Hampstead avenged it four years later, Freddie Young scoring a hat-trick in a 5–1 win. Golders Green won the last Amateur Cup encounter in 1933, 2–1, thanks to Bert Broadis and Freddie Evans goals. Two FA Cup ties went Hampstead's way, the first after 2–1 in a replay in October 1930, and the second 6–1 in September 1932. In the latter game, Ronnie Rowe bagged a hat-trick, Evans a double and Billy Breagan got the other. In Middlesex county cup ties, Uxbridge Town won the only Senior Cup meeting, and the Charity Cup ties after the 1913 final were shared one apiece, with the 1934–35 meeting requiring three games before the Reds won through. Golders Green enjoyed 6–2, 5–0 and 7–0 wins in Town's last three seasons in the Athenian League before they dropped out.

It is now more than 80 years since the clubs have met in league action but, as well as three friendlies, we have met in 16 cup-ties, once each in the FA Cup (a 3–1 Hendon win in 1952), Isthmian League Cup – Uxbridge were 1–0 winners in 1985, the Isthmian League Full Members Cup, Steve Heffer getting the only goal for Hendon on the way to winning the trophy for the first time in 1994, and in the 1998 London Challenge Cup, when it was the senior London competition, Warren Ryan scoring Hendon's goal in a 3–1 defeat at the Honeycroft.

In the Middlesex Charity Cup, both teams have enjoyed victory at the other's expense in the final once, Alan Campbell and Rod Haider scoring in a 2–0 victory at Claremont Road in 1977, while Dencell Green grabbed a consolation in Hendon's 2–1 loss at The Honeycroft in 1982. In both 1985 and 1990, Hendon came out on top, both times at Claremont Road, Steve Newing and George Duck netting in the former, a 2–1 win, and Lawrence Holmes getting the only tally of the latter encounter. Golders Green won a wartime Middlesex Senior Cup tie in 1945, Alan Cochrane, Harry Robshaw, two goals, and C Fair netting in 4–1 success. In 1960, Miles Spector scored for the Greens in a 1–1 draw at Southall before Terry Howard and a Jimmy Quail double at Hayes saw us win the semi-final. It would be 13 seasons before the next Middlesex Senior Cup tie, a 1–0 Hendon win thanks to Rod Haider's goal, and 24 more seasons before the teams clashed again. On 2 February 1999, Paul Whitmarsh grabbed an extra-time winner at the Honeycroft, but, two seasons later, the Reds avenged that result, winning 2–0.

In 2004, Hendon met Uxbridge in the final, at Yeading, when Eugene Ofori's opener was cancelled out by Mark Weedon's reply, both goals coming early in the second half. Hendon then had Dale Binns sent off for violent conduct, but the 10 men outlasted the 11 in extra time as Martin Randall and Dave Hunt scored late in the first of the 15-minute periods. The most recent meeting was in December 2011, at Vale Farm. The match was goalless after 90 minutes, and in extra time Uxbridge took the lead only for 38-year-old player-coach Junior Lewis to equalise with what was not only his first Hendon goal of the 21st century, but his 69th and final goal for the club. Hendon won the penalty shoot-out which followed 4–2, the final miss coming from future Greens player Howard Hall.

V

Victories – V famous ones

Victories – V famous ones

This piece focuses on victories, five (V in Roman numerals) famous ones.

29 December 2001 – Billericay Town 4 Hendon 6. Isthmian League

Twelve months earlier, Hendon had fallen to Heybridge Swifts at a frozen Scraley Road, losing 5–4 after extra time, a match I thought was great entertainment, but Simon Lawrence told me "It can't be great because we lost," or words to that effect. On the final whistle at New Lodge, he came up to me and said, "Now that was an all-time great game."

Mark Cooper opened the scoring after four minutes, but Simon Clarke and Micky Woolner scored own goals to give the Blues a half-time lead. Debutant Leon Woodruffe had been injured just before the interval, so Dale Binns replaced him for the second half. Byron Bubb set up Steve Forbes for an equaliser two minutes into the half, and Bubb, Paul Yates and Jon-Barrie Bates combined before Woolner scored a screamer at the right end. Martin Carthy equalised for Billericay before Cooper became the second Hendon player to score for both teams, restoring the Blues' lead. In the final eight minutes, Binns scored twice before, in stoppage time, Eugene Ofori added number six to seal an astonishing victory. My headline from the game? "Nine out of ten ain't bad!"

Saturday 12 October 1996 – Dover Athletic 0 Hendon 1. FA Cup

Dover Athletic were in mid-table in the Conference, Hendon were bottom of the Isthmian League Premier Division, so on paper at least, this was a banker home win. Thankfully, the afternoon was a little overcast because a solar eclipse was due late in the second half, which might have made things very interesting. Quite how the game was goalless at half-time no one knows. Mo Munden made three good saves for Dover while Jan Gert Wagenaar was outstanding between the sticks for the Greens. Ten minutes into the second half, a clearance from Wagenaar saw Richardson jump with a Dover centre-half and they seemed to clash heads because both fell to the ground. As the referee was checking that they were OK, the ball broke towards the Dover goal. Paul Kelly chased it and pushed aside the Dover player with him. Both the referee and his assistant were more concerned with the two players in the centre circle and missed the foul. Suddenly, Kelly had only the goalkeeper to beat, which he did at the second attempt. It proved to be the only goal of the game and Hendon went on to meet Cardiff in the first round proper.

Saturday 20 October 2012 – Corby Town 1 Hendon 2. FA Cup

A glorious victory against the odds saw Hendon beat a Conference second tier team for the second consecutive round. Eastbourne Borough had been beaten in dramatic fashion in a home replay 11 days earlier, and now the Greens were back on the road, this time to Conference North Corby Town. The Steelmen dominated the first 35 minutes, but had only a Josh Moreman goal to show for it. Berkley Laurencin had one of his best games in goal for the Greens and after another save, in the 37th minute, Hendon launched a counter-attack which ended with Greg Ngoyi holding

off an illegal challenge from Carl Piergianni before beating Paul Walker.

In the 63rd minute, a corner from Scott Cousins found Michael Murray, who drilled the ball into the net. Thereafter, Corby rarely threatened, but in stoppage time, their frustration blew over which resulted in Piergianni fighting with Elliott Charles, both players being dismissed. The Greens went on to lose to Aldershot Town in the first round.

For a small group of Hendon supporters the day was memorable for another reason. Corby has a large Scottish exile community, and this group, wearing their green and white scarves, went into the local branch of the Glasgow Rangers Supporters Club for a pre-match drink. After receiving some rather odd looks, they explained which team they supported, and that it was not Glasgow Celtic!

Thursday 3 April 1986 – Billericay Town 1 Hendon 4. Isthmian League

Hendon's great escape of 1985–86 was pivotal with the double over Billericay, who ended up joining Epsom & Ewell in falling through the relegation trap-door. The Blues were without giant goalkeeper Mark McCutcheon and his replacement was not in the same class. A superb performance was punctuated by a quartet of quality goals, with Steve Parsons the orchestrator-in-chief. He got the last goal in the 4–1 win,

255

with Colin Tate, Andy O'Brien and Bobby Harding having scored earlier. The Greens would hit four in the return at Claremont Road three weeks later, and in the season finale at Slough Town.

Saturday 15 December 2007 – Leyton 1 Hendon 11. Isthmian League

Hendon's biggest win in the Isthmian League came at the expense of a Leyton team riven by internal problems and managed by Vice-chairman Rowly Cray. The simple fact that Hendon took full and brutal advantage, and went to the top of the table too, showed a level of great professionalism.

Only 78 spectators were at the E10 Stadium on Lea Bridge Road to witness the slaughter. Wayne O'Sullivan with two, and Lubomir Guentchev gave Hendon a 3–0 half-time lead, but Billy Bricknell reduced the arrears early in the second half. Hendon's response was smash eight goals in the last 38 minutes. O'Sullivan with two more, Lubomir Guentchev, Sam Collins, Brian Haule, Jamie Busby with two, and Ivalio Dimitrov all beat the heroic Sam Tanner, who kept the score below 20. Nineteen seasons earlier, Hendon had lost 9–1 at the same ground; this was sweet revenge.

W

Curtis Warmington

Wealdstone

Wembley

Will Mather Cup

Richard Wilmot

Bobby Wilson

Wingate (& Finchley)

Danny Worley

Curtis Warmington

Curtis Warmington was a 'fans' favourite' as well as being a defender, captain, and player-coach. Curtis, it would be fair to say, wore his heart on his sleeve, and his honesty, passion and desire made him a fans' favourite pretty much everywhere he played. A very strange statistic of his Hendon career, which comprised six seasons, was that he never reached even 40 appearances in a season, but did have three with 39 and one with 37.

He was a midfielder when he left the West Ham United academy, but by the time he made his name in the Isthmian League it was as a defender. And, it must be said, few defenders have been as solid and uncompromising as Curtis – certainly in the modern era – and it brought him significant success in a career that lasted almost 20 years. His clubs, before joining Hendon for the first time in 1993, included Dulwich Hamlet, Yeovil Town and Carshalton Athletic. Curtis did not make his Hendon debut until the middle of September, coming on as a substitute for Bob Dowie in a League Cup loss at Boreham Wood. His first start came in midfield, at home to Heybridge Swifts in the FA Cup and he scored his first goal, too, in a 5–2 victory.

The turmoil of December 1993 to January 1994 meant a very different Hendon finished the campaign. Dowie was player-manager, Curtis was captain, and they were centre-back partners. Dowie's four months in charge ended with glory in the Full Members Cup Final, a 2–1 victory over Wokingham Town at Marlow and it was Curtis who lifted the trophy. Pretty much all of the squad left in the summer of 1994, Curtis included, and he spent time at Enfield and Walton & Hersham before returning to Claremont Road to play for Neil Price. The highlight of the season was a run to the first round proper of the FA Cup and Curtis played in the 2–0 defeat to Cardiff City, thanks to the Greens arranging a Middlesex Senior Cup tie two days before the big game, to allow him to complete a suspension.

Frank Murphy took over as manager in March 1997 and helped the Greens avoid relegation. It would be fair to say that the central defence at the start of Frank's first full season was experienced, the four main centre-backs, Curtis, Steve Bateman, Richard Nugent and Tony Kelly had an aggregate age of 131. It did mean that they all were a little frail, with only Kelly – 51 – despite chronic knee issues – reaching a half-century of appearances. The 1997–98 season was memorable on so many levels, especially the FA Cup first round proper victory over Leyton Orient and the Full Members Cup Final success against Basingstoke at Chesham. The second goal of that glorious evening, the one that gave Hendon the lead, was reminiscent of Tommy Smith in the 1977 European Cup Final – a veteran centre-half storming into the penalty area and smashing a header into the net – only this time it was Curtis who grabbed the glory.

The last goal of Curtis's Hendon career came the following season, and it was another key one, a shot from the edge of the penalty area at New Lodge, Billericay, then the home of Chelmsford United, and a 3–2 FA Cup qualifying round replay victory, completing a comeback from 2–0 down. The Greens went on to face Notts County in the first round proper, but Curtis was an unused substitute in the first game and the replay. At the end of that season, Curtis was captain when Hendon met Worthing in the Full Members Cup Final, against Worthing at Sutton United's Gander Green Lane. Matt Maran's goal was enough to allow Curtis to lift the trophy for the second time as Hendon skipper. It was also the second trophy of the year for him as Hendon had beaten Wembley at Enfield in the Middlesex Senior Cup Final a month earlier.

Frank Murphy appointed Curtis as player-coach for the 1999–2000 season and the additional responsibilities cut into his playing time, with just 22 appearances. Although he was involved in the three qualifying rounds of the FA Cup, he was simply the coach against Bath City and Blackpool. Curtis turned 36 during the weather-blighted 2000–01 season. He was very much a coach as opposed to player-coach, as proved by his three starts all coming in early rounds of cup competitions. His only other appearance came in the penultimate match of the season, a 5–0 loss at home to Aldershot Town, the second of three games on consecutive days, with two more left unplayed. Frank left at the end of the season, and both Curtis and Dave Anderson applied for the job. When Dave was appointed, Curtis quickly moved to join Frank who took over at Carshalton Athletic. He later was a coach with Bromley, managed Whyteleafe and was assistant manager back at Carshalton.

Wealdstone

Arguably Hendon's fiercest rivalry this century has been that with Wealdstone. There is certainly a case that, historically, Hendon's biggest rivalry has been with Enfield, but that club now languishes at the wrong end of the Essex Senior League under the guide of Enfield 1893 and they are currently based at Harlow Town's Barrow Farm ground. It should also be said that the Greens and Harrow Borough have met many more times since 2000, but this rivalry is much friendlier.

There is certainly no club that Hendon, in various guises, has met in more competitions than Wealdstone, an amazing 18, including the wartime Herts & Middlesex League Cup, the Middlesex Junior Cup, Centenary Cup and George Ruffell Memorial Shield, or in five different leagues, the Willesden, London, Middlesex, Athenian and Isthmian. Wealdstone's history dates back to 1899, but there was a two-year hiatus before the club reformed in 1908. The first time the teams met was back on 17 September 1910, when Hampstead Town travelled to Wealdstone in the Willesden League, and left on the wrong end of a 5–0 scoreline. There is no record, sadly of the return, but Wealdstone also won a Middlesex Junior Cup tie in January 1911. The following season, both clubs were in the London League, and Wealdstone won both matches, including a 7–5 triumph at home. Two seasons later, in the Middlesex League, which Hampstead Town won, we recorded a double, winning 3–2 and 2–0 in March 1914.

Hampstead joined the Athenian League in 1914, but football was put on hold because of the First World War. Wealdstone played in the London and Middlesex Leagues before joining the Athenian in 1928. However, before then, Hampstead won a 1921 FA Cup tie 1–0, Reg Kirby scoring, and a 1920 Middlesex Charity Cup tie 6–1, the highlight of which was a hat-trick, on his debut for F Cushing. He only played one more match for the club. The Second World War apart, the clubs met in Athenian League competition every season from 1928 to 1963, when Hendon moved to the Isthmian League.

A year later, the rivalry was resumed as the Stones – knocked back in their application in 1963 – were able to join the Isthmian competition. The annual contests continued for only a short time as Wealdstone turned professional in 1971 and entered the Southern League. Comparatively, going back to 1928, Hendon have the better League record, winning three Athenian League titles and one Isthmian crown, compared to a solitary Athenian title for Wealdstone. Since then, however, Wealdstone have enjoyed far greater highs and lows than the Greens, the highlight being in 1985 when they won both the Conference and FA Trophy. After losing Lower Mead, they spent many years travelling nomadically, with temporary homes at Watford, Yeading, Edgware and Northwood. They went into Ruislip Manor's Grosvenor Vale ground with the hosts in terminal decline.

However, the biggest match between the clubs came on 16 April 1966, at Wembley Stadium, in the FA Amateur Cup Final. The Greens were favourites to retain the trophy they had won 12 months earlier, being on their way to a runners-up spot in the Isthmian League, 13 points clear of sixth-placed Wealdstone – there were two points for a win in those days. The Stones upset the formbook by winning 3–1. Geoff Riddy gave Hendon the lead after just five minutes, but future Hendon favourite Bobby Childs equalised just before half-time. The game looked as if it was going into extra time, but Wealdstone scored against through Bobby Bremer after 85 minutes and, three minutes later, Childs followed up to score after John Swannell had partially saved a shot from Hugh Lindsay.

In fact, in 1965–66 the clubs must have been pretty sick of the sight of each other because there were seven meetings. Hendon won the two Isthmian League encounters, but the Stones won replays in both the London and Middlesex Senior Cups, the latter competition at the semi-final stage.

The biggest win in Hendon versus Wealdstone matches was on Boxing Day 1934, when Golders Green put six without reply past Wealdstone; a day earlier Wealdstone hit six, but Green had replied with four of their own. The 1911 London League match which Wealdstone was the highest scoring match, 7–5 to the Stones, but in 2005–06, Hendon recorded a pair of 5–4 victories over Wealdstone, mounting a famous comeback to win a league game at Northwood's Chestnut Avenue ground, then scraping a victory in the Middlesex Senior Cup at Claremont Road, which went into extra time. The last meeting was in February 2017, in the Middlesex Senior Cup semi-final, at Silver Jubilee Park, and Wealdstone won 3–1 in a penalty shoot-out.

As far as player movement is concerned, there has been a lot of it most recently in 2018–19 when the Stones sent centre-back Guri Demuria to Silver Jubilee Park. He performed excellently and his season-ending injury at Dorchester in late September certainly contributed to the Greens' problems in the second half of the season Hendon's league record against Wealdstone (in all five league competitions) is P96, W40, D22, L33 (one result is unknown), Goals for 200, Goals against 184. The cup records is also in the Greens' favour, P71, W30, D12, L19, Goals for 141, Goals against 115 (there was one abandoned Middlesex Senior Cup tie, at Edgware in February 2003). Thus, Hendon's overall record is:

Played 167	Abandoned 1
Won 70	Unknown 1
Drawn 34	Goals for 341
Lost 52	Goals against 297
(Goals include the abandonment)	

There have also been seven friendlies, which have also been split, two wins apiece and three draws.

Wembley

Wembley, both the Stadium and the football club, have both played significant roles in Hendon's history. Hendon were tenants at the latter's Vale Farm ground in Sudbury for the best part of four seasons.

Wembley Stadium

The official home of English football first opened in 1923, built in a matter of months. Hendon's first official visit to the Stadium came on 16 May 1945, a few days after the end of the Second World War, when Golders Green met our Claremont Road tenants Tufnell Park in the Middlesex Red Cross Cup Final – the Middlesex Charity Cup was renamed during wartime. The Green dominated the match, winning 4–1, with George Bucci and Alan Cochrane both scoring twice. Five of Hendon's next six appearances at Wembley were in the FA Amateur Cup final. In 1955, Bishop Auckland were 2–0 winners, the start of the Bishops' run of three consecutive final victories. The Greens played another game at Wembley in September 1955, at the invitation of the Football Association to test the stadium's new floodlights. A friendly between Hendon's first team and reserves ended 1–0 to the first team, Gordon Holden scoring the goal. Almost five years later, Hendon produced one of the greatest comebacks in the stadium's history. Playing Kingstonian, the Greens were losing 1–0 in the final couple of minutes; legend has it that the red and white ribbons Kingstonian ribbons were being tied to the trophy. Terry Howard equalised and then Laurie Topp broke Ks hearts with Hendon's winner.

Hendon's greatest season, 1964–65, included the Isthmian League title and the Amateur Cup, a 3–1 victory over Whitby Town with David Hyde grabbing a double and Jimmy Quail the other. A year later, it was a different story as Wealdstone won 3–1 after Geoff Riddy had given the Greens the lead. In 1972, Wembley hosted a Middlesex derby in the Amateur Cup final, Hendon and Enfield meeting. A John Baker shot, deflected by Mick Smith, and a header from Tony Bass gave Hendon a 2–0 win. Our last visit to Wembley came on 2 June 1988 and is the perfect segue into the second part of the piece, because our opponents in the Russell Grant sponsored Middlesex Charity Cup were Wembley FC. We won 2–0 in front of 3,715 fans, Iain Dowie and Dermot Drummy scoring. One memory I took from that night was the Hendon fans serenading the Wembley contingent with, "You're supposed to be at home."

Wembley FC

Hendon's history against Wembley FC has never included a first-team league fixture, but the clubs have been regular cup rivals. Formed in 1947, Wembley climbed up through the leagues, reaching Isthmian League Division 1, before dropping back down and the club now plays in the Molten Spartan South Midlands League, having transferred from the Combined Counties League. The first meeting between the clubs

262

was in January 1955, a 4–1 Hendon win in the Middlesex Senior Cup, with Eric Parker, Eric Beardsley, Erwin Bahler and Charlie Nock getting the goals.

While Hendon were in the Athenian League, they played Wembley on six further occasions, in the London Senior Cup (two wins, one defeat) and Middlesex Senior Cup (three wins). The Greens' biggest defeat, but not the most embarrassing, was in the Middlesex Senior Cup Final of 1984–85 when Steve Wilkins' goal proved little more than a consolation as Lance Cadogan ripped the Greens apart in a 5–1 win. The worst reverse came when Barrie Williams took his high-priced team to Vale Farm in the FA Cup and the Lions ended up 1–0 winners. As well as the aforementioned 1988 Middlesex Charity Cup Final at Wembley Stadium, the teams also met in the final at Claremont Road when Tony Field's extra-time goal won the trophy for the home side.

The clubs met in three Isthmian League cup ties, with Hendon losing once and winning twice, most recently in 1996. The last meeting was in October 2016 in the Middlesex Senior Cup, a 4–3 penalty shoot-out victory after Keagan Cole and Niko Muir had netted in a 2–2 draw.

But it is important to mention the almost four seasons Hendon spent as tenants of Wembley between 2008 and 2012. The tenancy arrangement gave Hendon time to stabilise the club after the abrupt departure from Claremont Road. And for supporters living near Claremont Road, there was a direct bus service back to Cricklewood.

Probably the most memorable of the games the club played at Vale Farm in that period was the FA Cup third qualifying round replay against Eastbourne Borough of the Conference South. A goal down early in extra time, Scott Cousins was then sent off, but then Michael Murray converted a penalty and Isaiah Rankin scored a stunning winner. Hendon's four biggest victories against Wembley all came in friendlies (there have been 11 friendlies between the clubs, only one at Claremont Road and one at SJP) between 2006 and 2010. The biggest was 10–1 and there were 7–0, 8–2 and 7–1 successes too, all at Vale Farm.

Will Mather Cup

The Will Mather Cup was an invitational trophy hosted by Hendon from the 1930s to the 1970s. Officially, the trophy was named the Golders Green Hospitals Cup for Manor House. The Manor House Hospital was on North End Road, close to Hampstead Heath and opposite the top entrance of Golders Hill Park, Golders Green. An independent hospital – funded by trade unions – it opened in 1917 and closed in around 2000, and, rebuilt, is now used for housing.

Golders Green played Casuals in the first match, and it was the Isthmian League club who triumphed 3–0 on 27 April 1938. After the match the Casuals captain received the special trophy from Mr Will Mather. The Green did a little better the following year, losing only 2–0. A couple of weeks later, the Cup went on its first journey, to Underhill, where Barnet beat Golders Green 4–2, the Green's goal scorers are not known. In four wartime years, 1941 to 1944, Golders Green chose local rivals for the Will Mather Cup matches, their tenants Tufnell Park. The first of these matches ended in 2–2, Roy Stroud and Jock Ellison scoring for the Green. A year later, the match ended 1–1, but went to extra time, during which time Les Pulling scored his second goal and it ended 2–1 to Golders Green. The matches in 1943 and 1944 both ended in Golders Green wins, 8–2 in the former year – Dave Chappell getting a hat-trick, Roy Stroud and Ron Mitchell each bagging doubles and R Webb getting the other – and 4–3 in 1944, as 36-year-old George Bucci scored twice and G Cox and V Henocq once each.

The most famous, and longest-lasting of the rivalries for the Will Mather Cup was against Arsenal, with whom the club had an arrangement, which included the Gunners junior teams playing midweek matches at Claremont Road and coaching and training there too. The teams met 11 times between 1946 and 1958, the first of these matches was played by Golders Green, and it went the way of the Gunners on nine occasions. Hendon won the 1947 encounter, Bill Reay, netting the only goal, and Pat Terry and Jimmy Quail were on target in 1957, when the match ended 2–2. Usually the Arsenal team was quite a strong one, including first team squad players.

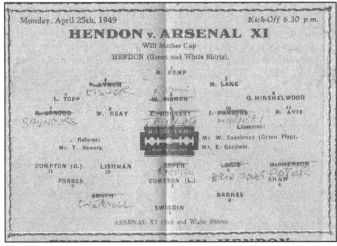

Hendon versus Arsenal in 1949 with Dennis and Leslie Compton playing for Arsenal.

Hendon began a friendship with Whitley Bay when the teams met in the 1965 FA Amateur Cup semi-final, and on August Bank Holiday Monday that year, with Bay's official Arthur Clark – later an FA Councillor and President of the Northern Football League – helping to set up the match, the teams met for the Will Mather Cup at Claremont Road. The Greens won 4–2, with Keith Mills scoring twice and Laurie Churchill and Quail getting the others. Bay avenged that defeat two years later, winning 2–0 in the north-east. Mickey Cannon bagged a double and the attacking Peter Anderson was also on the scoresheet on 1 September 1968 as Hendon won 3–1. It would be another five seasons before the Cup was contested again, and Hendon were 3–0 victors as Fred Pudney, Tony Bass and Jimmy Wilsonham found the net. The last time the Will Mather Cup was officially contested was in August 1983, when Hendon went up to Whitley Bay and just about came back with the trophy after Dermot Drummy, Billy MacMillan and Stan Alexander scored in a 3–1 win.

The reason I put "just about" in the last sentence is that the Cup was almost lost after the game. After the match, the players hurried back to their hotel, the infamous Royal on the sea-front – what happens on tour stays on tour – for a night on the disco floor. Such was their rush, however, that no one remembered to take the Cup with them. I was there and with another supporter, Des McManus, and we were just about to leave the bar at Hillheads Park, we had gone bowling in the ten-pin centre – and ice hockey arena – adjoining the stadium before leaving the ground, when we noticed a shiny silver cup sitting on a settee in the bar. A quick inspection showed it to be the Will Mather Cup and that no other Hendon people were left in the ground. After checking with the barman, we took the trophy with us and proudly walked back to the hotel, avoiding the temptation of taking it for a few rides at the funfair on the seafront. We got a few strange looks from people as we walked along the sea-front and it was with some relief that the Will Mather Cup was handed back to a Hendon official for safe keeping.

In July 2005, a little more than 50 years after Hendon's first FA Amateur Cup Final, the club was invited to play a friendly against Bishop Auckland at Claremont Road, who had won the Amateur Cup 10 times, the last in 1957. Hendon won 3–0 thanks to goals from Kevin Chakaodza, René Street and Troy Perfect. Hendon offered to contest the Will Mather Cup, but they brought a trophy with them, which they contested against Corinthian–Casuals and Wycombe Wanderers, the Bishops' Amateur Cup victims in 1956 and 1957, respectively.

Richard Wilmot

Richard Wilmot was one of my personal favourites – a goalkeeper whose bravery was maybe greater than any of the recent era. I first met Richard when he played for Hitchin Town in the Southern Counties Floodlit Youth League. He was one of the most affable goalkeepers around, and he had talent, too, as he was signed by Mansfield Town. It didn't work out for him and he returned to the south Midlands and Hitchin, though he also had a spell at Stevenage Borough. He was an excellent 'keeper, on more than one occasion earning points for his team with top performances against the Greens. Very tall and athletic, the nickname 'Stretch' seemed entirely appropriate.

Gary McCann's injury meant he was unavailable at the start of the 2000–01 season and Andy Iga lost form, so manager Frank Murphy hunted around for a goalkeeper. Hitchin had three and they considered Richard to be their third choice, so he came to Hendon for a month. Richard was also one of three police officers in the Greens' line-up – probationer Jon Daly and Paul Towler, both in the Met – and Richard, based in Stevenage.

Richard did well enough in the first month for the loan to be extended for a second month and then a third – the maximum permitted under the loan rules of the time. A trip to Carshalton was the last game of the loan spell, but it proved to be his final game for quite a while. Already trailing 1–0, Richard raced of his line to deal with danger from Jamie Pace and the two collided. He has subsequently told me that he knew immediately that his arm was badly injured – probably broken – but he stayed on the pitch. Think about this for a moment: a goalkeeper, in the final game of a loan spell, breaks his arm and refuses to come off. It was 100 per cent insanity, 100 per cent loyalty and 100 per cent bravery. By half-time, the pain was too much, so he went to hospital to get the break confirmed, while Bontcho Guentchev took over in goal, and Hendon came back to win 2–1. Come the end of the season, and although Gary was back playing, he had to be nursed through games and could not play three times a week. Richard was released by Hitchin and returned to Hendon for the final few weeks. Unfortunately, he then injured his groin, so Hendon finished the season with two crocked goalkeepers – both, semi-mobile at best, had a half each in a loss away to Gravesend & Northfleet.

Fast forward to 2006 and Gary, now the manager, was looking for an experienced goalkeeper, who could look after a very inexperienced team in front of him. The Greens had been reprieved from relegation during the summer and the team went through a difficult few months to start the season, failing to win any of the first 11 League games. They had just two points on the board before they went to Walton & Hersham and won 2–0. It was the start of a remarkable turnaround.

266

Richard was inspiring in goal, almost single-handedly defying some teams as the Greens found ways to snatch wins and points. Not only were his performances frequently top quality, he was respected and trusted in equal amounts by the defenders in front of him and their performances also improved.

Unsurprisingly, Richard's form was recognised by the fans and he finished the season with the Supporters Association Player of the Year in 2007. Hendon, in the end, finished just below halfway, 19 points clear of Worthing, who were the highest-placed Ryman League Premier Division club relegated. Richard was ever-present in the league and missed only one cup tie in what was his only full season for Hendon.

He celebrated his 38th birthday early in 2007–08 season, but over 20 years of goalkeeping were catching with up him and injuries took longer to heal, and he played in only 33 games. Richard was in goal, however, for the London Senior Cup final at Imber Court when Tooting & Mitcham United won 3–2, so he ended his Hendon career without any winners medals. He wasn't in the plans for the following season, but Luke Blackmore was injured in the second game, Joe Welch played three times and Berkley Laurencin four before Richard was recalled. He played in the final game at Claremont Road, but appeared only 10 times all season with Will Viner as the main goalkeeper. Richard went on to play for AFC Sudbury before become part of Barton Rovers' management team. Overall, he made 114 appearances for Hendon.

Bobby Wilson

Bobby Wilson scored loads of goals for Hendon in the 1960s and early 70s. However, Bobby Wilson, the Hendon football player, was definitely the second-best known sportsman in the borough with that name when he began his Hendon career. Finchley resident Bobby Wilson, nine years his senior, had spent many years as Britain's Number one tennis player and was a seven-times Grand Slam quarter-finalist. The footballing Bobby joined the club from Feltham in 1967, having been a junior at Brentford. He made his debut on the opening day of the 1967–68 campaign away to Dulwich Hamlet and scored the third of five Hendon goals in a 5–0 win. He was prolific at the start of the season, scoring eight times in the first nine matches – and failed to register in only two of them – and was on 11 goals by mid-October. He finished the season with 19 goals from a team-high 45 appearances, but was a dozen behind top-scorer Tony Harding. It was a disappointing cup season for the Greens, who despite losing only 1–0 to West Ham in the London Challenge Cup, were out of everything by the beginning of March.

For the following season, Bobby was the focus of the Hendon attack, and delivered 25 goals in 48 appearances, the most prolific of his four

Hendon seasons. Although the league form was disappointing, there was silverware at the end of the campaign season as Hendon beat Dagenham in the London Senior Cup final. Bobby appeared in all five ties and scored in the 4–0 win over Hounslow at the start of the run. But Bobby was not the out-and-out centre-forward in the style of Harding and although he scored all those goals, the Greens were not as dangerous in front of goal. At the end of the season, Bobby received representative honours in the form of selection for the famous Middlesex Wanderers touring team.

The striking issue was sorted out for the 1969–70 season with the arrival of John Baker – but Bobby had an injury-hit campaign and played in only 24 of 38 League matches. His goal tally in the league was also down to just nine, but he scored the same number in 21 cup ties. Amazingly, his 18 goals were good enough only for joint-fourth on the Hendon scoring charts. Baker was on 26, Peter Anderson on 24 and Rod Haider with 19 all bettered his total; Paul Collett matched it. To put this into perspective, Hendon's five top goal scorers in all competitions scored 105 goals between them. It didn't translate into much in the way of success as Hendon finished fifth in the Isthmian League, 12 points behind champions Enfield when there were two points for a win.

In cup competitions, Hendon didn't reach any finals, but did make it to the second round of the FA Cup, a run which saw the Greens net 21 goals including seven in a replay against Rainham – in which Bobby scored twice – and five in the first round proper against Carshalton Athletic. Hendon's problem was winning cup ties at the first attempt, though a 2–2 at home to a strong Millwall team in the London Challenge Cup was laudable. Four other ties needed replays to resolve them, and the same malaise was to be found in the league as Hendon recorded 12 draws in 38 outings – only Ilford with 15 enjoyed parity more often.

Bobby's final season was the one before the great run of success in the 1970s. Under new manager John Evans, Hendon tightened up their defence, and reduced their Isthmian League goals against from 44 to 37. They upped their goals tally, too, 77 to 81, but the numbers that really mattered were disappointing, with a sixth-place finish and one fewer win and draw than in 1969–70. Bobby did win his second Hendon medal, albeit a Middlesex Senior Cup runners-up one as the Greens lost 1–0 and 2–0 to Enfield in the two-leg final for a 3–0 aggregate loss. Bobby played in the FA Cup first round 2–0 loss at home to Football League side Aldershot and scored the only goal of the Middlesex Cup quarter-final victory over Hayes at Claremont Road. He scored 18 times in 42 appearances, his final goal – the 80th in four seasons – came at the beginning of May 1971, a 1–0 victory at home to Corinthian Casuals. His strike rate would be eye-opening in today's football, a goal every

2.25 games, but it was not that unusual in his time. Overall, he scored 80 goals for Hendon in 180 games.

Evans' rebuilding saw the arrival of John Connell and Tony Bass to join Baker up front, so Bobby decided to move on. He joined Kingstonian, but his time there was very short and he moved to Feltham and Hayes all before the end of October 1971. Business commitments limited Bobby's time at Church Road, and although an end-of-season review suggested he had "star quality", it took some spotting because he played in just six games, and scored three times.

Wingate (& Finchley)

This piece is about three clubs, who have all been Hendon's local rivals: Finchley, Wingate and the combined Wingate & Finchley.

Taking Wingate first, Hendon met the Hendon-based Jewish club, which was formed in 1946, on two occasions, once each in the Middlesex Senior and London Senior Cups, both at Claremont Road, and won both games, scoring 20 goals in the process. On 2 February 1957, Hendon enjoyed a club record 13–1 victory, with Dave Orr, John Rawlings with two, Pat Terry, Miles Spector with four, and Tommy Lawrence, five, getting the goals.

Miles Spector was one of the most storied players in club history. He was a 16-year-old sixth former at Hendon Grammar School, when Chelsea manager and former Hendon coach Roy Drake selected him for their first team. He later played briefly for Millwall and won England amateur and Athenian League representative honours. After scoring 151 goals in 280 games for Hendon in eight seasons, 1955–56 to 1962–63, then joined Wingate, as he had promised, where he played and also managed. Spector was still at Wingate for the second meeting, on 4 December 1965, and it ended 7–0 to Hendon, with Roy Drake, Danny Lakey, Jimmy Quail, Roy Sleap, Laurie Churchill and David Hyde with two, getting the goals. Hendon played one pre-season friendly, in Wingate's final season, 1990–91, at Arkley, and won 4–1, Andy Smith and Uche Egbe both scoring twice.

Hendon's rivalry with Finchley saw the clubs meet more than 100 times, 95 of the matches being competitive. The first games were 1913–14 county cup ties, a Middlesex Senior match in November, and a London Senior tie a month later. The Finches presumably won both ties, the former is known to be 4–0, the latter is not recorded, but Hampstead Town did not play in the London Senior Cup again that season. Hendon's cup record against Finchley was mixed. In the Middlesex Senior Cup both teams recorded six wins and a draw; in the Charity Cup, including the war-time Red Cross Cup, Hendon won 13 times, drew four, lost four and one match was abandoned; the Greens lost at home and away in the Middlesex Centenary Cup in 1962, while in the London Senior Cup, Finchley held the edge, five wins to Hendon's four. FA competitions saw six FA Cup ties, three wins each and four FA Amateur Cup meetings, with Hendon winning and drawing once each, but losing twice. However, the Hendon victory came at Highbury, Arsenal's home, in the 1965 semi-final and the final score was 4–1.

Founder members of the Athenian League in 1912, Finchley left after World War 1, played one season in 1929–30 and returned in 1939, only for World War 2 to cause the season to be cancelled. From 1945–46, however, Hendon played the Finches in 1929–30, then every season until leaving the competition in 1963. In those 19 seasons, the Greens won 22 times and drew and lost on eight occasions each – there was also one abandonment, while Golders Green won a Herts & Middlesex League Cup tie in 1945. Finchley were close to winning promotion a few times after they joined the Isthmian League in 1973, but by the end of the 1980s, they were struggling on and off the pitch. Peter Rebak, whose father Maurice and uncle Asher were among the founders of Wingate FC, decided to merge Wingate and Finchley into a single club, so Finchley ceased to exist in 1991.

While the ground at Summers Lane was being redeveloped, Wingate & Finchley played in the Spartan South Midlands League – Wingate had been members of the Herts County League until 1991 – at Arkley, before they stepped up to the Isthmian League in 1995, playing in the fourth tier for six of their first seven seasons. Placed in Division One North in 2001, the Blues spent two seasons in that competition before spending two campaigns in the Southern League East Division. From 2006 until 2011, Wingate & Finchley were back in the Isthmian North Division before winning promotion, through the playoffs, in 2011. A week after gaining promotion, the Blues beat Hendon 3–1 in the London Senior Cup Final after Greg Ngoyi had given the Greens the lead. There were 14 League meetings after 2011, both teams winning five times, with four draws. The Blues also won 4–2 in an FA Cup first qualifying round replay in 2017–18, but Hendon came out on top in the London Senior Cup, a 4–3 penalty shoot-out success after a 2–2 draw.

There were three memorable Isthmian League cup-ties, the first a 5–2 Hendon win when Rob Haworth was credited with a hat-trick, though he didn't get the final touch for any of the 'goals'. The Blues took revenge in November 2009, scoring twice in the last two minutes of extra time to force a penalty shoot-out, which they won 4–3. Finally in October 2014, Hendon trailed 3–0 at the Abrahams Stadium, before hitting back to win 4–3, the goals coming from Max McCann, Sam Murphy, Leon Smith and Ola Sogbanmu with an own goal.

Although in different leagues in 2018–19, both clubs enjoyed last day wins to avoid relegation from step 3 to step 4.

Danny Worley

Danny Worley died tragically young, but heroically. It takes a special kind of player to accept a role as substitute week-in week-out. One of those, and probably in the top two 'super subs' in Hendon's history, is Danny Worley. There were many things that made Danny, who was raised in Hendon, a special player, not just the acceptance of his place in the squad. Ask any manager about problems posed an opposing player, and the thing they all find hardest to deal with is exceptional pace. Danny was one of the fastest players ever to appear for the Greens and a succession of managers realised that his speed, against tiring defenders, was more effective late in a game than from the start.

Danny came to Hendon when youth club Princes Park FC was the club's midweek under-18 squad. It was an exceptional team, led by Steve Newing, with Phil Gridelet also a regular player. Steve was one of the country's top schoolboy footballers, while Phil went on to enjoy a long professional career and remains the last man to earn an England Non-League international cap while a Hendon player.

Newing was the first of the trio to make his first-team debut, doing so on 1 January 1985. Danny made his bow on 23 March 1985, partnering George Duck in a 2–2 draw away to Tooting & Mitcham United. It was the first of four appearances – all starts – he made in what was a troubled season. Despite the Greens' problems, Danny was never on the losing side in that campaign. The highlight was his magnificent individual performance in a stunning 3–1 victory away to Wycombe Wanderers, denting their title challenge – the Chairboys went up when the top two, Sutton and Worthing, declined promotion – while simultaneously bolstering the Greens in their battle against the drop. He didn't score in the game, but Newing finished off a move created by Danny for the decisive third goal.

Danny brought something different, a *joie de vivre* and almost naïve attitude, but he was steeped in sportsmanship, something his father demanded. Despite taking serious kickings from a number of defenders neither quick nor smart enough to stop him legitimately, he never retaliated. In the 1985–86 season, he scored Hendon's goal in a 2–1 defeat away to Yeovil Town; in the return at Claremont Road in March, a Glovers defender, once more beaten for pace, slowed Danny down by literally knocking him into the front row of the stand.

The only reason Danny didn't make many more appearances for the Greens was that he was already committed to joining the Royal Air Force and his studies often took priority. In March 1987, Hendon FC Supporters Association made a presentation to Danny on the pitch at Richmond Road after a 1–0 defeat of Kingstonian. He had been an unused substitute on what would have been his final appearance before

271

going to RAF training. Hendon could have done with Danny as the team had a frantic end to the season, which culminated in League and Premier Inter-League Cup final defeats. A player who could make a difference off the bench, he scored the winner the Inter-League Cup last-16 defeat of Dagenham, and there may have been a happier outcome if he had played in the 3–2 League Cup Final loss to Bognor Regis Town.

But Danny wasn't actually finished with football or Hendon. The following season, when on leave, he came back to play for the Greens nine times, seven as substitute, but he didn't reach the 10 goal career milestone. His 61st and final appearance, 40th as a substitute, came on 29 March 1988, a win – naturally – 3–0 against Croydon at home.

Danny travelled around the world with the RAF and when he entered civilian life, he was married and living in Derbyshire – by coincidence the Commissioner of Derbyshire's Police force was his former Princes Park and Hendon Youth coach, John Newing. On 2 May 2000, with his wife heavily pregnant with their second child, Danny was co-pilot in a Lear jet flying Formula One driver David Coulthard to Europe for a Grand Prix. The plane developed problems and crash-landed at Lyon-Satolas Airport in France. The efforts of Danny and the pilot, David Saunders, ensured that the three passengers escaped without serious injury; tragically, however, the cockpit caught fire and Worley, still only 35, and Saunders died.

X and Z

Xs and Zs

Xs and Zs

Every letter has been covered in this book, but none are harder to write about than X and Z. In terms of opponents, for the club, there has been one, Zephyr Athletic, and that was in a friendly early in our second season. It was played on 18 September 1909 and the final score was 5–1 to Hampstead Town but, sadly, the goalscorers are not known. A glance at the FCHD website shows that there has never been a senior club in English football beginning with X and, Zephyr apart, the only senior club beginning with Z was Zeneca, who changed their name from ICI Blackley in 1993 and then spent two seasons in the Manchester League before dropping out.

Moving to players, only two whose surname began with X have ever made first-team appearances and they were midfielder Tony Xavier, whose Hendon career encompassed three matches in early 1990, and Mark Xavier, who played between 1990 and 1994, and nearly made the Green & Gold series of Hendon Isthmian League players. Going back to Tony, he came through the ranks, having played for both the Under-18s and reserves, before making his debut – and only start – on 10 January 1990, in a 2–0 London Senior Cup defeat against Woodford Town at Snakes Lane. Two weeks later, he came off the bench to replace Gerry Mulhern in a 3–2 Middlesex Senior Cup victory at home to Southall. Tony's final appearance was also as a sub, coming on for Martin Duffield in Hendon's amazing 6–3 victory away to relegation-bound Dulwich Hamlet on the club's final visit to the old Champion Hill. Steve Baker got a hat-trick at Champion Hill, with Colin Tate, Uche Egbe and the other substitute Steve Bracken netting the other goals.

Striker Mark Xavier, not closely related to Tony, certainly didn't lack self-confidence. He watched Hendon train in Clitterhouse Playing Fields in July 1990 and told manager Alan Randall he was a better than any Hendon player he saw. With no senior level credentials to back him up, Mark started the season in the reserves and quickly lived up to his bluster. He made his debut as a substitute in a 1–0 Middlesex Charity Cup victory over Uxbridge at Claremont Road on 20 November 1990. Four days later, at home to Basingstoke, Mark was again a substitute, but he certainly made his mark, taking over from Colin Tate and scoring twice in a 4–2 Isthmian League victory. Mark ended the season with six goals in 32 appearances, but he came into his own in 1991–92, despite the club being in turmoil off the field, topping the goals chart with 18 in 49 matches. Mark's goals dried up in 1992–93, with Barrie Williams in charge, and he managed only three in 40 games, 32 of them starts. In 1994–95, Mark made one substitute appearance, his last for Hendon. In all, Mark made 122 appearances and scored 27 goals.

Finding players with Z was actually harder because Greg Zacharia, who joined Hendon from Kingsbury Town, is the only one to make it into the first team. Between them Ossie Zort (two in 2005–06) and Adam Zeniou (2008–09) made three pre-season appearances, but none competitively. Midfielder Greg stepped up a division in summer 1989, having been a part of Kingsbury's excellent team built by former Spurs winger Terry Dyson. Kingsbury hoped to emulate Hendon, 12 months earlier, and play the Russell Grant Middlesex Charity Cup final at Wembley Stadium, but the match could not played there and it was moved to the following season, when they travelled to Stamford Bridge and were beaten 6–2 by Chelsea. Greg was a hard-working, midfielder, who made his debut in the season-opening 4–1 win at Bromley. He missed only eight of Hendon's 65 matches that season and scored six goals. Living in Bedford, commuting to Cricklewood proved to be an issue and he did not re-sign after the season.

Even when expanding this feature to include players whose first name began with X or Z, there are very few. In 2016–17 the Greens signed Xavier Comas on dual registration with Kings Langley, but the French goalkeeper did not make a competitive appearance. In that pre-season, Zsabor Takacs made two second half appearances in friendlies but was not involved thereafter. In 2017–18, Zak Joseph, who father Francis and uncle Roger both had long Football League careers, joined the Greens from North Greenford United. He scored 18 times in 57 appearances before following Gary McCann to Hampton & Richmond Borough. Zaki Oualah was signed to be first-choice goalkeeper for the following season, but he went home to Algeria during pre-season and left without making a competitive appearance. That puts him one behind another Z, Zoran Radovic from what was then Yugoslavia. His only appearance was a 29-minute cameo as a substitute in a goalless home draw against Wokingham Town in April 1987.

Ys

Youth team football

Ys

So, we come to the letter Y. Hendon have had 11 players whose surname began with Y, and the club has played 45 competitive matches against three teams beginning with Y. Two of them no longer exist – Yiewsley and Yeading – the other is Yeovil Town.

The most famous player was one who played for Hampstead Town between the wars and, when he finally left the club, joined the original Hendon FC. Freddie Young signed from Chiswick Town in 1922, and spent three seasons at Farm Avenue before leaving for a couple of years. When he returned, the club had moved to Claremont Road. He gave four seasons of loyal service leading the club in appearances three times and finishing second in the other campaign. After the 1930–31 season, he fell out of favour and, in September 1931, joined the original Hendon FC, who went out of business a few years later. In all, Freddie Young made 169 appearances and scored 52 goals.

The only other "Y" player to make more than 45 appearances for the club was Paul Yates, in the early 2000s. A midfielder, he was one of Dave Anderson's best signings and in two seasons, 2001–02 and 2002–03, Paul played 107 matches and scored seven goals, including 56 in the latter campaign, when he netted six times. He also won Middlesex Senior Cup winners' medals in those two seasons, though as an unused substitute against Northwood at Hayes in 2002. Paul left the club for work and family reasons in the summer of 2003.

Dave Yerby and Stuart Young both played at either right-back or in the middle of defence, but they could hardly have been more different. Yerby's 44 appearances in 1974–75 and 1975–76 including appearances in the FA Cup victory over Reading and the defeat against Swindon Town in 1975 – his goal line hand ball gave Swindon the penalty, converted by David Moss for the only goal. A flame-haired cab driver, he had a very combative attitude and it sometimes got him into trouble. Young was a willowy 18-year-old when manager Dave Mawson gave him his debut. Never a regular over his three seasons, from 1988 to 1991, he played 34 times in all.

Two other players to mention are both called Young. Doug joined Hendon from FA Vase winners Billericay Town in 1979, and scored 10 goals in 28 games before he was forced to quit with arthritis in his hip. He still makes occasional visits to New Lodge. Alfie Young arrived at Silver Jubilee Park in the summer of 2016, but left to join Wingate & Finchley after 10 appearances. Alfie, now with Worthing, scored for the Rebels against Hendon in October 2017. Eddie Yates, 19 games, six goals, F. Yates, two goals in five matches, Eseyas Yhdego, two matches, and P Young and Terry Young both made a solitary appearance.

As for team Ys, we played Yeovil Town in five seasons, managed only two draws and eight defeats in the 10 Isthmian League fixtures, 1985–88 and 1996–97. In the League Cup, however, the Greens enjoyed a memorable 2–0 semi-final first leg victory at The Huish in 1986–87, Dermot Drummy and Micky Kiely getting the goals just before half-time. The second ended 2–1 to the Greens, with the same goal scorers. Hendon produced a magnificent shock in the 1995–96 competition, winning a first-round contest 3–1 at Huish Park, with Chris James, Steve McKimm and Junior Haynes on target.

Yiewsley became Hillingdon Borough in 1964, and the clubs never met in a league match. Our first cup tie was back in 1914, when Hampstead won a replay 3–0 after a 2–2 draw. Ten years later the clubs met in the FA Amateur Cup and Hampstead Town enjoyed a 9–0 victory at Farm Avenue, with Cecil Wise getting four goals, Freddie Young and Ken Seabrooke two each and Syd Sweetman the other. In the 1950s, there were FA Cup ties, three times in four seasons, Hendon losing twice, once in a replay, and winning the other. Hampstead beat Yiewsley 2–0 in the 1922 Middlesex Charity Cup and 1–0 in in 1950. There were also three Middlesex Senior Cup meetings, Hendon losing 2–1 in 1949, but winning 2–0 in 1956 and 5–3 the following season, the last meeting with Yiewsley.

Yeading were Hendon's most frequent opponents, though their history is far and away the shortest. Formed as a junior club in 1960, they gained senior status when joining the Spartan League in the mid-1980s. The Ding won the FA Vase in 1990 and gained promotion to the Isthmian League Premier Division in 1992. Hendon played Yeading 14 times in League action, from 1992 to 2005, winning five times and losing three, with six draws. Yeading won the only Middlesex Charity Cup tie in 1993, and dominated Middlesex Senior Cup ties, winning four of six with one draw and one loss. Hendon triumphed 3–2 in 2000 with Dominic Gentle grabbing a hat-trick. In 2007, Yeading merged with Hayes to become Hayes & Yeading United.

In 2019–20, there was another rival to join this list as Yate Town, near Bristol, won promotion to the Southern League Premier Division South.

Youth team football

This piece is about senior youth teams and players, that is Under-18s. Hendon have run youth teams at many levels for decades, but the first dedicated midweek league team dates back to 1977–78, when the club entered the Isthmian League Youth Cup, as well as the FA Youth Cup. Hendon lost in the first round of the FA Youth Cup, to St Albans City, who included future Glamorgan CCC wicket-keeper Terry Davies, who

278

had to rush from Lord's, where he was playing for Cross Arrows CC – the MCC Club & Ground team who played on the Nursery Ground in September – to Clarence Park. In the Hendon team that night was Devon Gayle, who scored the club's first ever FA Youth Cup goal, and went on to play 40 times for the first team.

In 1981–82, Hendon had a very strong team, which won the Middlesex and London Youth Cups. The London Cup Final, played at Mile End Stadium, was notable because Hendon beat Tigers FC and the decisive second goal was scored by the team's goalkeeper with a drop kick. He was so excited about scoring he developed a major nose-bleed and, at the final whistle, a few minutes later, his yellow shirt had a large red stain. That team, managed by committee member Ken Scarr and coached by future first-team boss Dave Mawson, provided a large number of players for the first team in the 1982–83 season.

The first really good youth team was the one put together by the late John Newing in the early-to mid-1980s. It contained three players who made it to the first team and played more than 45 games each: Phil Gridelet, Danny Worley and Steve Newing. Danny's Hendon career was cut short when he joined the RAF and – in 2005, as a commercial pilot/co-pilot, his and the pilot's brave actions saved the life of Formula 1 driver David Coulthard and other passengers, but at the expense of their own. Phil's career at Hendon was in two spells: his first saw him become Hendon's first England Non-League international before he went on to a long Football League career; his second was in 2000–01, when he played under Frank Murphy. Steve played only 45 times, but, uniquely, as well as playing for his father in the youth team, his brother Matt also made one first-team appearance and his sister Jackie was a mainstay of the Hendon women's team.

Fast forward to 1991–92, as members of the Southern Counties Floodlit Invitation League, Hendon had five standout players who went on to make more than 2,500 appearances for Football League clubs: Greg Heald, Junior Hunter, Micah Hyde (a Jamaican international), Scott McGleish and Darren Currie. For Hendon, however, Greg made one appearance and Junior six (five in 1991–92 and one in 1995–96). Darren made his debut just before his 37th birthday and went on to play 46 times between 2011 and 2013, while coaching at Dagenham & Redbridge. He was named manager at Barnet in spring 2019. Scott (who left early in that 1991–92 season) was appointed Hendon coach in late 2018 and finally made his Hendon debut on New Year's Day 2019, five weeks short of his 45th birthday – one of the oldest players ever to make his first-team debut. The player Scott marked was a former Hendon player Jefferson Louis, a spring chicken by comparison aged seven weeks short of 40! Micah – a team-mate of David Beckham at Ridgeway Rovers before joining the Greens – never made it to the first team.

After the 1992–93 season, the youth team was disbanded and it would be a number of years before the club returned to senior youth football. The best player of the reformed squad under Cecil Collins was Chris Moore, who got close to the first team squad, but decided to join Uxbridge and then went on to enjoy a 20-year career including a few seasons in the Football League. He took his first steps in management in 2018 and was in charge of Hanwell Town against Hendon in the Middlesex Senior Cup. In 2000–01, Hendon had an excellent centre-half, Kevin Amankwaah, who was discovered by Gary Hand, but he joined Bristol City before he could make a first-team appearance for the Greens. He appeared against Hendon for Bath City in the 2018–19 FA Trophy, having made more than 300 League appearances.

Hendon's move to Silver Jubilee Park was preceded by the setting up of a huge youth system a couple of years earlier. These teams, who play at all age groups, have done a fantastic job of developing players and this can been seen by the number of players from the Under-18s who have made first-team appearances in the past four seasons. Of the more than half a dozen to get into the first team, Keagan Cole is remarkable. On the final day of the 46-match 2017–18 Bostik League season, he came off the bench to make his 100th appearance. Born on 13 July 1999, he was 18 years and 299 days old when he reached his landmark appearance – certainly Hendon's youngest player ever to reach 100 first-team games – and there are probably only a handful of current players anywhere in the country who have made 100 first team appearances before their 19th birthday.

Part 2: Dream Teams

A strong team with several players who made major contributions to the club.

Scott Ashcroft: Scott made a deep impression in his 22-game Hendon career. Signed by Neil Price, the young goalkeeper was outstanding in helping avoid relegation in 1996. In the opening game of 1996–97, he suffered a career-ending knee injury. Notably David Speedie finished the 2–1 loss to Sutton United in goal.

Peter Anderson: Sunderland-born Peter was signed from Ilford along fellow north-easterner Dave Holden and Peter Deadman in 1976. He started as a right-back but also partner Alan Campbell at centre-back. A solid defender, in either position, his quality in the air helped him to score 31 goals in 265 appearances in seven seasons.

Eric Allinson: Eric was an under-rated defender who came out of the reserves run by George Rocknean after many years with Dulwich Hamlet. With Alan Campbell, Peter Deadman and Peter Anderson ahead of him, his first-team opportunities were limited, but he had good positional sense which frequently got him out of trouble.

John Ashworth: In April 1966, John captained Wealdstone to Amateur Cup victory over Hendon, six years after being on the losing side against the Greens for Kingstonian. The solid, uncompromising centre-half gave Hendon three good seasons before he moved to Hitchin, helping them to their best ever Isthmian top flight finish.

Dexter Adams: Dexter joined Hendon from Northampton Polytechnic and played for 11 seasons mainly at centre-half, but occasionally at right back. One of Hendon's finest defenders, he earned 20 England amateur caps, including some as captain, and also was selected for the Great Britain Olympic team at the 1956 Games in Melbourne. He captained Hendon in the 1955 Amateur Cup final and won three Athenian League championships, two as a player and one as coach. It was also as coach that he won the Amateur Cup in 1960 and, having retired through injury, he later managed Barnet when they turned professional and joined the Southern League.

Pat Austin: Pat spent nine seasons with Hendon, earning numerous honours, including two Athenian League championship medals and an Amateur Cup runners-up medal. He joined the club in 1949 and made

252 appearances, mainly at left-half. Pat was briefly reserve team coach in the 1960s and spent many years as a Middlesex FA Councillor.

Peter Anderson: Three players stand out in this team, winger Peter Anderson, Bob Avis and Dexter Adams. Peter joined Hendon from Barnet in 1968 and scored 58 goals in 125 appearances. He left in February 1971, signing for Luton Town, and he enjoyed a long professional career in England, Belgium and the USA.

Lee Angol: Striker or midfielder Lee had made his Football League debut for Wycombe before two loan spells at Hendon in 2013. He had joined Wycombe after playing for Tottenham's Academy team. His physical attributes were evident, but it took a little longer for his potential to come through. He has scored more than 20 goals in almost 100 games at four Football League clubs.

Bob Avis: Bob's 11 seasons with Hendon saw him score 163 goals in 257 appearances. The centre-forward made his debut for Golders Green in September 1945, scoring in a 3–2 defeat at Bromley. His most prolific seasons were 1950–51 and 1951–52, when he scored 60 goals in 82 games.

Belal Aite-Ouakrim: Belal was an enigma. A superb footballer technically, he should have played consistently at a higher level, but too many injuries – his knocks were never minor – kept him back. His strike rate of a goal almost every three games, 59 in 183 appearances, tells the story of what might have been.

Mark Adams: Mark Adams was a will-o-the-wisp type winger, who spent parts of two seasons at Claremont Road. His first spell lasted only three games but he returned in 1985 and played 25 times for Gary Hand and Ted Hardy. Working for the Metropolitan Police, he later played against the Greens for the Blues.

Substitutes

Dave Abrey: Dave was only the first-choice goalkeeper in the 1962–63 season, when he made 26 appearances. John Swannell's arrival for the start of the 1963–64 season ended his first-team aspirations.

Ricardo Alves: A student from Brazil, Ricardo was more Dunga than Zico as a midfielder, but his touch, passing ability, passion and energy were typically Samba.

Alan Anderson: Winger Peter Anderson's nephew, his father delivered the post to Claremont Road, but after midfielder Alan had moved to America on a football scholarship.

Gary Allen: Fox in the box-type striker, Gary signed from Carshalton Athletic and scored 29 goals in 54 matches, a fine return given the team's struggles in the mid-1980s.

Takumi Ake: Japanese striker, from Kobe, who contributed much to Hendon's battle to avoid relegation in 2006–07. He later played for Chelmsford City.

B

Several important players for the club in this team.

Mark Broughton: Goalkeeper Mark was magnificent in his 15 months at Hendon. Not that big off the pitch, he was a giant on it. His superb work in 55 first team matches in the 1984–85 and 1985–86 seasons helped to prevent the club being relegated, especially the first-half save against Slough in his final game.

James Burgess: James gave Hendon outstanding service and was willing to play in a multitude of positions. An identical twin of Mark, who also played for Hendon, James won both Supporters Association and Clubman of the Year awards. He occupied every defensive position or in defensive midfield and scored three times in 324 appearances.

Eric Beardsley: Eric joined Hendon from Eastbourne in 1952 and won both England and Great Britain Olympic honours in his five seasons at Claremont Road. The left-back scored the goal in the semi-final against Hounslow, aided by a deflection, that took Hendon to their first Amateur Cup final in 1955.

Jamie Busby: Jamie was only 26 when he quit semi-professional football, having made 258 Hendon appearances in just over six seasons from 2006 to 2012. The midfielder averaged almost 10 goals per season, many with powerful strikes. A bad injury in the FA Cup at Luton Town in 2011 curtailed his effectiveness.

Steve Bateman: Kevin Ratcliffe's arrival at Everton denied Bateman a top-flight career and he went to Harrow where he won the Isthmian League title in his first season. He joined Hendon under Frank Murphy, aged 31, and was a key member of the Greens' defence when Hendon beat Leyton Orient in the FA Cup in 1997, with over 100 first team appearances.

Elliott Brathwaite: Elliott was probably Hendon's best centre-half since the 1970s. Knee injuries ended his career at 27 – after 97 appearances between 2011 and 2017, including 58 in 2014–15 – denying him the chance of a long Football League career. His partnership with Charlie Goode was the foundation of Hendon's fantastic 2014–15 season.

George Bucci: The son of one of the club's founders, George gave Hampstead and Golders Green almost 20 years of loyal playing service and marked his final appearance in memorable fashion, netting twice in the Green's 5–1 Middlesex Red Cross Cup Final victory against Tufnell Park at Wembley in May 1945. He started his career as a forward, but ended as a half-back, though he actually played in every position –

including once as a goalkeeper. George made 433 appearances, many as captain, for the first team and scored 75 goals. After retiring he spent many years on the Hendon committee.

Billy Breagan: Right-winger Billy joined Hampstead from Southall in 1932 and passed the 20-appearance mark in all of his 10 seasons at Claremont Road, finishing with 71 goals from 310 games. He played against Southend United in the FA Cup, and his injury was keenly felt in a 10–1 defeat.

Tony Bass: Tony, who was six feet three inches tall, dominated defences in his two Hendon seasons, scoring 55 goals in 102 appearances - he played in the opening game of the 1973–74 season before leaving. His most important goal probably was the second in the 1972 Amateur Cup Final, a typically powerful close-range header.

John Baker: John was a key member of the great Hendon teams from 1969 to 1974. He had two further spells at Claremont Road and enjoyed five 20-goals seasons. At Hendon, John won almost medal available, including the Isthmian League, Amateur Cup and Barassi Cup and played in both games against Newcastle in the FA Cup in 1974.

Dale Binns: Dale was an electrifying winger who gave Hendon five superb seasons, from 1999 to 2004 before returning in 2016. Blessed with great touch and dribbling ability, many of his 41 goals in 217 appearances were spectacular. Dale's game-changing talent meant he was often, over 80 times, used to great effect as a substitute.

Substitutes

Rikki Banks: Goalkeeper Rikki commuted from Sussex to play for Hendon. He enjoyed a long Isthmian League career. He had two spells with Hendon, 2005–06 and 2011–12, making 14 appearances.

Rian Bray: A dominant central defender, signed from Millwall in 2017, the switch to the Southern League in 2018 hastened the Bromley-based teenager's departure from SJP.

Steve Butler: The son of fan favourite striker Roy, Steve was an excellent centre-back and occasional midfielder under Dave Anderson. He played in 114 matches over three seasons, from 2001 to 2004.

Michael Banton: South African Michael had the happy knack of scoring important goals, despite some bad luck with serious injuries. He scored 27 goals in 80 matches in the mid-1990s.

Fred and Bill Boston: Between them the Bostons, Bill, a defender, and forward Fred, made almost 400 appearances for the club in the 1930s and 40s. Fred scored 84 goals in 169 games.

George Blackburn: A young forward for Hampstead Town, after scoring 30 goals in 21 first team appearances, George turned professional with Aston Villa in December 1920. He was the first former Hampstead player to play for the full England team, which he did in 1924.

C

This team is an unusual mixture and the bench contains three full internationals.

Bob Chambers: The goalkeeper cupboard is very bare and Bob gets the nod mainly because neither Paul Cotter nor Simon Chang were significantly better. Bob joined Hendon in 1955 and made 34 appearances in his only season, including the FA Cup defeat at Exeter.

Micky Cooper: A fantastic club servant and excellent defender – good enough to play for the England Amateur team – Micky scored one of the most famous goals in Hendon history. He shot from close to the half-way line in the dying seconds to equalise against Skelmersdale in a 1967 Amateur Cup semi-final. Hendon eventually lost after two replays.

Simon Clarke: Opposite Micky Cooper, at left-back, is another very loyal Hendon man. Simon made three Football League appearances for West Ham United before joining the Greens in 1995. He went on to make more than 350 appearances in seven seasons. He was a two-time Supporters Association Player of the Year.

Darren Currie: Darren starred in Hendon's Under-18 team in 1992–93 before enjoying a very long Football League career. Paul Currie's son – and Tony's nephew – Darren was on Dagenham & Redbridge's coaching staff when made his first-team debut just before his 37th birthday and gave Hendon two seasons of consistent excellence.

Alan Campbell: One of the finest centre-halves ever to play for Hendon, Alan joined the club from Finchley in 1976 and spent five seasons, with 28 goals in 249 games, at Claremont Road before moving to Dagenham. He returned in 1986 and gave three more seasons of continued excellence under Ted Hardy. Aged almost 38 he was back in 1991–92, but could barely train and spent the warm-up on his own, stretching just to get through a game. Alan was also Barrie Williams' assistant, but left in early 1993. In all, Alan played 395 matches for the Greens and scored 31 goals.

Micky Cannon: Thirty goals in 168 games for a centre-back is exceptional, but Micky Cannon also played as a striker at times. He was a London Senior Cup winner in his debut season, 1968–69, but Alan Phillips had replaced him at centre-back by the 1972 Amateur Cup Final.

Bobby Childs: A double Amateur Cup winner, once with Hendon in 1972 and once against, for Wealdstone in 1966), Bobby was one of my favourite players when I started watching the Greens. A winger or wide midfielder, Bobby joined Hendon in October 1971 and in 221 appearances across six seasons scored 43 goals, many from set-pieces, especially penalties. He died prematurely from leukaemia aged 42.

John Connell: Irish Amateur international John Connell won his third Amateur Cup winner's medal in 1972, having won two with Enfield in 1967 and 1970. Having often scored against the club for Enfield, he joined Hendon for the 1971-72 season. The Greens' three-pronged strike force that year, Tony Bass, John Baker and Connell, amassed 70 goals between them. John left in Autumn 1972.

Ricci Crace: Ricci joined Hendon from Ware in summer 2001, but a knee injury in September side-lined him for almost half the season. He still scored a goal every three games including 21 in 2002–03. Ricci returned for a second spell at the end of the 2005–06 season.

Roger Connell: Roger scored 19 goals in 44 games in his only Hendon season, joining – with Keiron Somers – from Walton & Hersham. He scored a hat-trick against Barnet in the 1973–74 FA Cup fourth qualifying round replay, but broke his ankle and was out until the Newcastle replay.

Scott Cousins: Scott's dad, also Scott, played a couple of reserve games for Hendon, but his son came close a career at Chelsea before joining the Greens in the summer of 2003. He returned after one season for a longer spell, 2009 to 2017, the last three years as a player-coach.

Substitutes

Simon Chang: Simon was an athletic young goalkeeper, but lacked the physique to play in the Isthmian League. He played one first team game in 2002.

Tony Currie: The Sheffield United legend grew up close to Claremont Road, and enjoyed a long professional career, including England caps before spending an unsuccessful month with Hendon in 1985.

Jeff Campbell: Jeff was a full New Zealand international when he joined Hendon in 2005–06 on loan from AFC Wimbledon. He lived less than a mile from Claremont Road.

Elliott Charles: A talented striker, Elliott played in a World Cup tie for Grenada just days before joining Hendon in 2011, where he spent part of three seasons. He briefly returned in 2018-19, but work commitments intervened before he could challenge for a team place. In three spells at the club he made 48 appearances, scoring 16 goals.

Simon Clark: Simon was a solid central defender, who joined from Kings Lynn after moving down to London from Lincolnshire. He was in the Leyton Orient team beaten by Hendon in 1997.

Bobby Cantwell: One of the key players in the mid-1960s, Bobby was a half-back in the successful Hendon teams of that period and was captain in the 1965 and 1966 Amateur Cup Finals. He played in 170 matches from 1964 to 1969, scoring 13 goals.

D

A veritable treasure trove of riches; the final 11 was hard to choose.

Malcolm Dalrymple: Malcolm had a Football League career, appearing in the pre-season Watney Cup for Bristol Rovers, having also played for Luton Town. He was slightly above average height, but had all the necessary goalkeeping attributes. After leaving Hendon he played for the short-lived Colne Dynamos. For the Greens, he made 105 appearances from 1975 to 1977.

Iain Duncan: Solid and unspectacular would sum up Iain. He did his job as a right-back, occasionally on the left side too, without fuss. He had a good football brain, was rarely caught out of position and had the technique to keep even the best wide players quiet. He made his debut in August 2000, and played in 162 matches over five seasons.

Frank Dean: Frank's career straddled the Hampstead and Golders Green era, though mainly in the former. He made his debut in late April 1930 and made 105 more appearances over the next three seasons. In days when full-backs didn't attack much, his five goals in 1931–32 was a notable achievement.

Peter Deadman: Peter's loyalty to Hendon came ahead of an England Non-League international cap in spring 1974. A magnificent defender and winner of 45 England Amateur caps, 25 while at Hendon, Peter was a West Ham junior, played 552 times for Hendon and had a non-league career lasting almost 25 years. He won the Amateur Cup, Barassi Cup and Isthmian League with Hendon. His winning goal in the 1972 Amateur Cup semi-final against Wycombe Wanderers at Brentford's Griffin Park was particularly memorable.

Bob Dowie: Bob's oil-business commitments limited his availability, but Ted Hardy dreaded his teams playing against him. In 1993 Peter Taylor appointed him Hendon captain, he was player-manager later that season, and in 2004, as Director of Football at Crystal Palace, became Peter's boss. England striker Natasha Dowie is Bob's daughter. His brother is Iain Dowie. He made his debut in February 1987 and played 65 matches over four seasons.

Jon Daly: Jon played in the last-ever matches at both Enfield and Wealdstone, but not Claremont Road. A no-nonsense midfielder he joined the Police while at Hendon and played for the Metropolitan Police team in his 40s. Jon spent six seasons at Hendon, from 1992 to 2001, scoring 26 goals in 203 appearances.

Dermot Drummy: Dermot joined Hendon in 1980, aged 19, after being released by Arsenal. An old-fashioned winger, his skills quickly made him a fan favourite. His party trick, dummying to pick up a stationary ball, but instead sprinting clear of the confused full-back, caught out many players. He joined Enfield in 1984, but returned two years later a better player, playing more centrally. Dermot and Iain Dowie scored when Hendon won the 1988 Middlesex Charity Cup at Wembley. Dermot left Hendon in 1989 after scoring 62 goals in 348 games. His death in 2017 left the club in shock.

Martin Duffield: Martin – who played once for QPR – did not take a backward step in midfield, but wasn't a negative ball-winner. Instead he was a creative driving force and ideal captain. His style of play led to many injuries, but he did score 25 goals in 188 games across six seasons in two spells from the late 1980s to mid-1990s.

Iain Dowie: Iain was a phenomenal striker, scoring twice on his debut in November 1986. He completed his rocket engineering degree in his first season, scored at Wembley in his second, and after training through summer 1988, turned pro with Luton in December after scoring 27 goals in 30 games for Hendon. He went on to have a successful playing and managerial career at several clubs, and was capped regularly by Northern Ireland.

Cyril Drinkwater: Cyril starred in Golders Green's first two seasons before turning professional for Aston Villa in 1936. He made his debut in Hampstead's final Athenian League game, was a regular for the next two seasons and scored in the 10–1 FA Cup loss to Southend in 1934.

Dave Diedhiou: On 20 September 2008, Dave scored his first competitive Hendon goal and the Greens' last-ever at Claremont Road. The Senegalese midfielder spent 10 seasons at Hendon playing in almost every defensive and midfield role before leaving in 2018 after 380 games and 43 goals, many of huge importance.

Substitutes

Derek Dawson: Derek spent only one season at Hendon, 1958–59, but the goalkeeper had a long and successful career elsewhere, particularly at Enfield.

Mick Dalton: Mick was the calm captain of Mick Browne's team which somehow avoided relegation in 1994–95, the first Arbiter-era season. He played 74 times over two seasons.

Mark Dawber: Mark was Michael Banton's striker partner for parts of three seasons, but injuries limited his appearances to 68, with 16 goals.

Roy Drake Senior and Junior: Roy senior played 41 times in the hugely successful mid-1960s team as a winger. His son was a goalkeeper who played a few times in the 1980s.

Peter Dean I and II: The first Peter Dean was a squad player, with six goals in 11 matches in four seasons. His debut was in April 1963. The second Peter was a midfielder or striker from 2009 to 2010, and again in 2014, making 109 appearances with 12 goals overall.

E

This is not the strongest of squads, but two strikers stand out.

Ken Ellis: Ken was one of John Swannell's back-ups, so rarely saw first team action for Hendon. He was, however, one the youngest players on record at Hendon, debuting as a 16-year-old in January 1968. He left in 1970, but his son was in Hendon's Sunday Under-18s team in the late 1990s. He made eight first-team appearances over four seasons.

Jake Eggleton: One of the stars of the 2017–18 season, 18-year-old Jake arrived from West Ham United and quickly made the right-back position his own. A tigerish tackler, his total of 48 appearances would have been more, but for an injury in spring 2018.

Bobby Ellison: By coincidence, Bobby was 16 when made his Hendon debut in September 1958, and was playing for Wembley in 1968, when 16-year-old Ken Ellis made his Hendon bow. Bobby played at least once in seven seasons between 1958 and 1966, and finished with 59 games and a season high of 17.

John Evans: Midfielder John left an indelible mark on Hendon, first as a player from 1964 to 1967, then as manager from 1970 to 1973. A Loughborough College graduate – and mentor to Peter Deadman – he won Welsh Amateur international caps at Claremont Road before overseeing 1972 Amateur Cup win. He emigrated to South America in 1973. He made 95 first team appearances, including two in 1971–72.

Colin Edwards: Colin played occasionally at centre-half, but his finest moment in seven Hendon seasons – he made 100 appearances – was the 1954 Middlesex Charity Cup Final against Southall at Hayes. He replaced injured goalkeeper Don Archer just after half-time, didn't concede a goal and Hendon won 1–0 after extra time.

Bryn Evans: Bryn was one of the legion of players who left Malden Vale with Mick Browne in 1994 to join Hendon. The two-step climb was probably a little too much for the defender or midfielder, but he was intelligent enough to play to his strengths. In his two seasons, he made 15 appearances.

T E Edwards: Before the Second World War, many players were known by their initials rather than their first name and T E Edwards falls into this category. The former Tufnell Park captain joined Golders Green in the summer of 1934, scoring nine goals in 22 appearances that season, and played twice in the following campaign.

L A 'Jock' Ellison: Jock joined Golders Green in 1938 and had an excellent first season, scoring 10 goals in 21 appearances, including in the 4–0 Middlesex Senior Cup Final victory over Wealdstone at

Summers Lane, Finchley. He stayed for another three seasons, so mainly played for the club during the Second World War.

Uche Egbe: Uche was at his most prolific in 1988–89, scoring more than 100 goals at three levels, one coming in the Isthmian League. Noted for strength, power and spectacular celebrations, he was top scorer in 1989–90 and 1994–95 and finished with 46 goals in 186 appearances for the club.

Freddie Evans: Freddie is a club legend. The club's second England Amateur international, he is the all-time leading goal scorer, with 181 goals in 175 appearances, from known figures. He scored twice on his 1 September 1926 debut for Hampstead Town against Botwell Mission, spent a couple of seasons at Hendon Town and returned in January 1930. Over the next six years, he made 160 appearances and netted 168 goals. In 1931–32 his 49 goals was the club's second best all-time tally in a season. Injured soon after Golders Green's FA Cup loss to Southend, he did not play for the club again.

Roy Evans: Roy made his debut in March 1939 for Golders Green and his final appearance for Hendon in October 1952. The winger was a regular in only one season, 1951–52, when he made more than half of his 80 appearances and scored 12 of his 21 goals.

Substitutes
Cyril Evans: Cyril made his debut in the 1921 Middlesex Charity Cup Final 3-1 loss to Botwell Mission at Brentford. He played 18 times in three seasons at Hampstead Town.

A Elwell: A full-back, he made his debut in a 6–0 rout of Cheshunt at Claremont Road in September 1930, but never held down a regular place at Hampstead, playing 21 first team matches over three seasons.

Steve Eley: The long-time captain of Hendon Reserves, Steve got his chance with 15 games in 1980–81, mainly at right back.

Tommy Evans: Tommy spent parts of two seasons at Golders Green, during which time he was a prolific goal scorer, grabbing 28 in 57 appearances between 1934 and 1936.

Nathan Edwards: Nathan, a Junior Lewis lookalike, scored the winner against Hampton in his second League game. One referee booked Nathan and bragged about cautioning "Junior". He played 13 games over two seasons, from 1999 to 2001.

This is a defensively strong team, but with limited goalkeeping and striking options.

Bill Farlam: Bill, a Middlesex County representative player, joined Hendon from Uxbridge in December 1960 and played most of the rest of the season, but missed the Middlesex Senior Cup Final replay against Hounslow because he was on holiday. His 24 appearances are the most by any 'F' goalkeeper for Hendon.

Bill Fisher: Including friendlies and reserve team games, for which records are incomplete, Bill probably played in more than 1,000 games for the club between 1941 and 1962. A right-back or half-back, Bill – along with Laurie Topp – played in Hendon's first two Amateur Cup Finals, including the 1960 victory over Kingstonian. Bill's dedication to Hendon continued after he retired as a player with spells as first-team and reserve team manager. His death aged 56 in November 1978, just before an FA Cup tie with Hitchin, rocked the club and deprived Hendon of a man frequently referred to as 'Mr Nice Guy' and 'Mr Hendon'.

Mark Furneaux: Mark signed from Enfield in 1987 and spent four seasons at Claremont Road, making 50 appearances in each of his first two campaigns. Although not the finest left-back in club history, he was a great presence in the dressing room and a much-respected team-mate.

John Field: John, a former Tottenham Hotspur junior, signed for the club at the start of the 1974–75 season and spent two seasons with Hendon. A versatile player, he appeared at right-back, centre-half, midfield and, occasionally, up front. In all, he made 101 appearances and scored 11 goals.

Sam Flegg: Sam was a more than useful member of the Hendon squad in his four seasons, 2012 to 2016, though overseas work commitments limited his games to only 118 matches. He was the epitome of a steady centre-half, his football intelligence frequently getting Hendon out of trouble. He won the FA Vase with Chertsey Town in 2019, along with several other former Hendon players.

Phil Fry: A superb defensive midfielder, Phil joined Hendon from Dagenham in 1972. His talent was breaking up play and letting the ball-players around him go forward. After winning the Barassi Cup, Isthmian League and Middlesex Senior Cup, and playing against Newcastle, he left for Enfield in March 1974. His departure, along with Derek Baker and Tony Jennings on a familiar route round the North Circular Road, undermined the club's chance of retaining the Isthmian League title.

Tony Field: Playing alongside his brother John, Tony joined Hendon in March 1975, too late to play in that season's Middlesex Senior Cup Final against Staines. A skilful attacking midfielder and dead-ball specialist formerly with Fulham, he stayed two seasons longer than John and scored 29 goals in 153 appearances.

Steve Forbes: Hendon's second Steve Forbes, he joined in 2001 having played in the Football League for Millwall, Colchester and Peterborough. A powerful and graceful midfielder, his three Hendon seasons brought 13 goals in 112 games – maybe the best of which was in a 6–0 demolition of Heybridge Swifts.

John Frendo: John was a prolific goal scorer in his short time at Hendon, netting 28 goals in 75 appearances. He was leading goal scorer – 12 goals – in 2005–06, despite leaving in January. His final scoring appearance was the 7–0 London Senior Cup rout of Redbridge when he netted four.

Dave Flint: Dave's best days came long before he joined Hendon in September 1994. He scored nine goals in his only Hendon season, but five late ones brought seven points – more than the difference between safety and going down. His thunderbolt strike at Yeading had fans believing relegation wasn't inevitable.

Brian Figg: Brian spent only 13 months at Hendon, December 1959 to January 1961, but left with an Amateur Cup winners' medal and was part of the Athenian League Championship squad the following year. The inside forward scored in his final Hendon match against Southall.

Substitutes

Ashley Fisk: Goalkeeper Ashley was the brother of talented central defender Mason and the son of Under-18s manager Jack. All three moved to Wingate & Finchley from Hendon. He made his debut in 1989 and played six games over two seasons.

James Fisher: James was a classy, calm defender or midfielder, but injuries caused his early retirement in 2015 after 134 appearances in four seasons.

Lee Flynn: Lee joined Hendon in August 1994 and left that Christmas. An excellent left back, he played non-league football until his mid-40s.

Gary Fitzgerald: A tough tackling defender or midfielder, Gary joined Hendon from Enfield in 1998 and spent three seasons – plus two games – at Hendon, making 149 appearances and scoring 10 goals.

Leo Fortune-West: Striker Leo enjoyed much success almost everywhere else he played, including for nine Football League clubs, amassing more than 100 goals and 400 appearances. For the Greens, he scored six times in 21 matches in 1992–93.

G

This team is the only to contain England Non-League internationals who were capped while at Hendon.

Ernie Goodwin: Ernie replaced goalkeeper E McCracken, who retired because football clashed with his career as a professional tenor, and spent three seasons at Hampstead, making his debut in September 1924. After playing 59 times in two seasons, Ernie didn't play the following year, but returned for 16 games in 1926.

Warren Goodhind: Warren, a full-back or central defender, enjoyed a stellar career, predominantly at Hayes before joining Hendon in the spring of 2013. He contributed to a strong end to the season and returned for the following pre-season, but did not play in a competitive game.

Ron Graves: Ron made his debut for Golders Green at left-back against Southall in September 1937. He left in the autumn of 1939, after the Athenian League's suspension because of the Second World War. He made 56 appearances and scored eight goals, having played mainly at centre-half, but also at both centre-forward and in goal.

Phil Gridelet: Phil won a Middlesex Charity Cup winner's medal on his debut, against Feltham in May 1985, and was almost ever-present for the next four seasons as a central defender. An England Non-League international at Hendon, he left to turn full-time professional in 1989, with Barnet, and played in the Football League for Barnsley, Rotherham and Southend. He came back to the club in 2000 as a midfielder. Overall, he made 264 appearances for Hendon, scoring eight goals.

Charlie Goode: Charlie's six months partnering Elliot Brathwaite – after signing from AFC Hayes in late 2014 – gave Hendon an outstanding centre-back pairing. Technically sound in the air and on the ground, scouts were soon chasing him. The 19-year-old played for the England Non-League team just days before signing for Scunthorpe.

Tony Gibson: Hendon was Tony's last club at the end of a great career. He played for Hendon from 1986 to 1988. A midfield minder, he broke up play and let others be expressive. But he also was masterful doing dark deeds out of the officials' sight – and those deeds were often rather bloody.

Robbie Garvey: Robbie played top-level non-league football for many years, including two half-seasons at Hendon, in 1992 and 1993 when Victor Green funded the club. Tall and powerful, he would stride forward from midfield to great effect. When he was a Grays Athletic player, he bought a flat overlooking the Rec Ground pitch.

Bontcho Guentchev: Bontcho, when playing at Luton Town, bought a house 200 yards from Claremont Road so he could commute to Luton and his boys could attend the Chelsea FC Academy. In summer 1999, aged 35, he asked to join Hendon. A Bulgarian World Cup USA 1994 semi-finalist, Bontcho was a dressing room mentor, adored by younger players. He left after two seasons, but rejoined as player-coach under Gary McCann. In all, he made 83 appearances and scored 12 goals. He also played with both his sons and, in November 2000, played 45 minutes in goal at Carshalton.

Melvyn Griffiths: Melvyn joined Golders Green at the start of 1945 and spent parts of three seasons with club as it became Hendon in 1946. He had a hand in three of the Green's four goals in the Middlesex

Red Cross Cup Final at Wembley in 1945 and was a prolific scorer, with 45 in 73 games.

Micky Garrini: Micky was recommended to Hendon by his close friend Roy Butler in 1978. A near Minor Counties-standard cricketer, he was a livewire striker, not biggest or strongest, but had an eye for goal, especially feeding off scraps. In 102 games for Hendon, he scored 33 goals.

Lubomir Guentchev: Lubo played with his father Bontcho a few times in his four Hendon seasons. He took special toll on AFC Hornchurch, scoring the winner at Bridge Avenue in 2008 and a hat-trick there in 2009. At Vale Farm, at the end of that season, he netted with an audacious lob.

Substitutes
Arthur Godding: Arthur played regularly in goal in Golders Green's 1934–35 campaign, and in the club's first FA Cup 1st round proper tie, away to Southend United. He played a handful of matches in the 1945–46 season.

Kenny Gayle: Solid and uncomplicated, Kenny played within his limits in either defence or midfield in a struggling team between 1990 and 1992.

Dean Green: Dean spent two seasons at Hendon, bring his wealth of experience to a squad which was filled with young players in the late 2000s.

Gil Gomes: Gil Gomes was Man-of-the-Match for Portugal in the 1991 FIFA Under-19 World Cup Final. After one game at Hendon in January 2001, he later coached at Manchester United.

Glenn Garner: Many other 'G' strikers have better credentials, but none would cause the mayhem Glenn could with his old-style, physical centre-forward play. He made his debut in February 2008, and made 64 appearances with 20 goals over four seasons.

There are some all-time Hendon greats in this team.

David Hook: Desperately needing a goalkeeper with Gary McCann's knee problems keeping him out, Dave Anderson brought in the very experienced David Hook from Harrow Borough in 2001. He played 109 games in his two seasons with the club.

David Hogwood: David played for Hendon from 1962, making his debut at the age of 18, to 1971, before returning briefly in 1974. He won every domestic honour with the club and represented England Amateurs and Great Britain, playing at Claremont Road when Great Britain lost 1–0 to Germany, but won on aggregate in a 1968 Olympic Games qualifier. He made 440 first team appearances, and scored 24 goals, mainly from penalties.

Gary Hand: Gary joined Hendon in summer 1971 and, apart from spending 1974–75 at Wycombe, left in autumn 1986, when he was sacked in his second spell as manager. He played 619 games, winning the Amateur Cup in his first season and the Isthmian League title the following year.

Mark Hill: Mark, a solid full-back or central defender, joined Hendon from Slough in 1992. One of the few who stayed loyal to the club during the turmoil of 1993–94, Mark scored his only goal, the Full Members Cup Final winner against Wokingham, in the 63rd of his 64 appearances.

Jeff Harris: The 17-year-old Jeff joined Hendon from Arsenal in 1959, and in his three seasons at Claremont Road, he won the 1960 Amateur Cup, 1961 Athenian League, four England Amateur caps and Athenian League representative honours. He left Hendon in the autumn of 1961 to join Enfield, and later turned professional with Leyton Orient. He made 91 appearances for Hendon.

Rod Haider: Rod is among the greatest of all Hendon players. He joined from Kingstonian in 1967, having won 10 England Amateur caps, but he added 55 while at Hendon to become England's most capped Amateur ever. A brilliant midfielder, he had a sixth sense, knowing where to be when it mattered. This talent brought him the FA Cup equaliser against Newcastle United in January 1974, and the only goal of the 1977 League Cup Final. He left the club after being sacked as manager in November 1989, refusing to continue as a player, having made 696 appearances and scored 165 goals.

Steve Heard: Steve didn't need to play non-league football, as he earned a six-figure salary as a computer salesman. He joined Hendon from Aylesbury in 1996 – having been part of their "duck-walk celebration" team – and spent three seasons at Hendon, playing in the 1997 FA Cup win over Leyton Orient, and making 143 first team appearances.

Freddie Hyatt: One of the great characters of non-league football, not least because he was a rat-catcher, Freddie joined Hendon in 1997 and left 21 years later. A skilful midfielder, his Greens playing career lasted three seasons, scoring 18 goals in 163 appearances, before he returned as Gary McCann's assistant manager for 12 years.

David Hyde: David was Hendon's most prolific goal scorer of the Isthmian League era. Between 1963 and 1966, he scored 118 goals in 140 appearances, including two in the 1965 Amateur Cup Final, one in the Isthmian League Championship Play-off and three against Arsenal in the 4–3 London Challenge Cup victory. He had one of the hardest shots in amateur football. He joined Wimbledon in the Southern League after leaving Hendon.

Tony Harding: Tony remained an amateur at Barnet before joining Hendon in 1966. Brought in to replace David Hyde, he reached the 30-goal landmark in both of his Hendon seasons, finishing with 61 goals in 85 games. Hendon, however, didn't have a 20-goal man to partner him.

Terry Howard: Left-winger Terry scored the winning goal in the 1960 FA Amateur Cup Final against Kingstonian in a magical year for him. It also included caps for Great Britain in the Rome Olympic Games and for England Amateurs. Signed from Harwich & Parkeston, he later played at Leyton Orient. He made 82 appearances with 31 goals in his two seasons with the club.

Substitutes

Reg Hill: Goalkeeper Reg played in two pre-war seasons for Golders Green, making his debut in January 1937, and two for Hendon from 1949 to 1951, when he weighed 16 stone and wore glasses. He played 52 first team matches in his two spells with the club.

Matthew Howard: Matt was the victim of a nasty accident in the Hendon dressing room in 1999. A fine full-back, he played 130 games in his three seasons.

Rakatahr Hudson: Midfielder Rakatahr was on every Hendon team sheet in his debut season, 2006–07. He played in parts of four seasons making 108 appearances.

Arthur Humphreys: Arthur, scored on his debut, against Barnet & Alston in 1912 and got Hampstead's first ever Athenian League goal in 1914, also against Barnet. The club records show that he scored 31 goals in 25 first team games, spread over three seasons,

Brian and Davis Haule: The Haule brothers gave Hendon loyal service in multiple spells. Striker Brian scored with his first touch for Hendon. Both played more than 140 games.

Almost every decade of the club's history is represented here.

John Jacobs: John was an unpopular signing when brought in by Ted Hardy to replace fans-favourite Dave Root in summer 1987. Past his best, he played only 17 games before Root returned. He was Jewish, played on Yom Kippur (a major Jewish holy day) and was sloppy in a 4–1 defeat against Slough.

Robyn Jones: A graduate of three universities, Welshman Robyn played at right-back for Barrie Williams at Sutton when they beat Coventry in the 1989 FA Cup. Williams brought Robyn to Hendon when he took over as manager in 1992, but Robyn endured an injury-hit campaign, playing only 34 times.

Bernard Joy: Bernard also appears in the Internationals Dream Team, having won a full England cap as an amateur. His played twice for Hendon, once each in 1932 for Hampstead and 1934 for Golders Green. His son, Chris, who spent decades at Corinthian-Casuals in various roles, made three Hendon appearances in 1968–69.

Tony Jennings: Hendon saw a very good player become a great one after Tony left Claremont Road for Enfield in March 1974. He was the right-back in the 1972 Amateur Cup Final, 1972–73 Isthmian League championship-winning team and in the two games against Newcastle United in 1974. He played 155 times for Hendon, scoring seven goals. Tony won a couple of England Amateur call-ups at Hendon without winning a cap, but went on to become England's Non-League team captain and later manager. Soon after retiring, he returned to Hendon as Dave Mawson's assistant manager, but left in late 1982, citing travel problems from his north Essex home. He died in June 2015 at the age of 65.

Alan Jones: Alan joined Hendon right at the end of the 1960–61 Athenian League Championship season, playing two League games and the Final – his debut – and replay of the Middlesex Senior Cup, when Hounslow eventually triumphed 3–2. He played 26 times in 1961–62 before moving on.

Paul Johnson: Paul made his Hendon debut as an 18-year-old in September 2000, but was never able to nail down a regular place – something he achieved after leaving for Ashford Town (Middlesex) in 2001. He played in a variety of positions in his 20 matches for Dave Anderson.

Danny Julienne: Danny was a combative midfielder, who played under Tony Choules, Gary Farrell and Gary McCann after signing from Northwood in summer 2004. He was one of the few players who stayed at Hendon beyond the end of 2004–05, but returned to Northwood early in 2006.

Oscar James: Inside forward Oscar joined Hampstead Town in the Middlesex and London Leagues in September 1913 after Kilburn FC's demise. Partnering Arthur Humphries, Oscar scored twice on his debut in the 5–1 Middlesex League defeat of East Ham Town, but played only nine more times scoring six goals.

Eggie James: Hendon fans mused on which body part Eggie would use to score a goal, and legs or head were not necessarily among the favourites. In one-plus seasons, from 1974 to 1976, the tall, gangly, awkward forward averaged almost one goal every three appearances, before returning to Staines Town. Overall, he scored 22 goals in 69 appearances.

Zak Joseph: The son of former Brentford striker Roger Joseph, Zak earned a degree in sports journalism before joining Hendon from

Hanwell Town in June 2017. His only season was a huge success as he scored 18 goals in 57 games, helping Hendon finish third in the Isthmian League.

Keith Jameson: Keith joined Hendon in the 1968–69 season and played four times. He became a first team regular the following season and won an FA Amateur Cup winner's medal in 1972. The hard-working midfielder left for Hayes that summer, having played 138 times and scored six goals.

Substitutes

Micky Janes: Micky succeeded Ted Hardy as manager in September 1987 and led out the team in the 1988 Russell Grant Middlesex Charity Cup Final at Wembley.

John Jacobs: By strange coincidence, John was also a goalkeeper, but he made only three appearances for Golders Green, all in September 1937.

Romario Jonas: Centre-half Romario made his Hendon debut in the second game of 2018–19 and, early indications are that he looks a real prospect.

F Johnson: The club does not have his first name. He made his debut at Wealdstone on Christmas Day 1929 in a 1–1 draw, and made 21 appearances in all.

Steve Jefferies: A real fan favourite, Steve was Hendon's first super sub. A police officer, he had blistering pace and terrorised tiring defences with it. He made 141 appearances, scoring 30 goals, between 1974 and 1978.

Chris James: Both of Chris's goals were as a substitute, against Yeovil on his debut in 1995 and, five seconds after coming on against Northwood.

K

There are some very interesting characters in this Special-K squad.

Dave King: Dave was not everyone's cup of tea as a goalkeeper and – given his size – might have done more with his career. He joined Hendon after starring for Hastings Town in the 2002 FA Cup and made 142 appearances in three seasons before signing for Tooting & Mitcham United.

Charlie Kuehn: Charlie spent three seasons with Hendon and played in more tournaments for England – in both Futsal and Socca (five- and six-a-side) – than he made appearances for the Greens, three, all in cup ties. At a Socca World Cup, Charlie was joined by six other former Hendon players.

John Knapman: John, the left-back in Enfield's glorious 1970s and 1980s era, was 35 when signed by Ted Hardy in January 1986 as Hendon battled to avoid relegation. He spent one year with the Greens, playing 44 games and scoring three goals. He has been a local councillor in Epping for 20 years.

Paul Kelly: Paul joined Hendon on loan from Fulham in April 1994 and signed permanently in the summer of 1996. The high-energy midfielder won two Full Members Cup winner's medals in his three Hendon seasons. He scored nine goals – most importantly the FA Cup winner at Dover in 1996 – in 121 appearances.

Mark Kirby: Ask any Haringey Borough or Enfield Town fan about Mark and they will get positively dewy-eyed as they marvel at his quality. In two Hendon spells, across parts of three seasons, this was rarely evident, but the no-nonsense surrounding cast of this team might make a difference. He first played for Hendon from 2008 to 2009–10, and returned in 2015–16. Overall, he made 68 first team appearances, and scored twice.

Warren Kelly: Warren was a superb central defender or sweeper, who was 32 years old when signed by Frank Murphy in January 2000. A knee injury in a pre-season game away to Hillingdon Borough, 18 months later, ended his playing career. He had played 52 times for Hendon. He was Dave Anderson's coach throughout his three-year tenure.

Tony Kelly: Quite how Tony made 136 Hendon appearances – and scored 15 goals, from February 1996 to April 1999, is a mystery, because his knee problems were debilitating. He played at centre-half in the win over Leyton Orient and was equally as effective in midfield, where he thrived as an enforcer.

Gary Keen: It would be damning Gary with faint praise to call him versatile, but he played at left-back, left and central midfield, and occasionally up front. A scorer in Hendon's 1991 FA Cup loss at Reading, Gary made 185 appearances and scored 39 goals between January 1987 and September 1993.

Mick Kiely: Mick, an MA in history from the University of California at Berkeley – he played for the Golden Bears – a Bachelor of Education from the University of London and a former football coach at Eton College, is now head teacher of Cardinal Wiseman School. Before he joined Hendon, Mick played for Slough when they beat Millwall in the 1982 FA Cup and he calmed the dressing room by quoting and acting out *The Charge of the Light Brigade* poem. He scored the key second goal in Hendon's 4–1 win at Slough the night the club avoided relegation in 1986. Overall, he made 131 appearances over four seasons for Hendon, scoring 25 goals.

 Reg Kirby: Reg had a prolific 1921–22 season for Hampstead Town – 23 goals in 20 games – but his exact career statistics are unknown. His first recorded goal was in a 3–0 FA Cup win over Barnet at the Avenue Ground in September 1921. He returned briefly in 1923.

Walter Koller: Swiss national Walter was working in London in autumn 1972 and played in Hendon's Isthmian League title-winning squad. His only two cup-ties for the Greens were in the Barassi Cup, when Hendon beat UC Valdinievole 3–1 on aggregate. He still follows the club from afar.

Substitutes

Ray Kemp: Ray made his goalkeeping debut in Golders Green's final ever Athenian League match versus Southall, May 1946, and was Hendon's first choice until 1949, making 103 first team appearances.

Ray Kingsland: Ray was Hendon's centre-half throughout 1958–59, but left for Enfield in autumn 1959 and missed out on 1960 Amateur Cup glory. He played 53 times for Hendon.

Mark Kane: Another with Enfield links, Peter Taylor signed 'Kipper' from Southbury Road in 1993. Mark won a 1994 Full Member Cup winners medal, and played 24 matches in his only season with the club.

Herbert Knott: Former Arsenal junior Herbert, from Goole, Humberside, spent two prolific seasons at Golders Green, scoring 47 goals in 45 games from 1932 to 1934.

Tony Knox: Tony scored 20 goals in 68 Hendon games over three seasons from 1963, but was on the losing side for Whitley Bay against the Greens in the 1966 FA Amateur Cup semi-final.

The most amazing thing about this Dream Team is that no player whose surname began with this letter appeared for Hendon in the 1970s, in fact between spring 1968 and spring 1981.

Tom Lovelock: Tom spent only 16 months at Hendon, but played key roles in the Greens' escape from relegation in 2017 and run to the Bostik League Premier Division play-off final in 2018. He produced countless outstanding saves to join a long list of top quality goalkeepers to play for the club. He made his debut on New Year's Eve 2016, and played 77 games.

Pat Lynch: Pat joined Golders Green at the end of the Second World War and gave seven seasons of loyal service, mainly at right-back. He was there for the club's start of a glorious quarter-century at the top of amateur football, playing in both FA Amateur Cup semi-final games against Pegasus. Overall, he played 241 games, scoring 11 times.

Micky Lane: Hendon were very fortunate that they did not have to worry about the full-back positions for five seasons as Micky played alongside Pat, normally on the left side. He joined the club in April 1948 and left in September 1953, retiring to run his pub in West Ham, having appeared 205 times for Hendon.

A Lovell: Another player whose first name is lost in time, he joined Golders Green from Southall in December 1938, quickly become a key contributor from half-back. He served in the Army in the Second World

War and thus lost a large part of his football career. He left the Green in 1945. Of his 65 appearances, 45 were during the War.

Marc Leach: Marc's first two spells at Hendon were on loan from Yeading – he signed permanently at the end of the second one. A tall, commanding central defender, he was also dangerous taking free-kicks, most memorably the one which started the 3–2 comeback win against Tonbridge in August 2007. Between 2005 and 2009 he made 155 appearances in five seasons.

Arthur Lee: Arthur, a heart-on-his-sleeve central defender, made his debut on the opening day of the 2016–17 season, in the first Bostik League game played at SJP. Frequently named captain, he made 105 appearances in his two seasons, but was part of the exodus in summer 2018, joining Tonbridge.

Tony Lynch: Although his best days were at a higher level than the Isthmian League – and earlier in his career – Tony showed flashes of his qualities in his only season at Hendon. He was a substitute in the home FA Cup tie against Leyton Orient, replacing Colin Simpson late on. He played 38 times for Hendon in 1997–98, his only season at the club.

Fred Long: Fred's career was interrupted by the Second World War. He made his debut at inside-forward in April 1938 and played 12 times for Golders Green in 1938–39. His final goal came in the Middlesex Red Cross Cup defeat of Wood Green Town in 1945.

Tommy Lawrence: Although better known for his Enfield career, Tommy spent three prolific seasons at Hendon in the late 1950s. He scored 37 goals in 41 appearances in 1956–57, his first season at Claremont Road and added 67 goals in 89 games before joining the Es in 1959.

Junior Lewis: Junior played in England's top 10 tiers from non-league step 6 to the Premier League. He joined Hendon in 1996 and was at his best partnering Paul Whitmarsh under Frank Murphy. Peter Taylor signed him for Gillingham, and Junior followed him to Premier League Leicester City – and many clubs thereafter. He played 149 times for Hendon, three of which were as player-coach in 2011–12, in his late 30s. He scored 69 goals.

Danny Lakey: Danny's Hendon career began in statistically the club's greatest ever season, 1964–65, when the Greens did the Isthmian League and Amateur Cup 'double', plus the Middlesex Senior Cup. Ostensibly a winger, thus a creator of goals rather than an out-and-out scorer, he scored 30 goals – fourth highest for the club – in 49 games that season, including in the 4–3 victory over Arsenal at Highbury in the London Challenge Cup and at Dulwich in the League play-off final against Enfield. In December 1967, no longer a first-team regular, Danny, after 105 games and 55 goals, joined Ramsgate.

Substitutes

Berkley Laurencin: Berkley had all the attributes for a top goalkeeper, but never fully made it at Hendon. He registered 169 appearances between 2008 and 2017.

Richard Langley: One who slipped through the net, full-back Richard joined from Dulwich, left for Corinthian–Casuals and ended up as a regular at Fulham. He made 59 appearances in the 1984–85 and 1985–86 seasons.

Freddie Langdale: Loyalty was the key to Freddie Langdale's selection here as he played in 10 seasons from 1946 to 1957, but finished with only 29 first team appearances.

Bill Little: Bill made a scoring debut against Sutton Court in October 1919. Not a regular, he scored 10 goals in 27 games, leaving in 1927.

Jefferson Louis: Maybe football's ultimate journeyman with over 40 clubs at the time of writing, Jefferson's six months at Hendon, 2013–14, were his most prolific, with 22 League goals in 25 games.

The M versus Mc & Mac game would certainly be exciting with all the attacking options in this team.

Melvin Minter: Melvin was another goalkeeper with all the attributes to be absolutely top-class, but somehow, he could not make that leap (pardon the pun). Tall and agile, he could make miraculous saves, but also errors, and these affected both his confidence, and that of the defenders in front of him. He played nine times in the 2015–16 season.

Tom Murphy: Tom was one of Ken Payne's first signings in January 1981. A steady, unfussy player, equally effective at full-back or in midfield, he featured in all the remaining league games that season. He scored four times in 97 appearances in four seasons including a brief return in 1985.

Tommy Mason: Tommy won New Zealand eight caps after emigrating there to continue his football career. It didn't work out for him, so he returned home and signed Hendon, managed by Peter Taylor, in 1993. He stayed loyal when many left and scored Hendon's opening goal in the Full Members Cup Final. He played 44 times in the 1993–94 season.

Stewart Mitchell: Stewart was unveiled as a 30-goal-a-year midfielder when moving south from Gateshead and signing for Hendon in 1983. This bemused him as he had scored 13 the previous season – lost in translation! He was not that prolific with Hendon, managing only five in 58 games across two seasons.

Charlie Murphy: Charlie, the first Hendon captain to lift the Amateur Cup – the 2–1 defeat of Kingstonian in 1960 – enjoyed a meteoric rise. Signed from St Mary's, who called Clitterhouse Playing Fields home, in the summer of 1958, he made his debut on 20 April 1959. Soon appointed skipper, 369 days after his senior debut, he led out Hendon at Wembley. Not tall for a centre-half, he barely missed a game in his three full Hendon seasons, finishing with 136 appearances and three goals. Charlie led Hendon to the Athenian League title in 1961. Tragically, he hit hard times and died homeless.

Dean Murphy: Dean joined Hendon in January 1996 and spent two seasons in relegation battles. His only league goal was the 88th-minute equaliser in a 2–1 comeback win away to Aylesbury United, a pivotal result in the escape of 1997. A dominant, fearless central defender, he was terrified of being interviewed. He made 67 appearances over two seasons.

Sam Murphy: Sam spent four seasons – 184 games, 20 goals – during which he metamorphosed from a right-winger into a left-back. His Twitter account @SilkySam11 sums up his attacking talents as shown by his first season, 2014–15 when he scored 11 times. He played in the 2018 Socca World Cup.

Dave Metchick: An England Youth international who played more than 250 Football League games, joined Hendon in 1975 and brought inventive class to central midfield. His dead ball accuracy led to the Greens' FA Cup victory over Reading – Alan Phillips scoring from John Baker's flick-on. Sadly, he only stayed for one season at the club, making 46 appearances

Niko Muir: Niko spearheaded Hendon's fantastic attack in 2017–18, scoring 40 goals and earning a move to Hartlepool United. His first Greens spell in 2012–13 saw no appearances, but he netted 11 in 27 games in 2016 before joining Leiston. He was almost unstoppable third time around.

Frank Murphy: Frank played with a smile. He scored with his first Hendon touch, an audacious lob in an 8–1 League Cup win over Staines Town at Chertsey. A hugely skilful striker, he made only 11 appearance in four seasons, but turned around the club's fortunes as manager.

Matt Maran: Matt made his Hendon debut in February 1997 but came into his own in 1997–98. The highlight was the only goal in the 1998 Puma Cup Final against Worthing at Sutton. He left the following season as work commitments as a wildlife photographer took him to Africa. Overall, he played 61 times for Hendon, scoring seven times.

Substitutes

Nick Morgan: Goalkeeper Nick spent a month on loan from Billericay in March 2011. Seven months later he was temporarily paralysed when assaulted in Essex.

Ted Moore: Ted was the Hendon substitute in the 1972 Amateur Cup Final. He played 21 times in his only Hendon season, having joined from Dagenham.

Michael Murray: Talented midfielder who was superb at set-pieces. His FA Cup fourth qualifying winner at Corby in 2012 was worth thousands to the club.

He played 51 times in three seasons at the club, never fully establishing a first team place.

Stan Moore: Left-winger Stan joined Hampstead in 1928 and spent three seasons with the club scoring a more than respectable 35 goals in 82 appearances.

Junior Morais: Junior, from Mill Hill, spent two spells on loan from Wycombe Wanderers in 2013. His tenacious aggression brought him six goals in 15 games. He subsequently played for Peterborough United and Northampton Town, then moved to Scotland in the summer of 2019, signing for St Mirren.

Mc and Mac

One of the most fertile letters in Hendon history, the team of Mcs and Macs may be stronger than the M team.

Gary McCann: One of Frank Murphy's first signings, Gary, the manager's goalkeeper at Dulwich Hamlet, made his Hendon debut on 31 March 1997. Not the tallest for a goalkeeper, but he was a good shot-stopper, brave off his line and a very good talker. His last-kick penalty save away to Hitchin Town, a month later, confirmed the Greens' escape from relegation. Starring in the 1997–98 FA Cup run was probably the highlight of his time at Hendon, especially the replay win away to Leyton Orient. He suffered a career-curtailing injury in April 2000 and comeback attempts proved in vain. He played 196 games for the club. Subsequently became the longest-ever serving Hendon manager from February 2005 to 2018.

Roger McKay: Roger had a cameo career at Hendon, but was effective and important in battles against the drop. Roger, a schoolteacher who signed after a long career at Sutton, was a dressing room joker, but serious on the pitch where it really mattered. He played 36 games in two seasons after making his debut in January 1983.

Graeme McVie: A dead-ball specialist, Graeme had Scottish League experience before work commitments brought him to London in spring 1995, late in the 'kick-in' season – his brother Gary joined Hendon too and stayed longer. Graeme's 15 games, with his solid defensive play and quality at kick-ins were key in saving the Greens from relegation.

Casey Maclaren: Casey overcame a multitude of long-term injuries to join the ranks of Hendon all-time greats. In 11 seasons, he played in every position – including goalkeeper – and passed both the 350-appearance and 50-goal landmarks. He was probably at his best in midfield, but very good at centre-back too. He left the club in 2018 to join Gary McCann at Hampton & Richmond.

Josh McLeod-Urquhart: A loan signing from Wealdstone in February 2017, Josh's performances in the last dozen games of the Ryman

League season were another vital part of Hendon's escape from the abyss of relegation. As well as being a dominant centre-half and good passer, he brought calmness to the defence.

Martin McCayna: Another veteran defender, Martin joined Hendon in August 1989, but he left early in 1990 after losing his place following an injury a couple of months earlier. He made 31 appearances and scored four goals, all of which were in victories, and three in FA Cup or Trophy ties.

Kevin Maclaren: Kevin followed Casey to Hendon and emulated his brother in becoming the youngest ever – by one day – green badge London Taxi driver. A hard-as-nails midfielder, and occasional full-back, all too often Kevin's talents were overshadowed by his emotions getting the better of him, resulting in numerous red cards. Following a year-long suspension for an off the pitch incident, he returned to the side, but was then released after being sent off in January 2017.

Steve McKimm: Eighteen-year-old Steve joined the Malden Vale to Hendon exodus in summer 1994, scoring a pre-season goal soon after turning 19. He scored 10 goals in 61 games from midfield, leaving on manager Mick Browne's departure, and then enjoyed a long career at the top of non-league football.

James 'Jock' McGleish: James – or Jock as everyone called him – joined Hendon in the summer of 1979. Short and stocky, he was a terrier of a forward, forcing defenders into errors and capitalising on them. Sadly, after two good seasons, he suffered an injury away from football ending his career at Hendon. He played 78 games for the club, scoring 24 goals.

Carl McCluskey: Carl joined Hendon in summer 2011 and was one of four players to score 10 goals in 2011–12, along with Elliot Charles, Greg Ngoyi and Isaiah Rankin, but injuries limited his next two campaigns. He returned in 2015–16 and finished with 25 goals in 116 appearances.

Jason McKoy: Jason joined Hendon from Wembley in 1998 and spent two seasons under Frank Murphy, playing 47 matches for the club. Like many youngsters in an experienced squad, much of his two seasons was as a substitute or an occasional starter, but he was dangerous out wide and quick enough to upset tiring opposition midfielders.

Substitutes

Ben McNamara: Australian Ben was outstanding in goal in Hendon's glorious 2014–15 season, and pushed his manager Gary McCann hard for this Dream Team's starting spot. He played 50 times for the club before moving on.

Steve McGrath: Former youth-teamer Steve was aged 35 when he made a scoring debut in February 2005. The centre-back was vital to Hendon's survival that spring. He made 14 appearances in two seasons.

George McCluskey: Carl's younger brother, George joined Hendon on work experience from Barnet in September 2012. He was as a good at left-back as centre-half. He played eight first team games, mainly cup matches.

Max McCann: Manager Gary's son, Max was around Hendon's squad from his youth. Regularly an unused substitute, he still made 37 appearances in four seasons.

Gavin McPherson: Gavin McPherson, now a serving police officer, didn't score in eight Hendon appearances in two spells, but enjoyed success with Metropolitan Police FC.

N

Sadly, the N squad is rather lacking in options, the five goalkeepers combined for less than 20 appearances.

Andre Nolan: Andre spent most of the 1994–95 season as Dave Hudson's back-up, but missed two months with a dislocated shoulder, an injury he suffered diving for the finish line in a training session sprint. He started the following season as first choice while Hudson recuperated from knee surgery. Overall, he made seven appearances for the club.

Reg Nelmes: Full-back Reg appeared for Hendon in four seasons between 1949–50 and 1953–54, but was only ever an occasional first-teamer, playing 18 first team games in four seasons. He made his debut in February 1950, and was an emergency winger against Wealdstone on Boxing Day 1951, scoring his only goal in a 2–2 draw.

David Nolan: David came through Hendon's youth team in the early 1990s, but did not appear for the first team until Tony Choules signed him in the summer of 2004. He was promoted to player-coach under Gary Farrell, limiting his playing time, and left the club with Farrell in early February 2005, after playing 25 games.

Neil Norman: Neil, a talented midfielder, knew his own worth. He left Hendon after only 14 appearances in 1984, and starred as Fisher Athletic reached the Conference. When Millwall offered him a two-year deal, IT specialist Neil is believed to have asked for £2m, to cover lost income and compensation for leaving his lucrative profession.

Richard Nugent: The garrulous centre-back from the Midlands was a close friend of Frank Murphy and, thus, his first signing in March 1997. Richard switched to centre-forward in a September 1997 League Cup tie against Staines Town, replacing the injured Michael Banton, and scored four of Hendon's eight goals. He played 48 times over three seasons, scoring 13 goals.

Albert Nash: Albert joined Hendon the season after the club changed its name from Golders Green to Hendon, one of three players who arrived from Leyton – Bert Gibbs and Jock Watson being the other two. He played six games at centre-back, scoring once, while Bill Fisher was absent, but lost his place when Bill returned.

Youness Nabil: Youness was signed by Dave Anderson in 2001–02, but saw no competitive action. Gary McCann brought him back in 2005 effectively as bait for a bigger fish – this being Belal Aite-Ouakrim. Once Belal had signed, Youness was allowed to leave, having scored once in seven games.

Steve Newing: Steve, with Phil Gridelet and Danny Worley, stepped up from his dad John Newing's Princes Park and Hendon Under-18s to play in the Isthmian League. He debuted on New Year's Day 1985, but left after 45 appearances and four goals. Steve later became a legend at Edgware Town.

Greg Ngoyi: Greg was another former Hendon youth-teamer who later contributed to the first team. He built his senior reputation as a prolific goal scorer with Edgware then Wealdstone. At Hendon, he scored 29 goals in 71 games between January 2011 and December 2012, before joining St Albans City.

Cliff Nock: Cliff was recommended to Hendon by the Secretary of the Army FA and signed before the 1951–52 season. His 37 goals in 81 matches came across four seasons, but only in 1953–54 was he even a semi-regular, 35 games and 16 goals. He joined Finchley in 1955.

Ashley Nathaniel-George: Ashley joined Hendon in the summer of 2017, having scored 17 goals for Potters Bar Town the previous season. He made a slow start at SJP, but quickly became a key member of Gary McCann's squad, being one of four forwards to score at least 17 goals. Many of his strikes were spectacular, with the one that settled the game at Thurrock being possibly the best. Ashley scored Hendon's goal in the Bostik League Premier Division play-off final against Dulwich. In June 2018, he left Hendon to turn full-time professional with Crawley Town.

Substitutes

Brendan Norris: Canadian goalkeeper Brendan came to England – his family had emigrated in the 1940s – to further his career. He played four times for Hendon in 2016.

Matt Newing: Matt's only Hendon game was against Finchley in December 1987, playing against big brother Steve. Their sister Jackie played for Hendon Ladies.

Joe Nartey: Joe, a prolific goal scorer, had two spells at Hendon, both of them very short. In all, he scored three goals in 11 games.

Mark Nicholls: Mark won the European Cup Winners Cup with Chelsea before his career was derailed. At his best he was brilliant, at his worst, awful. He scored 24 goals in 35 games for Hendon.

O Neale: On 21 September 1912, he made his only appearance for Hampstead Town and scored a hat-trick against Kilburn. His first name is not known.

O

I knew that this was going to be a tough selection and have had to use a player who did not make a single appearance for the Greens.

Zaki Oualah: Zaki is the first dream teamer who never played competitively for Hendon – but there is no 'O' goalkeeper. Zaki was one of the first players signed by James Gray in 2018, but during pre-season went home to Algeria and never regained his place once Danny Boness arrived.

Jason O'Connor: Jason was a commanding defender brought in by Gary Farrell at the end of 2004 and made his debut on New Year's Day 2005, a 1–0 win away to Dover Athletic. When Gary McCann took over in February, Jason stayed, but left after the end of the season.

A Owens: His first name is another lost in time, Owens made his Hampstead debut in January 1928 and he stayed until the end of the following season. Although he was normally a left-back, his final performance was in the number 10 shirt as Hampstead enjoyed a best-ever second place finish.

Lee O'Leary: Midfielder Lee – appointed joint manager of Potters Bar with Scott Cousins in autumn 2018 – spent a decade at Hendon, but suffered a multitude of injuries, the worst of which was a broken leg against Horsham in March 2009, after being knocked unconscious while challenging for a header. He played 290 times for Hendon and scored 27 goals.

Andy O'Brien: Andy was a loyal Hendon servant in three spells, making 370 appearances and scoring 26 goals. Promoted from the reserves to first team aged 18 in November 1981, he continued to play for the Greens while commuting from his studies at Nottingham University. A clever central defender, he left early in 1987 and returned two years later, but only until 1991. Back in summer 1995, he played under Mick Browne and Neil Price, the latter appointing him reserve team manager a year later. When Price was dismissed, Andy had three games as first-team boss before Frank Murphy arrived.

Pat O'Donnell: Pat had the physique to be a top central defender, but not the self-confidence. The former Leyton Orient youth team captain joined Hendon aged 18 in September 2009. His biggest contribution in 12 games was the 18th and winning penalty in the FA Cup shoot-out against Ashford Town (Middlesex).

Ray O'Callaghan: Ray played in four consecutive seasons at Hendon, 1976 to 1980, during which time he also had a brief spell playing in Australia. Predominantly a reserve, he was a semi-regular first-teamer in the 1978–79 campaign. A self-confident winger or attacking midfielder, he made 60 appearances and scored four goals.

Eugene Ofori: Eugene, an under-21 international from Ghana, made his debut in September 2001 and quickly became a regular first-team goal scorer – his bustling, aggressive running reminding management of compatriot Tony Yeboah. He scored 27 goals in 2003–04 and netted 71 times in 196 Hendon appearances before joining Braintree in 2005.

Gerry O'Rourke: Gerry spent only one season at Hendon, the Greens' first in the Isthmian League. As centre-forward, he finished as top goal scorer with 39 goals in 47 appearances – including the 1964 London Senior Cup Final winner – as the team finished runners-up behind Wimbledon, who signed him as they turned professional.

Wayne O'Sullivan: An exciting attacking talent Wayne played at Arsenal, Exeter, Canvey Island and Torquay before joining Hendon in 2006. His second season was his best, earning him a move to Stevenage Borough in January 2008. Back at Hendon in 2009 he finished with 103 appearances and 24 goals.

Mick O'Donoghue: Mick scored one of my favourite ever Hendon goals, the third – a 30-yard run and 25-yard shot – in a 3–0 defeat of Wycombe Wanderers in August 1976. West Ham scouted him against Southall, but their Alan Devonshire was more impressive. The Wycombe goal was Mick's career high-point.

Substitutes

Glyn Owen: Glyn was a steady left-back who played briefly at the end of the 1973–74 season and left early in the following campaign.

Bob and Sean O'Leary: Striker Bob scored three goals in 30 games in 1984–85. Midfielder brother Sean played sparingly in Ted Hardy's 1986 relegation battle.

Ted Owen: Inside-forward Ted made his Golders Green debut in December 1938 and finished with Hendon in 1951 after 79 appearances and 18 goals.

Ben Odeje: Ben was England's first ever black football international when selected as a schoolboy in 1971. He played in three Hendon games in 1975.

Karl Oliyide: Karl debuted in April 2014, but played regularly in the first half of 2016–17, when he scored 12 times in 35 games.

This team has some famous names in what is a very strong squad.

Mike Pinner: One of the most interesting players ever to appear for Hendon, Mike left the RAF where he had been a pilot, to become a solicitor, having studied law at Cambridge University. A winner of 52 England Amateur caps – nine at Hendon – and three for Great Britain in the 1956 and 1960 Olympic Games, his professional clubs included

Aston Villa, Arsenal, QPR, Manchester United, Chelsea, then Hendon – a game at Swansea Town – and Leyton Orient, mainly as an amateur. The goalkeeper joined the Greens in August 1961 and played 34 times that season, plus seven the following campaign. He was used to the professional game, and admitted later that he was not happy in senior amateur football.

David Poole: David made his debut in April 1971 and, for four of his five Hendon seasons, first team appearances were rarities. In the 1974–75 season, however, the dogged full-back was a regular, making 48 appearances and scoring his only Hendon goal in a 3–1 win at Barking.

Ray Poole: There is no record of Ray and David being related though both were defenders and near contemporaries. Ray's first game was the home London Senior Cup replay against Cheshunt – a 7–2 win after a 5–5 draw – in December 1966 and he made 136 appearances in four seasons.

Harold Pearse: Harold was a half-back for Hampstead Town in the 1920s. In two full seasons, and part of a third, he scored eight goals in 71 matches, the most notable of which was the 4–3 FA Cup victory over Berkhamsted – the first ever match at Claremont Road.

Alan Phillips: Welsh international centre-half Alan starred in Hendon's greatest days in the 1970s. He played in the 1972 Amateur Cup and Barassi Cup victories, won the Isthmian League in 1973, played against Newcastle in 1974 and scored the goal to beat Reading in the FA Cup in 1975.

James Parker: Full-back or centre-half James made his debut in Gary Farrell's last game in charge, in January 2005, and he added 299 games for Gary McCann, despite persistent ankle problems after an injury at Bromley in April 2006. Duties as an Enfield schoolteacher caused his sudden retirement in September 2012.

Steve Parsons: Steve matched outstanding skill with outrageous roguishness. He went to Finland near the end of the 1985–86 season, but was back the following season. Desperate to watch a big race on FA Cup 4th qualifying round day, he brought a television set into the dressing room.

Arthur Phebey: A long-time player for Kent County Cricket Club, Arthur was also a fine football inside-forward, earning Middlesex representative honours. He scored the London Challenge Cup winners against Arsenal and West Ham in 1951, two of 21 goals in 83 games between November 1950 and December 1953, leaving to rejoin Dulwich Hamlet.

Fred Pudney: Fred came through the Hendon youth team, making his first team debut in 1962, but was never a regular and left in the 1965–66 season. The striker returned in the Greens' Isthmian League

Championship and Middlesex Senior Cup-winning 1972–73 season, playing in the Barassi Cup in Italy.

Henry Pennifer: Henry joined Hampstead Town for their Middlesex League and London League Division 1 championship campaigns in 1912, and left to join QPR in 1913. Appearance and scoring records are incomplete, but show 22 goals in 19 games. He died in action in the First World War in 1918.

Arthur Peel: Arthur made his Hendon debut in March 1964 and was a key part of the squad – rather than a first-team regular – for the all-conquering Greens the following season, earning Middlesex County honours. If substitutes had been allowed in that season, his appearances would have been more than 25.

Substitutes

Arthur Paisley: Capable goalkeeper Arthur was a very loyal back-up, mainly to John Swannell in the early 1970s. In six seasons, he made 62 appearances.

Roy Parkyn: A fine winger or occasional full-back, Roy had terrible luck at Hendon; a summer 1992 shoulder injury ended his Greens career.

Sam Page: Sam joined Hendon on loan from MK Dons – earning boos from AFC Wimbledon fans – but the centre-back left in 2008 due to travel difficulties.

A Potter: Potter, whose first name is unknown, arrived in October 1927 and spent five seasons at Claremont Road, mainly as a back-up. He made 36 appearances, scoring four times.

Ross Pickett: Ross's versatility as a centre-back or, mainly, a striker made him a fine squad player. In five 2000s seasons, he scored 39 goals in 189 games.

There are 90 years of stars are in this squad.

Dave Root: Dave was one of Hendon's best-ever goalkeepers, but it nearly was very different. Manager Ted Hardy felt he was responsible for the 1986–87 cup final defeats, his first season with the club, and let him go. He got a second chance when John Jacobs made too many mistakes, and Dave grabbed it with both hands. His kicking was a weakness, but he more than made up for it with the rest of his game. In 1993–94, the last of his eight seasons with the Greens, Dave was awarded a testimonial. He left Hendon after making 442 appearances.

Dave Robotham: Dave joined Hendon towards the end of the 1987–88 season and ended up – as an unused substitute – with a Russell Grant Middlesex Charity Cup winners medal at Wembley. A full-back or centre-half, he moved on when he could not make the starting line-up in early 1988–89.

Alan Roughan: Alan spent parts of eight seasons at Hendon, in three spells. Like Dave Robotham he was an unused substitute at Wembley in June 1988, but he did make 123 appearances, scoring seven goals, almost all at left-back. He worked as joint-player-manager at both Ware and Finchley with Dermot Drummy.

Rodney Richards: Midfielder Rodney came over from Malden Vale with Mick Browne in 1994. He only scored one goal and suffered a serious knee late in the season. His son, Colin Kazim-Richards, won 37 caps for Turkey.

Geoff Riddy: Geoff came through the reserves to make his debut in December 1961. It took him three seasons to be become Hendon's first-choice centre-half, and he won FA Amateur Cup, Isthmian League and Middlesex Senior Cup winners medals in 1964–65. He left the following season after making 129 appearances.

P A Rees: Rees, whose initials were P A, but his given name is not recorded, joined Hampstead in March 1931 and spent the next two full seasons with the club, playing as a half-back. He scored only one goal, in an AFA Cup tie in February 1933, after making 64 appearances.

Finbarr Robins: Finbarr joined Hendon from Ware in November 2015 and left after around a year. A talented attacking midfielder, he was unfortunate to play in struggling squads, which clearly affected his confidence. He scored five goals in 46 games, before leaving to join Enfield Borough, then returning to Ware.

Bill Reay: Bill joined Hendon from Erith & Belvedere in 1946 and did not miss a competitive match - Will Mather Cup included - until what would have been his 165th and final appearance, 11 short of Bill Fisher's club record. A prolific goal scorer, he netted almost 70 in four seasons.

Oscar Reinke: Oscar shares the club record for most competitive games with a goal, netting 18 times in eight consecutive matches in September and October 1925 – Leon Smith equalled it in autumn 2014. Oscar played 55 times, from 1925 to 1928, interrupted by a brief spell at Clapton, and scored 52 goals.

Martin Randall: Martin spent almost three seasons at Hendon, joining from Hayes in 2001, and scored 32 goals in 100 appearances, despite a drought in 2003–04 when he netted only six times. He joined AFC Wimbledon under Dave Anderson, who was his manager at Hendon.

Isaiah Rankin: Isaiah joined Hendon in August 2011, having played in the Premier League for Arsenal and Bradford City. Hugely experienced, he was joined by Darren Currie and Frank Sinclair that autumn. The following season, his spectacular FA Cup winner against Eastbourne Borough led to a first-round proper appearance.

Substitutes

James Reading: James, and identical twin David, were released by Wycombe in 2009, and the goalkeeper spent two seasons at Hendon, joining Northwood in 2011.

Jack Richardson: Left-back Jack joined Hampstead in March 1932, and made 116 appearances, including Golders Green's 10–1 FA Cup loss to Southend in 1934.

George Rocknean: Although he played only 16 times for the first team, from 1964 to 1973, George was an integral member of the club and a key player for the reserves. He later enjoyed much success as reserve team manager.

Charlie Richardson: Charlie was an outrageously talented midfielder, but being the son of the notorious South London gangster Charles Richardson hampered his football career.

John Richardson: John scored on his Hendon debut in September 1996. The striker led the attack in that year's FA Cup first round at Cardiff.

S

This is arguably the most prolific of all the dream team attacks, the defence isn't bad either.

John Swannell: Hendon have been blessed with great goalkeepers and John was best of all. This outstanding keeper won everything at Hendon, from 1963 to 1974, after joining from Corinthian-Casuals where he learned his craft. His honours included: 61 England Amateur international caps, Great Britain Olympic caps, two Isthmian League titles, two FA Amateur Cups and the FA Cup matches against Newcastle United. In a 1967 Amateur Cup-tie at Leatherhead, John saved a penalty and set up a counter-attack goal for Tony Harding. John spent six years at Leatherhead then, aged 41 in 1980, briefly returned to Claremont Road, finishing with 594 appearances.

Erskine Smart: Erskine was a fine right-back who made a scoring Hendon debut in a 3–1 League Cup victory at Feltham. He managed only two more goals in his final 230 Hendon games and was a near ever-present in the three seasons 1986–87 to 1988–89.

Oliver Sprague: Ollie joined Hendon from Northwood in spring 2014. A defensively sound left-back, with a good attacking instinct, he was signed by both Welling United and Billericay Town, but didn't settle at either club and returned to Hendon. He moved to Hampton in 2018 after making 148 appearances, scoring seven goals for the club.

Roy Sleap: Roy, a teak-tough full-back or midfielder, won the Athenian (1961) and Isthmian (1965) Leagues with Hendon. Training sessions with good friend John Swannell were so physical that manager Ron Burgess insisted they didn't go head-to head. For a defensive specialist, 31 goals in 288 games was a prolific return. He also won England Amateur honours and, as a Barnet player, was in the 1960 Olympic squad.

David Shacklock: David played for Cheshunt in a London Senior Cup shock win against Hendon in November 1964, joined the Greens soon after and debuted before Christmas that year. A solid, reliable defender, he was a regular in only two of his seven Hendon seasons until 1971, David played 215 times without scoring a goal.

Chris Seeby: Chris's best Hendon season was at right-back in 2013–14, but was a fine centre-back as well. A knee injury, in a friendly against Harrow Borough in February 2015, kept him out for 14 months – he made a scoring return – but another serious knee injury later in 2016 ended his football career.

Roy Stroud: Roy was aged 14 when joined Golders Green in 1940, and played more than 420 matches, including 120 during the Second World War and netted 212 goals. An outstanding winger, he won England Amateur international caps before playing for West Ham United as amateur. He turned professional for the Hammers in November 1953 at the age of 28. Injuries meant that he never established himself as a regular first teamer at Upton Park. He died, aged 90, in 2015.

Peter Slade: Known as "Gurney", inside-forward Peter spent only two seasons at Hendon, but scored 55 goals in 102 appearances, winning the FA Amateur Cup, Isthmian League and Middlesex Senior Cup – he scored in both the League play-off and County Cup Final. He married and moved to Oxfordshire in 1965.

Harry Shearcroft: Harry marked Hampstead's first home game at Claremont Road – against Berkhamsted in September 1926 – with a goal. He had also scored on his debut at Enfield a week earlier. He scored 71 times in 72 games, 1926 to 1929, and finished with 80 goals in 89 appearances.

David Swain: David joined Hendon from Tooting & Mitcham United in November 1962 and scored on his debut in a London Charity Cup tie against Dulwich Hamlet. He spent five seasons at Claremont Road, but was in the reserves for the next two seasons. Nonetheless, he scored 49 times in 101 games for the first team.

Miles Spector: Winger or centre forward Miles spent eight seasons at Hendon between September 1955 and June 1963, amassing 151 goals in 280 games. He was part of the team that won the Amateur Cup in 1960 and the Athenian League in 1961. A Chelsea first-teamer as a schoolboy before joining Hendon, Miles scored four times in Hendon's record 13–1 win over Wingate, the club he left the Greens to become their player-coach. He won two England Amateur caps, and is fondly remembered by both Chelsea and Hendon supporters.

Substitutes

Peter Shearing: A fine goalkeeper, Peter's availability to Hendon was limited as he was doing National Service. He played in the 1960 Amateur Cup Final, but then turned professional with West Ham United in 1960. He did not win a regular first team place at Upton Park, and also played for Portsmouth, Exeter

City, Plymouth Argyle, Bristol Rovers and Gillingham, making 245 Football League appearances.

Dave Stephenson: Dave, a solid but mobile centre-back, stepped up from Malden Vale with Mick Browne and spent three seasons at Hendon.

Bobby Southam: Bobby was a mid-1970s box-to-box midfielder from Corinthian-Casuals who made more than 150 appearances, scoring 25 goals.

Graeme Sewell: Graeme sadly died too young a few years ago. The tall winger from Childs Hill suffered back problems which limited him to 50 games, from 1978 to 1981.

Leon Smith: Leon equalled the club record of scoring in eight straight games in autumn 2014. He scored 43 goals in 110 appearances.

T

The star of the T Dream Team is a legend of non-league football.

Sean Thomas: Diminutive for a goalkeeper, Sean had four spells at Hendon between signing as a youth loanee from QPR in November 2005 and his final appearance, a 5–0 FA Cup defeat against Bishop's Stortford in September 2013. He never made more than 10 appearances in any Hendon spell, often due to work commitments.

Luke Tingey: A current player, Luke deserves inclusion in this squad. He joined from MK Dons, where he attracted Manchester United's interest, and, aged only 22, now is one of the more experienced members of the current squad. Darren Gough's nephew, he is equally effective at full-back, centre-back or in midfield.

Peter Terry: Peter Terry made a scoring debut – at Enfield – as a 16-year-old in April 1954. He left after that season and returned two years later, converted from a forward to left-back. The regular penalty-taker, he scored nine times from 1956 to 1958, but left six games into the 1958–59 season.

Paul Towler: Police officer Paul played for Met Police against Hendon in a pre-season friendly and told Greens manager Frank Murphy he could do a job for him. The full-back or centre-half proved it in four seasons, from 1999 to 2003, during which time he played 169 times and scored 12 goals.

Bradley Thomas: Bradley joined Hendon from Sutton in November 2009, and scored twice in his 25 games for the club. He was sent off on his debut, at Aveley, but his foul probably preserved a 2–1 win. A solid and uncompromising centre-back, he was released in summer 2010.

Laurie Topp: Laurie was, in many experts' eyes, the finest amateur footballer of his era and probably the club's best ever. He won 32 England Amateur international caps, played in the 1952 and 1956 Olympic Games and gave the club almost 20 years of service. Having turned down Arsenal's overtures, the half-back – defensive midfielder in modern football – signed for Golders Green in 1942 and won three Athenian League titles, the 1960 FA Amateur Cup and numerous county cups. Including matches during the Second World War, Laurie made almost 600 appearances and scoring 16 goals. He retired in 1961, and coached Enfield for a year or so. He died, aged 93, early in 2017.

Roy Thomas: One of three attacking Thomases in the squad, Roy was a right-winger or centre-forward. His goal tally of 40 in 86 games from spring 1957 to spring 1959, suggests he was an out-and-out goal scorer, but he was equally good as a creator from wide positions.

Anthony Thomas: Anthony – no relation to contemporary Bradley – made his debut on loan from Farnborough in February 2010 and signed permanently in summer 2013. He was the FA Cup player of the first round qualifying in September 2013, scoring a seven-minute hat-trick as a substitute against Biggleswade United.

Bob Thomas: Bob made his debut on 31 December 1938 and scored in the 4–2 defeat of Leyton at Claremont Road. A fine goal scorer, he finished the season with 14 goals in 22 appearances. It was enough for Brentford to offer him a professional contract, ending his amateur career.

Colin Tate: Colin grabbed a debut double in a 5–3 defeat away to Epsom & Ewell in August 1985 and netted over 20 goals in each of his first two Hendon seasons. His only appearance of 1987–88 brought him a Russell Grant Middlesex Charity Cup winner's medal in the final at Wembley.

Peter Taylor: Soon after being appointed Hendon manager, Peter rejected Glenn Hoddle's offer to become Chelsea's assistant boss. He played in almost every game in the first half of 1993–94, before becoming Southend United's manager. In a star-studded team, even aged 42, he was easily Hendon's best player.

Substitutes

Martin Taylor: Martin was a very capable goalkeeper, who left Hendon in summer 1982, and then gave Bishop's Stortford many years of excellent service.

John Tone: John, outstanding as Enfield's left-back, was past his best when signing in 1984. He left when new manager Gary Hand returned to playing in 1985.

A Thorlby: His first name is unknown and playing records are incomplete, but Thorlby was a half-back in five seasons between 1925 and 1929. He made 34 appearances for the club, 23 of which were in the 1925–26 season, but never scored a goal.

Alec and Alfred Tompkins: Club records for both players are incomplete, but they were regular goal scorers for Hampstead Town in the pre-Athenian League era.

Tony Taggart: Tony joined Hendon in 2013. An excellent left-sided full-back or winger, he also was a great dressing room influence in his three seasons. He made 115 appearances, scoring 12 goals.

For this team there were so many midfielders and strikers to choose from, but so few defenders.

Richard Wilmot: Richard proved the old adage, "you must be mad to be a goalkeeper" when, in his last game on loan from Stevenage in October 2000, he played 15 minutes at Carshalton with an arm he knew was broken. An excellent goalkeeper, he made 114 appearances in four Hendon spells.

John-Simon White: Devonian John-Simon, signed after being released by Watford in the summer of 1996, spent four seasons with Hendon. It was his cross, on 25 November 1997, that Junior Lewis headed past Paul Hyde to given Hendon victory over Leyton Orient in the FA Cup. He played 177 times, scoring six goals.

Jock Watson: Jock joined newly-renamed Hendon in 1946 and made 68 appearances in two years at Claremont Road. A good left-back, his first-team time at Hendon ended in late summer 1948 when he took a job overseas.

Roger Wade: Roger was team leader on and off the pitch. He made 119 appearances with seven goals, often important ones, between January 1986 and June 1988. He captained the team at Wembley in the Russell Grant Middlesex Charity Cup Final win against Wembley, and returned briefly after a season away.

Curtis Warmington: Curtis wore his heart on his sleeve and played with a passion that made him a fans' favourite. Strong and powerful, few attackers got the better of him. First signed by Peter Taylor in 1993, he returned to play under Neil Price and Frank Murphy, before becoming player-coach. He played 180 times, coring five goals, having made his debut in 1993.

Ryan Wharton: Ryan spent three months at Hendon in autumn 2006, making his final appearance in the first win of the season late that October. The centre-back or full-back has since had three spells with the Greens, most recently in 2015–16. Overall, he made 96 appearances and scored one goal.

John Wilson: John was one of Hendon's shortest players, but the midfielder scored one of his nine goals with his head – against former Fulham keeper Tony Macedo, who was on his knees at the time! He made his debut in March 1967 and left in March 1975, after making 154 appearances.

Jimmy Wilsonham: Jimmy, an unsung, no-nonsense midfielder who kept the ball well, joined from Leytonstone in 1972 and won Barassi Cup and Isthmian League medals in his first Hendon season. A regular squad member, if not starter, for three seasons, his positional sense and powerful shot brought him 14 goals.

Bobby Wilson: Bobby had a tough act to follow when he joined Hendon from Feltham in 1967. His predecessors at number nine were David Hyde and Tony Harding, but he was no slouch in the goalscoring stakes, notching 80 in 180 matches before moving to Kingstonian in the summer of 1971.

Cecil Wise: Cecil was the club's first real star. An inside forward, he joined Hampstead Town in 1920 and was selected for the England Amateur team that November against Ireland in Belfast. He made a spectacular debut scoring a hat-trick in a 4–0 victory. As well as scoring at prolific rate – 144 goals in 153 recorded appearances 1920 to 1927 – Cecil was equally adept at creating chances. He was captain when Hampstead Town won the 1922 Middlesex Charity Cup and also was the first player from the club to score five goals in a game, against Enfield in 1923.

Neil Wolstenholme: An unflashy midfielder, Lancastrian Neil was a more attacking force, averaging better than a goal every five games. Signed from Walthamstow Avenue in September 1986, he was a Russell Grant Middlesex Charity Cup winner at Wembley in June 1988, but returned home for work reasons later that year.

Substitutes

Ron Whiteaker: Ron's Hendon debut was in November 1962 and, from the following season, was John Swannell's back-up. He made 34 first team appearances in six seasons.

Freddy Webb: Left-back Freddy joined Hampstead from Southall in 1928 and spent two seasons at Claremont Road, making 43 appearances before joining Wealdstone in 1930.

Paul Whitmarsh: Prolific striker Paul scored 70 goals in 120 Hendon appearances between November 1997 and 2000, including 42 in the 1998–99 season.

Josh Walker: Josh had the happy knack of scoring match-winning late goals, netting 17 in 42 appearances in 2017–18. He joined Barnet in 2018.

Danny Worley: A true super-sub, 40 of Danny's 61 appearances were off the bench. The former youth teamer, who enlisted with the RAF, and died in a 2000 plane crash having left the forces.

QUIVXYZ

QUIVXYZ is a made-up word or name, but it does contain the seven letters so far unused.

Reg Ivey: Reg, a serving Police officer, was a near-ever-present in goal in his first two seasons, 1950 to 1952, and played in the 1951 FA Amateur Cup semi-final against Pegasus, the FA Cup tie against Northampton Town and, aged 39, in the 1955 Amateur Cup Final against Bishop Auckland. Overall, he played 128 first team games.

Dave Yerby: From one regular non-league occupation to another, cab driver Dave Yerby joined Hendon from Hayes and made his debut in February 1975. He played in the team which beat Reading in the 1975 FA Cup first round. But it was his goal line handball which gave Swindon their late winner in the second round. Overall, he made 44 first team appearances.

Craig Vargas: Craig qualifies for this team as he first joined the team as Vargas and later changed his name to Carby. He had four spells with Hendon, between 2006 and autumn 2011, making 176 appearances and scoring four goals. He played in the Claremont Road finale in September 2008.

John Ugbah: John Ugbah was signed by Neil Price in January 1997 season and was a key player in the Greens' battle to stay in the top flight. A powerful and mobile defensive midfielder, he contributed three vital goals in 21 games. He later enjoyed many years at Crawley Town.

Jerel Ifil: Jerel made his Hendon debut aged 16, in November 1988. He added only one more appearance before Watford snapped him up and he went on to enjoy a long Football League and Scottish League career, mainly with Swindon Town and Aberdeen.

Stuart Young: Stuart was capable of playing at right back or centre-half. He was only 18 when he made his debut, having been a success in the Under-18s team. The step up was tough and he was not a regular, but finished with 34 appearances across three seasons.

Dan Uchechi: Dan first came to Hendon's attention, painfully, as one of Boreham Wood's stars when they beat the Greens in the 2016–17 FA Cup fourth round qualifying. He joined Hendon early the following season, but suffered an injury-hit campaign before moving to Hampton in summer 2018. He played 33 games and scored three times. He has wide experience in the professional game, both in England and abroad, and was capped by Nigeria at under-20 and under-23 levels.

Mark Xavier: Striker Mark saw Hendon train in Clitterhouse Playing Fields in the summer of 1990 and told manager Alan Randall he was better than anyone there. He spent three months in the reserves before stepping up. His best season was 1991–92, when he scored 18 times in 49 games.

Kezie Ibe: Kezie was a prolific goal scorer throughout his career. He was at Hendon for four seasons, 2014 to 2017, and netted 28 times in 62 games in the joyful 2014–15 campaign. Zak Joseph and Niko Muir's form limited his opportunities and he joined Harlow Town in December 2017. His overall record was 72 goals in 147 games.

Jimmy Quail: Jimmy is in the top handful of Hendon players ever to play for the club and was good enough to be considered for a full international call-up by his native Northern Ireland. He made his Hendon debut in February 1955, aged 19, became a semi-regular in the first team in 1956–57 and was indispensable for the following four seasons. An inside-forward, he won pretty much everything there was to win with Hendon between 1956 and 1967 – he spent two seasons at Enfield – and also managed and coached the club until the 1980s. He played 383 games and scored 174 goals, just less than one every two games. Jimmy is still an occasional visitor to SJP.

Paul Yates: Paul debuted in August 2001 and was an integral part of Dave Anderson's squads for two seasons, playing in more than 100 matches. A solid, unfussy midfielder, with a powerful shot, he came into his own in 2002–03, when he made 57 appearances and scored six goals.

Substitutes

Will Viner: Will's first and last games for Hendon were in the 2008–09 London Senior Cup and the goalkeeper won both in penalty shoot-outs. He made 34 appearances in that season.

Greg Zacharia: Signed from Kingsbury, midfielder Greg commuted from Bedford to play for Hendon in 1989–90. He made 57 appearances in his only season.

Eric Irwin: Right-winger Eric scored on his Hampstead Town debut in September 1924. A regular that season, he played occasionally in two other campaigns, the last one being 1929–30. He scored seven goals in 30 first team appearances.

Doug Young: Doug joined Hendon from Billericay in 1980, but arthritic hips ended his career after half a season, having scored 10 goals in 28 games.

Freddie Young: In 1931, almost uniquely, Freddie left the club to join Hendon FC, but the current Hendon Football Club was still Hampstead. A prolific centre-forward from 1922 to 1925, he returned as a midfielder in 1927. He was a mainstay of the inter-war period for the club. Overall he made 169 first team appearances, and scored 52 goals.

Special select teams

Dermot Drummy

To mark the special day of memory the club held for Dermot Drummy, this dream team comprises the cream of the Hendon squad in the late 1980s, when Dermot returned to the club.

Dave Root: Dave will be remembered as one of the finest and most loyal of Hendon goalkeepers. When he signed, his profession was chandelier cleaner – think *Only Fools and Horses* – and his handling was excellent. He had moved to Cornwall with his family and began his career with Barking after returning to London. In eight seasons, 1986 to 1994, Dave finished with 442 appearances, but was never an ever-present. His importance can be seen when Leytonstone-Ilford wanted to buy him, but a tribunal valued him at £1,500 and the offer was withdrawn. Dave himself was shocked at the valuation.

Roger Wade: If you listened to Roger, you would be amazed that he played for as long as he did and at the level he achieved. It isn't true. An England schoolboy and Republic of Ireland youth international, he signed for Spurs at the same time as two future Greens – Gary Hyams and Fred Barwick – and Glenn Hoddle. He made his Hendon debut on New Year's Day 1986, scoring in a 1–1 home draw against Bishop's Stortford. The regular captain, most of his seven goals in 125 appearances were of the vital kind.

Erskine Smart: Erskine came through the ranks and went on to make 231 Hendon appearances. His debut was a scoring one, in a 3–1 extra time Isthmian League Cup victory at Feltham. He was a fortnight past his 21st birthday and, at the time, equally comfortable at full-back, occasionally on the left side, or in midfield. By the end of the 1986–87 season, his second with the Greens, he was a regular. Solid in the tackle and blessed with both pace and positional awareness, he was almost indispensable and few wide players consistently got the better of him.

Duncan Hardy: Duncan was an extremely versatile player, apparently equally comfortable in defence, midfield and up front, during had three spells with the Greens. He first joined in 1982–83, returned between 1987 and 1989, and was brought back by Bob Dowie in 1993–94. He was denied a Wembley appearance in the 1988 Russell Grant Middlesex Charity Cup Final because of a bad knee injury. A long-time feud with Reg Leather blew up in an FA Trophy tie in December 1988, resulting in five red cards. Duncan won a Carlsberg (Isthmian Full Members) Cup medal in 1994.

Alan Campbell: An outstanding centre-half, Alan played 395 times for the Greens and scored 31 goals in three spells between 1976 and 1992. A 22-year-old triallist from Finchley in summer 1976, Alan earned a first-team spot and spent almost five seasons at Hendon before Ted Hardy brought him back in 1986, after spells at Dagenham and Barnet. Battle-hardened, he was the epitome of a strong central defender: good in the air, strong in the tackle and someone not to be messed with. He was briefly Barrie Williams' assistant manager in 1992–93, after a brief third playing stint.

Bob Dowie: Working in the oil business in the Middle East, Bob played only occasionally when Dermot was at Hendon – and brother Iain was leading the attack. Bob was a no-nonsense centre-back, who never held back, and such was his quality that manager Ted Hardy considered him to be one of the best Isthmian League defenders around at the time. Bob became player-manager midway through 1993–94, having been signed by Peter Taylor, and took the team to success in the Carlsberg (Isthmian Full Members) Cup. He later became Crystal Palace's Director of Football, working with Iain and then Peter.

Dermot Drummy: Dermot was a true Hendon legend. His death in November 2017 shocked the club and was the defining issue for the club's focus on mental health treatment and support. Dermot made 348 appearances for Hendon, and scored 62 goals in seven seasons, 1981 to 1984 and 1986 to 1989. His assists total that would go with the gaudy goal numbers is not recorded, but counting them in hundreds is realistic. A tricky winger when he arrived, Dermot became a superb attacking force, either behind the frontmen or deeper in midfield. London-born, to Irish parents, Dermot was very close to making it as a professional, but he couldn't quite fill the boots of Liam Brady at Arsenal and his Football League career comprised a handful of appearances on loan at Blackpool. He was also an exceptional youth team coach with Arsenal and Chelsea before he spent a year managing Crawley Town.

Tony Gibson: Tony Gibson was possibly the last true enforcer Hendon have had. The Burgess and Maclaren brothers were modern-day midfield hard men; "Gibbo" was harder, stronger, a better footballer, and much, much more challenging. He allegedly got opponents booked as he broke their noses and was not punished himself. The key words in those two sentences were "a better footballer", because, even at the very end of his career, when knee problems limited his playing time, he would dominate in midfield. Tony made his debut in February 1986 and left in late 1987 after recording 98 appearances with seven goals.

Iain Dowie: Iain arrived at Hendon, much to St Albans City's disappointment, a raw-boned, gangly striker. He left, 25 months later, a Football League-ready attack leader. Working incredibly hard with the late Ronnie Duke in the summer of 1988, Iain bagged FA Cup hat-tricks against Harwich & Parkeston and Bishop's Stortford during a run of scoring in 10 out 11 games. Professional clubs chased him and after scoring 27 goals in 30 games Luton signed him in December 1988, from whence he enjoyed a long professional and international career. In all, he scored 78 goals in 132 Hendon games.

Colin Tate: Thanks to the 1988 Russell Grant Middlesex Charity Cup Final, Colin played in seven consecutive Hendon seasons 1985–86 to 1991–92, during which time he scored 83 goals in 284 appearances. His 21 goals in the relegation dogfight of 1985–86 and 23 in the 76-game marathon the following campaign, were his most prolific seasons, but he reached double figures in goals twice more. Not the tallest, strongest or quickest striker around, he was, nonetheless, a fine finisher and had the instinct to be in the right place at the right time when chances arrived.

Gary Keen: Gary joined Hendon from his hometown club, St Albans City, in January 1987 and filled a number of roles in the crowded end to the 75-match season. Although at his most effective either as a left-winger or attacking left midfielder, he could fill in at left-back as well. Gary left briefly at the end of 1987, having scored 11 times in 24 appearances, but was back the following season and scored in the FA Cup defeat at Reading. In parts of seven seasons at Hendon, 1987 to 1993, Gary made 185 appearances and scored a more than creditable 39 goals.

Substitutes

Mark Broughton: None of Dave Root's four understudies, 1986 to1989, were close to Mark's talent, and Dave replaced Mark when he returned to the Midlands. An excellent goalkeeper, Mark was a key performer in 1985–86's relegation battle. It is unlikely Dermot would have returned if Hendon had gone down.

Alan Roughan: One of Dermot's closest football friends, fellow cab-driver Alan was a very competent left-back, with a powerful left foot. Although he played in eight seasons between 1978 and 1989, Alan made only 123 appearances. Dermot and Alan were joint-managers at both Finchley and Ware in the early 1990s.

Mark Furneaux: Mark was never one of the team's best players, but was a perfectly adequate defender. A former Spurs junior, he was at Enfield before moving across north London to join the Greens, playing 173 times in four seasons. A dressing room joker, he was considered great for morale.

Phil Gridelet: Phil's debut was Hendon's 5–1 Middlesex Charity Cup final victory against Feltham in May 1985. Combative and aggressive, Phil was an outstanding central defender – winning England non-league honours before joining Barnet. After a long Football League career Phil returned to Hendon in 2000 to play in midfield.

Neil Wolstenholme: The Lancastrian, an attacking midfielder, was living in Golders Green when he joined Hendon from Walthamstow Avenue. When at university in Preston, Neil rejected the chance of a Football League appearance for Rochdale at Plymouth. He scored 21 goals in 99 appearances between September 1986 and April 1989.

Andy O'Brien: One of the most loyal Hendon players, he commuted from the University of Nottingham to continue playing for the Greens. A midfielder or, more frequently, defender either at right-back or centre-half, he had numerous spells with the club, even spending a month as manager early in 1997.

Danny Worley: Danny died in 2000, the co-pilot in an aircraft crash carrying Formula 1 star David Coulthard. From Princes Park's youth set-up, Danny made 61 appearances, 41 as a "super sub" (nine goals). He retired, aged 21, to join the RAF in 1987, but played a few times while on leave.

Steve Scott: Midfielder Steve scored 15 goals in 99 appearances, 1988 to 1991. His first season was eventful, playing in the FA Cup first round, FA Trophy against Hayes – sent off for being assaulted by Paul Hyde – and a 9–1 loss to Leyton when injured and hospitalised in the first half.

Manager – Ted Hardy: One of non-league's most famous managers, Ted was Hendon boss from 1985 to 1987, saving the Greens from relegation in 1986 and reaching two cup finals in 1987 – the 75-game season. A decade after leaving Hendon, aged 70, Ted managed Dagenham & Redbridge in the 1997 FA Trophy Final.

Internationals

This squad of internationals, either full or Under-21 or Under-23, is based more on their international careers than time at Hendon.

Mike Pinner: Mike played for the Great Britain team at the Rome Olympics in 1960 and England amateurs, as there are no eligible full or Under-21 international goalkeepers. He played parts of two seasons at Hendon, having also played for Aston Villa, Sheffield Wednesday, QPR, Manchester United, Chelsea, Swansea and Leyton Orient, mainly as an amateur.

Bernard Joy: Bernard, who spent 25 years as journalist after football, was the last amateur to win a full England cap – in 1936. He played twice for the club in the early 1930s. Most of his 12 Amateur caps came as an Arsenal and Casuals player – he played for both. His son Chris also played a handful of games for Hendon.

Tommy Mason: Tommy, a Londoner, moved to play football for Papatoetoe in New Zealand and was selected for the All Whites four times. He returned to England and later was signed by Peter Taylor. Tommy converted a penalty to open the scoring in the 1994 Full Members Cup Final.

Michael Duberry: Michael's Hendon career was very brief, one game shorter than his England Under-21 time. The former Chelsea, Leeds and England Under-21 defender was nearly 38 when he played four times for Hendon in August 2013, debuting alongside Dream-team-mate Jefferson Louis in a 4–0 win over Thamesmead Town.

Frank Sinclair: Another player with World Cup Finals experience, France 1998, Frank did Hendon coach Junior Lewis a favour by signing in November 2011, a month before his 40th birthday. Frank commuted from his Bolton home to play for Hendon, appearing 10 times. He won 28 caps for Jamaica.

Jeff Campbell: New Zealand midfielder Jeff was living in Cricklewood when he joined Hendon from AFC Wimbledon in September 2005. He was not far from selection for the All Whites' 2010 World Cup squad, having returned home in 2006 after a difficult Hendon campaign when the club was spared from relegation.

Bontcho Guentchev: Bontcho was a World Cup semi-finalist with Bulgaria in 1994 and joined Hendon in 1999, having scored for CSKA Sofia in the UEFA Cup nine months earlier. He spent two seasons with us before returning as player-coach under Gary McCann. He, like Speedie, made one goalkeeping appearance.

Tony Currie: A fan at Claremont Road, Hendon Boys representative and Whitefields schoolmate of Dave Bedford, Hendon was a big part of Tony's youth, but it took until 1985 – aged 35 – for him to sign and then he only played five times. Tony was the antithesis of what England boss Don Revie wanted in midfield so he won only 17 caps. He played for Watford, Sheffield United, Leeds – post Revie – and QPR, where he helped Hendon beat Taunton in the 1982 FA Trophy, giving brother Paul access to the boot room so Hendon were correctly shod for the Loftus Road Astroturf pitch.

Iain Dowie: This team's most capped player – 59 Northern Ireland caps with 12 goals – Iain spent 25 months at Hendon from November 1986, scoring 78 goals in 132 games. Tall, quick and powerful, non-league defences could not cope with him. This helped him secure a deal with Luton Town in December 1988 and Hendon a record transfer fee.

Jefferson Louis: Many players from the CONCACAF region made fleeting appearances at Hendon and internationally. Jefferson gets the nod because in his 42 moves in a 23-season career, nowhere does he have a better League strike rate than with Hendon, 2013–14, when he scored 22 goals in 25 games.

Peter Taylor: Hendon player-manager May to December 1993 – 22 games, seven goals – Peter also played for and managed England (four games and one). Southend United and Crystal Palace, where he earned an England call-up as a third-tier player. While at Hendon, Peter declined the chance to be Glenn Hoddle's assistant at Chelsea.

Substitutes

Pat Morrissey: Pat won one Republic Ireland Under-23 cap. His Football League career began with Coventry City at Old Trafford and included a spell at Crewe when fans on the wing opposite the dugout would feed him chips. He played 41 times for Hendon in 1981–82, scoring six goals.

Luke Gambin: Luke made his debut against Aldershot – on loan from Barnet – in the 2012 FA Cup, but played only twice more. He has 16 Malta caps.

Otis Roberts: Otis joined Hendon in 2001 having won two Grenada caps in 2000. Jason Roberts' uncle, he is related to the Regis family through marriage.

David Speedie: David finished his Hendon debut – against Sutton – in August 1995 as a goalkeeper, having replacing the injured Scott Ashcroft. The Scotland striker won 10 caps, double the number of his Hendon appearance total – in those five matches, he was cautioned five times, twice in his last appearance.

Matt Ball: Northern Ireland Under-21 international with six caps, Matt helped Hendon stay up in 2017 and left in 2018 after 60 games and 11 goals.

Jack Connors: A Republic of Ireland Under-21 squad player, Jack was at Hendon in 2013 on work experience from Dagenham & Redbridge.

Elliott Charles: Elliott scored on his Hendon debut at Wealdstone in September 2011. Just days earlier he had represented Grenada in a World Cup qualifier.

Michael Bryan: Michael won two full international caps for Northern Ireland, and played for their under-21 side. He played 42 games for Hendon in the 2013–14 season, scoring once, before joining Harrow Borough. He played for Watford and Bradford City in the Football League.

Smiths

The most common surname in Britain is Smith and so here is a team of Hendon Smiths. By the way, the world's most common forename is Mohammed (various spellings) and surname is Li (Lee or Leigh).

Sid Smith: Sid's Hampstead Town debut in December 1927 was in an 8–2 loss to Leyton. However, he went on to make 215 appearances for the club in seven seasons, leaving in the summer of 1934.

Jamie Smith: Full-back Jamie joined on a dual registration from Sutton United as an 18-year-old. In a struggling team, he brought a classy calmness, but returned to Gander Green Lane after making 15 appearances, all except one in the Ryman League in 2016–17.

J Smith: J Smith's first name is not recorded, but he was mainly a reserve in 1945–46. His only first team, appearance was certainly memorable as the left-back played in a 5–5 draw against Barnet.

Adrian Smith: Adrian played mainly in midfield, but also as a central defender or forward. His debut, aged 19, came in a 4–4 Isthmian League Cup draw with Bognor Regis Town in December 1982. He played more frequently in 1983–84, before enjoying success at Wembley FC.

Lewis Smith: Lewis was never a first choice at Hampstead Town, and started his time as a forward, scoring on his debut in a 3–1 defeat against Luton Clarence in 1921. In 1923–24, he played in more than half of the Town's Athenian League campaign as a centre-half.

Charlie Smith: Charlie is one of the few current players to make a dream team, but these are mainly retrospective pieces. Formerly with Luton, Hitchin and Welwyn Garden City, his debut was in January

2019's draw at Beaconsfield. He is equally comfortable in midfield or as a wing-back.

Andy Smith: Andy's pace was a strength, but the whole-hearted attacker often didn't know when to slow down, so crossing was not a strong point. He made 115 appearances with 24 goals, including at Wembley in the 1988 Russell Grant Middlesex Charity Cup Final.

Steve Smith: Roy Ruffell signed Steve from Harrow Borough in early in the 1983–84 season. A clever ball-player, he played in a talented midfield alongside Dermot Drummy and Steve Wilkins, but suffered from ankle problems and missed almost one-third of his only Hendon season.

Leon Smith: Leon was football Marmite. Two Football League scouts watched him playing for Wingate & Finchley and, at half-time, one said, "I don't know what people see in him. He's overweight and lazy with terrible body language." The other said, "Two goals in 45 minutes; I'll take that." Looking overweight, he joined Hendon in January 2014, and netted 12 goals in 21 appearances. Fitter in 2014–15, he equalled Oscar Reinke's 1925 club record of scoring in eight consecutive matches. When not starting regularly, his weight could rise and it resulted in his departure in autumn 2016 after scoring 43 goals in 108 games.

Denny Smith: Denny made his Hendon debut in November 1961 and scored in his second match, a 3–1 win at Hitchin. He was not a first-team regular, which, on the face of it was surprising in that he scored 10 times in 14 appearances, his only Hendon season.

Stanley Smith: Stanley, a left-winger, joined Hampstead Town in August 1924 and spent just the one season with the club. His exact contribution is unknown because the club's records for the season are incomplete, but he is known to have scored seven goals in 30 appearances.

Substitutes

Peter Smith: England's last Amateur international goalkeeper, Peter struggled under floodlights, if the pylons were down the side. He played for Hendon in 1974–75.

Kambo Smith: Kambo, a striker previously with Dulwich Hamlet, impressed in friendlies in autumn 2012. He made only seven appearances and scored once.

G H Smith: G H (first name unknown) signed for Hampstead in 1927, playing at least 20 matches and scoring 13 times – but records are incomplete.

Bill Smith: Bill debuted in a September 1961 9–1 FA Cup win over Leyton. He didn't score in any of his six Hendon appearances.

C Smith: C Smith (first name unknown) scored in Hampstead Town's 3–0 FA Cup defeat of Barnet in 1921. He played only twice.

Hendon Football Club is one of the most famous names in non-league football. This club history, published in 2008, marks the club's first 100 years. It covers from their early days as a junior team before the First World War to their development in senior football in the Athenian and Isthmian Leagues.

ISBN: 9781903659-42-7. Cover price: £16.95

Available from London League Publications Ltd, www.llpshop.co.uk or by post @ £16.50 post free in the UK from PO Box 65784, London NW2 9NS, or from Amazon and AbeBooks or can be ordered from any bookshop.

Walter Tull 1888 to 1918 – Footballer and Officer
By Phil Vasili

Walter Daniel John Tull was one of Britain's first Black infantry officers – a Black Briton in a society where there were few others. As a footballer for Clapton, Tottenham Hotspur and Northampton Town he was praised, idolised, denigrated and abused. As a soldier and then officer he was loved, respected, ridiculed and humiliated. He led White troops into battle on the Western and Italian fronts at a time when Army regulations and Military Law forbade 'non-Europeans' from becoming combat officers. Recommended for a Military Cross – that was never awarded – for his bravery and leadership in Italy, he died on 25 March 1918. Since then, his life has featuredin documentaries, a drama on television and a play by Phil Vasili. First published in 2010, this **new edition** includes further research and illustrations.

Published in February 2018 @ £14.95. ISBN: 9781909885172
The book is available on Amazon, Abe Books and for credit card orders from the London League Publications Ltd website: www.llpshop.co.uk
Or: Send a cheque for £14.50 (post free in the UK) payable to London League Publications Ltd, to PO Box 65784, London NW2 9NS. Please include details of where you want the book to be sent. It can be ordered from any bookshop.